THE SPECTER OF RELATIVISM

Northwestern University
Studies in Phenomenology
and
Existential Philosophy

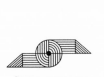

THE SPECTER OF RELATIVISM

Truth, Dialogue, and *Phronesis* in Philosophical Hermeneutics

Edited by Lawrence K. Schmidt

Northwestern University Press
Evanston, Illinois

1995

Northwestern University Press
Evanston, Illinois 60208-4210

ISBN 0-8101-1256-6 cloth
      0-8101-1257-4 paper

Library of Congress Cataloging-in-Publication Data

The specter of relativism : truth, dialogue, and phronesis in
    philosophical hermeneutics / edited by Lawrence K. Schmidt.
          p.   cm. — (Northwestern University studies in phenomenology
    and existential philosophy)
    Includes bibliographical references.
    ISBN 0-8101-1256-6. —ISBN 0-8101-1257-4 (paper)
    1. Hermeneutics. 2. Gadamer, Hans Georg, 1900–   Contributions in
hermeneutics. 3. Relativity. 4. Truth. 5. Dialogue.   I. Schmidt,
Lawrence, 1949–   . II. Series: Northwestern University studies in
phenomenology & existential philosophy.
    BD241.S69   1995
    121'.68—dc20   95-16129
                                                                              CIP

The paper used in this publication meets the minimum requirements of the
American National Standard for Information Sciences—Permanence of Paper
for Printed Library Materials, ANSI Z39.48-1984.

For Monika and Kassandra

Contents

Part 2: On the Truth of the Word

Part 3: On Dialogue and *Phronesis*

Acknowledgments

This collection emerged from an international symposium, "Grund-probleme der Hermeneutik im Anschluß an Hans-Georg Gadamers *Wahrheit und Methode*," that was held 8-10 July 1989 at the Internationales Wissenschaftsforum Heidelberg. For all the participants I wish to express my gratitude to the Stiftung 600 Jahre Universität Heidelberg and the Ministerium für Wissenschaft und Kunst Baden-Württemberg for their support. This volume represents only one of the many directions of questioning that occurred in this symposium and have continued, almost yearly, in workshops held in the Philosophisches Seminar at the University of Heidelberg, organized by myself, James Risser (Seattle University) and Prof. Dr. Reiner Wiehl (University of Heidelberg).

Hendrix College has provided me with further assistance in the intervening time. The manuscript was completed during the National Endowment for the Humanities Summer Seminar for College Teachers, "Postmodernism: A Philosophical Genealogy," directed by Bernd Magnus. I am thankful to all those who have aided me in Heidelberg, Conway, and Riverside. My deepest gratitude goes to Hans-Georg Gadamer, whose participation, concern, and gracious hospitality have enabled this collection.

Abbreviations

BT   Martin Heidegger. *Being and Time.* Trans. John Macquarrie and Edward Robinson. New York: Harper and Row, 1962.

DD   *Dialogue and Deconstruction: The Gadamer-Derrida Encounter.* Ed. Diane P. Michelfelder and Richard E. Palmer. Albany: State University of New York, 1989.

GW   Hans-Georg Gadamer. *Gesammelte Werke.* Tübingen: J. C. B. Mohr (Paul Siebeck), 1985–95. The number represents the volume of this collection.

PH   Hans-Georg Gadamer. *Philosophical Hermeneutics.* Trans. David E. Linge. Berkeley: University of California, 1976.

SZ   Martin Heidegger. *Sein und Zeit.* Tübingen: Max Niemeyer, 12th ed., 1972.

TM   Hans-Georg Gadamer. *Truth and Method.* Revised translation by Joel Weisenheimer and Donald Marshall. New York: Crossroad, 1989.

WM   Hans-Georg Gadamer. *Wahrheit und Methode.* Tübingen: J. C. B. Mohr (Paul Siebeck), 1960, 4th ed., 1975.

These abbreviations are used throughout. See the notes to the specific contributions for additional abbreviations used by that author.

Introduction:
Between Certainty and
Relativism

Lawrence K. Schmidt

Is the natural scientific method of verification the only way to secure and guarantee truth? Is truth properly defined as *adaequatio intellectus ad rem?* Are all claims to knowledge that are *not* founded upon scientific verification to be rejected? Hans-Georg Gadamer responds decisively and negatively to these questions in his magnum opus, *Truth and Method.* His stated purpose is to search out and examine those experiences of truth—in art, history, philosophy and the human sciences—that cannot be justified by means of the scientific method and to provide a philosophical justification for them (*WM*, xxviii; *TM*, xxii). Although the positivistic claims for the scientific method have been modified within the philosophy of science during this century, the investigation of other ways of experiencing truth is still a valuable corrective, for "if verification—in whatever form—first determines truth (*veritas*), then the criterion for the determination of cognition is no longer its truth but its certainty" (*GW*II, 48). By exposing the conditions under which one can vouch for these other experiences of truth, Gadamer proposes a new theory of understanding—philosophical hermeneutics. "Hermeneutics" refers directly to Heidegger's "hermeneutics of facticity" (*GW*II, 495) and indicates Gadamer's central thesis that all understanding necessarily involves interpretation and application. Gadamer's theory is termed philosophical in order to differentiate it from traditional forms of hermeneutics, which concern a methodology of interpretation, and to emphasize that the uncovered process of understanding applies universally.

Both scientific and hermeneutic truth concern a linguistic expression that says something about the world in the broadest sense. Truth-claims result from human thinking and purport to be knowledge concerning the subject matter under investigation. However, the truth of verification is limited to those knowledge-claims that can be guaranteed

1

by the scientific method that accepts only intersubjectively testable, empirical facts (stated in the protocol sentences in one standard version) and develops inductive generalizations based upon these facts. In contrast, hermeneutic truth occurs as an event where one comes to experience truth through an uncovering of the proper linguistic expression for that subject matter. It is the speculative emergence of the subject matter into the temporally bounded, linguistic horizon of the participants of the dialogue, so that cognizers in different situations, while correctly experiencing the "same" subject matter, will experience differing and yet correct truths. The hermeneutic claim that all understanding necessarily involves an interpretive and applicative moment implies that scientific truth-claims are themselves derivative, a misunderstood form of hermeneutic experience.[1]

Whereas scientific truth claims temporal independence and ideally complete correspondence, hermeneutic truth is conditioned by the temporal horizon and involves multiple, partial, and differing expressions of a subject matter. This situation raises the specter of relativism for philosophical hermeneutics. After a review of the argument in *Truth and Method*, the major critiques of hermeneutic truth will be introduced along with a discussion of the first set of contributions to this volume (those contained in parts 1 and 2). I will then discuss the final set of contributions (those contained in part 3), which expand the question to the possibility of a hermeneutic conversation and ethics.

In *Truth and Method* Gadamer initiates the search for those experiences of truth in the humanities that are not justifiable by the scientific method by examining four concepts from the humanist tradition. These concepts demonstrate what is required of a cognizer in such an experience of truth. This way of understanding, Gadamer argues, was limited and subjectivized by Kant, when he relegated taste and a sense of judgment to the realm of aesthetic judgments (*WM*, 40; *TM*, 43). Through a critical examination of Kant, aesthetic experience is returned to the realm of human existence so that "art is knowledge and the experience of the work of art allows participation in this knowledge" (*WM*, 92; *TM*, 97).

To explicate the mode of being of the work of art and the occurrence of truth therein, Gadamer examines the concept of play. He argues that "the primordial sense of playing is the medial voice" (*WM*, 99; *TM*, 103) and so overcomes the subject-object dichotomy. The play brings itself into being by involving the players within its structures. So the actual subject of the play is the play itself (*WM*, 102; *TM*, 106).

Human play attains its highest form in art, which Gadamer terms the "transformation into structure [*Gebilde*]" (*WM*, 105; *TM*, 110). The temporality of this mode of being of the work of art is demonstrated through the example of the festival. Although different participants and variations in the activities of the festival may be involved, each celebration calls forth the same meaningful whole. The ontological valence of a work of art refers to its capacity to bring forth its subject matter in different temporal situations (*WM*, 134; *TM*, 141). As in the case of a festival, the differing specifics of each presentation do not imply that something else has come to be—the determination of meaning exclusively through the work's reception would be an "untenable hermeneutic nihilism" (*WM*, 90; *TM*, 95). Rather each presentation is of the one universal that is the work of art—but there exists no perfect performance, no teleologically approached finality, and no work of art "in itself" (*WM*, 140; *TM*, 148). There exists a historical series of realizations of the work of art like Hegel's discussion of the dialectic in art (*WM*, 93; *TM*, 98). Unlike Hegel, however, this series cannot be said to be approaching a final synthesis. Hermeneutic truth is better described as the "bad infinite," since this series never reaches completion (*GW*II, 505).

The experience of truth in the work of art anticipates several features of the concept of hermeneutic truth. The experience of truth is an event. One is taken up and belongs to the event of truth, as the spectators and actors belong to the presentation in a performance. Through the double nondifference of mimetic presentation the same subject matter is realized in each historically different presentation. The ontological valence of the work of art allows for this emanation of the subject matter that had been transformed into the structure of that work of art. There is no perfect realization of the truth of the work of art as there is no perfect performance. There is no truth in itself. On the other hand, as each successful performance, although differing in detail, brings the subject matter of the play to presentation, so each realization of truth, although differing, is nevertheless the realization of the "same" truth.

The next question is whether the discovered mode of being for the work of art may be applied to literature. Are texts also transformations into structure with ontological valence? To answer this question Gadamer examines the history of hermeneutics. This historical review demonstrates a move away from an attempt to understand the subject matter, still found in Spinoza and Chladenius, to an increasing reliance on the scientific methodology. In each case a positive contribution toward a philosophical hermeneutics is made, but at the cost of a flawed assumption. Heidegger, Gadamer contends, is first able uncover the ontological ground for the explication of hermeneutic experience through his hermeneutics of facticity and destruction of the metaphysical tradition. In Heidegger understanding is discovered to be "the *original form of the realization of Dasein*" (*WM*, 245; *TM*, 259). All understanding is an interpreting that begins with the fore-structures of understanding and moves toward completion by refining these fore-structures. This interdependence constitutes the hermeneutic circle as an ontological structure of Dasein. One cannot escape this circular structure, for there is no possible cognition free from the conditioning influence of these fore-structures. Since the circle cannot be allowed to become vicious, the continual task of understanding is to revise the fore-structures according to the subject matter (*Sache selbst*) and not to permit them to be determined by fancy and popular opinions (*SZ*, 153).

Gadamer initiates his theory of philosophical hermeneutics by extending Heidegger's description of understanding. He introduces the concept of prejudice, *Vorurteil*, to designate Heidegger's fore-structures of understanding (*WM*, 254; *TM*, 270). The problem of hermeneutic truth in relation to the circular structure of understanding can be stated in two fundamental epistemological questions: "What is the ground of the legitimacy of prejudices? What differentiates legitimate prejudices from those numerous other prejudices whose overcoming is the undoubted task of critical reason?" (*WM*, 261; *TM*, 277)

The central thesis of philosophical hermeneutics is: "Being, which can be understood, is language" (*WM*, 450; *TM*, 474). Since the publication of *Truth and Method*, Gadamer has clarified this thesis, stating that it does not imply that the one who understands determines what is by creating concepts, but that being happens and informs the subject (*WM*, xxiii; *TM*, xxxv). It also means that "what is, can never be completely understood," for what is said always points beyond itself to what is not said (*GW*II, 334). Nor does this thesis deny the actuality of prelinguistic interaction and nonlinguistic conditions for human life. However, it does mean that "the communality, which we call human, is based upon the linguistic composition of our life-world" (*GW*II, 496–97) and "everywhere where something is experienced, where unfamiliarity is overcome, where enlightenment, insight and appropriation succeed, there the hermeneutic process of bringing into the word and into common consciousness has occurred" (*GW*II, 498).

How does Being come to be expressed in language? Gadamer argues that neither the conventionalist sign theory nor a natural copy theory of language correctly presents the relationship between a word and its referent. Experiencing is a process influenced by language where the correct words to express the experience are realized as the experience is recognized for what it is (*WM*, 394; *TM*, 417). Experiencing is the coming-to-be-in-language of the subject matter or referent. The expression of the subject matter in language is partial, since Gadamer agrees with Humboldt that each linguistic perspective (*Sprachansicht*) presents a perspective of the world (*Weltansicht*) (*WM*, 419; *TM*, 442). However, "the multiplicity of such world perspectives does not imply a relativization of the 'world.' Rather, what the world itself is, is no different from the perspectives in which it presents itself" (*WM*, 423; *TM*, 447). A prejudice is a partial expression in language of the subject matter. One's set of inherited prejudices form one's world horizon (*WM*, 289; *TM*, 306).

One inherits a set of prejudices through acculturation in primarily a passive manner. This inherited set of prejudices embeds one within a tradition (*WM*, 261; *TM*, 277). To test a prejudice one must be faced with a question, which may be posed by a tradition or an other. The question horizon establishes the openness wherein the legitimation of prejudices, the experience of hermeneutic truth, occurs. In order to be confronted with a competing prejudice, the other must be allowed to speak and one must listen. The horizon of the other must be constituted in relation to one's own horizon. This is accomplished by means of what Gadamer terms the preconception of completion (*WM*, 278; *TM*, 294). In this manner the text may be brought to speak as an other.

Gadamer identifies one of three possible relationships between the "I" and the other as adequately reflecting the hermeneutic experience of truth (*WM*, 340; *TM*, 358). In the truly human relationship the other must be acknowledged as another person whose views are to be taken seriously, in the sense that his or her truth-claims are, for the moment, supposed correct, thereby allowing one's own to be questioned. This clearly does not mean that the other is to be blindly followed (*WM*, 343; *TM*, 361). In terms of a conversation each conversant must have the "good will" to listen and acknowledge what the other has to say (*GW*II, 343; *DD* 33). The temporal distance between the interpreter and a text within a tradition is important since it represents a likely source for conflicting and perhaps legitimate prejudices (*GW*I, 304, fn. 228; *TM*, 298).

Inasmuch as one can speak of the two horizons, the horizons of the "I" and the other or of the interpreter and the text, the event of hermeneutic truth, where one of the conflicting prejudices is legitimated, can be said to be the fusion of horizons. On the other hand, since this event occurs in the openness of the question horizon and the text's horizon is projected by the interpreter using the preconception of completion, Gadamer argues that one should speak of the continual development of one, contemporary horizon (*WM*, 289; *TM*, 306).

The exemplary model for this type of questioning is the Platonic dialogue. Gadamer's purpose is to return to the Platonic dialogue and examine the necessary conditions for its possibility as established by language in the conversation (*GW*II, 369). "To engage in a conversation means to place oneself under the leadership of the subject matter [*Sache*] towards which the conversants are directed" (*WM*, 349; *TM*, 367). In the discussion of the experience of the work of art, this guiding function of the subject matter was connected with the concept of the game. In the same sense the conversation is not directed and controlled by one or more of the conversants, but the subject matter as it evolves and is experienced carries the conversants along. So it is more correct to say "that language speaks us, than that we speak it" (*WM*, 439; *TM*, 463).

The origins of prejudices and role of the subject matter indicates the central concept of philosophical hermeneutics, effective history (*Wirkungsgeschichte*). One's prejudices come from one's cultural and linguistic past. In this way history, as accumulated human experience, affects the present. History is also effective in another sense, since the subject matter may be said to guide a conversation in the tradition. So, "in fact history does not belong to us, but we belong to it" (*WM*, 261; *TM*, 276).

In addition to the necessary interpretive element in all understanding discussed by Heidegger, Gadamer insists that there exists a necessary applicative element in all cases of understanding (*WM*, 292; *TM*, 308). To have correctly understood involves allowing the subject matter in its truth to speak to the present situation as determined by the linguistic horizon of the conversants. So correct understanding can be said to be the application of the subject matter to the historically determined situation of the one who understands. Application does not mean that one first correctly understands something and then later "applies" it to a particular situation. Rather application necessarily occurs in the process of understanding itself (*WM*, 323; *TM*, 340). Since understanding necessarily involves application, Gadamer can argue that the correct understanding of a text changes in time due to changes in the historically and linguistically determined horizon where understanding occurs (*WM*, 292; *TM*, 309).

For Gadamer, the actuality of Aristotle's analysis of *phronesis* lies in its exemplification of the logical process of hermeneutic understanding and specifically of application. Aristotle has demonstrated the possibility of truth in ethical understanding where this is neither the subsumption of a particular under a universal rule, as in science, nor merely the carrying out of a plan (method) as in technology. Gadamer argues by analogy that hermeneutic truth is equally possible. The essential point of comparison is that both the actor and the one who understands are

involved in a situation where understanding depends upon the application of a general scheme to a specific situation and where that particular
understanding affects one's own being (*WM*, 295; *TM*, 312). The inherited understanding of a subject matter may be viewed as analogous to the
virtues, in being "guiding images" (*WM*, 300; *TM*, 317) that aid in the
realization of the truth of the subject matter in that particular horizon of
understanding. The hermeneutic truth discovered occurs as the concrete and particular application of the subject matter to that individual
situation. The event of hermeneutic truth can now be viewed as experiencing the correct application of the subject matter.

Due to effective history the consciousness of the one who understands is itself an effective historical consciousness. This means, in the
first place, that every consciousness is embedded in a tradition due to
one's inherited set of prejudices, whether one is aware of this inheritance or not. In the second place, effective historical consciousness
refers to that consciousness which is reflectively aware of its status as a
consciousness embedded within effective history (*WM*, xxii; *TM*, xxxiv).
In this narrower sense, one is aware of the hermeneutic circle in understanding and one's own effectivity through the applicative moment.
However, such an effective historical consciousness, by means of its own
self-reflectivity, cannot become completely aware of its historical determination and thereby escape the effects of its inheritance to achieve a
historically independent understanding (*WM*, 324; *TM*, 341).

Gadamer makes three essential points concerning the concept of
experience. With reference to Aristotle, he argues that experience is
something that happens to a subject. From Hegel he acknowledges that
to have an experience means to discover that what one thought was the
case is, in fact, not the case. In opposition to Hegel's dialectical synthesis, Gadamer argues that philosophical consciousness, through the
observation of the experiences of consciousness, must acknowledge that
"the truth of experience always contains a reference to new experience"
(*WM*, 338; *TM*, 355). This breaks the dialectical progression. Therefore
the experienced consciousness is fundamentally open to the possibility
of future experiences. Aeschylus's statement, "to learn from suffering,"
bears witness to this fundamental finitude and fallibility in human experience (*WM*, 339; *TM*, 356). The reflexivity of effective historical consciousness is, therefore, bounded by the truth of experience so it is
"more being than consciousness" (*GW*II, 247).

The experience of hermeneutic truth is properly described as an
act of the subject matter itself (*WM*, 439; *TM*, 463). The subject matter,
as experienced in its coming to be in language, overturns one's previous
experience. "This act of the subject matter is the authentic speculative

movement, which grasps the speaker" (*WM*, 450; *TM*, 474). The Being of the subject matter itself is, therefore, its ever changing speculative self-presentations in the changing linguistic perspectives. Unlike Hegel, this speculative movement represents a "bad infinite." Each perspective is a mirroring of the subject matter in so far as it can exist within that linguistic perspective (*WM*, 450; *TM*, 475).

How is this speculative self-presentation recognized as a legitimate prejudice in this experience? To answer this question Gadamer refers to Plato's concept of the beautiful, which is able to present itself in its truth. The self-presentation of the subject matter overcomes the cognizer in the significant sense of experience. As the beautiful, the self-presentation is "enlightening" (*WM*, 460; *TM*, 485). The human "suffers" the appearance of the beautiful as it does the truth of the subject matter in the event of understanding. The concept of the game, which was used to explicate the experience of the truth in the work of art, applies to the experience of hermeneutic truth. It is a language game where the players become involved in the conversation, in the openness of the questioning. It is "the play of language itself that addresses us, proposes and withdraws, questions and completes itself in the answer" (*WM*, 464; *TM*, 490). As the players in a game, the conversants do not have complete freedom of action, but are incorporated in "an event where the meaningful is able to establish itself" (*WM*, 465; *TM*, 490). The conversants are embedded in their linguistic horizon within effective history and cannot attain an independent position where the linguistic expression of the subject matter could be objectively tested. "We are, as cognizers, involved in an event of truth and come too late, as it were, if we want to know what we should believe" (*WM*, 465; *TM*, 490). The experience of hermeneutic truth overcomes and enlightens the conversants. Therefore, Gadamer is justified in concluding *Truth and Method*: "What the tool of method cannot accomplish, must rather and can truly be accomplished by means of a discipline of questioning and investigating, which authenticates [*verbürgt*] truth" (*WM*, 465; *TM*, 491).

With the publication of *Truth and Method* several questions have been raised concerning hermeneutic truth. Traditional hermeneuticists charge that Gadamer's analysis of textual understanding is mistaken and opens the door to relativism. They argue that only a hermeneutic methodology is able to preserve the concept of justified interpretation. Although critical theorists agree with Gadamer's critique of methodology, they charge that he has underrated the critical power of reflective thought to develop criteria for truth and so escape from the hermeneutic circle. They too raise the specter of relativism. On the other hand, postmodernists charge that Gadamer has not gone far enough, since Gadamer's claimed justification for hermeneutic truth depends on unjustifiable logocentric assumptions he makes in his analysis of language and the speculative event of understanding. Gadamer is simply not relativistic enough. Perhaps in being charged with being both too relativistic and not relativistic enough, Gadamer has laid open a middle ground. This volume continues this discussion of the place of hermeneutic philosophy with respect to the question relativism.

From the position of traditional hermeneutics Emilio Betti maintains that Gadamer's reintroduction of the applicative moment in understanding is his fundamental mistake. In reference to Gadamer's discussion of "the exemplary significance of legal hermeneutics," Betti argues that one can and must distinguish between the legal historian's as opposed to the judge's understanding of the meaning of a law. Only the judge must discover the law's application, i.e. its significance (*Bedeutsamkeit*), since he or she must use this law in the contemporary situation. The legal historian, on the other hand, must use a hermeneutic methodology to attempt to avoid all influence of his or her own prejudices or those of the time in order to discover the original meaning (*Bedeutung*) of that law. For Betti a text is an objectification of mind so that the correct interpretation of a text can be established as the author's intention. Betti concludes that Gadamer's insistence upon a necessary applicative moment in all understanding "opens the door to subjective caprice and threatens to conceal historical truth, if not to bend it and distort it, even if only unconsciously."[2]

E. D. Hirsch, Jr. raises a similar objection, arguing that Gadamer's development of Heidegger's radical historicality for the interpreter results in an internal contradiction as well as the destruction of any meaningful sense of truth.[3] Following traditional hermeneutics, Hirsch argues that the meaning of a text is determined by the author's intention as embodied in his or her choice of linguistic symbols. This is the meaning of a text and its understanding is to be taken at least as the regulative principle for truth. It is quite another thing to ask what the text means for an interpreter; this is the text's significance and does involve an applicative moment. Hirsch argues that Gadamer's theory of the fusion of horizons presupposes this distinction since the past horizon of the text is its meaning without application. If Gadamer insists on application, Hirsch concludes, the result would be the "indeterminacy of textual meaning" so that a text would mean "nothing in particular at all."[4]

This collection begins by examining the charge of relativism from the position of traditional hermeneutics. In "On the Composition of *Truth and Method*" Jean Grondin argues that the earliest manuscript of *Truth and Method* demonstrates that this work was conceived as one whole and is not a compilation of various works. The original argument is apparent in this manuscript and requires the modification of the dominant opinion that the three parts of *Truth and Method* deal with art, history or the humanities, and language, respectively. He demonstrates that the first part does not primarily concern art, but concerns, as the whole, "the problem of the methodological self-clarification in the humanities." The discussion of art is only a necessary detour. The second part concerns a humanistic hermeneutics. Grondin argues that the third part really concerns philosophy and not language as such. He concludes that *Truth and Method* should be understood as a unitary discussion of the methodology of the humanities that leads to a rehabilitated humanistic hermeneutics and an examination of the motivational background and constraints in philosophical understanding. The development of philosophical hermeneutics as such begins in *Truth and Method* but is continued in Gadamer's writings thereafter.

In "Hermeneutical Truth and the Structure of Human Experience: Gadamer's Critique of Dilthey," Tom Nenon continues the discussion of truth in traditional humanities by examining Gadamer's critique of Dilthey. His purpose is to demonstrate that Gadamer's concept of truth is either similar to the later Dilthey's or, if not, the problem of relativism arises. Although the charge of subjectivism might be correct for the earlier Dilthey, it is not for the later Dilthey. The central problem Gadamer discusses in Dilthey is the idea that a work is an expression of the life of its author. However, in his later period, Nenon continues, Dilthey spoke of "the structures of human life" in a technical sense that was meant to include more general and not just individualistic elements. The question Nenon poses is whether Gadamer's sense of "world" or "Being" can be reduced to Dilthey's "structures of human life." If Gadamer does not intend a Heideggerian "history of Being," then his concept of world is very similar to Dilthey's structures of life. In Dilthey there are "fundamentally constant general structures of human life" that are accessible to competent interpreters and so guarantee the "possibility of human sciences as *sciences.*" In Gadamer what comes to be understood is not fixed but changing. However, it is exactly this flexibility, Nenon concludes, that leads to the charge of relativism.

The second group that charges Gadamer's theory is relativistic may be represented by Jürgen Habermas and Karl Otto Apel. Although both agree with Gadamer's critique of methodology, they claim he has overlooked the power of reflective thought to provide a criterion for truth within interpretive, historical understanding, so that philosophical hermeneutics becomes conservative and dogmatic in the final analysis. Habermas's central point is that Gadamer does not acknowledge the power of reflective consciousness to escape the historical conditioning of understanding.[5] Although Habermas agrees that one is conditioned by prejudices and that one must become aware of and critically question them if one is to understand, he argues that once one has become aware of one's prejudices, they will no longer function prejudicially. Rather reflective consciousness can critically examine the history of these prejudices and examine the truth-claims embodied in them with reference to ahistorical conditions for rationality.[6] Apel also agrees with Gadamer's critique of Hegel that the interpreter must allow for the possibility that he or she could learn from an inherited text.[7] However, Apel argues that Gadamer goes too far in emphasizing the passive or secondary position of the interpreter in relation to the text. Therefore Gadamer transfers all authority to the text and ignores the power of reflective consciousness to critically examine the text and find it wrong.[8] By means of a reflection on reflection, Apel argues that a universally valid standpoint can be discovered and legitimized by reflective consciousness.[9] Further, the general standpoint of Gadamer's own analysis and his universal claims are only possible presupposing such a nonhistorical, nonembedded position for self-consciousness. In this collection this direction of questioning is developed by Tom Rockmore and Joseph Margolis.

Tom Rockmore examines the epistemological implications of *Truth and Method* and the problem of relativism in his essay "Gadamer's Hermeneutics and the Overcoming of Epistemology." After examining Gadamer's reading of Dilthey and his addition of the concept of effective historical consciousness to Heidegger, Rockmore argues that history has become "a vehicle of truth." In attempting to surpass the philosophy of reflection in an experiential hermeneutics, Rockmore argues, Gadamer did not realize the epistemological price that had to be paid for denying reason its "pristine" character. Gadamer has confused (1) the idea of possible prejudices, which could be tested in a dialectic between the subject and object of experience; and (2) those prejudices, which as presuppositions, are not even questionable. What is lacking in Gadamer is "anyway to know that at a given time a given prejudice is true and not false." Gadamer's mistake lies in a misreading of Hegel and the post-Hegelian anticipation of the hermeneutic circle of understanding. Therefore, Rockmore concludes, Gadamer was wrong in arguing that phenomenology overcomes the epistemological problem.

In "Uncovering Hermeneutic Truth," Lawrence Schmidt provides an answer to the question of how hermeneutic truth can be justified by demonstrating how prejudices can be recognized as true and not false. Referring to Gadamer's discussions of Humboldt and Husserl, it is argued that what comes to be expressed in correct understanding can only be a perspective of the thing itself or subject matter under discussion. Schmidt then claims that the correct perspective of the subject matter can be recognized by the interpreter, since this perspective is enlightening. The enlightening quality is proposed as the hermeneutic truth-criterion enabling one to differentiate truth from falsity. This criterion is defended from Grondin's argument that there is no hermeneutic truth-criterion. Schmidt's conclusion is that this enlightening quality of the subject matter, which the cognizer experiences, allows Gadamer to justify hermeneutic truth, thereby escaping the charge of relativism without falling back into a traditional foundationalism.

Joseph Margolis presents "Three Puzzles for Gadamer's Hermeneutics" and turns the discussion of hermeneutic truth to the question of the metaphysical status of the hermeneutic subject. The problem is to reconcile the nature of human understanding with the nature of human being. Margolis refers to a passage where Gadamer denies that the "I" and "Thou" are isolated, substantial realities, since they are preceded by a common understanding. So to each self is predicated a necessary collective or historical nature, and yet the universal linguistic relation between man and the world requires individual selves. So Margolis asks how these hermeneutic subjects can remain distinct if "their nature can and must change under hermeneutic efforts and self-understanding." He finds no answer in Gadamer. According to Margolis the classical represents cases of historical invariance. The first puzzle asks how a historically effected self can know that what appears to be an invariance in the classical is not a "mere artifact" and so not a discernible universal. Without the classical, Margolis argues, Gadamer's theory is in danger of slipping into the position of radical relativism, which Gadamer wishes to avoid.

The postmodernists charge that Gadamer has not gone far enough in recognizing the radical relativism in the analysis of historicity and language. Gadamer's conclusion that hermeneutic truth may be justified indicates, rather, that he is still trapped within the logocentric tradition of metaphysics.

Jacques Derrida's explicit criticism of Gadamer appears in their 1981 encounter (*DD*, 52). Both philosophers are working from the thought of Heidegger and both look to an analysis of language in their criticism of Hegel. The essential difference concerns the speculative relationship between the word and its referent. Derrida argues, in his criticism of Husserl in *Speech and Phenomena*, that all linguistic signs are infected with a difference that undercuts their pretended referencing to a thing or some presence. Signs, and so written expressions, contain multiple traces to other signs, so that no determinant interpretation or truth may be claimed for any expression. For Derrida there can be no speculative recapturing in the sign or an interpretation of some supposed reference. Even Heidegger in his later works is suspect of searching for some particular meaning for Being, instead of acknowledging the radical indeterminacy of all references. From this perspective Derrida has raised three questions for Gadamer. Derrida charges that Gadamer has presupposed a certain "good will" in order for the conversants to allow the subject matter to guide the conversation. This implies Gadamer has succumbed to a hidden but nevertheless foundational "metaphysics of the will" (*DD*, 53). The second objection concerned the context of interpretation and its possible enlargement. Derrida means that if one attempts to enlarge the conversation to include more and more otherness what results is not a coming to agreement under the influence of the subject matter, but rather increased discontinuity and restructuring (*DD*, 53). Finally Derrida charges that Gadamer's concept of experience, which he used to break the Hegelian dialectic, may itself be a metaphysical importation. Instead of an experience in the event of truth where agreement is reached, there is, rather, a discontinuous series of interruptions (*DD*, 54).

Richard Rorty and John D. Caputo develop this line of criticism. Rorty applauds Gadamer's criticism of the correspondence theory of truth and his universal claim that all understanding is rooted in tradition. Rorty differentiates between what he terms a weak and a strong textualist. The strong textualist, a Rortian pragmatist, recognizes the complete contingency of language. There are merely different vocabularies. To argue that one has understood is merely to argue that this way of speaking, this vocabulary is more useful. The weak textualist is still a decoder and "victim of realism, of the 'metaphysics of presence.'"[10] The weak textualist still thinks that the meaning of a text can be discovered and that a consensus can be established concerning the correct interpretation. Rorty charges that this is Gadamer's position. Although Rorty does not identify the problem in Gadamer explicitly, it is clear that for him Gadamer's discussion of the active role of the subject matter in informing the interpreters and his conclusion that a hermeneutic truth may be authenticated, do prevent Gadamer from being a strong textualist. Rorty does charge Heidegger with making "language into a kind of divinity, something of which human beings are mere emanations."[11]

In *Radical Hermeneutics* Caputo argues that Gadamer's conception of hermeneutic truth "turns on a principle of creative repetition, of the endless reenactment of the tradition."[12] But at a critical point Gadamer turns from the more radical position of the later Heidegger and remains "attached to the tradition as the bearer of eternal truths."[13] Caputo charges that Gadamer does not provide for the criticism of tradition and does not see the dangerous side of tradition. Gadamer is concerned with "the *verum, alethea*, what is true here and now and ready for our consumption (application), and not *a-letheia*, the event of concealment and unconcealment" as the later Heidegger was.[14] In the end Gadamer's hermeneutics is "the most liberal possible version of a fundamentally conservative idea."[15]

Francis Ambrosio's "Caputo's Critique of Gadamer: Hermeneutics and the Metaphorics of the Person" responds indirectly to Margolis's puzzle of historical invariance through an examination of Caputo's critique. He argues that philosophical hermeneutics does not contain hidden universals, but rather Caputo has misunderstood the dialogical character of Gadamer's theory, his relation to the later Heidegger, and the role of application. Gadamer's concept of truth concerns an "emergence into language of the human relationship to the world as a virtual whole of meaning." Gadamer transformed Hegel's concept of the wholeness of truth, so that truth is virtual, of language, and never reaches full determinacy. So the unchanging in Gadamer is only the transmission of shared questions and not universals. Truth is an event of unconcealment amidst concealment. The difference from Heidegger's concept of truth lies in its relation to freedom. In Gadamer this relation is expressed in the willingness to hear truth and "allow it to make its claim in the universal play of conversation." Gadamer's hermeneutics is Platonic not because of a relationship to ideal truths but because of a relationship to Plato's discipline of dialogue, where the aim is to take responsibility for and assimilate Socrates's questions. By responding to them one continues the conversation. Ambrosio suggests "double-crossing" Caputo and Gadamer and that this could lead to a metaphorics of the person that would be neither a philosophical nor a radical hermeneutics.

In "Hermeneutics of the Possible: On Finitude and Truth in Philosophical Hermeneutics," James Risser indirectly takes up Margolis's question of the hermeneutic subject by defending Gadamer from the criticisms of Rorty and Caputo. Risser develops an ontology by arguing that possibility is higher than actuality. He defends Gadamer by exploring the idea that language is movement, *kinesis*, which occurs in its lived execution and produces meaning. In a conversation no prefigured potentiality, no hidden essence, as Caputo charges, comes forth and is actualized, but rather a common sphere of meaning emerges. Within the conversation sense emerges and transforms itself—a language game controlled by no individual will, but a play of language. Turning to Rorty, Risser demonstrates how truth occurs within an ontology of the possible. In *mimesis* there is an image-making without a distinction between image and original. The result is "thick images in which the intelligible and the image are entangled." These thick images "seep with possibility." So the question of truth will be concerned with a metaphoric of surface and depth—the playing out of thick images. Risser concludes by identifying two determinations to the moment of truth in philosophical hermeneutics. First, truth is something fitting, a fitting answer to the question, a certain disentanglement. There is falsifiability in the sense that the *Sache* breaks through to show itself to be other than was thought. Secondly, following an interpretation of *mimesis* and the thick image, truth occurs within a continuum of empty and full. An incorrect interpretation is empty and leads nowhere, whereas a correct one indicates an overflowing, an increase in being, and the possibility of saying more. So although the traditionalist's mark for truth, correspondence, is absent, one may nevertheless speak of truth—truth as *veritas*, as making real.

Hans-Georg Gadamer's essay, "On the Truth of the Word," provides an important development after *Truth and Method* concerning the ability of words to express hermeneutic truth. In this essay Gadamer is responding to the charges of relativism and has not yet taken up postmodern criticisms. In this volume his essay marks the conclusion of the discussion of the possibility of hermeneutic truth. The constitution of the word in the life of language as conversation, which Gadamer presupposes in this essay, frames the questions for the final set of contributions. How can dialogue form the conversation where the event of truth occurs? What is the role of *phronesis* in conversations?

In "Toward a Discursive Logic: Gadamer and Toulmin on Inquiry and Argument," P. Christopher Smith presents the logical structures involved in deliberative discourse by modifying Toulmin's account of practical logic to accommodate Gadamer's theory of question and answer. Smith examines Gadamer's synthesis of Plato's *dialegesthai*, talking something through, and Aristotle's *bouleuesthai*, taking counsel, in order to establish Gadamer's dialogical model. Smith translates Toulmin's set of analogous procedural rules into the dialogical structure, since Toulmin, in clinging to the ideal of apodictic inference, suppresses the dialogue between claim and counterclaim. To remedy this deficiency, Smith incorporates the structure of scholastic arguments. He then presents a modified version of Toulmin's structures in accord with this scholastic model. Since coming to an understanding is a cooperative process and not the adjudication of rival claims, one must move from a speaker playing the language game to the center of language, the play of language, where language speaks through us. This reflects Gadamer's emphasis on the subject matter in dialogue—Plato's "happening of arguments to us." Smith concludes that his logical schema must be modified to include this third element so that at "the provisional close of the language event . . . they had both been given something to understand."

Robert Bernasconi's essay, "'You Don't Know What I'm Talking About': Alterity and the Hermeneutic Ideal," focuses on the question of alterity in hermeneutic dialogue. It concerns the possibility of coming to agreement within dialogue and concentrates on the case of dialogue where understanding is sought across temporal and cultural difference, which he takes to be paradigmatic for hermeneutics. Bernasconi relates the question of alterity to Gadamer's own self-critical question concerning the extent to which Gadamer was able to preserve and not simply sublate the otherness of the other in the event of understanding. After examining three models of dialogue in *Truth and Method*, Bernasconi questions whether the notion of openness is the same in the experience of the claim of tradition and in the experience of the Thou. Tradition appears to be employed by Gadamer in a Hegelian sense, as is evidenced by the monolithic way it serves to bridge the temporal distance. He worries that "the Other of its Own," the reflected other, the other of myself, that the text becomes for the interpreter, appears to indicate the standpoint of the second and not the third model of the I-Thou relation. Although the otherness of the past may be a beginning point, the aim appears to be its overcoming. This has led to the charge that Gadamer's dialogue, like Hegel's and Heidegger's, is really a monologue. Bernasconi resists the temptation of reducing the tension between mutuality and alterity within Gadamer's writings. He examines several more recent essays where Gadamer acknowledges the otherness of the other. But the question is posed "whether Gadamer could insist on the importance of attending to the saying of the other without shifting his focus from the object of discourse." Genuine alterity lies in the *experience* of the radical challenge where one is addressed and put into question. This experience of alterity, however, cannot be incorporated into hermeneutic theory, since the theory depends on mutuality and a model of understanding directed to agreement. So, Gadamer's writings must be read not only in terms of the hermeneutic theory they enunciate, but as juxtaposing this theory with the testimony of certain experiences of alterity that the theory does not and cannot accommodate.

In "Understanding and Willing," Kees Vuyk examines the relationship between the good will toward the other (which Gadamer claims is a precondition for understanding) and a metaphysics of the will (which Derrida suggests underlies Gadamer's hermeneutics). He approaches this question by examining the relation between the will and resoluteness (*Entschlossenheit*) in Heidegger. Willing to know is the resoluteness to be able to stand in the openness of entities or truth, and is connected to a departure from the captivity of entities. In authentic understanding Dasein is not-at-home (*unheimlich*) and holds itself open for the abyss. Vuyk argues that Gadamer must presuppose the good will, since to understand the other in its otherness and to know one does not know, are required in order to place something in the open. Therefore Gadamer's presupposition of a good will in dialogue does not imply the will as the subject of a contemporary metaphysics. It is not a Nietzschean will to dominate. Vuyk concludes that Heidegger's concept of the will is more radical than Gadamer's. The good will in Gadamer attempts to make the other as strong as possible, but in completed understanding there is a unifying of self and other. In Heidegger, authentic understanding reveals Dasein as originally without foundation. In Gadamer willing is primarily a relation between entities and not a mode of Being, so that Gadamer could be said to have an illusion too many, "the illusion of truth."

Marc J. LaFountain questions whether the hermeneutic conversation can occur at all in today's postmodern culture in "Play and Ethics in *Culturus Interruptus*: Gadamer's Hermeneutics in Postmodernity." With this contribution the question concerning the relationship between ethics, especially Aristotle's, and the possibility of hermeneutic truth occurring within the conversation is broached. LaFountain begins with an analysis of play and its relation to the fusion of horizons. Today, according to LaFountain, hermeneutic experience finds itself interrupted and deferred. The to-and-fro motion of play has been "overwhelmed by postmodernity's code of speed." The playing motion has become a "helter-skelter" and the game a "speedy con-fusion." The primary hermeneutic situation has become distorted. "We have become decentered in a way not envisioned by Gadamer." The situation in ethics is especially bleak. Since play has been disrupted, the mediation with tradition, which gave our finite and temporal ethics its support, no longer exists. Ethics is now an excess, not phronetic but the "pathetic, phrenetic grasping and wandering of a nomadic life." History has become histories so the temporal flow of tradition necessary to preserve the ethos and polis has disappeared, and now there is a "radical separation of ethos and polis" that is beyond transformative unification. The result is that Gadamer's hermeneutics is only "a pleasing way" to present the call that today has been interrupted.

Michael Kelly, on the other hand, argues for the possibility of hermeneutic conversations in today's world. In "Gadamer, Foucault, and Habermas on Ethical Critique," he maintains that Gadamer's hermeneutics and Foucault's genealogy are "complementary in certain important respects in ethics." Kelly examines Habermas's critique of Gadamer and Foucault and argues that for Gadamer a hermeneutic ethics requires the synthesis of Aristotle and Kant. To explain the possibility of philosophical critique of the norms of an ethos, Gadamer turns to Kant's categorical imperative as a test. The difference between Gadamer and Habermas concerns the justification of this universality principle. For Gadamer the historically conditioned structures of practical reason cannot be overcome to result in an unconditional justification, whereas Habermas insists this is necessary. At this juncture Kelly finds that Foucault compliments Gadamer. To explain the possibility of ethical critique Foucault turns to the Enlightenment and especially Kant, to the surprise of many. Kant introduces the ethos of a permanent critique of our norms that becomes Foucault's "genealogical-archaeological critique." Since we have not yet attained complete freedom, Foucault requires one to disturb the immobile, to fragment the unified, and to demonstrate heterogeneity in the imagined homogeneous. This ethos presupposes that the actor is "committed to freedom." But such a commitment need not be universal as Habermas claims. It may be local. Kelly concludes that what unifies the ethical theories of Gadamer, Foucault, and Habermas is "solidarity on the Enlightenment ideal of moral freedom, which Gadamer calls the highest principle of reason."

In "*Phronesis* as Understanding: Situating Philosophical Hermeneutics," Günter Figal examines the central role of Aristotle's concept of practical reason in Gadamer's reinterpretation of practical philosophy. He argues that Aristotle's concept of *phronesis* is more important for philosophical hermeneutics than Heidegger's analysis of Dasein, since *phronesis* demonstrates the moment of application to the particular, inherent in all understanding. Philosophical hermeneutics presents a new relation to the later Heidegger and his path toward language by means of a reinterpretation of the tradition of practical philosophy. That understanding is an event within language means that language is a work (*ergon*) and not just an activity (*energeia*). This preserves the foreignness of tradition. Experiencing in the event of understanding has "the character of an apprehension [*Vernehmen*]." There is a "difference between the apprehension of tradition and the completion of understanding." The place of hermeneutics is in this difference. This leads to the reinterpretation of practical philosophy. Tradition is experienced as an event. The text or tradition presents something that shines forth and claims to be meaningful without completing understanding. So language has the character of an open space of a playing (*Spielraum*) that is never completed. Philosophical hermeneutics is more than a practical philosophy since it attempts to make clear the openness of language and one's involvement in the space of a playing of acting and understanding. It first presents the free space in which any practical act can occur, and it demonstrates *phronesis* to always be effective historical consciousness. The relation of philosophical hermeneutics to the inherited is "neither *phronesis* nor historicality," for neither of these correctly acknowledges the foreignness of the inherited. Therefore, the place of philosophical hermeneutics is in the "between." It sees itself in this place and is able to place the inherited in this openness between the foreign and the accessible.

This volume seeks to situate philosophical hermeneutics in the contemporary conversation. The voices raised here question the place of hermeneutics between certainty and relativism. Is there a specter of relativism that is avoided or entertained? Resolution was not the aim; rather, questions and perspectives are opened for a continuing conversation.

PART   1

ON HERMENEUTIC
TRUTH(S)

On the Composition of
Truth and Method

Jean Grondin

Translated by Lawrence K. Schmidt

n its thirty-year effective history the book *Truth and Method* (hereafter: *TM*) has been primarily discussed as a hermeneutic theory or philosophical conception. It is completely correct and most important that philosophical books be considered as proposed theories. However, we will here be concerned with another, and perhaps less frequented, approach that one could term purely "philological." The work *TM* will be discussed in terms of its composition and the history of its development. Hitherto *TM* has hardly been discussed as a text that has a history. There are philologies for Plato, Kant, and even Wittgenstein and Heidegger, but not yet one for Gadamer. Is one needed? Philosophers have the habit of considering philology to be less important: they are concerned with the spirit, not with the letter. Due to the common disdain for philological work, an interest in Gadamer philology must first be aroused. What is at stake? Can the philological viewpoint expose something that the philosophical reader would miss?

In spite of its prosaic character, *TM* is a very complicated work, especially as concerns its organization. Is there a stringent compositional development in the series of chapters and sections? Over time *TM* has earned the reputation of being a rather heterogeneous work. It is true that it offers many historical studies (e.g., concerning Greek tragedy, the beautiful in Plato, Augustine's doctrine of the *verbum*, Hegel's concept of experience) about which one could often be of the opinion that they stand disconnected next to each other. Sometimes the suspicion even arises, and Gadamer has at times nourished it, that *TM* originated from *different* investigations—perhaps from works on art, history, and language. In the beginning of his "self-critique" of 1985, Gadamer speaks of *TM* as "a theoretical project that united the initiated investigations from various sides into the unity of a philosophical whole" (*GW*II, 3). Does *TM* then consist of three different analyses that came together, perhaps by chance, to form the unity of a philosophical opus? For each individual investigation the question also arises whether it was created as a whole, for many chapters in *TM* read like individual essays.

One recognizes what is at stake here: the question whether *TM* is a heterogeneous whole. This suspicion, which will not be supported here, implies the further question of whether *TM* was conceived as a unified hermeneutic theory and, therefore, can be read as a coherent philosophy. If *TM* is to be understood as a unity, it remains to be demonstrated how the individual parts relate to the whole of the work. More simply expressed: What is the basic thesis of this work and in what manner is it argumentatively developed in the individual chapters? Clearly these are also *philosophical* questions. How can a philological discussion contribute to their solution?

What sources are available for such a philological examination of the text? There are different ones. First, a philology must pay attention to the specific conjunctions of the parts of the work. How is each transition from one part to the next, from one chapter to the next, accomplished? One must ask whether these transitions are arbitrary or consistent. Second, a philological analysis must pay special attention to the "preliminary stages" of the work. Before *TM*, Gadamer published several individual investigations that disclose his original intuitions at that time. Some of these essays are brought together under the title "Preliminary Stages" in the beginning of the second volume of his collected works. For example, one should be struck by the fact that Gadamer was then concerned with questions, such as the problem of truth in the humanities, which concerned him to a far lesser extent after the publication of *TM*, when the debates with Betti, Habermas and Derrida presented his hermeneutics with completely new challenges. Third, Gadamer's autobiographical statements concerning the composition of his major work are to be consulted, including the oral ones.[1] For *TM* itself says relatively little about the most important conjunctions of its parts. Our fourth and most informative source, however, is the longhand manuscript of *TM*. On the occasion of his eightieth birthday, Gadamer presented this manuscript to the University of Heidelberg Library for an exhibit that took place from 11 February to 15 April 1980. Until now, this manuscript has been neither examined nor even noticed by scholars.[2] It consists of approximately eighty closely written pages, forty-five of which were numbered by Gadamer. This first draft of *TM* does not greatly depart from the published work of 1960 in either its development, its formulations or, for the most part, in its theoretical standpoint. What is most important is that this manuscript may illuminate the original theme of *TM*, due to its short length. On the basis of these four sources I wish to submit in the following a few theses concerning the composition of *TM* and especially the major conjunctions of *TM*. For corroborative purposes, our argument will be based on the published texts of Gadamer insofar as is possible.

To begin, a few formal particulars concerning the genesis of the work are to be recalled. Gadamer presented his first systematic, major work relatively late in life, when he was sixty. This is understandable due in part to the historical circumstances. After the publication of his habilitation in 1931, in the time between 1933 and 1945, Gadamer could not consider a larger publication. During this time he worked on a commentary on Aristotle's *Physics*, a part of which may be published (*GW*II, 487). Also, a larger study on Sophistic and Platonic politics was at that time "prudently" discontinued (*GW*II, 489). After the war he was appointed rector in Leipzig, which must again have delayed any plans for a demanding publication. After a two-year teaching appointment in Frankfurt am Main, he became the successor of Karl Jaspers in Heidelberg in 1949. Caring for the intellectual rebirth of Germany, he dedicated himself, as a "passionate teacher" (*GW*II, 492), during this period to his teaching and pedagogically oriented publications (e.g., the translation of Aristotle's *Metaphysics*, Book Lambda, and a new edition of Dilthey's *Outline of the History of Philosophy*). In addition to these trying historical circumstances, it is also the case that Gadamer found writing difficult. Concerning this period, he writes in his actual autobiography, the "self-presentation" of 1975 (the *Philosophical Apprenticeship* of 1977 clearly discusses Gadamer's encounters with others more than himself): "Otherwise writing remained a real torment for me for a long time. I always had the damnable feeling that Heidegger was looking over my shoulder" (*GW*II, 491). In the semester vacations between 1950 and 1959, he wrote his "Hermeneutics" (this was clearly the general working title). There exist three drafts of this work. The first is that eighty-page manuscript which can be found in the University of Heidelberg Library. Its exact dates are difficult to determine. Perhaps this is not so important, but presumably it was written in the year 1956, before the Löwen essays of 1957. The latter were published in French under the title, "Le problème de la conscience historique." (In the meantime there exist Italian and English translations of this French text. The German manuscript, which may be considered a further draft of *TM*, has been lost.) The second draft of *TM* is an interim editing, which we do not know, but which can be recognized in its first part from the end of the manuscript of the original draft. The third was published as *TM*.

The original draft demonstrates first that *TM* was written as a whole. It has neither a title nor titled sections. Nevertheless, the major argument, the original argument of *TM*, may be grasped in it and will be summarized here. It begins with the problem of the methodological self-understanding of the humanities in Dilthey, Droysen, and Helmholtz. This is followed by the essence of the discussion of the humanistic guiding concepts of education and taste. In the same breath, it discusses the abstractions of the historical and aesthetic consciousnesses, before it deals separately with the aesthetic. The central point here concerns the isolation of the aesthetic image from the context of life out of which it sprang. This isolation leads to an uneasiness in the Romantic and a new appreciation of hermeneutics in Schleiermacher (whose task of reconstruction is criticized, although without the reference to Hegel's task of integration as occurs at the end of the first part of *TM*). From this point on, the original draft follows the development of the hermeneutic question in Schleiermacher and Dilthey up to the new formulation of the problem in Heidegger. Then, within one and the same paragraph the transition is made to the systematic and central part of *TM*, namely, by means of the doctrine of the hermeneutic circle. Already in this original draft one finds next the idea of a mediation between history and the present, which the classical is called upon to illustrate. Here as well, the theory of the fusion of horizons builds the central aspect of the principle of effective history. On the basis of this principle, the critique of the philosophy of reflexivity is conducted. (The 1960 sections concerning application, judicial hermeneutics and *phronesis*, which occur between the chapters on effective history and the philosophy of reflexivity, are absent in the original draft.)[3] From this position the universal aspect of language is developed. The important *Cratylus* und *verbum* analyses follow, the latter, however, without reference to the Thomistic reception. The logic of question and answer is first discussed here, before the "third" part of *TM*. Further, the reference to Humboldt is missing in what will be the third part of *TM*. Gadamer's discussion of the universal character of language often confronts the problem of relativism and the hermeneutic character of philosophical statements, to which we will return. The proof of the metaphysical character of the beautiful in Plato—the actual conclusion of *TM*—also occurs near the end of the original draft. However, the manuscript, as it now exists, returns finally to the problem of the humanities. But it soon becomes clear that one is concerned with a new editing of the first pages of the work. Sketched summaries follow, certainly as indications of further working plans. So much on the general structure of the first draft, which we are unable to discuss in detail here.

The absence of subdivisions in the development of thought in the first draft often makes it difficult to follow, but it does permit the unified character of the work and its original intention to be grasped in outline. Due to the later introduction of the tripartite division of the book, it is the ruling opinion that the first part concerns "art," the second "history" or the "humanities" (as if they were the same), and the third "language." Following the original draft we will have reason to relativize this opinion. We will turn first to the thematic of the "first" part.

It is also true for the printed version that the first part does not only, and perhaps does not primarily, concern "art." The point of departure for the first part, and certainly for the whole work, is the problem of the methodological self-clarification in the humanities. The title of the first section of the first part is proof: "The Meaning of the Humanistic Tradition for the Humanities"—whose subsections are: "(a) The Problem of Method; (b) Humanistic Guiding Concepts." In the first fifty pages of *TM*, art is not even mentioned. Gadamer's problem is rather that of the correct self-understanding of the humanities in opposition to the natural sciences. For this Gadamer situates the discussion around Helmholtz's commemorative speech of 1862 on the relationship between the natural sciences and the humanities. It is the speech, by the way, that Helmholtz delivered upon becoming pro-rector of the University of Heidelberg—it constitutes a wonderful relation to Gadamer's own place of work. In his presentation Helmholtz finds the natural sciences to be characterized by the practice of logical induction that leads to universal rules and laws. The humanities, on the other hand, achieve their knowledge more by means of a psychological feeling of tact. Helmholtz speaks here of an artistic induction, of instinctive feeling and artistic tact, which proceed without clearly defined rules. With only a little exaggeration, one could claim that Gadamer's privileged conversation partner in the first part of *TM* is Helmholtz. At strategic points in the first part reference is made to Helmholtz.[4] Should it be the case that one has understood a book when one has grasped the question to which it is the answer, then one could say that it was Helmholtz's question concerning the manner of cognition in the humanities that gave the impetus to *TM*.

It is especially evident that Gadamer is essentially in *solidarity* with Helmholtz. As is stated toward the end of the original draft:

> At the end of all attempts to justify the unique method of the humanities, one finds oneself returned to the straightforward conclusions that Helmholtz made. What one terms method in modern science is exemplarily effective in the natural sciences. The method of the humanities has, fundamentally, actually nothing of its own. But the question arises as to how important method is here and whether there do not exist other conditions, which supervene here. Helmholtz correctly indicated exactly this point when he emphasized memory and authority and spoke of psychological tact, which here replaced conscious demonstrations. What is the basis of such tact? How is it attained? Does not the scientific nature of the humanities lie finally more in this than in the use of "method"?[5]

Gadamer and Helmholtz agree that the humanities are fundamentally much more concerned with practicing a tact than with applying some sort of method. Although Helmholtz proceeded from the exemplary status of the natural scientific method—nothing else was possible in the second half of the nineteenth century—he still correctly grasped in Gadamer's sense the uniqueness of the humanities in 1862. One can thereby judge the provocation of Gadamer's solidarity: In returning to a discussion of 1862 by the *natural scientist* Helmholtz, Gadamer skips over the epistemological discussions concerning the methodological uniqueness of the humanities that were conducted toward the end of the nineteenth and in the beginning of the twentieth century by authors such as Dilthey, Misch, Rothacker, Weber, and those influenced by the ruling Neo-Kantianism. The point is surely that these protracted debates were possessed by the idea that the humanities must somehow also have their own method in order to elevate them to sciences. It appears to Gadamer, who follows Helmholtz here, much more appropriate to trace the uniqueness of the humanities back to something like tact, a "*je ne sais quoi*" that cannot be methodized. Helmholtz, not Dilthey,[6] becomes thereby the silent representative of a hermeneutics that correctly exemplifies the specific mode of cognition in the humanities. In this spirit, *TM* conducts a fundamental critique of the methodological obsession apparent in their concern for the scientific nature of the humanities.

Accordingly, the initial thesis of *TM* is that the scientific character of the humanities may be "better understood from the tradition of the concept of education [*Bildung*] than from the idea of modern science" (*GWI*, 23). Here the meaning of the recourse to the humanistic tradition at the beginning of *TM* is uncovered. In the lap of this tradition, the concepts were developed which are able to correctly express the particular claim to knowledge of the humanities. According to Gadamer, this tradition was very much alive before Kant, previous to its being supplanted by the heteronym rule of the concept of method. So Gadamer must pursue the question: "How did the deterioration of this tradition happen and how did the claim for truth in humanistic knowledge thereby fall under the criterion of the methodological thinking of modern science, which is essentially foreign to it?" (*GWI*, 29). How did this deterioration of the humanistic tradition occur that lead to the sole rule of the idea of method dominated more and more by the natural sciences? Gadamer answers: by means of the ominous aesthetization of the basic concepts of the humanistic tradition, especially judgment and taste, which previously were acknowledged to have a *cognitive* function. This was the act or effect (Gadamer varies somewhat in the characterization) of Kant's *Critique of Judgment*, which subjectivized and aestheticized taste and, what amounts to the same thing, denied it cognitive value. What could not satisfy the criteria of the objective and methodological natural sciences, was now seen as merely "subjective" or "aesthetic," i.e., separated from the realm of knowledge. Since the Kantian subjectivization of the concept of taste "discredited every other theoretical cognition besides those of the natural sciences, it forced the self-understanding of the humanities towards the doctrine of method in the natural sciences" (*GWI*, 46). The humanistic tradition, in which the humanities could have recognized itself, was thereby abandoned and the path of the aesthetization and subjectivization of judgment followed. One measures the loss for the humanities:

> The significance of this is not easily overestimated. For what was given away is just that wherein philological-historical studies lived and from which they could alone have achieved their complete self-understanding, as they sought to methodologically justify themselves under the name of the "humanities" next to the natural sciences. (GWI, 46)

This development also has consequences that cannot be underestimated for the textual structure of *TM*, because art or aesthetics must first be considered here in the discussion of *TM*. Specifically, the exposure of the subjectivization and aesthetization of the fundamental supports of the humanistic tradition does not lose sight of the *guiding question* concerning the self-understanding of the humanities. Gadamer avidly pursues this guiding question when he decisively criticizes the development that led to the creation of a completely new and specific aesthetic consciousness. The center of the first part of *TM*, therefore, consists in a "critique of the abstraction of aesthetic consciousness."[7] If we may be permitted the expression, it may be said that, according to the subject matter, the path into the aesthetic represents, rather, a kind of detour. In spite of all the positive insights into art, the initial move of *TM* is rather anti-aesthetic than aesthetic. The creation of the aesthetic is nothing more than an abstraction, which needs—in the words of the early Heidegger—to be destroyed or relativized, in order to (re)gain an appropriate understanding of the mode of cognition in the humanities.

This regaining of the hermeneutic specificity of the humanities is accomplished in the following part of *TM*, especially in its systematic and major subdivision, which is preceded by a historical review. How stringent is the textual transition from the first part to the second part of *TM*? The opposition of Hegel and Schleiermacher constitutes the transitional point in the published version. While Schleiermacher understood the fundamental task of understanding to be a reconstruction and reproduction of a past act, Hegel saw it in the task of integrating history and the present. In this, Hegel more adequately presented the historical productivity of understanding than Schleiermacher. Gadamer wishes to follow "more Hegel than Schleiermacher" and therefore "accentuates the history of hermeneutics in a completely new" manner.[8] For this reason the "dogmatic presuppositions" of the development of hermeneutics are to be exposed in the second part. The transition is somewhat different in the original draft. There, the reference to Hegel is completely missing. Schleiermacher's position is alone decisive. Gadamer especially emphasizes the discomfort that follows the creation of the artistic consciousness and the thereby associated isolation of the work of art from the horizon of its creation. Schleiermacher was still clear about the "organic interdependence of the work of art and its situation of origination" in his lectures on aesthetics.[9] The task of historical understanding was, therefore, to reconquer this original world. Accordingly, he saw the historical understanding of the work of art "as a reconstitution of the uprooting that influenced the understanding of the work, therefore, history as a means to completely grasp the artistic meaning of the work—a restitution in and for the aesthetic consciousness."[10] The interest in the reconstitution of the original work was still a normative one: it concerned the rewinning of an exemplary stylistic ideal. Gadamer discusses primarily the interest in the stylistic ideal of antique simplicity, which Winckelmann and Herder pursued, and which called classical studies into life as well as the romantic interest in the middle ages. Exactly at this point the transition to the second part of *TM*, which is still not yet one, occurs:

> In this situation of a historical-normative interest in the romantic Middle Ages, an old discipline of Biblical theology and classical philology regains a new life: hermeneutics. And the whole future of historical sciences will be influenced by it. On both paths, the theological and the philological, this art of understanding and interpretation developed from an analo-gous impulse: Theological hermeneutics, as Dilthey has beautifully shown, developed as a self-defense of the reformation's understanding of the Bible against the attack of the Tridentine theologians and their appeal to the indispensability of tradition; the philological hermeneutics developed as an instrument for the humanistic claim to re-discover classi-cal literature."[11]

The last lines are identical with the beginning of the second part in *TM*. Only the point of departure is somewhat different.

For reasons of space, we must forgo a presentation of the very rich second part, as it appears in the original and published versions. Two remarks must suffice. *First,* the systematic second subdivision of the sec-ond part is to be viewed as a type of conclusion for the question of *TM* concerning the appropriate self-understanding of the humanities. This is not only due to the fact that the concepts are explicated there that stand at the center of the discussion about philosophical hermeneutics (such as effective history, fusion of horizons, rehabilitation of prejudices, authority and tradition, application, as well as the logic of question and answer). This point is already present in the title of the systematic subdi-vision, "Fundamentals of a Theory of Hermeneutic Experience," because this title is almost identical with the original title of the book, which was relegated to the subtitle during the printing: "Fundamentals of Philosophical Hermeneutics." There can be no doubt that in this sub-division *TM* attains its goal as stated in the introduction, i.e., to situate the truth-claims of the humanities.

Our second remark is precisely that this second part still concerns the problem of the humanities. In both the published as well as in the original version, Gadamer speaks, in this second part, continually and consequently of his project as one of a "hermeneutics of the humanities" (*geisteswissenschaftlichen Hermeneutik*).[12] This must be emphasized because *after TM* the problem of hermeneutics was considered to be one of a gen-eral theory of historicity, facticity, the lifeworld, and dialogue. This development is quite correct, but the work of 1960 remains completely influenced and ruled by its initial problem, the humanities.[13]

Nevertheless, the development toward a *philosophical* hermeneutics, which leaves the "bounded" problem of the humanities behind it, is already present in 1960. This is, however, to be accomplished in the third part of *TM*. There, the universal dimension of hermeneutics is to be brought to light. The basis of this universal aspect is, however, not immediately evident. The sure, but limited, means of philology alone certainly do not permit its discovery. Nevertheless, there exists a certain consensus that this universality is to be accredited to "language." So the third part of *TM* should be a discussion of "language."

The means of philology do permit this consensus to be questioned to some degree. For some texts indicate that the actual discussion of the third part is to be about "philosophy." On the very first page of *TM* (in the introduction) one reads, for example, about the goal of the investigation:

> Its purpose is to seek out those experiences of truth, wherever they may be encountered, which transcend the area of control of the scientific method and to question them concerning their own legitimacy. So the humanities are brought together with other ways of experiencing that lie outside science: with the experience of philosophy, with the experience of art and with the experience of history itself. (*GWI*, 1–2)

Right at the beginning of *TM* this passage confronts us with the triad: philosophy, art, and history. Is this perhaps a mistake by Gadamer, who forgot to emphasize language as the third and fundamental area of experience in his hermeneutics? Or does Gadamer thereby hit the nail on the head, namely the subject matter that is considered in the "ontological" turn of hermeneutics *following the guide* of language (the title of the third part)? What does "ontological" mean here? Primarily, following the paths of Heidegger, a turn of hermeneutics toward the philosophical is envisioned. The closing section of *TM* concerns hermeneutics' becoming universal, *that means* philosophical. Here the transition is achieved from the "hermeneutics of the humanities" of the second part to an authentic "philosophical hermeneutics" of the third part, which is to be accomplished following the "guide" of language. Following the text, a (hermeneutic) self-understanding is to be initiated here that draws on the consequences from the hermeneutics of the humanities in the second part.

This turn of hermeneutics toward the philosophical, I believe, is much clearer in the original draft than in the published work. Already on the first page of the original draft, the task of the investigation is determined to be the unification of a new basis for philosophy with the self-understanding of the humanities. Since it has not yet been published, it is of value to quote the first paragraph in its full length:

> It is not only a need for logical clarity that connects the humanities with philosophy. To a greater extent the so-called humanities present philosophy itself with a problem. What one has stated and could say about their logical, epistemological foundation and about the justification of their scientific independence in opposition to the natural sciences, remains far behind what the humanities are and what they mean for philosophy. It could be nothing—or everything. Nothing, if they are considered as only an incomplete realization of the idea of science. For it follows from this that the idea of "scientific philosophy" will also be measured in terms of the complete determination of this idea of science as it is presented in the mathematical natural sciences, i.e., understood only, however, as a tool of these sciences. On the other hand, where the idea of the humanities is recognized as an independent type of science, whose reduction to the ideal of natural scientific knowledge is impossible, and where the idea of the greatest possible approximation to the methods and certainty of the natural sciences is even recognized as absurd, there philosophy itself and all of its concerns are brought into play. It is doomed to fail, if the discussion of the methodological particularity of the humanities is limited to the methodological: it does not concern another, unique method, but rather a completely different idea of knowledge and truth. And philosophy, if it acknowledges this claim, will project for itself completely different goals than are demanded by the concept of truth in science. A true foundation for the humanities, as Dilthey sought to achieve, is, with inner necessity, a foundation for philosophy.

TM opposes the determination of the scientific character of philosophy that orients itself according to the methodological natural sciences. Philosophy can learn from the humanities, properly understood, that knowledge in the humanities is not based upon methodological distance, but rather upon the belongingness of the interpreter to its object and to its history. It is clear that a philosophy that accepts this "completely different idea of knowledge and truth" will also "project for itself completely different goals." Based upon the self-understanding of the humanities (in the first two parts), a new, hermeneutic foundation for philosophy is to be made possible in the third part.

This becomes evident in the development of the original draft. As

soon as the principle of effective history is established, Gadamer pro-
gresses to the determination of the limits of the philosophy of reflexivity. With this move, the third part of *TM* actually begins, the becoming
philosophical of hermeneutic self-understanding that has been freed
from methodological prejudices. The principle of effective history clearly implies becoming conscious of the continuing efficacy of tradition
beyond our conscious awareness of these effects and, therefore, the
impossibility of a complete self-awareness of consciousness about itself.
This Gadamer opposes to the absolute claim of the philosophy of reflexivity. The power of history makes unattainable the speculative self-pos-
session of consciousness, which the philosophy of reflexivity has envisioned up to the present.

> But, properly considered, the power of history does not depend upon its
> being acknowledged. The power of history over finite human conscious-
> ness is exactly that it has its effect even when one, through the belief in
> method, denies one's own historicality. The demand to become con-
> scious of this effective history is so urgent precisely because of this situa-
> tion.[14]

The next task is to convince philosophy about this urgency.

Philosophy, hermeneutically understood, is not exhausted by a system of true sentences. Its propositions may only be understood when
one has referred them back to their motivational background. The content of philosophical propositions, as all propositions, cannot be read
from their semantic-logical character. To understand philosophically
and in language one must proceed to the motivation of the spoken. In
the classical terminology of Augustine, from whom alone the hermeneutic claim to universality in Gadamer's sense may be understood, one is
concerned with the *actus exercitus*, with the completed meaning of the
statement, i.e., with the significance that speaking has for the speaker
and for the listener,[15] with the *verbum interius* or the *logos endiathetos* (i.e.,
that which is expressed) and not with the *logos prophorikos* alone (i.e., that
which is logically determinable in the statement). This fundamental
intuition, which is derived from Augustine as seen by the early Heidegger,[16] is already to be found in the preliminary studies to *TM*, for example in the important essay of 1957, "What is Truth?," where Gadamer
wrote:

> I believe that one can principally state: there can exist no statement that
> is absolutely true. . . . There exists no statement that one can grasp only

from the content that it presents, if one wishes to grasp it in its truth.
Every statement is motivated. Every statement has its presuppositions that
it does not express (*GW*II, 52).

This *universal hermeneutic* character of philosophical sentences is the
actual theme at the end of *TM*. Here Gadamer uses the adjective
"hermeneutic," as he later recognizes, "with reference to a manner of
speech that Heidegger developed in his early period."[17] As we can learn
from the only recently available lectures of the young Heidegger, the
hermeneutic is to be understood as the opposite word for the apophantic. While the apophantic retains only the level of sense that constitutes
the form of the logical proposition, the hermeneutic envisions the
opposing, more original sphere of the unstated self-interpretation of the
sense of Dasein that motivates the apophantic. Through the universal
hermeneutic character of philosophical sentences, Gadamer supports
the thesis that philosophical sentences are not to be reduced to their logical content, but are to be comprehended in their total meaning only
from their motivational background. We quote again from the original
draft and indeed from one of the last paragraphs, its *conclusio*, if one will:

> It is necessary to also understand the propositions of philosophy in their
> propositional character, i.e., they are also not to be organized as separat-
> ed, absolute, and in a system of true sentences, but are to be understood
> in their "meaning." This meaning is in every proposition, as is to be
> remembered, a direction of meaning that results from its motivation.
> This reference of all philosophical propositions to such a motivational
> background does not at all imply that, therefore, every proposition—as
> always motivated—is correct. Rather, what is more important is to estab-
> lish the motivational niveau as such.[18]

The actual meaning of the claim for the universality of hermeneutics lies in this motivational structure of language, in the *verbum interius*,
which is to be received as the *actus exercitus* in its complete meaning. The
dialectic of question and answer is called upon in order to clarify this
motivational structure. No surprise that it is contained in the original
draft in the section on language (the later third part). In the printed version it enables precisely the *transition* from the hermeneutics of the
humanities of the second part to the philosophical, and thereby the universal, hermeneutics of the last part. This dialogic, which replaces
Hegel's dialectic aiming toward completion, embodies "the hermeneutic primordial phenomenon, that there exists no possible proposition

that could be understood as anything else but an answer to a question."[19]

This hermeneutic primordial phenomenon legitimizes the universality of philosophical hermeneutics. It makes sense that this "universal aspect," as *TM* almost paradoxically states, primarily concerns "language." For this reason language enjoys the guiding function in the last part of *TM* and so constitutes its central theme. But the discussion of a *philosophical* hermeneutics means more, namely a new understanding of philosophy that is to result from the hermeneutics of the humanities (in part 2), which clearly presents its historical motivational structure. The textual unity of *TM* becomes evident here in that "the methodological self- understanding of philology pushes towards a systematic questioning of philosophy."[20] One will understand and appreciate that this hermeneutics that has become universal, i.e., philosophical hermeneutics, and that has its location in the dialogical element of language, will develop for itself completely different goals than would be suggested by the concept of a methodological, self-certain, scientific philosophy of reflexivity. Its direction of attack will certainly include the need to "break the rigidity of the so-called chemically pure concepts" (*GW*II, 90).

The well-known three part division of *TM* ("art," "history," "language") thereby receives a new coherence. As we saw, it is also somewhat inexact. For the first part does not primarily concern art. Its point of departure is much more the methodological problem in the humanities, and, due to the ominous aesthetization of the concept of taste, the deterioration of the humanistic tradition wherein the humanities could have been able to recognize itself. The aesthetic, and even art, constitute abstractions that are criticized in the first part for the purpose of a better hermeneutic evaluation of the humanistic guiding concepts. After this "detour" the second part is dedicated to the problematic of a hermeneutics of the humanities. With all the emphasis on historicality and effective history, it does not concern "history" in general and avoids speculations on the philosophy of history. The third part certainly deals with "language" and its universal hermeneutic dimension (in the sense of the early Heidegger), but implies the unspoken motivational structure of language, the dialogic of question and answer that conditions every proposition—in short, the *verbum interius*—a hermeneutic view that finally aims at a new self-conception of philosophy.

Clearly with these remarks the domain of pure philology has been transgressed here and there. In order not to break the boundaries of this project, I will now return to the textual evidence of *TM* and its third part. In relation to the corresponding discussions of the original draft, the final part of *TM* might appear somewhat unsatisfying. Even without reference to the original draft, this is apparent in a certain vagueness of its use of language, which other critics have already had reason to fault. In this third part Gadamer employs extremely imprecise formulations, which contrasts sharply with the conceptual precision of the second part. The thesis, that "Being, which can be understood, is language," speaking about an "ontological turn" and a "universal aspect" of hermeneutics are formulations that are not very often understood. Why, in addition, were these theses presented as historical interpretations of Augustine and Plato? What Gadamer wanted to say in this third part remains very difficult to pinpoint, if one does not consider the motivational background of the original draft. This background permits the deciphering of many of the formulations of the third part, since Gadamer essentially proposed the same positions here as in the original draft.

But what accounts for this indistinctness in the published third part? Viewed purely philologically, the comfortable expediency about an earlier or later writing of the third part could suggest itself. It is clearly customary in philology to explain away differing textual editions by means of periodizing. In order to discover whether our private feelings were perhaps misleading us here, we finally asked Professor Gadamer himself about this vagueness in the third part. He answered completely sincerely that this third part even appears to himself as linguistically very indistinct. He explained this in that perhaps he had run out of breath at the end of the work on so long a text, so that the third part was composed more hastily, whereby the precision of the formulations was given less attention. Each is free to accept or reject this self-explanation. Until further notice, it has something to it.

Gadamer has provided another small hint. Although the third part might appear often elusive, he has made up for this in the years after *TM* and has continued to work on the theme of language, which was discussed in general in the work of 1960.[21] In fact, after 1960 Gadamer has turned his attention, to an increasing degree, to the theme of language, which previously was less the subject matter of detailed publications. At that time the theme was certainly the humanities, which still dominated in *TM,* and which primarily occupied his attention as well as the study of Greek philosophy.[22]

If that is the case, one must recognize that the text of *TM* does not end in the year 1960, but continues beyond. This is supported by the interesting history of the title "Truth and Method." As one can learn from *Philosophical Apprenticeship* the book was originally to be called "Fundamentals of a Philosophical Hermeneutics."[23] Gadamer's publisher found the title somewhat exotic. "Hermeneutics" was then clearly not a common term. So Gadamer decided to make the original title the subtitle. We should remember that the original title was "Fundamentals of a Philosophical Hermeneutics." Gadamer also announced his work to colleagues under this title. The book was also sometimes reviewed under this old heading. In his debate with Gadamer, Emilio Betti continually quotes the book as "Fundamentals of a Philosophical Hermeneutics" as if the title "Truth and Method" did not exist.

At that time Gadamer considered the title "Event and Understanding," which he perhaps rejected because of its similarity to a title of Bultmann's (*Belief and Understanding*). Only during the printing did the new, Goetheske title, "Truth and Method" occur to him. That, however, is not the end of the matter. The book appeared between the years 1960 and 1975 in four editions. A fifth edition appeared in the year 1986 as volume 1 of the *Collected Works*. Until now it has been overlooked that the title was then silently somewhat modified. In fact, besides the first volume that presents the revised and corrected text of 1960, a second volume appeared with "Supplementary Material" that consists primarily of essays on philosophical hermeneutics, which were published before and after *TM*. This second volume also bears the title "Truth and Method." This title literally stands on the title-page of the *two first* volumes of the complete edition. The only thing that differentiates the first volume, with respect to the title, is the heading "Fundamentals of a Philosophical Hermeneutics." Thereby the text of 1960 regains, de facto, its original title. The title "Fundamentals . . ." applies only to the first volume, the one from 1960. Surreptitiously, "Truth and Method" became the title for the two volumes. In this manner the prefaces and postscripts of the earlier editions could be accommodated in the second volume.

In this Gadamer gives an important hint for the understanding of his work, namely that one should not limit *TM* to the work published in 1960. Also after 1960, Gadamer continued to work on *TM*, on his hermeneutics.[24] Only its "Fundamentals" remained, necessarily, the same. Those who wish to understand, to truly read, *TM* must deliberate upon the works after, but also before *TM*. The composition of *TM* did not end in 1960. It still continues.

2

Hermeneutical Truth and the Structure of Human Experience: Gadamer's Critique of Dilthey

Tom Nenon

The general outlines of Gadamer's estimation of Dilthey and the latter's contribution to hermeneutic philosophy are fairly well known.[1] Dilthey is seen as a crucial figure in the development of twentieth-century hermeneutics; he is viewed as the synthesizer of the nineteenth-century historical school and romantic aesthetics who thereby prepared the way for contemporary hermeneutical thinking. His positive contribution consists in his propagation and popularization of central concepts developed by previous hermeneutic theorists, in particular the concept of understanding, and in the key role he played in emphasizing the unique character of the human sciences; his chief failing was his psychological orientation and the resulting blindness to the claim to truth inherent in human communication and especially in works of art. According to Gadamer, his own hermeneutical philosophy corrects this flaw by shifting the focus from the speaker or the artist back to what is said in speech or the work of art, its truth-claim, thereby overcoming the psychological orientation that Dilthey had inherited from romantic aesthetics.

The exact details of Gadamer's interpretation and critique of Dilthey and their justification (or lack of justification) are less clear—perhaps not in the least because Gadamer's own remarks are for the most part rather general and oftentimes ambiguous as well. Moreover, much of his critique is conveyed indirectly—either by the tone in which his remarks on Dilthey are expressed, or by the way he emphasizes what he considers to be the novel insights of contemporary hermeneutics, thereby indicating what he thinks was lacking in his predecessors. And perhaps even more significantly, the view of Dilthey advanced by Gadamer has come to be the predominant, indeed almost unquestioned view adopted in the broad movement that has recently come to be known as "hermeneutics."[2]

In what follows I would thus like to examine more closely Gadamer's critique of Dilthey, filling in some of the details and examining the justification for his critical remarks. The issue is less the philological accuracy of his characterization of Dilthey than the systematic motives behind Gadamer's depiction and evaluation of his predecessor. In particular, I would like to concentrate on the notion of "truth" at work in Gadamer's major work *Truth and Method*, and examine whether the function it fulfills in Gadamer's "system" places him as far from Dilthey as his criticisms seem to imply. The thesis that will emerge is that Gadamer's position is much closer to that of the later Dilthey than the image he projects of Dilthey might suggest. For if one is to make sense of Gadamer's notion of truth, the content of the various forms of truth must be expressible in terms of possible structures of human experience. Gadamer himself fails to draw this conclusion. However, I will argue that the only way to avoid it would be to reduce the truth of art and communication back to the kind of objectivist, propositional truth that is the object of the natural sciences, or to look for the origin of truth in some nonhuman source such as the History of Being, or "language" taken as a historical agent. Since the first of these alternatives is clearly unacceptable for Gadamer and the second is also fraught with serious difficulties, the remaining possibility leaves him closer to Dilthey than his own comments and the common view admit. Unless he chooses to go the way of the History of Being or make language an independent agent in history, Gadamer's position ends up being related to that of the early Heidegger in *Being and Time*, where the primordial structures of the world and of truth can still be expressed in terms of fundamental possibilities of human existence, or to use Dilthey's term, structures of life.

I

A persistent theme throughout *Truth and Method* is Gadamer's contention that, in spite of intentions to the contrary, Dilthey remains too closely wed to the goals of the natural sciences and is thus led to espouse a kind of objectivity inappropriate to the human sciences. The means Dilthey chooses to establish such an objective foundation for the human sciences, however, is a unique version of psychology, i.e., he provides the human sciences with an objective foundation in the subjective structure of human life. Thus, in Gadamer's eyes, Dilthey turns out to be at one and the same time too much of an objectivitist with regard to the goals and possibilities of the human sciences and too much of a subjectivist with regard to its subject matter.

Let us turn first to his criticism of Dilthey as an objectivist. Dilthey's intention, Gadamer says at the outset of *Truth and Method*, is to find a different method for grasping the sociohistorical world than the inductive method of the natural sciences (*WM*, 2). Nonetheless, his aim is still to establish the humanistic disciplines as *sciences*, so that the methodology he ends up adopting is much closer to the method of the natural sciences than he realizes. It assumes the same distance from oneself and one's own surroundings that the natural sciences take as a requirement for objectivity (*WM*, 5) and it ends up adopting the same methods as the natural sciences—with the simple difference that it has a different kind of subject matter:

> No matter how much Dilthey advocated the epistemological independence of the human sciences—what is referred to as method in modern sciences is everywhere one and the same, and is exemplified best of all in the natural sciences. There is no special method for the human sciences. (*WM*, 5)

Dilthey is said to follow Helmholtz in his admiration of Mill's inductive method as a model for the human sciences as well (*WM*, 6); and in another place he is criticized for speaking of an "inductive procedure" to be employed in the human sciences: "the concept of an inductive procedure which is modelled on the natural sciences is just as insufficient. Historical experience, which is what he basically has in mind, is not a procedure and does not possess the anonymity of a procedure" (*WM*, 228).

An examination of Dilthey's writings, however, shows that the inductive method does not play a dominant role in his analysis of the products of the human mind; and that where it does play a role, the meaning of the term "induction" is altered. Where Dilthey does speak of the "inductive method," for instance in the opening sections of his essay "Das Wesen der Philosophie," it is employed as a kind of fact-finding tool, as a starting point for historical investigations, but it is by no means the kind of detached external observation of individually discrete, measurable occurrences that is supposed to result in statistical regularities; it is far removed from the methods of the natural sciences.[3] Nor is it a codifiable procedure or method in the sense that Gadamer suggests. Rather, the necessity for employing the inductive method for Dilthey arises quite simply from the impossibility of deriving the course of human affairs and the particular character of the results of human production from a priori "laws."[4] To stress the importance of the inductive method is just to emphasize that one must start from the individual phenomena and not from general theories in analyzing history and human behavior. This hardly seems to be something that Gadamer would want to contest, but that is, on the other hand, not the real point of Gadamer's critique.

Behind his—if the above is correct, misleading—criticisms of Dilthey's reliance upon the inductive method is a critique of the belief that there can be an objective science of the historical world after the model of the natural sciences. Can Dilthey's search for human *sciences*, can the notion of "distance," the impartiality, the external viewpoint that natural science takes to be necessary for objectivity, not be seen as the real target of Gadamer's criticism? In addition to the passage quoted above, numerous statements in *Truth and Method* seem to indicate that this is the case.[5] But how can this be? Was it not above all Dilthey who employed the notion of *Verstehen* to emphasize that the object of the human sciences is not something alien to us, an objectivity that we are confronted with as an external observer, but rather a form of life, a kind of second self, an other that we think we understand only when we have ourselves been able imaginatively to reexperience it (*nacherleben*) on our own? Is Dilthey not at the same time the object of Gadamer's critique precisely because he is not objective enough, because he still sees understanding as a kind of aesthetic process in which one recreates the experience and feelings of the other who is our partner in a dialogue or who creates a work of art?

II

In the Foreword to the second edition Gadamer writes: "However, I believe that I have correctly demonstrated that this kind of understanding does not at all understand the 'you' but rather the truth you tell us. I am thereby referring to that kind of truth that can become apparent only if one allows oneself to be told something by you" (*WM*, xxiii). This is not limited just to normal communication, but to art works as well:

Whereas we saw that not even the poetic work of art is grasped in its essential truth if one proceeds according to the standard of aesthetic consciousness. What a work like this shares with all other literary texts is rather that it speaks to us in terms of a meaningful content. Our understanding is not specifically directed to the guiding form that is proper to it as a work of art, but rather to what it tells us. (*WM*, 155)

This insight, which Gadamer considers one of the central shifts in contemporary hermeneutics, is what Dilthey, due to his position at the end of romantic aesthetics, failed to grasp. Dilthey has failed to direct his attention to the "immediate truth" contained in art, religion, and philosophy because he sees them as "forms in which life is expressed [*Ausdrucksformen des Lebens*]" (*WM*, 215).

The object of and basis for the human sciences in Dilthey's view was then human life. Just as the natural sciences trace natural appearances back to their genuine sources in the laws of nature, so too must the human sciences trace communicative utterances and works of art back to their source in the structures of human life. And just as there are natural laws that hold always and everywhere for all natural phenomena, so too are there definite structures to be discovered in all expressions of human life. In Dilthey's earlier writings, these are interpreted in terms of individual psychology, in his later writings in terms of more general structures which the particular artist or thinker instantiates. But in either case, to understand a work of art or any other product of the human mind is for Dilthey equivalent to understanding a structure of life.

Gadamer consistently and repeatedly distances himself from this subjective, "psychologistic" side of Dilthey's thinking. Gadamer depicts the consequences of Dilthey's historical approach which views art, philosophy, and religion as "expressions" (*Ausdrücke*) of life: "To this extent, for historical consciousness the entire tradition becomes an encounter of the human spirit with itself" (*WM*, 216). For him, however, this is anything but a positive development: "Even philosophy counts only as an expression of life. To the extent that it becomes aware of this, it abandons its ancient claim to be knowledge through concepts" (*WM*, 216). If all that were lost were metaphysics' illusion that we can capture all of reality in concepts, then this would hardly be a loss to be bemoaned. But the loss extends further than this: Gadamer notes that all claims to "immediate truth" are abandoned in favor of a historical understanding of forms of life (*WM*, 217).

As Gadamer himself recognizes, Dilthey's position on what it means to understand art, philosophy, religion, and other products of the human mind as expressions of human life changes as his thought develops. Whereas in the earlier writings, it involves what can well be called a "psychological" approach that aims to understand the work by imaginatively reenacting the experience of the author as a particular individual, the later writings place a stronger emphasis on the notion of "structures" of human life, basic possibilities of seeing and valuing things as well as of acting that each represent some one basic possibility for human living. Gadamer follows the scholarly literature on Dilthey in distinguishing between an earlier "psychological" and a later "hermeneutic" phase.[6] But on the whole, Gadamer concludes, Dilthey's primary emphasis was too strongly tied to the subjective realm as the proper subject for objective human sciences:

> His point of departure, the "inner awareness of experiences," could not provide the bridge to historical realities because the two great historical realities, society and the state, are always in truth prior determining factors for any "experience." . . . In truth, history does not belong to us, but rather we to history . . . . The focus of subjectivity is a distorted mirror. Individual self-reflection is merely a flickering in the closed circuit of historical life. That is why the prejudices of an individual are—much more than that individual's judgments—the historical reality of his being. (*WM*, 261)

The criticism voiced in this quotation is directed to two distinct yet interrelated aspects of Dilthey's "subjectivism." The first of these is its concentration on the individual. Gadamer contends that this leads—against Dilthey's own intentions—to a kind of ahistoricality, for by concentrating on the individual as the locus of significance, the broader context on which the individual draws in order to attach a particular meaning to various experiences can be easily lost from view. According to Gadamer, Dilthey's approach removes the subject from the "circuit of historical life [*Stromkreis des geschichtlichen Lebens*]," ignoring its situatedness in a concrete historical situation and placing each individual equally close to that secular successor of the position formerly occupied by God in earlier historicist thought, namely to the totality of life. Furthermore, since for Dilthey each individual, including the present-day interpreter, is him- or herself a participant in this process of life, and the basic structure of human life is a constant, this seems to make it possible to overcome problems of historical distance and make judgments about a work and its author that can find their place in an objective body of knowledge that can be called science. We shall return later in section 4 to the reasons why Gadamer thinks that this prospect is an illusion.

Secondly, Gadamer also seems to be accusing Dilthey of committing a kind of "intentionalist fallacy" by concentrating on the subject's conscious judgments instead of upon those prejudices which reflect the historical reality in which the individual is immersed. An emphasis on self-reflection and autobiography follows naturally from Dilthey's starting point in the "awareness of experiences [*Innesein der Erlebnisse*]" (*WM*, 261). In all of this, Dilthey is said to be captive of an Enlightenment tradition that holds out the possibility of absolute rationality, of a consciousness that has purged everything alien from itself and has thereby attained complete self-transparency and freedom from the shackles of historical prejudices.[7] Dilthey's "subjectivism" thereby also involves rationalist assumptions concerning the autonomy and perspicuity of human consciousness that Gadamer relegates to the realm of those unjustified historical prejudices that genuinely critical reason must unmask as such.

There can be no doubt that at least in many respects this critique does apply to Dilthey's earlier "psychological" approach. Here the emphasis was indeed, as Gadamer repeatedly points out, on the work as an expression of the life of the individual author, and much of Dilthey's analysis of literary, theological, and philosophical works is guided by the authors' own statements about their works and the relationship these works bear to their own lives, in letters, personal documents, and most especially in their autobiographies. The dominant influence of Goethe, the paragon of the artist for nineteenth-century Germany, is more than obvious here. Yet even in his earlier phases, Dilthey was not an "intentionalist." The point is not to discover what the "author was trying to say" and by no means does the author's own opinion about the meaning of a work necessarily coincide with its genuine meaning.[8] Rather, what the interpreter tries to understand is the "meaning" as a connective structure, a *Zusammenhang*, that unites all of the elements of a work of art just as it unites and forms all the elements of a particular human life. The author is not necessarily consciously aware of this "meaning," in fact it is not any kind of propositional knowledge, a judgment or set of judgments that one could state either apart from or within a work of art— that is the very point of the notion of genius as a kind of pre- or unconsciousness production. And for that reason, the author's statements about his work are not necessarily complete or even reliable guides to its "real" meaning. The advantage of the autobiography for Dilthey is not that it is an infallible test of the correctness or incorrectness of various interpretations, but rather that in the autobiography there is an explicit attempt to articulate the connectedness of a life as a whole and to see artistic production in relationship to this ordering structure. Every human life *exhibits* such connectedness or meaning, artworks *express* it, and autobiographies *explicitly thematize* and try to capture it. This does not mean, however, that the autobiography or the author's own reflections on the connection between one's life and one's work must necessarily be successful in their attempt to capture it, that there cannot be a difference between the meaning expressed in the works and the meaning that the author thinks is contained there. Thus, the suggestion that Dilthey can be equated with any simplistic form of intentionalism is at best misleading.

What about the two other charges, i.e., that Dilthey's position is too strongly oriented on the individual who creates the art work and not enough on the immediate truth which the work intends to convey (Dilthey's subjectivism), and the claim that he is still too strongly oriented on the model of the natural sciences in his conviction that there is some one meaning contained in a statement or a work of art, and that the human sciences can discover what this objective meaning (i.e., the connection which unites the various elements of the work) is once and for all time? The two claims, as we have seen, are closely related, but we should deal with them separately, for each has different implications for Gadamer's own position.

Concerning the first charge, i.e., Dilthey's subjectivism, the answer depends on how the charge is interpreted and the period in Dilthey's thinking to which one is referring. In the quotation cited above, Gadamer raises the problem of Dilthey's emphasis on the individual and the individual's own conscious judgments. The emphasis on conscious judgments is related to what we have called the suggestion of "intentionalism"; the accuracy of this suggestion has been shown to be questionable. In addition to this, however, Gadamer seems to be making a further point. The real agents in history, the "*großen geschichtlichen Wirklichkeiten*" are not individual human beings, but rather institutions—family, society, and the state—in which we live. It is only against the background of such institutions that the individual comes to be the person he or she is. Yet certainly, at least in his later periods, Dilthey would not deny that human beings are influenced, perhaps even in a certain sense determined by the age in which they live and the institutions in which they participate. He too speaks of the "spirit" of an age that permeates all of the individuals living in it and the works that they produce. Indeed, even in earlier writings, Dilthey outlines how the rise of great institutions, such as the

Church, or the breakdown of others, such as the Greek polis, were the causes of various views that were expressed and particular kinds of art-works that were produced. Indeed, the very notion of a *Weltanschauung* conjures up the notion of a common view, the view of an age, a nation, or a culture much more than that of an individual, and seems to imply a structure that underlies all of an individual's conscious reflection rather than being the result of it. However, throughout his work Dilthey focuses on individuals as the actual carriers of life, as the basic units out of which such institutions as family, society, and state are comprised. In this respect, it does not appear that he is as far from Gadamer as the passage cited above might indicate. For in Gadamer's own works, the consciousness of the pervasive force of institutions and historical epochs does not lead him away from an analysis of individuals and their works, but rather back to them as the loci where these forces become apparent. Therefore, it cannot be the program of individual psychology as opposed to institutional analysis or a history of culture that constitutes the genuine difference between them.

The alternative which remains, then, is that the real problem lies in Dilthey's focus on the work as an expression of the life of the author and not on it as a repository of truth or at least of claims to truth in its own right. This is the most pervasive and significant theme that Gadamer stresses as the difference between himself and previous theorists, including Dilthey in particular: "To the extent that what is intended is not individuality and its intentions, but rather the substantive truth, a text is not understood merely as an expression of life, but rather taken seriously in its claim to truth" (*WM*, 280–81). Taken together with the passages cited at the outset, it becomes clear what Gadamer takes to be the biggest difference between Dilthey and himself. Dilthey's "subjectivism" consists in his failure to see the "truth claim" of art because he sees it as an expression of human life, in particular the life of the artist who produces the work. Is this a fair characterization of Dilthey?

For Dilthey in his earlier, psychological phases this is certainly accurate. The connection between life and work, the fact that the real meaning of the work is identical to the "meaning" of the life that gives all of its particular aspects significance and order, these are unmistakably prominent themes in Dilthey earlier writings, both in his more theoretical works and in his actual interpretations. In his later writings, however, the technical use of the notion of meaning as a "structure" emphasizes meaning more in terms of a unifying element in a work of literature or art than as the unifying element in the life of the artist who produces it. The work can incorporate some one aspect or phase of an artist's life that is no more the expression of the whole of this life than the artist's life itself is a complete expression of the whole of human life in general. In the later writings Dilthey's primary attention is directed to the structure of human life as it is expressed in the work itself, and he does not attempt to trace the meaning of the work back immediately to the experience of the artist who produces it; but he never completely severs the tie between the structure that constitutes the meaning of the work and the life of the person who produces it. For, even in this hermeneutic phase, it is structures of human life, general structures that represent possibilities of human life as a totality, and not just idiosyncratic features of the artists' mental life, that are expressed in art, philosophy, and religion. However, it is important to note that the life structure expressed in the work is no longer produced or understood through the idiosyncratic and nonreproducible experience of some one individual, but rather in terms of general structures in which all human beings participate to some degree. Thus, even in the phase in which Dilthey distanced himself most from his earlier, psychological approach, his notion of what it means to understand a work of art still remains in Gadamer's eyes improperly "subjectivist," since it still refers not to some immediate truth but rather back to the structures of life out of which it arises and to which it gives objective form.[9]

III

What does Gadamer offer in its place? To what extent can Gadamer be taken to have overcome this kind of subjectivism that Dilthey, even in his latest stages of development, did not choose or was not able to leave behind? Since the answer to this question necessarily also involves an inquiry into what Gadamer means by "truth," especially in the case of an artwork, it turns out that an investigation of Gadamer's critique of Dilthey also leads us to the heart of his own hermeneutic position. In particular, the question we must ask ourselves is to what extent Gadamer's emphasis upon the truth of the work of art really involves a departure from the interpretation of art in terms of structures of human experience.

At the heart of Gadamer's description of artistic truth in *Truth and Method* is the notion of "*Darstellung*" or "presentation." Two points are important to note here. The first point concerns what Gadamer sees as his difference with Dilthey. What is presented in a work of art (or in a statement) is not for Gadamer the artist (or the speaker) but rather what the artwork or the statement is about, the truth of the statement, its message. The charge of an overly "psychologistic" orientation in Dilthey can be traced back to just this mistake, i.e., that Dilthey's aesthetic approach shifts the emphasis from what is conveyed in the work or in a statement back to the person who makes it. Against this subjectivist approach, Gadamer opposes his notion of communication in general and in particular in art as a direct presentation of the truth:

> To understand is to understand an expression. In an expression, what is expressed is present in a different way than the way in which a cause is present in an effect. It is itself present in the act and is understood whenever the expression is understood. (*WM*, 211)

And what he means by "understanding an expression" becomes clear if we recall the passage quoted in section 1:

> Whereas we saw that not even the poetic work of art is grasped in its essential truth if one proceeds according to the standard of aesthetic consciousness. What a work like this shares with all other literary texts is rather that it speaks to us in terms of a meaningful content. Our understanding is not specifically directed to the guiding form that is proper to it as a work of art, but rather to what it tells us. (*WM*, 155)

It thus appears that this turn away from the form that is given to the work by the subject who creates it toward the content that it conveys, represents a turn away from subjectivism back to an objective truth that is contained in the work.

The question that must be asked then is how this kind of "truth" differs from the "objectivism" that Gadamer criticizes in Dilthey. Does it not seem to lead us back to just the sort of truth that the natural sciences have as their goal? If the "truth" about the things depicted in art is the real issue, how is this to be distinguished from the truth about them that is discovered in the sciences? Does this not ultimately lead us back to another common view of art, according to which art is a figurative way of stating truths in images or metaphors that can also be expressed in simple propositions that do not employ pictures and images? And if this is so, must it not in the end lead to a subordination of artistic truth to the "real" truth that is expressed perhaps less effectively, less vividly, but nonetheless more clearly in simple statements made outside of the realm of art—statements whose reliability (if they are true) consists in the fact that they can be verified by the standard means available to any impartial observer, and in particular by the systematic and reliable means that are accepted for verification in science outside of art? How is art to avoid becoming just a picturesque way of representing truths whose reliability or lack of it—i.e., whose genuine status as truths—must be established outside of art. Put briefly: How does the notion of artistic truth differ in a positive way from scientific truth, which also purports to tell us how things really are?

The difference turns on the second important point to be made concerning Gadamer's notion of "*Darstellung*," namely that "*Darstellung*" is not to be confused with mere "representation." The traditional notion of truth as correspondence with the thing underlies the common interpretation of objectivity. According to this notion, a statement is true or objective if it tells us how things really are, if it represents the facts as they are "in themselves," undistorted by subjective viewpoints and distortions. Without committing himself in any way to such a notion for "scientific" truth, Gadamer makes it plain that artistic truth as *Darstellung* is not a mere representation of some sort of objective "facts." Rather, art brings to light the essence of things:

> The primordial mimetic relationship that we are explicating not only involves the presence of what is presented but that it has more properly come into presence. Imitation and presentation are not merely representative repetitions, but rather knowledge of the essence. Since they are not mere repetition (*Wiederholung*), but rather "bringing forth" ["*Hervorholung*"], the audience is also part of what is intended in them. (WM, 109)

What is here called essence thus includes something like a perspective from which the artwork is able to bring the thing forth in its essence, and this for Gadamer not only does not preclude an implicit reference to the subject who does the viewing, but rather involves such a reference as one of its essential elements, which is why the "audience [*Zuschauer*]" is also said to be simultaneously and essentially intended as well.

The emphasis on the content of the work of art as opposed to its form, on the truth of art or of statements rather than on their authors, therefore seems to lead us back to something subjective after all, if it is not to be equated with the kind of representationalism that would make artistic truth just a less exact form of scientific truth. This, it would seem, makes Gadamer seem less distant from Dilthey than the talk of "truth" as opposed to "artistic experience" might imply. Is there an alternative way of interpreting Gadamer's position so that such subjectivist readings can be avoided? If so, the most promising avenue would seem to be by emphasizing the notion of "world" that Gadamer adopts from Heidegger. For world is what in the most proper sense is presented in a work of art:

> The world that appears in the play of presentation stands not as a reproduction next to the real world, but is rather this world in the elevated truth of its being. . . . The concept of mimesis . . . means less reproduction than the appearance of what is presented. Without the mimesis of the work the world is not present as it is present in it, and without this rendering [of the world] the work in turn also fails to be present. In the presentation, the presence of what is presented completes itself. (*WM*, 130)

The measure for truth in Gadamer's *Truth and Method* may indeed be the "*einleuchtende Ansicht der Sache selbst*," as Lawrence Schmidt argues in a recent work,[10] but at least in the case of the work of art, the "*Sache*" or the issue is not in this case an individual object, but rather the world or what Gadamer in another place calls "*Sein*" or "Being" (e.g., *WM*, 137). Whether one speaks of a perspective or *Weltanschauung* (Dilthey) or a world or Being (Gadamer), the concern of the work of art is not the neutral depiction of some object, but rather the expression, the illumination of the total context out of which it can be experienced as or be the kind of object that it is. The difference between Gadamer and Dilthey can be better understood not in terms of an emphasis on content or form, upon immediate objective truth as opposed to subjective experience or the worldview of the author, but rather in terms of the difference between such structures of life seen as perspectives and the substantiality of "world" or Being. As opposed to the term "perspective," the term "world" and more particularly the term "Being" imply a substantiality that goes beyond the merely subjective. We do not make the world, we do not make Being, but rather live in a world and are immersed in or surrounded by Being, so that they have a kind of objectivity that is different from that of individual objects but is at the same time something nonsubjective as well. This at least is what Gadamer would need to establish if the difference between himself and Dilthey is to be as marked as his remarks on Dilthey suggest.

Two distinct although related questions are at issue here. The first is whether the terms "world" and "Being" as Gadamer uses them can be reduced back to structures of human Being or—to use Dilthey's phrase—to structures of life or not; and the second is whether, if so, they are then something particular and individual or something more general, something like social practices or historically devolved institutions. This distinction is important because if the structures are general, then that would make them very different from the subjective experiences that the early Dilthey took to be the subject of art, but not necessarily from the structures of life that are emphasized by the later Dilthey; if they were not reducible to structures or ways of human Being, then that would indeed be a significant departure not only from the early, but also from the thinking of the later Dilthey as well.

Regarding the second question, the answer is clear. "Being" or "world" is not something created by the individual for Gadamer. Like the "play" of language, it is rather something in which one finds oneself, a backdrop against which statements are made and actions are undertaken. This is what unites the Heideggerian notion of "world," the classical rhetorical notion of the "common sense," and the Hegelian notion of "*Sittlichkeit*," all of which are cast in a positive light in *Truth and Method.* "World," "common sense," and "*Sittlichkeit*" are structures in which individual human beings participate, they have the character that Hegel refers to as "substantiality"; they are not something that human beings as subjects, i.e., as conscious autonomous agents, create or voluntarily decide upon (see above, *WM*, 18).

Yet, to return to the first question, does that necessarily imply that they are not at the same time structures of human life? Gadamer himself is not unambiguous on this point, but I believe that ultimately the only way to make sense of his use of the term "world" is to trace it back—as Heidegger does in his early thinking in *Being and Time*—to structures of human being or *Dasein*. Quite certainly, "common sense"—or the lack of it—is a structure of human life. In the rhetorical tradition, of course, this is not something possessed as much by an individual as by a community, something that a speaker and an audience must share if genuine communication is to transpire. Gadamer's repeated references to the "ethical dimension" of art can be seen in the same vein—less in terms of the kinds of moral decisions that an individual makes than in terms of the shared values of a community that find their most vivid and explicit expression in great deeds, but just as well perhaps also in works of art or great oratorical achievements that bring to the fore and make evident the genuine values of a people or an age. These values also serve as the "prejudices" that serve as the background against which truth-claims can be made, understood, and evaluated. Since such values, such shared assumptions are to be found, "exist" only in the actions, views, and works of human beings, to refer to them as structures of human life seems appropriate.

But what about the notion of "world"? Was it not Heidegger's express purpose to establish world as a third kind of thing, a non-object that is neither subject nor object, as the horizon out of which it is at all possible for anything to emerge as the thing it is? And is not Gadamer's determination of world, and perhaps even more clearly, his determination of language—in which the world presents itself—meant in just the same way as a means of avoiding at one and the same time the objectivist, naturalistic approach of the sciences and representational theories and the subjectivist accounts forwarded by Dilthey and his predecessors?

One recalls, however, that the status of the determination "world" in Heidegger is significantly different at different stages in his thinking. Whereas it is certainly true that "world" in Heidegger's middle and later writings is increasingly taken to be a nonhuman force in which human beings dwell (even if in the modern age in a form of withdrawal), something that takes on the particular forms that it does due to the *Geschick* of Being to which mortals at best respond, in *Being and Time* world is still determined as a structural moment of Being-in-the-world as the Being of Dasein or human Being. Without overlooking the ontological significance of the concept of world as developed in *Being and Time*, and without falling back into a psychological interpretation of the insights Heidegger attains there, it is nonetheless important to emphasize that unless one is willing to take the further step into a history of Being as the true agent in history, world as a structure of Dasein is not as far as it may seem from what the later Dilthey calls a structure of life. Both have what one might refer to as "ontological" implications in the way that they determine what sorts of beings and above all as what sorts of beings things can appear. Yet both are structures of what had traditionally been referred to as subjectivity—in this case, however, a kind of subjectivity that no longer is seen as autonomous consciousness, but rather as a dynamic process prereflectively immersed in historical developments and institutions.

IV

In this sense one can see Gadamer following both Dilthey and the early Heidegger in a kind of transcendental philosophy, where it is the structures of subjectivity that make possible the kinds of objects that can present themselves to us at a given time.

Wherein does the real and basic difference between Gadamer and Dilthey lie—if there really is such a pronounced difference between them? First of all, there are the different emphases that their respective terminologies evoke: the more subjective bent of terms like "experience" and "life" in Dilthey, as opposed to the objective or ontological ring of terms such as "world" or "horizon." Such terminological differences are not without genuine philosophical importance. Additionally, however, there are genuine differences in content that cannot be traced back to their terminology.

We recall that for Dilthey, Kant's project of reestablishing a new version of critical metaphysics by means of transcendental philosophy was doomed to failure because the subjective concepts that Kant took to be the necessary and thus invariant basis for all objectivity are themselves historically conditioned and thus variable. Historical consciousness, the successor to transcendental philosophy, has as its general goal the demonstration that and how all cultural achievements including science and religion as well as philosophy and art can be traced back to structures of human life, and has as it particular charge the examination of the specific origins of various worldviews, concepts, and artistic creations. Yet, even historical consciousness assumes a fundamentally constant general structure of human life, which guarantees the possibility of understanding from culture to culture and across the ages. And it assumes that the particular structures which a work, concept, or practice expresses are fixed so that it possesses a determinate meaning that can be captured in the process of understanding, and is thus at least potentially accessible as the same to any competent observer.

Here is where the most significant difference between Gadamer and Dilthey lies. Whereas for Dilthey the definite meaning contained in an expression of life guarantees the possibility of the human sciences as *sciences*, Gadamer's notion of *Wirkungsgeschichte* points toward a kind of meaning that is not once and for all fixed, since it involves not only the horizon against which the work is created, the statement made, or the act performed, but also the horizon of the person who wishes to understand it as well. Moreover, rather than emphasizing the fundamental sameness of the general structure of human life as a guarantor of possible understanding, as Dilthey does, Gadamer stresses the mutability of historical horizons and thus the constant process of change in the meaning of a text or work of art.

While Dilthey in his historical analyses does take this phenomenon into account, he nonetheless fails to recognize its significance for a theory of the human sciences. The most important difference between Dilthey and Gadamer thus concerns the latter's notion of *Wirkungsgeschichte* and his recognition that meaning is not something fixed at the point of origin for a statement, a deed, or a work of art, but rather an ongoing process in which the interpreter plays every bit as much an active role as the original speaker, agent, or artist. This then turns out to be the real point behind Gadamer's critique of Dilthey's objectivism. The illusion of distance that Gadamer criticizes in Dilthey can be traced back to the belief that the interpreter can somehow ascertain the "original" meaning of a text, deed, or work of art by locating its place in the context from which it arose—and that this is not only fixed, but that this, its "meaning," is also determinable as the same for any interpreter.[11]

In closing, it should be pointed out that Gadamer's gain is not without its costs. For it is precisely Gadamer's abandonment of the constancy of meaning that leads to the charge of relativism and questions concerning the possibility of objectivity that have been raised so often. One might note as well that at least the word *Horizontverschmelzung* seems to imply that the work does bring with it something of its own, some determinate context in terms of which it must be viewed if it is to be properly understood, that the work has its own horizon that confronts ours, even if we may not know what this horizon is when we first encounter the work, but discover it only through the resistance which the work offers to our initial attempts to understand it. In the end, then, Gadamer's "difficulties" derive precisely from the fact that he rejects as inadequate the assumption that Dilthey clung to in order to make it possible for the human sciences to be sciences. Those who are convinced that Gadamer's conception of *Wirkungsgeschichte* and the rejection of a primacy of anything like an original and fixed context of meaning for a work of art are justified, must then face the question whether there is something that can be substituted in place of what has been left behind, or whether the idea of literary and artistic interpretation and criticism as sciences must not rather simply be abandoned as well.

3

Gadamer's Hermeneutics and the Overcoming of Epistemology

Tom Rockmore

Any discussion of the problem of knowledge does well to note the ancient roots of this concern. Obviously, epistemology has played an important, perhaps even a central role in philosophy since its origins in ancient Greece. The term "epistemology" is not used by the Greeks; but it is clear that like later thinkers they were concerned with various aspects of the problem of knowledge, above all in Plato's *Theaetetus*, which has arguably never been surpassed in the later discussion. The widespread tendency to date modern philosophy and epistemology from Descartes should not confuse his effort to make a new beginning for an older problem with an invention of the problem as such. It is sometimes said that epistemology comes to an end in Kant's transcendental turn. But this view—which echoes the Young Hegelian claim, familiar in Marxism, that philosophy as such terminates in Hegel's system—fails to do justice to the many later post-Kantian views concerned with epistemology. Such movements include post-Kantian German idealism, the Vienna Circle, the phenomenological movement that dates from Husserl, American pragmatism, and Anglo-American analytic thought. Each of these tendencies recasts the epistemological problem from its own angle of vision, and each of them offers its own solution, or a related series of solutions, to its revised version of the theory of knowledge.

There is no single view of epistemology, since the understanding of the problem of knowledge changes over time. But there is a small series of basic epistemological doctrines that are restated by Descartes for modern times, and later reflected in various ways through the views of his successors. A short list of such epistemological doctrines, whose roots lie in ancient thought, would include at least seven fundamental ideas. They include (1) the belief that claims to know require justification or legitimation; (2) the view that ultimate justification requires a method adequate to yield truth and knowledge in the full sense; (3) the idea of philosophy as a science which justifies all other claims to know as well as its own; (4) the distinction between opinion and knowledge; (5) the claim that the other sciences are grounded in philosophy; (6) the view that knowledge is universal, certain and necessary; and (7) the conviction that any philosophy worthy of the name can admit no presuppositions whatsoever, and must hence form a seamless web. Each of these doctrines is characteristic of the modern form of the problem of knowledge, and in different ways each of them is challenged by later thinkers as the view of the nature and conditions of knowledge evolves.

Modern philosophy is characterized by the view that it is possible to go beyond philosophy, either by putting an end to it, by realizing it, by making a new beginning once and for all, or by revealing it as a sterile enterprise. From the epistemological point of view, one of the more interesting ideas in modern philosophy is the claim that it is possible to overcome the epistemological problem. This idea is widespread in modern philosophy as early as Descartes. It was later restated by a number of thinkers, including Husserl, and most recently by Hans-Georg Gadamer in the context of his wide-ranging investigation of hermeneutics. Here, from his hermeneutic perspective Gadamer makes the epistemological claim that phenomenology overcomes the epistemological problem. Accordingly, the aim of this paper is to consider some of the epistemological implications of Gadamer's *Truth and Method.*

Gadamer's hermeneutic theory belongs to the post-Husserlian phase of the phenomenological movement, in the strand which issues from Heidegger's fundamental ontology, with secondary influences that derive from Dilthey and a host of other hermeneutic thinkers, particularly Aristotle. Now Husserlian phenomenology is largely centered on a particular view of and solution to the problem of knowledge with close links, as Husserl came to realize, to the views of Descartes and Kant. Husserl is an original thinker, who holds a series of often traditional epistemological views, which he defends in often novel ways. Certainly each of what I have called the traditional epistemological dogmas is still maintained in Husserl's phenomenology. But equally certainly, each of them is later denied in the post-Husserlian evolution of the phenomenological movement.

With the possible exception of Sartre, post-Husserlian phenomenology maintains an interest in the problem of knowledge, which it reinterprets in different ways. In general, the post-Husserlian phase of phenomenology leading up to Gadamer's theory of hermeneutics records the decline and fall of phenomenology understood as a method for absolute knowledge in the Husserlian sense. Sartre is a special case, since his earlier existentialism was only incidentally concerned with epistemology, and when he turned to this problem in his later phase it was from a different, Marxist orientation. More generally, the post-Husserlian phase of phenomenology—as witness the writings of Heidegger, Sartre, Merleau-Ponty, Ricoeur, Derrida, and others—records a transformation of the Husserlian idea of phenomenology, in the course of which each of the fundamental epistemological dogmas, to which he still subscribed in his thought, is denied.

Beginning with Heidegger, the problem of epistemological justification, which Husserl initially resolved through repetition, is abandoned. There is a general turn away from method, as witness Merleau-Ponty's objection to the very idea of the phenomenological reduction that Husserl considered as the indispensable cornerstone of phenomenology, Ricoeur's turn to texts and narrativity, and Derrida's concern to deconstruct what he calls the metaphysics of presence. None of the later phenomenologists insist on knowledge as universal, certain and necessary, which Heidegger, perhaps influenced by Aristotle's concept of practical theory, replaces through the phrase proximally and for the most part. The problem of presuppositionless theory is no longer on the agenda. Husserl's concern with philosophy as science persists as long as Heidegger's *Kehre*, which is also a turn away from the traditional, even "foundationalist" view of philosophy initially elaborated by Plato toward a concept of thought which no longer founds the various sciences but merely exists alongside them.[1] Finally, the sciences no longer need philosophy and it is no longer held to justify the other sciences.

Gadamer's hermeneutics draws on many sources, but mainly on Heidegger's theory of the hermeneutic circle of the understanding, which he develops in a turn to history, through a theory of the historical character of consciousness. Like the Husserlian movement in phenomenogy in general, Gadamer's thought preserves the concern with knowledge, although the view of the problem of knowledge has clearly changed. In his treatise on hermeneutics, the theory of knowledge is never far from view. Gadamer is clearly aware of the epistemological content of his discussion, which surfaces throughout the book in various ways, beginning with the title of the treatise.

The title of the book draws attention to an obvious connection to the Cartesian epistemological tradition in which truth was meant to follow from an adequate method correctly applied. Now Gadamer's discussion is meant to challenge the idea of a method as the source of knowledge. In that sense, the term "method" is surely meant in ironic fashion since from the hermeneutic perspective there is and can be no method adequate to secure knowledge. A problem which arises in the second noun in the title of the work is whether and in what way we can still speak of truth, that is as truth meant to follow in a manner which does not depend on method. Gadamer further makes a clearly epistemological assertion in the title of a chapter of his book, appropriately entitled "The Overcoming [*Überwindung*] of the Epistemological Problem through Phenomenological Research."

Since Gadamer is deeply influenced by Heidegger, his intention to overcome, and not merely to surpass (*verwinden*) epistemology is significant. In this way, Gadamer signals his desire to come to grips with, not merely to turn his back on, or to dismiss, the epistemological problem. It is well known that Heidegger offered a response to the problem of knowledge in his analysis of the hermeneutic circle of the understanding, although in his later phase he claimed to go beyond philosophy, which he regarded as moribund, and beyond the metaphysical tradition, indeed beyond Platonism, through thought that is not philosophy. Heidegger's later effort to surpass philosophy survives in Derrida's effort to deconstruct the metaphysics of presence and, by implication, to deconstruct philosophy itself from a vantage point presumably beyond the philosophical tradition. Gadamer's epistemologically more moderate position is meant to come to grips with the epistemological problem. Although Gadamer is certainly not an epistemologist in a Cartesian or even the Kantian mold, he does not flee the question of knowledge. He is well aware of and not concerned to avoid the history of epistemology, which in a sense is his subtext or at least a major theme in his book. He raises the epistemological question at a number of points in his discussion, particularly in the second of the three main parts of *Truth and Method*, perhaps most directly in the section entitled "The Overcoming of the Epistemological Problem through Phenomenological Research."

Let us recall the main lines of Gadamer's approach to epistemology. In the context of his extension of the question of truth to understanding in the human sciences, these include discussions of historical preparation and the foundations of a theory of hermeneutic experience. In the analysis of historical preparation, he considers the Enlightenment, romantic and historical approaches, Dilthey's relation to historicism, and the overcoming of the epistemological problem through phenomenology. In the discussion of the foundations of a hermeneutic theory of experience, he studies the elevation of historicality to the status of a hermeneutic principle, the rediscovery of the so-called fundamental hermeneutic problem, and the analysis of effective historical consciousness. Gadamer develops his argument in the course of a detailed historical analysis.

Gadamer's view that phenomenology overcomes the problem of epistemology has a deep similarity with Heidegger's view that metaphysics culminates in Nietzsche's thought, but which must be transformed in order to surpass metaphysics. In effect, Gadamer regards Heidegger as transforming hermeneutics in a way that overcomes epistemology. We can reconstruct Gadamer's argument as follows: Different forms of hermeneutics culminate in Dilthey's position, which is caught up in historicism. Going beyond Dilthey's *Lebensphilosophie*, and drawing on Husserl and Graf Yorck, Heidegger supposedly overcomes the problem of epistemology in his hermeneutic phenomenology, above all in the hermeneutic circle of the understanding. Gadamer insists on the significance of Heidegger's concept of the fore-structure of the understanding and further insists that the concept of prejudice, which was rejected by the Enlightenment, can be positively reappropriated through the principle of effective history, which he elaborates as the idea of effective historical consciousness. In sum, according to Gadamer the epistemological problem is not resolved by any thinker prior to Dilthey, nor by Dilthey, but it is resolved in phenomenology, more precisely in Heidegger's analysis of the hermeneutic circle of the understanding, or in that analysis as supplemented through Gadamer's own form of historical hermeneutics.

Let us examine Gadamer's argument. His argument can be interpreted in either a strong or a weak sense, that is, as a claim to overcome the problem of knowledge in general, or as a claim to overcome a particular form of the problem. It is difficult to defend the strong interpretation of Gadamer's argument. It is unclear at this late date that it is appropriate to attempt to overcome the epistemological problem in general. Although his text can be interpreted in a strong sense as the overcoming of the problem of knowledge in general, there is no reason to believe that this is Gadamer's intention. Despite his perhaps careless statement of what seems to be precisely the strong version of the claim,

Gadamer does not seem to think that Heidegger shows us how to argue for claims to know in the traditional sense of the term.

The ambiguity in the sense in which Gadamer means to overcome epistemology through phenomenology parallels an ambiguity in Heidegger's view of phenomenology in *Being and Time*. Here we can differentiate between a strong, or Husserlian form of phenomenological essentialism, and his own weaker effort to elicit what we can call the relative essence, which mainly obtains; but he finally argues for a weaker view, for which he is best known. In the same way, Gadamer does not pretend to resolve the epistemological problem in its classical form. He simply assumes that the problem of knowledge can no longer be raised as it was by a long series of thinkers through Descartes and Kant, arguably culminating in Husserl's thought. Despite his statement that phenomenology overcomes the problem of epistemology, Gadamer seems to be making a claim restricted to a form of the problem. More precisely, Gadamer seems to be making a more restricted claim, namely that the analysis of the hermeneutic circle of the understanding overcomes the problem of knowledge as it arises out of Dilthey's position.

In starting with Dilthey, Gadamer simply dismisses without argument, arguably correctly dismisses, much of the epistemological tradition. Obviously, unless we desire to resurrect ancient Greek ontology it is no longer possible to argue for direct, intuitive knowledge of the real. If we link the traditional formulation of the epistemological problem to the Cartesian position, then Gadamer is correct to infer that the problem of knowledge can no longer be raised in the traditional manner. It is well known that the form of epistemological foundationalism proposed by Descartes depends on a linear form of epistemological strategy. The problem with this strategy is that neither Descartes nor his followers ever discovered how to argue for an indubitable first principle from which the remainder of the theory could be rigorously deduced. The criticism leveled in the idealist tradition, e.g., Fichte's observation that an initial principle cannot be demonstrated precisely since it comes first—which Hegel reformulates in the point that Descartes cannot provide for the transition from certainty to truth—has been amply confirmed in the later discussion through a manifest failure to provide a viable form of foundationalism. This same problem persists in later views, for instance in the well-known inability in Husserl's position to return from the plane of transcendental subjectivity to the lifeworld. Gadamer further supposes that there is no other solution to the problem of knowledge than through Heidegger's analysis of the hermeneutic circle of the understanding.

Gadamer argues in favor of hermeneutics as overcoming what he calls the epistemological problem in three ways: in his historical analysis of the transition from Dilthey to Heidegger, in his systematic remarks on the implications of Heidegger's hermeneutics, and his own view of the concept of effective historical consciousness (*wirkungsgeschichtliches Bewußtsein*). One of the most interesting aspects of philosophy since Descartes is the emergence of the idea of the historical subject—in reaction to the abstract Cartesian concept and its restatement by Kant and others—for instance in the views of Fichte, Hegel, and Marx. Gadamer chooses Heidegger's alternative route, mediated by the writings of Dilthey, Husserl, and Graf Yorck, each of whom attempted to think life in a way leading up to the Heideggerian notion of Dasein, to arrive at a concept of the historical subject. Gadamer properly disregards Heidegger's own claim that his thought derives directly from the pre-Socratics in order to stress the sense in which Heidegger's thought was determined by the contemporary discussion. He regards the early Heidegger's hermeneutics of facticity as continuing the tendency to return to life through the innovative separation between epistemology and the hermeneutics of facticity. According to Gadamer, Heidegger's existential analysis of Dasein rests on a projective analysis of understanding as exhibiting a transcendence beyond Being. He considers his own task as the further development of Heidegger's view in a hermeneutics of the human sciences (*TM*, 259) or the constitution of a historical hermeneutics (*TM*, 262).

The assumption that the epistemological problem has not been overcome in prior philosophy is an ingredient in Gadamer's discussion of Dilthey. Now there is an ambiguity in Gadamer's way of posing the question, which apparently refers both to the overcoming of the epistemological problem as it arises in Dilthey's historicist effort to go beyond idealism, on the one hand—in the sense that phenomenology follows upon and takes up the problems left by historicism—and the divorce, or attempted divorce, between epistemology and what succeeds it, on the other. In the present paper, I am less interested in his reading of Dilthey than in the significance of his reading of the relation of later theories as a response to Diltheyan historicism, in order to inquire into the relation in general between epistemology, idealism, and phenomenology. In the section in question, following his well-known historical bias, Gadamer lets the epistemological problem arise out of his discussion of Dilthey. More precisely, Gadamer examines Dilthey's understanding of the distinction between Hegel's theory and his own as a distinction without a difference in order to suggest that, like Hegel, Dilthey means to provide an epistemological explanation.

In his interesting account, Gadamer challenges the alleged break between Dilthey and Hegel, corresponding to Dilthey's view of the relation, on several grounds. On the one hand, he objects that Dilthey merely repeats in different language, often in almost the same language, a number of basic Hegelian views. On the other hand, he claims that Dilthey's effort to substitute historical knowledge for spirit comprehending itself on the level of absolute knowledge is unsuccessful. According to Gadamer, there is no way in Dilthey's position in which the admission of relativism can be defeated in order to justify the fundamental claim to knowledge. And he regards Dilthey's own position as inherently contradictory, since from the beginning point within life, in a meditation on life, Dilthey's observations are not really compatible with his starting point.

For present purposes, Gadamer's way of reading Dilthey is particularly interesting for at least two reasons. First, it shows that he avoids the frequent assertion that epistemology ends in Kant. This is a deep misunderstanding, recently repeated by Habermas, but based on a lack of acquaintance with, or at least understanding of, the history of the tradition. This type of reading is problematic for a variety of reasons, for instance because it deprives the Fichtean and Hegelian views, to name only those, of their important epistemological force through an overly narrow paradigm of the epistemological problem. It is to Gadamer's credit that he takes a wider view of the problem of knowledge, which he does not restrict merely to its Cartesian-Kantian formulation.

Second, it is clear that Gadamer bases the weak version of his claim that phenomenology overcomes the problem of epistemology on a supposed opposition between the idealist view of epistemology and the phenomenological approach. From his angle of vision, the phenomenological approach culminates in his own concept of hermeneutics. From this perspective, like Lask's view of Fichte as a mere mediating link between Kant and Hegel, Dilthey is no more than a transition between the epistemological view in Hegelian idealism and the hermeneutic view of Heideggerian phenomenology.

Although Gadamer presents hermeneutics as the successor to epistemology, the continuity is strong, indeed so strong that it is clear that he has epistemological pretensions in mind for an allegedly postepistemological form of phenomenology. Now Gadamer is correct not to argue for a nonepistemological status of phenomenology as such. In evident ways, Husserl is a modern epistemologist. Husserl was certainly correct to regard his own position as the continuation of the Cartesian impulse in epistemology. Gadamer is further correct that in Heidegger we find a concerted effort to undercut the possibility of epistemology as ordinarily understood on a Cartesian model, for instance in the attack on the Cartesian idea of subjectivity, the insistence on the hermeneutic circle, the analysis of the problem of the ground, the discussion of the difference between readiness to hand and presence at hand, and so on.

But there is a price to be paid for any effort to defeat philosophy. As Heidegger later recognized, and as Derrida has made central to his view, the attack on philosophy necessarily draws one into the philosophical orbit. The attempt to defeat philosophy requires one to provide a philosophical argument, in effect to do what one in principle refuses. Heidegger's early hermeneutic argument against epistemology is itself epistemological in character. He does not escape from epistemology, but rather restates the epistemological problem in a different way. Certainly, this is one of the motives which later led Heidegger to turn away from philosophy in any traditional sense and toward thought, conceived of as an alternative to philosophy as such. In the same way, we can note that although Gadamer regards hermeneutics as a development of a postepistemological form of phenomenology, there is a strongly epistemological character to his view.

Gadamer's view of hermeneutics is similar in part to Heidegger's view of philosophy in *Being and Time*. To begin with, he follows Heidegger's claim that hermeneutics plays a basic, even a foundationalist role, since it is presupposed by science as something which cannot be demonstrated within science by scientific methods but which science cannot do without. In this way, Gadamerian hermeneutics makes the claim, familiar at least since Plato, that philosophy underlies and makes possible all other forms of knowledge. Second, again following Heidegger, hermeneutics demonstrates the familiar, self-reflexive character of epistemology, in Gadamer's view of hermeneutics as understanding in the effort to develop an understanding of understanding. This self-reflexive character is an ingredient since Hegel in the effort to perfect the Kantian transcendental turn through consideration of the real possibility of the theory.

Gadamer's remark in passing that Heidegger's *Daseinsanalytik* breaks with epistemology is valid only from a narrow perspective. In fact, Gadamer is careful to note the traditionally epistemological, transcendental residue still present in *Being and Time*. His specific contribution to the goal of overcoming epistemology through phenomenology lies in the systematic development of the Heideggerian view of hermeneutics through his own concept of effective historical consciousness, under the general heading of the foundations of a theory of hermeneutic experience. Through the analysis of the idea of the hermeneutic circle and the notion of prejudice, he claims to rediscover the fundamental hermeneutical problem, which he supplements through the introduction of his own conception of the role of history as a vehicle for truth. The systematic phase of the discussion develops in three moments, including the uncovering of the historical character of understanding through the scrutiny of the hermeneutic circle and the rehabilitation of the idea of prejudice, the establishment of a link between a historically minded hermeneutics and Aristotelian *phronesis*, and the effort to surpass the philosophy of reflection in an experiential hermeneutics. The latter argument constitutes Gadamer's most direct effort to demonstrate his contention that phenomenology in fact overcomes the problem of epistemology.

Gadamer's discussion of Heidegger's analysis of the hermeneutic circle stresses the way in which the analysis of the fore-structure of understanding shows how hermeneutics freed from the scientific concept of objectivity can grasp the historical character of understanding. He is most original in his effort, against the Enlightenment, to rehabilitate the concept of prejudice (*Vorurteil*) as intrinsic to historical understanding. His aim is to break down the absolute wall that has grown up between reason and tradition (*TM*, 281). Just as Hegel argued that skepticism was a necessary part of the process of the phenomenological growth of knowledge from experience, so Gadamer holds that prejudice is a necessary part of the hermeneutics of experience. His argument can be reconstructed as follows: Man is finite and his understanding is also finite. A finite being is in principle incapable of infinite, or absolute, reason. Finite reason is subject to prejudice, which Gadamer interprets as the historically determined bias exhibited in the fore-meaning (*TM*, 269). But we need to reject the Enlightenment bias against prejudice (*TM*, 270), since true prejudices can be justified by rational knowledge, even if this process may be infinite (*TM*, 242).

The problem of prejudice is another version of the problem of presuppositions. This theme goes back in the tradition at least until Plato, who maintained that philosophy was necessarily presuppositionless. Gadamer's assertion, although not his historical analysis, recalls Husserl's claim in the "Author's Preface" to the English-language edition of *Ideas* that phenomenology is free from presuppositions. Similarly, Descartes's entire theory rests on the claim that it is free from presuppositions, which is the basis of the Enlightenment effort to oppose reason to tradition. Gadamer is correct to point to the traditional character of the prevalent view of reason as untainted by prejudice, as devoid of presuppositions. He is insightful in his awareness of the historical character of prejudice, which transmits the history of the tradition in terms of which we construe the items of experience. In that sense he goes beyond Heidegger, who arguably lacks a satisfactory view of history, and perhaps beyond Hegel as well. Perhaps only Marx among his German predecessors is as aware as Gadamer of this point.

But Gadamer arguably fails to grasp the epistemological price to pay when reason cannot maintain its pristine character. Like Husserl, and in another context Popper, he can be taken as implying that we can be aware of and hence immunize ourselves to our prejudices. Now this line of argument fails for at least two distinct reasons. On the one hand, if we agree that the process of the verification of presuppositions is infinite, then the introduction of the concept of prejudice suffices to defeat the very possibility of knowledge. On other hand, there is an evident failure to take the idea of a possible prejudice with sufficient seriousness, present in Husserl as well, in the suggestion that we can be aware of and test prejudices.

Now in Gadamer's argument, this suggestion reflects a serious confusion between the conception of fore-understanding, which clearly presents an initial bias in the way in which we approach experience, and the presuppositions which underlie and, for that reason, cannot be demonstrated within a position. If we grant that something like an initial bias can be examined and tested in the dialectic between the subject and object of experience, it does not follow that on a deeper level we are even aware of, much less able to test, our prejudices, suppositions, hypotheses, or presuppositions. It does no good to ask us to discard the so-called Enlightenment prejudice against prejudice, since that request might itself only be an instance of a further, deeper prejudice, which, however, must be defeated if knowledge is to be possible. Descartes, who set the standard of the modern concept of epistemology, clearly realized this point in his introduction of the fictitious concept of the evil demon.

In his analysis of effective historical consciousness, Gadamer does not overcome the problem of epistemology, but rather largely turns his back on it. Yet he does not therefore escape from epistemology. In epistemological terms, the problem which concerns him is the possibility of a historical hermeneutics. He apparently intends his discussion as an overcoming (*Überwindung*) of the problem of knowledge. But I believe we can consider it as a suggestion for a different kind of knowledge, which takes into account the finite, historical character of human experience as its basis. The central concept in the discussion is the idea of the effective historical consciousness (*wirkungsgeschichtliches Bewußtsein*), which Gadamer comprehends as the effectivity of history within understanding (*TM*, 300).

As this concept suggests, Gadamer's focus lies in the way in which

the historical dimension informs our understanding. Interpreting prejudice in a historical sense, he suggests that temporal distance enables us
to distinguish true from false instances (*TM*, 298). Lacking here as elsewhere is any way to know that at a given time a given prejudice is true and
not false. According to Gadamer, who continually privileges historical
over systematic considerations, we are always subject to the effects of
effective history (*TM*, 300). Left unclear is whether this claim is itself
wholly systematic, or whether it is historically based, in which case we
could entertain the possibility of a time at which one might choose to
reject it, for instance through the assertion that it is purely systematic in
character or else cannot be maintained as true. According to Gadamer,
understanding provides the fusion of horizons (*TM*, 306) and consciousness of this fusion is the central problem of hermeneutics (*TM*,
307). It follows, as he points out, that understanding is a kind of effect
(*TM*, 341). After insisting on the need to be open to a tradition, from
which one can never escape (*TM*, 360), Gadamer sums up his understanding of what this means in his conviction that an openness to history
renounces what he calls the chimera of perfect enlightenment in the
fusion of the horizons of the understanding mediating between text and
interpreter (*TM*, 377–78).

Although Gadamer repeatedly refers to the concept of a historical
hermeneutics, he also tends to concentrate on textual interpretation.
The consequences of his argument go well beyond the problem of textual reading to the insightful suggestion of the historical component in
all cognition. This is an important point, which he does not fully develop, in part because he limits himself to an approach following mainly
from Heidegger's thought. But his view is problematic, beginning in the
claim that understanding is an effect. Obviously, he cannot admit that
his own understanding of understanding is an effect without giving up
the ability to argue for his position. To that extent, he needs to insist on
the distinction between historical and systematic approaches which he
otherwise attempts to undercut in his historical approach to hermeneutics. Now he can respond to this criticism by differentiating between the
interpretation of a text and the interpretation of interpretation, at the
cost of reintroducing a concept of epistemology which is constantly lurking in the background. But there is a deeper problem, which results in a
kind of paradox. For on Gadamer's own analysis, either there is no
knowledge, since epistemology is impossible, and accordingly he fails to
overcome the epistemological problem; or there is knowledge, and he
does not provide it since he fails to overcome the epistemological problem. I see no way within the framework of Gadamer's view to escape from
this paradoxical result.

TOM ROCKMORE

My main criticism of Gadamer's claim that phenomenology over-comes the problem of epistemology is that it rests on a clearly faulty read-ing of the history of philosophy. In his analysis of Dilthey's position, the supposed failure of the idealist approach is taken as a given, which Gadamer does not further examine. He merely assumes, without argu-ment, that the form of epistemology that reaches a peak in Hegel's posi-tion does not resolve the question of knowledge. This is a serious lacuna in his analysis. He simply fails to provide the analysis of Hegel's view nec-essary in order to show that it offers a deficient theory of epistemology. The closest Gadamer comes to an argument on this point is his frequent, unsupported statement that Hegel argues for infinite knowledge on the basis of a finite conception of human being.

Gadamer's assumption is false on at least three grounds. To begin with, as I have argued elsewhere, Hegel's argument contains a profound analysis of the problem of knowledge, whose full resources have arguably still not been perceived.[2] I do not want to repeat this argument at pre-sent. Suffice it to say that it is inconsistent for a thinker such as Gadamer, who correctly insists on the importance of the history of the tradition, to fail to grasp, or even to make a real effort to understand, the Hegelian view of knowledge. This is even more surprising since Hegel's position provides a main anticipation of Gadamer's own effort to rehabilitate the historical dimension of philosophy against the purely systematic efforts of Descartes and Kant, or the dismissive, often fantastic readings found in Heidegger.

Second, as part of his failure to consider Hegel's theory of knowl-edge, Gadamer appears to underestimate the extent to which others, such as Dilthey,[3] Fichte,[4] Friedrich Ast,[5] perhaps Lask, and certainly Hegel largely anticipate Heidegger's discussion of the hermeneutic circle of the understanding. Following Fichte's rejection of the concept of an ini-tial principle, or ground of knowledge, in favor of a circular concept, Hegel elaborates a little known, but powerful view of knowledge as intrinsically circular. According to Hegel, who makes a qualified return to the pre-Aristotelian view of knowledge as circular, a claim to know is justified, not through an initial principle, but through the elaboration of the entire theory. Now it is arguable that Hegel was mistaken in his effort to argue for knowledge in the traditional sense on the basis of a circular epistemological theory. But he clearly anticipates Heidegger's concept of what Gadamer calls the fore-understanding (*Vorverständnis*) in his analysis of the dialectic of subject and object. In this basic respect Hei-degger's view—whose claim to originality here as elsewhere is largely based on the concealment of his sources—which Gadamer ably summarizes, is mainly a restatement of Hegel's. Now one might object that Heidegger displaces what was earlier an epistemological discussion to an ontological plane, in line with his focus on the question of the meaning of Being. But even if his focus is ontological, the antifoundationalist argument he advances in his discussion of the hermeneutic circle is clearly epistemological in intent. In fact, Gadamer realizes this point as the basis of his claim that phenomenology overcomes the epistemological problem.

Third, Gadamer seems to rely on a false dichotomy between idealism and phenomenology. This is a distinction without a difference, since phenomenology is closely rooted in German idealism. Gadamer follows the general tendency, present even in such informed observers as Sartre, to regard phenomenology as arising in Husserl's thought. But this reading of the evolution of phenomenology is substantially incorrect since it overlooks or otherwise minimizes the phenomenological dimension of idealism, arguably present in Fichte's position, whose phenomenological aspect is strong, but not often noticed, and certainly present in Hegel's thought. If we prescind from discussion of Fichte and if we grant the phenomenological status of Hegel's position, then at most one can claim a new beginning, or a significant difference, in that part of the phenomenological tradition which originates in Husserl's thought and continues over Heidegger to Gadamer. What one cannot claim is that there is an epistemological difference in kind between idealism and phenomenology.

If Gadamer is incorrect to assume a distinction between idealist epistemology and the phenomenological analysis of the hermeneutic circle, then he cannot maintain that the phenomenological analysis of the hermeneutic circle overcomes the problem of knowledge in the sense that he intends this to be the case. Gadamer regards Heidegger as unlocking the epistemological potential of Dilthey's analysis in order finally to overcome the epistemological problem. But if, as I maintain, Heidegger's view of the hermeneutic circle is largely based on Hegel's, then we arrive at the following paradox: either phenomenology does overcome the epistemological problem, but this overcoming occurs in Hegel's position, not in either Heidegger's or Gadamer's; or phenomenology fails to overcome the epistemological problem. If Gadamer means to claim that phenomenology overcomes the problem of epistemology, and if this overcoming lies in the hermeneutic circle of the understanding that derives from Hegel's position, there is no other possible conclusion.

We can sum up the results of this examination of Gadamer's contention that phenomenology overcomes the problem of epistemology in five main points. First, it is a mistake to hold that the epistemological problem, or even epistemology as such, which in different ways has long been the focus of the philosophical tradition since its origins in ancient Greece, comes to an end in phenomenology or even prior to it. If phenomenology can be said to overcome this problem, it is only because it puts forward a new theory of knowledge, which arguably represents an advance on earlier views.

Second, to make out his claim that phenomenology overcomes the problem of epistemology, Gadamer provides an arguably tendentious reading of the history of philosophy, in particular through an exaggeration of the difference between idealism and phenomenology. With respect to the problem of epistemology there is no break between idealism and phenomenology. It is only through inattention to the history of philosophy by the author of the concept of effective historical consciousness that we can arrive at this strange interpretation, which does not preclude the conclusion that there is a change, even a major change, in the post-Hegelian form of phenomenology.

Third, after Kant there is a change in the problem of knowledge in two senses. On the one hand, because of the intrinsic circularity of the process of knowledge, the awareness that the linear form of epistemology, what later came to be known as foundationalism, was an unsatisfactory approach led to a qualified return to circular strategies for knowledge. On the other hand, as a result of the rehabilitation of the concept of the historical subject, Heidegger notwithstanding, philosophy moves from the a priori to the a posteriori plane, to society and to history, on whose level knowledge in the traditional sense of the term is not possible. Gadamer's stress on the historicity of hermeneutics is most original within the hermeneutic tradition, but is at least partially anticipated by others in the widespread turn to history.

Fourth, the problem of knowledge, which is central to the thought of both Fichte and Hegel, is still strongly present in later phenomenology: in Husserl's position, which centers on how to make out the ancient distinction between knowledge and opinion; in Heidegger's view of circularity, whose concept of what Gadamer calls *Vorverständnis* is a working out of the Hegelian view in the introduction to the *Phenomenology*; and in Gadamer's effort, following Heidegger and Dilthey, to stress the concept of history and of effective historical consciousness. Against Dewey, who held that there was no problem of knowledge, as well as writers in the analytic side of philosophy, who sometimes imply that there is only one problem of knowledge and a single possible solution, we must emphasize that there are different problems of knowledge which occur in different ways in different types of thought, and which admit of different possible solutions. Even if one were to grant the validity of the historical approach to hermeneutics as a solution to the problem of textual exegesis, at most that would represent the overcoming of one variant of the epistemological problem.

Fifth, phenomenology does not overcome the problem of knowledge in the general sense, if indeed that is possible at all. But Gadamer's analysis provides a lesson that surpasses his end in view. Through his further development of the Heideggerian form of the hermeneutic circle in a historical sense, he in effect demonstrates that knowledge, if there is any, cannot be justified in a traditional, foundationalist manner and hence cannot be traditional, as he shows in his analyses of language, Aristotelian *phronesis*, the social sciences, and so on. In this manner he perhaps unwittingly demonstrates that and how the problem of knowledge recurs within phenomenology, but that in virtue of its limitation hermeneutic phenomenology is unable to overcome the epistemological problem. I conclude that even if Gadamer does not show that phenomenology overcomes the epistemological problem, he at least illustrates the way in which the problem of knowledge arises in a different manner within later phenomenology.

4

Uncovering Hermeneutic Truth

Lawrence K. Schmidt

A response to the question concerning the legitimation of prejudices is required in order to understand the concept of hermeneutic truth. This question is posed with reference to Gadamer's concluding remark in *Truth and Method*, "What the tool of method does not achieve must—and actually can—be achieved by a discipline of questioning and investigating, a discipline that authenticates (*verbürgt*) truth" (*WM*, 465; *TM*, 491). How does one come to be able to authenticate, attest to, vouch for, guarantee, stand behind or warrant—all possible translations of *verbürgen*—a truth by means of a disciplined conversation? To begin this investigation an interpretation of the epistemologically relevant structures of *Truth and Method* will be developed. Next the question of the possibility of a hermeneutic criterion for truth will be considered. In conclusion the concept of the enlightening, which will be argued to be the hermeneutic truth-criterion, will be compared to Husserl's concept of evidence.

The Legitimation of Prejudices

Gadamer's philosophical hermeneutics centers around the problem of the legitimation of prejudices within the process of understanding (*WM*,

261; *TM*, 277). Basic to Gadamer's and Heidegger's hermeneutics is the idea that all cognitive acts begin in a pre-understanding. Whatever is to be examined is initially grasped by one's pre-understanding. The ever-present effect of the pre-understanding prohibits any possible direct or immediate cognition. The elements of the pre-understanding are one's *Vorurteile*, prejudices or prejudgments.

To begin his theoretic discussion of hermeneutic experience (*WM*, 251; *TM*, 266), Gadamer quotes Heidegger's statement that a vicious circularity within understanding can be avoided and positive possibilities of knowing can be revealed only when the prejudices are founded on the *Sachen selbst*, i.e., the things themselves or the subject matter, and not on fancies or popular conceptions. Gadamer's task, therefore, is to explain the legitimation of the prejudices during the process of understanding by demonstrating how they are grounded in the things themselves. That which permits such a grounding, I will argue, is the hermeneutic truth-criterion.

Prejudices are inherited during acculturation and especially in learning a language. They form one's horizon of possible meaning. To be able to criticize or legitimate prejudices one must be able to call them into question. This occurs when one prejudice is faced with an opposing one. In *Truth and Method* the primary way in which one is confronted by opposing prejudices is through the examination of past texts. In interpreting a text, one must project (that is, infer) the meaning or prejudices of a text. Every projecting of a text's meaning is relative to a particular question horizon and set of prejudices contained in the interpreter's linguistic and historic horizon. Further, Gadamer argues that reflective consciousness cannot transcend its own position in history. It is unable to escape from the influence of its horizon of prejudices to some absolute horizon of meaning. So consciousness remains always an effective historical consciousness. Therefore, one is unable to discover and justify a historically independent truth.

What Gadamer does conclude from the experience of interpretive understanding is that the projecting and comparing of prejudices is a dialectic of question and answer. It is a dialogue between interpreter and inherited text. All understanding occurs in the medium of language, and prejudices are linguistic. Inasmuch as every correct understanding of a text consists in the process of bringing the meaning of the text into the interpreter's language, and in as much as the language of different interpreters at different times can be significantly different, and since there is no absolute position, Gadamer concludes: "there cannot therefore be a correct interpretation 'in itself' precisely because every interpretation concerns the text itself. The historical life of tradition consists in its dependency on ever new appropriations and interpretations" (*WM*, 375; *TM*, 397).

How can the interpreter claim one prejudice to be correct or true as opposed to the other? In order to answer this question the relationship between language and the things themselves must be understood. Concerning the word and the object referred to, Gadamer claims that the subject does not already know the truth (that is, the referent of the word) and then search for the correct word to express this truth either in the sense of agreeing upon a sign or in the sense of discovering its natural image or copy in language. The interpreter does not discover some existing thing and give it meaning. "Rather the ideality of meaning lies in the word itself. It is always already meaning" (*WM*, 394; *TM*, 417). He or she does not first experience and then, only later, discover the words to express this experience. The essential point is that experiencing is itself a linguistic event.

> Experience is not wordless to begin with, subsequently becoming an object of reflection by being named. . . . Rather, experience of itself seeks and finds words that express it. One seeks the correct word, that is, the word that truly belongs to the thing [*Sache*], so that thereby the thing itself comes into language. (*WM*, 394; *TM*, 417)

Gadamer argues further that the event of understanding is primarily an act of the thing itself to present itself in language. It is the speculative act of self-presentation by the thing itself—its coming-to-be-in-language (*WM*, 450; *TM*, 475). This is what is experienced by the cognizer.

In order to understand the extent to which a thing can come into language, it is necessary to briefly examine Gadamer's discussions of Wilhelm von Humboldt and Edmund Husserl. Humboldt's thesis, which Gadamer incorporates, is that differences among languages cause different worldviews (*Weltansichten*) to be experienced (*WM*, 419; *TM*, 442). So each individual language, linguistic perspective, each *Sprachansicht*, presents a specific perspective of the world, a *Weltansicht*. Inasmuch as there is a common language, the speakers already have a common perspective. It is their linguistic inheritance and founds the *sensus communis*.

The relationship between the cognizer and the thing itself is accomplished in the medium of language. Any particular language is only a particular perspective of the world, and although it may be expanded to include any other, it cannot completely express the thing itself in its totality. There is no perfect human language. The essential point is that the interpreter can cognize only that aspect of the thing which is expressible in that particular linguistic perspective.

To clarify the idea that only a perspective of the thing is expressible, Gadamer refers to Husserl's analysis of the perception of a table. Just as each sense perception is different, if ever so slightly, so too each linguistic perspective can express only a perspective of the thing itself (*WM*, 424; *TM*, 448). This means that each particular linguistic perspective presents a different and incomplete picture of a theoretic or possible "world in itself." It presents only a perspective of the world in itself, just as each different sense perception presents a different perspective of the transphenomenal thing-in-itself, e.g., the table. Gadamer notes two essential differences to Husserl in this analogy. First, Husserl has a transcendental consciousness constituting the intentional object (table), while for Gadamer there is no such consciousness (analogous to an ahistorical, absolute point of view) able to connect the differing perspectives of the thing to form the thing-in-itself. There is no absolute position. Secondly, for Husserl the different perspectives in sense perception are distinct; one particular perspective cannot change to include others. The unification of the perspectives is an act of intentional consciousness. However, for Gadamer each perspective is linguistic and it is a characteristic of language to be able to develop and include other perspectives. The possibility of expanding any linguistic perspective by means of its confrontation with another, and thereby constituting a new perspective in dialogue, permits language to express any development in knowledge. So any one perspective may contain any other one potentially.

This discussion demonstrates that the hypothetical "whole" truth concerning a subject matter is only partially experienceable and expressible. It is only a perspective of the thing itself, an *Ansicht der Sache selbst*, that may be experienced and expressed in the language of that linguistic perspective (*WM*, 448; *TM*, 473). The ontological significance of language is that the thing itself presents itself and its truth, insofar as it is realizable, as a perspective of itself. What remains is to connect the prejudices with this expression in language.

How does the cognizer come to recognize the correct expression of the thing itself that is the truth of that thing in his or her language? How is this expression as truth to be distinguished from other expressions that are false since they do not express this thing? And, finally, how does the cognizer legitimize the prejudices by founding them on the thing itself? The essence of Gadamer's answers to these questions is that the perspective of the thing itself is enlightening (*einleuchtend*). In other words, the self-presentation of the thing in the event of understanding is something expressed by this concept, *die Einleuchtende*, "that which shines forth." Gadamer writes: "The *eikos*, the *verisimile*, the *Wahr-Schein-liche*, the *Einleuchtende* [the enlightening] belong to a series that defends its own correctness against the truth and certainty of the proven and known" (*WM*, 460; *TM*, 485).

The concept *enlightening* has been adopted from the metaphysical tradition of light in classical Greek philosophy. It has been adopted without any overtones concerning some sort of transcendental source of light (*WM*, 459; *TM*, 484). Rather it is the power of light to illuminate. It allows the illuminated to be seen. Gadamer attributes this power to language. It is "the light of the word" (*WM*, 458; *TM*, 483). The word as light permits the thing to be seen in its self-presentation in language. In this sense the self-presentation of the thing is self-evident. It presents itself to the cognizer as it is. So "Being, which can be understood, is language" (*WM*, 450; *TM*, 474).[1] Therefore, the enlightening may throw a new light upon what was thought to have been the case. "The enlightening is also clearly always something surprising, like the dawning of a new light" (*WM*, 460; *TM*, 486). Furthermore, the enlightening is more authentically true than what had been proven and thought to be true and certain.

Gadamer's conclusions (1) that the thing itself presents itself in every particular language as a perspective of itself, (2) that this is the most complete expression of the thing possible in that particular language horizon, and (3) that the perspective of the thing is enlightening, allow him to philosophically legitimize his conclusion that a discipline of questioning and investigating can authenticate truth.

Within the discipline of questioning and investigating, differing and conflicting possibilities present themselves to the interpreter who has opened a space for them. The inherited text may present prejudices different from the interpreter's. Creative development of new prejudices may occur in this clearing. The different prejudices are linguistic expressions concerning the subject matter, *Sache selbst*, under discussion. They are possible perspectives of this thing itself. Differing interpretations are probed. Finally, if there is an event of truth, one interpretation (one prejudice, one perspective) will shine forth since it is the enlightening perspective. It is a partial truth, the hermeneutic truth, the perspective of the thing itself relative to that linguistic perspective. In this way the prejudice may be founded upon the *Sache selbst* or subject matter and one may authenticate this truth. This is part of what I think Gadamer means when he writes: "As one who understands we are incorporated within an event of truth [*Wahrheitsgeschehen*] and come too late, if we wish to know what we should believe" (*WM*, 465; *TM*, 490).

The enlightening is evident; it shines forth. If a prejudice is enlightening and this is experienced in the event of truth, there is no possibility of wondering whether this is to be believed. If one questioned it, it would not be enlightening; we would have come too late. Later, in another experience, another perspective may appear as enlightening in a different linguistic perspective. Therefore, the enlightening quality of the perspective of the thing itself is the hermeneutic truth-criterion, since it alone enables the cognizer to found the prejudices on the things themselves. Further, the enlightening perspective of the thing itself permits the differentiation of truth from falsity within the linguistic perspective. This prevents a total relativism where truth and falsity are indistinguishable. And yet, since the enlightening perspective is only a perspective of the thing itself, the truth realized in the event of understanding is not an absolute truth but a truth relative to the linguistic perspective, which forms our present horizon of meaning and knowledge. This preserves the possibility of new knowledge and recognizes our human finitude and fallibility.

Hermeneutic truth is a human truth, but truth nevertheless. There is a mark or criterion for this truth; it is the enlightening quality of the perspective of the thing itself.[2]

Questioning the Truth Criterion

One may well question whether Gadamer is even interested in affirming a hermeneutic truth-criterion and, if he were, whether this proposal of the enlightening perspective would be acceptable. Nowhere in *Truth and Method* does Gadamer define a truth-criterion. In fact, in his 1971 essay "Replik" he writes: "Hermeneutic reflection is limited to opening possibilities for knowledge that without it would not be perceived. It does not itself convey a truth criterion" (*GWII*, 263).

To interpret this passage let me first examine in what sense a criterion is denied by eliciting the assistance of Jean Grondin's discussion in his important work entitled *Hermeneutische Wahrheit?*, whose epigraph is the above quotation.[3] In chapter 5, section 10, Grondin presents five arguments against a hermeneutic truth-criterion. I will briefly mention these because they help to show exactly what is being denied and what may still be possible as a truth-criterion.

First Grondin argues that the criterion of contradiction (i.e., the traditional coherence criterion) cannot be the hermeneutic truth-criterion, since the experience of hermeneutic truth may contradict what was before a coherent unity (*HW*, 177). This is quite correct, for we have seen that the power of the enlightening is just to present itself as true over and against what might have been proven coherent by some method. The essence of Gadamer's discussion of hermeneutic experience is just that an experience in its genuine sense corrects what had been considered a coherent unity by exposing an illegitimate prejudice (*WM*, 336; *TM*, 353).

Grondin's second argument is that a truth-criterion must claim universal validity and such universal validity is not possible for hermeneutic consciousness, since it is necessarily bounded by its historical horizon. Each epoch will have its own questions and therefore, Grondin continues, its own truth (*HW*, 177). This argument is also correct on one level. It is clearly the case that every interpretation and every truth-claim is bounded by the linguistic epoch in which it is asserted. However, on the "meta-level" of philosophical hermeneutics Gadamer seems willing to, and in fact does, make some universal truth-claims—I am thinking of such principles as the necessity of prejudices effecting all cognitions, the principle of effective history, effective-historical consciousness, and the unconditional claim concerning the conditioned nature of human cognition (*WM*, 424; *TM*, 448). I would also argue that the enlightening perspective belongs to this level and so may be claimed to be a truth-criterion. This means the content that appears to a cognizer as enlightening, the perspective of the thing itself, is clearly bounded by the historic and linguistic epoch and can never be claimed to be absolutely valid. However, it is always the case that the enlightening does shine forth and does correct mistaken prejudices and that the enlightening perspective is the self-presentation of the thing itself for that particular horizon. These may be said to be as universally valid as the principle of effective-historical consciousness itself. Clearly, since philosophical hermeneutics is itself a historically and linguistically bounded experience, it, as all experiences, must be open to the possibility of being questioned.

Grondin's third argument is that truth cannot be the correspondence of understanding to a stable criterion, since Gadamer denies that there exists an ahistorical consciousness that could measure the historically different truths. This implies, for Grondin, that there cannot be a stable criterion, whether it be the being-in-itself or the opinion of the author (*HW*, 177). I agree that neither the opinion of the author nor the being-in-itself of the subject matter is the criterion or what is to correspond to correct understanding. However, as I have mentioned, the speculative unity of the coming-to-be-in-language of the thing itself does guarantee that the enlightening perspective is the true expression of the subject matter for that linguistic perspective. The enlightening is experienced by the cognizer as enlightening, so there is no question here of making some further judgment concerning a correspondence or not. In this sense Grondin is correct that a judgment of correspondence cannot be the hermeneutic truth-criterion.

In the fourth argument Grondin raises the traditional problem that the criterion of truth must itself be true (*HW*, 177–78). According to Grondin, Hegel has proven that a truth-criterion cannot be discovered outside consciousness. Therefore, the criterion is itself dependent on the historical changes that consciousness undergoes. Grondin concludes that if an unchanging and so finally true criterion were asserted, it must be supported from a nonhistorical, i.e., nonhermeneutic, position and this is impossible (*HW*, 178). Again I would agree with Grondin if one accepts Hegel's position. But isn't the absolute position of subjectivity itself being called into question in Gadamer's philosophical hermeneutics? Gadamer concludes his examination of Hegel's dialectic of consciousness by demonstrating that prior to any dialectical synthesis is the hermeneutic truth of experience—i.e., that any conclusion may be overturned by a future experience (*WM*, 339; *TM*, 357). Such an experience that asserts itself, I maintain, does so exactly by means of the experience of the enlightening perspective.

Grondin's last argument states that the search for a criterion leads to an infinite regress in the sense that if the criterion is thought of as a measuring rod then one would need another measuring rod in order to measure the truth of the first rod, and so on (*HW*, 178). However, Gadamer's reference to the classical metaphysical theories of the beautiful and light demonstrates that the enlightening does not require a further testing (*WM*, 460; *TM*, 485). It carries within itself the power to illuminate itself. It shines forth and convinces one. In this sense Gadamer states that one arrives too late to ask what one should believe. The experience of the enlightening perspective requires no further justification; it is enlightening. To ask what one should believe is to presume that what was experienced was not enlightening.

Grondin has shown us important senses in which hermeneutic reflection does not provide us with a truth-criterion. But has the possibility of a hermeneutic truth-criterion been eliminated in all senses? I have tried to demonstrate why I believe it has not. My interpretation of Gadamer's statement in the "Replik," quoted above, is that Gadamer is primarily concerned to demonstrate that hermeneutic reflective consciousness (in a sense, what remains of subjectivity itself) is limited by the historical and linguistic epoch, or the linguistic perspective, in which it finds itself. It is limited but not powerless. The essential function of an effective-historical consciousness, which is aware of its own nature, is to follow the call of the question, to enter into a dialogue, to question one's prejudices, and so to open a new space into which the thing may speak, wherein prejudices may become founded in a truth-event by the enlightening perspective—where Being as *physis*, in Heidegger's sense, may arise and stand out in the gathering together of the *logos*.[4] Gadamer's point is to limit the idealist presupposition of the power of reflective consciousness. Reflective consciousness cannot provide a method or way toward the truth. It cannot provide a truth-criterion. Rather, hermeneutic reflection must acknowledge its own finitude, fallibility, and the infinite possibility of new experiences—experiences that, when enlightening, open up new vistas of what may be called hermeneutic truth.

What Is the Enlightening?

What does the concept *enlightening* entail when it is claimed to be the hermeneutic truth-criterion? Is Grondin correct, and to what extent, when he argues that an enlightening interpretation may not be correct? (*HW*, 166) Does the concept of the enlightening imply some subjective emotive state, so that if it were the truth-criterion, truth would be grounded in one's subjective emotions?

To initiate a discussion of the concept of the enlightening let me contrast this interpretation of Gadamer's concept of the enlightening with Husserl's concept of evidence. In the *Logical Investigations*, Husserl writes:

> Inner evidence is no accessory feeling, either casually attached, or attached by natural necessity, to certain judgments. . . . [It] is rather nothing but the "experience" of truth. . . . *Truth is an idea, whose particular case is an actual experience in the inwardly evident judgment. . . . The Experience of the agreement* between meaning and what is itself present, meant, between the actual sense of an assertion and the self-given *state of affairs*, is inward evidence.[5]

It is quite clear that Husserl's concept of evidence is not an affective state that attends to or occurs with some set of judgments. Not that such an affective state does not exist; I have all too often had such a feeling of surety or self-confidence. But it is clear that Gadamer's concept of the enlightening, like Husserl's concept of evidence, does not concern such an emotive state. In an experience, in its genuine sense, we come to see that we were mistaken; a very important type of experience is just to come to see that one was mistaken about what one accepted as self-evident. And this occurs by means of the legitimation of prejudices through the experience of the enlightening perspective of the thing itself. Only an inexperienced person would replace the feeling of self-evidence before such an experience with another feeling of self-assurance after that experience. What Aeschylus was to have taught us is that the fundamental truth of experience is just that one is fallible (*WM*, 339; *TM*, 356).

For Husserl inward evidence is the experience of the agreement between the meaning and the meant, or the assertion and the self-given state of affairs. Husserl presupposes here, as does Hegel in the beginning of the *Phenomenology of Mind,* that it is a fact of human consciousness that it is able to provide itself with its own criterion of truth since both notion and object, being for another and being in itself fall within consciousness. Consciousness is able to examine with certainty, self-clarity, or evidently what is presented to it and decide on the match or the extent of the match. The meaning or assertion is an intention of consciousness and the meant or self-given state of affairs is what is presented to consciousness, by perhaps the senses or by the imagination. What consciousness is able to do with certainty is to judge the extent of the match between these two—the greater the match the higher the fulfillment of the intention.[6] Husserl writes in the sixth investigation:

> The discussion of possible relationships of fulfillment therefore points to *a goal in which increase of fulfillment terminates, in which the complete and entire intention has reached its fulfillment,* and that not intermediately and partially, but ultimately and finally. . . . *The object is actually "present" or "given," and present as just what we have intended it;* no partial intention remains implicit and still lacking fulfillment.[7]

In the sense that one can speak of an intention being only partly fulfilled one can also speak of "degrees and levels of self-evidence," but

> the *epistemologically pregnant sense* of self-evidence is exclusively concerned with this last unsurpassable goal, *the act of this most perfect synthesis of fulfillment,* which gives to an intention, e.g. the intention of judgment, the absolute fulness of content, the fulness of the object itself.[8]

This epistemologically pregnant sense of self-evidence can be contrasted to Gadamer's concept of enlightening. For Husserl human consciousness has this innate ability to compare with absolute clarity and certainty two elements within itself (i.e., the intended and the given) and a perfect match is then said to be self-evident. There can be no questioning as to the ability or clarity with which consciousness makes this particular type of comparison. For Gadamer such an event within consciousness is not implied in the experience of the enlightening. In consciousness there are not two separate things, a linguistically formed intention and a nonlinguistic, experienced state of affairs. Rather the ontological significance of language is that experience, as noted above, is already linguistic. The legitimation of prejudices is not an internal judgment of consciousness comparing two states. Human consciousness is least in control and least active in the enlightening truth-event. Consciousness's activity has already been accomplished in the important sense of clearing a space for this event of truth. There is a more active role for the subject matter or thing itself in this truth-event (*WM*, 439; *TM*, 463). The thing comes to be in language, it "informs" consciousness of its being in an experience whose power is just to be enlightening. This event is primarily an act of the thing itself and not a judgment of consciousness. As noted above hermeneutic reflection does not provide a truth-criterion, rather it experiences truth.

This I would argue is the essential difference in concepts. The self-evident for Husserl is a "pure seeing" or "pure apprehension" by consciousness of a correspondence of two elements within itself that is indubitable. The enlightening, for Gadamer, is a shining forth from the thing itself that overcomes and informs consciousness. It presents consciousness with an experience.

However, one must note a similarity between Husserl's and Gadamer's concepts in spite of this fundamental difference. Both the enlightening and the self-evident present themselves in such a manner that they are accepted without requiring any external justification by means of a method or anything else. To this extent Grondin is wrong if he claims that the enlightening experience *as such* can be incorrect. On the other hand, it is correct that for Gadamer the enlightening is never final—what once was enlightening may be overcome in a new experience. In another truth-event, in a new linguistic perspective, a different perspective may be enlightening.

These investigations have argued that Gadamer does demonstrate how one's prejudices are legitimized, and therefore he is justified in concluding that a hermeneutic discipline of questioning and investigating can authenticate truth. The enlightening quality of the perspective of the thing itself shines forth and is experienced by the cognizer. This experience legitimizes a prejudice for that particular linguistic horizon. This enlightening quality may be said to be the hermeneutic truth-criterion, since the examination of Grondin's arguments against a hermeneutic truth-criterion were seen not to apply to the enlightening. The examination of Husserl's concept of evidence showed that the enlightening was experienced by consciousness as beyond question within that horizon, although it was not an internal judgment of the correspondence of an intention and a self-given state of affairs. Therefore, the enlightening quality of the thing itself permits the differentiation of hermeneutic truth from falsity, thereby avoiding the charge of radical relativism, while its dependence on the temporal, linguistic horizon preserves the historicity and finitude of human understanding and so avoids the charge of essentialism.

5

Three Puzzles for Gadamer's Hermeneutics

Joseph Margolis

W e owe to Hans-Georg Gadamer the clear articulation of a fully historicized hermeneutics of man. *Truth and Method* is often unceremoniously characterized as a post-Heideggerian reading of the questions of classical hermeneutics. It is certainly decisively influenced by Heidegger's sense of the radical historicity of human existence. But it is also true that Gadamer attempts to restore a certain conservative strain in the hermeneutic process that is not really found in Heidegger; and it is true that Gadamer is not committed to Heidegger's ontology of Dasein (in *Being and Time*) or to the displacement of Dasein in Heidegger's treatment of historical time in the period following the *Kehre*. In a fair sense, he is a tactful and indirect critic of Heidegger; at the same time it must be said that *Truth and Method* could probably not have been written had not Heidegger developed his own account of time and history. Certainly, Gadamer does not subscribe to any totalized or teleologized or absolute-idealist reading of hermeneutics; in this sense, he joins Heidegger in opposing what both take Hegel to have intended by his history and hermeneutics. Furthermore, Gadamer opposes the objectivism of classical metaphysics; and in this sense, once again, he joins Heidegger in locating the very question of objectivity in the space of the historicized symbiosis of human self-understanding. But, as Gadamer himself observes, Heidegger pursues the matter in order to be clear about the ontology of Dasein; whereas he, Gadamer, is primarily interested in "the historicality of understanding" itself.[1]

There is, therefore, a certain risk in speaking of Gadamer's metaphysics. There is no question that Gadamer is interested in the metaphysics of human existence. That is the very point of his prioritizing what he calls "contemporaneousness" and "the universal linguisticality of man's relation to the world," why he insists (for instance, against Jürgen Habermas) that "hermeneutics is not to be viewed as a mere subordinate discipline within the arena of the *Geisteswissenschaften.*"[2]

Nevertheless, it would be a mistake to treat the metaphysics of Gadamer's theory of hermeneutics in the same way in which Heidegger's conception of Dasein invites a comparison with classical metaphysics. It may even be that Gadamer's originality lends itself to a variety of more systematic metaphysical options—more options, possibly, than he himself would care to consider. Certainly, the very idea that man's existence is "hermeneutical" has attracted theorists of every conceivable persuasion and is hardly confined to the tradition moving through Hegel and Nietzsche that, in German philosophy, has produced Heidegger and Gadamer. For example, many have observed a distinct convergence between such utterly dissimilar minds as Gadamer's and the American pragmatist Charles Peirce's.[3]

Be that as it may, Gadamer's oeuvre does not constitute a sufficiently systematized vision of its own, such that one may begin to test the prospects of a hermeneuticized metaphysics centered on just the themes that rightly distinguish his thought, whether in agreement, say, with Heidegger's notions of *Temporalität* and *Historizität* or in opposition to or independence from them. And there, in a spirit entirely congenial to the executive thesis intended, a number of nagging puzzles demand an answer before we can responsibly go much further along Gadamer's own line of argument. The pretty thing about these puzzles is that they confirm the sense in which Gadamer's and Heidegger's thought (and Hegel's and Nietzsche's, for that matter) must still adhere to certain dialectical constraints that link canonical metaphysics and the liberating options historicity makes possible, in a way that belies the radical novelty of the latter. That is, these puzzles need not detract from their originality or their break with past practices; but they show that any such departure—as far as we can tell—must still adhere to deeper conceptual conditions that accommodate quite straightforwardly both the old and the new. There would actually be an advantage in showing this, since it would strengthen (against the derogating doubts of the old guard) the prospect that these more adventurous lines of speculation are quite capable of escaping paradox and incoherence.

I

Three puzzles seem particularly insistent. As it happens, they may be fixed in one stroke by juxtaposing two well-known remarks of Gadamer's. They interpenetrate one another, though they can be sorted; and they bear on nearly all contemporary and classical philosophy with as much force as on Gadamer himself.

Put compendiously—hence, opaquely, at first—they are these: (1) the apparent impossibility of overcoming the incompatibility of *historicism* (construed in Heidegger's and Gadamer's general sense of *historicity*) and *universalism* (or any historicized analogue of same, for instance, *traditionalism*); (2) the apparent impossibility of employing any notion of the preformative *symbiosis of subject and object* in a way that bears *distributively* on discursive acts to which we assign cognitive or hermeneutic standing; and (3) the apparent impossibility of resolving the puzzles of (1) and (2) without providing for the *ontic adequation* between cognizing or hermeneutic subjects and their capacity to make particular claims about cognizable or interpretable objects.

Here, our general thesis is that (1)–(3) constitute notably persistent constraints on any theorizing leading to a metaphysical hermeneutics—a hermeneutics, that is, that would reconcile the nature of human understanding and the nature of human existence. Since that *is* Gadamer's purpose, (1)–(3) are essentially unavoidable puzzles. But the point of collecting them in this frontal way is to draw attention as well to their unavoidability vis-à-vis nearly every large contemporary philosophy. As a matter of fact, what we have cited just a moment ago from Gadamer's paper on the scope of hermeneutics clearly implicates all three puzzles. That in itself is a good sign, because it may be reasonably argued that (1)–(3) are, effectively, the defining problems of contemporary philosophy.

Well, then, let's have the two citations promised. Take them neat, first, without comment:

> We say . . . that understanding and misunderstanding take place between I and thou. But the formulation "I and thou" already betrays an enormous alienation. There is nothing like an "I and thou" at all—there is

neither the I nor the thou as isolated, substantial realities. I may say "thou" and I may refer to myself over against a thou, but a common understanding [*Verständigung*] always precedes these situations.[4]

The classical is fundamentally something quite different from a descriptive concept used by an objectivizing historical consciousness. It is a historical reality to which historical consciousness belongs and is subordinate. What we call "classical" is something retrieved from the vicissitudes of changing time and its changing taste . . . it is a consciousness of something enduring, of significance that cannot be lost and is independent of all the circumstances of time, in which we call something "classical"—a kind of timeless present that is contemporaneous with every other age.[5]

There is a benign equivocation embedded in the first remark; but it poses a serious difficulty for Gadamer, both by itself and in tandem with the second. The denial that there is an "I and thou *at all*" could mean: (a) that selves are not individual substances at all, not "substantial realities"; or (b) that selves are not ever "isolated" from some "common understanding," some "comprehensive life-phenomenon that constitutes the 'we' that all are"—"the hermeneutical *Urphänomen*"[6]; or (c) that selves, however designated under the conditions of (b), still conform with (a).

The reason the equivocation is benign is because Gadamer clearly wishes to emphasize the societal and historical precondition within the space of which selves (the "I and thou") *are* sorted; and because he wished to emphasize the contingency and plasticity of selves that, under the conditions of hermeneutic formation and transformation, *are not* to be taken as fixed substances of any sort. Put in alternative terms, Gadamer wishes to *predicate* of selves (whatever they may be) an ineliminable social or collective or historical "nature"; and he wishes to *individuate* and *identify* plural selves only within the space of the "hermeneutic *Urphänomen*." But then, it is not at all clear whether he is also willing to say that the "I and thou" are "substantial realities"—individual substances *of some sort*—though not, to be sure, Aristotelian substances. The truth is, he never quite says. But the issue demands an answer. The question takes this form: How can an "I and thou" remain distinctive selves, if their nature can and must change under hermeneutic efforts and self-understanding?

It is not a negligible observation, therefore, that in *The Idea of the Good in Platonic-Aristotelian Philosophy*, which follows the second edition of *Truth and Method* by more than ten years and pursues the essential theme of *phronesis* featured in the earlier book, Gadamer does not come to terms with the problem of the "substantial" nature of the self (the "I and thou") that his hermeneutic metaphysics requires.[7] On the contrary, the book exacerbates the worry posed by (1)–(3), because it reviews the most important ancient efforts to account for the universal structure of practical reasoning under the conditions of man's finitude and contingency. And yet, though there is, indeed, plain evidence of Gadamer's concern with the relationship between *Being* and *goodness* in Plato and Aristotle, there is no actual analysis given of Aristotle's primary category of substance or of the nature of a human being or of the bearing of the radical hermeneutic issues *on* what Plato and Aristotle claim in this respect. So the apparent continuity of these essays and the essential theme of *Truth and Method* is difficult to fathom.[8]

Look a little more closely now. The "we"—the focus of the "hermeneutical *Urphänomen*"—can only point to the preformational condition under which the "I and thou" emerge and function, or to the societal (or collective or historical) predicables that hold of the "I and thou," or of both. There is, in context, no other possible option. Which is to say, the "we" cannot function as a cognizing or hermeneutic subject except as an *aggregated* collection of "I's and thou's"; but in that case it would presuppose Gadamer's own hermeneutic thesis, it would not help to explain it. So the thesis of the "we" obscures the question of accounting for the characteristic *function* of the "I and thou," namely, to be able to act discursively, to speak, to make distributed claims about what is true and false, and to act in nondiscursive ways that are, nevertheless, linguistically informed. That surely is the point of Gadamer's insistence on "the universal linguisticality of man's relation to the world."

There cannot be such a "universal linguisticality" unless functioning selves *are* individual agents. Even Heidegger's notorious extravagance in the "Letter on Humanism" means to come to terms with that condition, that is, even when Heidegger says:

> But man is not only a living creature who possesses language along with other capacities. Rather, language is the house of Being in which man exists by dwelling, in that he belongs to the truth of Being, guarding it. . . .
> In the determination of the humanity of man as ex-sistence what is essential is not man but Being. . . .[9]

Heidegger adds of course: "In its essence language is not the utterance of an organism, nor is it the expression of a living thing. . . . Language is the lighting-concealing advent of Being itself."[10] But that would be hopeless nonsense, were it not also true that he means to speak in a mythic mode about the preformative conditions *of* human utterance. Gadamer has a much more sensible use for the "we" of hermeneutic experience; but he does not quite explain the *nature* of the speaking and active self, and he needs to.

II

We have been proceeding in a soft way with the puzzles chiefly of (2) and (3) of our tally. The symbiotized preformative condition *from which* and *in which* functioning selves emerge as distinct, linguistically competent individuals cannot itself function as a functioning agent of any sort (there is no discoursing "we," except aggregatively; and there is no sense in supposing that "Being" discourses at all or in any way absolutely prior to the linguistic competence of the members of a natural society of humans). In a word, there is no *point* to a hermeneutic metaphysics unless the preconditions of discourse are brought to bear on the ontic status of human selves. But that, curious as it may seem, Gadamer never directly addresses. It is clearly an urgent matter, because the essential themes of *Truth and Method*—*Horizontverschmelzung* and *wirkungs-geschichtliches Bewußtsein*—make no sense without such an analysis. That is, those concepts would make no sense, given the benign equivocation on the expression, "I and thou" that we have been tracking, unless we were suitably reassured that "I's and thou's" *are* particulars of some sort apt for discourse and related acts. The reason is simply that the two themes mentioned are essentially concerned with the defeat of all canonical forms of objectivism and with their replacement by a resilient conception of just how the agents of hermeneutic practice are affected by their own ongoing hermeneutic work. Only a resolution of (2) and (3) can satisfy us here.

Consider, now, the bearing of all this on our second citation. What Gadamer intends, worrying about the fixity and isolation of the "I and thou," is to ensure the radical historicity of the human being—the agent (we have been calling him, the "self") *of* discourse and of whatever is infected by "linguisticality." Whatever his sympathies for Plato's reliance on mathematics and Aristotle's on biology in analyzing human nature, Gadamer certainly never conflates the hermeneutic powers of man with the merely physical and biological gifts of *homo sapiens*. How to understand the connection between the two may well be the single most important unanswered question in philosophy. In any case, the radical hermeneutic thesis Gadamer propounds accepts no compromise with the "historicality of understanding." The "I and thou," therefore, are "individual substances" (if they are "substances") whose intrinsic properties are subject to some sort of significant transformation under the condition of hermeneutic exertions—a transformation that parallels the effect of the historical contingency and plasticity of the symbiotized preconditions (the "we," the "hermeneutical *Urphänomen*") facilitating the first appearance of the "I and thou." That is the reason Gadamer avoids a straightforwardly Aristotelian or Platonic account of the self: his intended replacement is too radical for the idiom of individual substances in the old canon. Nevertheless, even the posit of hermeneutically symbiotized preconditions is the work of a discursively competent agent who cannot be entirely swallowed up by that symbiosis. Gadamer obviously does not wish to go to the extremes of Michel Foucault's constructivism regarding the self.[11] But he does not sufficiently mark out the required middle ground. That is clearly a failing with respect to (3).

There is a further difficulty that surfaces at once. *If* the self (the "I and thou"), emergent and functional in hermeneutic space, is whatever it is as a result of its "historicality" and "linguisticality," then, apart from an analysis of its would-be nature, we cannot fail to be puzzled by Gadamer's theory of "the classical"—because the classical escapes "the vicissitudes of changing time and its changing taste," and the self appears to be the creature of just such variability. How, then, is it that the hermeneutic endeavor can ensure a mode of "significance that cannot be lost and is independent of all the circumstances of time"? There is no answer in Gadamer. Without it, it is difficult to see how he means to escape the force of a radical perspectivism (of Nietzsche's sort) or of the radical relativism he feared lay threatening in Heidegger; or how, resisting such possibilities, he could make his own doctrine appear less arbitrary than it seems to be. This is not the right place to attempt an answer.[12] But we may at least observe: first, that it seems impossible to reconcile the historicism of Gadamer's hermeneutic view of the self and the universalism of his theory of the classical; and second, that any possible resolution of that puzzle would require a full-fledged theory of the metaphysics of the "I and thou."

This is not to say that Gadamer intends to recover the "mathematical" or "natural" universals of Plato and Aristotle. He is clearly opposed to any explicitly canonical essentialism.[13] But he does claim—as of course he must, if he means to support his theory of the classical—that "Practical philosophy . . . certainly is 'science': a knowledge of the universal that as such is teachable." He expressly says that this "holds true for hermeneutics as well"; although he rightly cautions that hermeneutic self-under-standing, like ethics, "presupposes its concretization [that is, the con-cretization or any relevant 'reference to self that is essential to practical philosophy'] within a living ethos."[14] He also, however, pursues the seem-ingly opposed line of argument, for instance against Hegel, maintaining:

> Just like all other history, . . . universal history too always must be
> rewritten insofar as it does not possess its absolute datum as does
> *Heilgeschichte*; and each projection of universal history has a validity that
> does not last much longer than the appearance of a flash momentarily
> cutting across the darkness of the future as well as of the past as it gets
> lost in the consuming twilight. That is the proposition of hermeneutical
> philosophy that I dared to defend against Hegel.[15]

To put the point dialectically, Gadamer does not succeed, here or elsewhere, in demonstrating *how* to distinguish, in a plausible way, his own view of historicality from Hegelian *historicism* (which might be con-strued as a version of relativism, by way of isolating, in the nineteenth-century manner—in Reigl's, for instance—one historical *Geist* from another) or from canonical *essentialism* (Aristotle's, for instance), in which the historical is merely the contingent or accidental among phe-nomena housing discernible universal invariances. Of course, we know that Gadamer opposes both; but we don't know how he manages to make the opposition convincing. After all, he could yield in a forthright way *to* relativism, to the denial of universal invariances, by way of a hermeneutics of radical historicity. He opts instead for what may be called *traditionalism*, the historically open-ended recovery, under the conditions of historical change and hermeneutic plasticity, of *effective* universal invariances that moving history itself confirms.[16] His formula in this regard is: the "timelessness [of the classical] is a mode of historical being."[17] What is invariant appears as a historical artifact; it is "timeless" because it recurs invariantly in all historical cultures.

The question that must nag here asks: How can we know that the invariances *of* the "classical" are not mere artifacts of a certain stubborn-ness that refuses to entertain any departure from would-be classical norms? Also, how is it possible for there to be such discernible universals if, whatever they are, they are cognitively accessible *only* through the sym-biotized formation of "I's and thou's"? The concept of the classical is "normative" for Gadamer.[18] He thinks of it in terms of ethics and practi-cal life, but he develops his notion primarily by considering classical style. The idea of classical style is paradigmatic, in the sense that "the classical is seen as the concept of a stylistic phase, of a climax that articulates the history of the genre in terms of before and after." Given that notion, Gadamer generalizes:

> As this kind of historical stylistic concept, the concept of the classical is capable of being extended to any "development" to which an immanent telos gives unity. And in fact all cultures have high periods, in which a particular civilization is marked by special achievements in all fields. Thus the general value concept of the classical becomes, via its particular historical fulfillment, again a general historical stylistic concept.[19]

This is not really satisfactory. For one thing, it does not address at all the doubts we were just collecting. How, for instance, are we supposed to know that there is "an imminent telos" to be discerned in a congeries of cultural processes—that gives the appropriate normative unity to the "before and after"? The formula is a charming one, but one that is peculiarly subject to conservative manipulation. In fact, the most recent articulation of just this notion appears—obviously tendentiously—in Alisdair MacIntyre's *After Virtue.*[20] MacIntyre there attempts to recover something like the "imminent telos" of a social practice (its inherent virtue, in fact), at the same time he admits historical variability, the untenability of Aristotelian essentialism, and the indefensibility of teleologism. MacIntyre's error lies, very simply put, in supposing that the specification of a viable social *practice*, under historical circumstances, invariably or regularly yields a discernible *virtue* that normatively orients the "before and after." Gadamer offers no evidence for supposing that the required normative idealization he has in mind—the recovery of the classical—would escape the sort of reasonable criticism that MacIntyre's thesis invites. In any event, it is difficult to see how he would proceed, without having explained the metaphysics of the hermeneutic self.

Secondly, the meaning of the classical, as Gadamer develops it, has a certain plausibility when it is linked to the hermeneutic circle and to conditions of understanding. That is certainly part of what Gadamer intends by his use of the notion. But it gains its plausibility just insofar as it remains formal, or regulative in a formal sense, that is, *without any substantively normative force at all.* This is just the point of his remarking, in context, that "the movement of understanding is constantly from the whole [of a text] to the part and back to the whole. . . . Full understanding can take place only within this objective and subjective whole."[21] Now, then, understanding (even self-understanding), the articulation of the hermeneutic circle in interpreting any text (including oneself and one another), takes place only within an actual tradition:

> The [hermeneutic] circle . . . is not formal in nature, it is neither subjective nor objective, but describes understanding as the interplay of the movement of tradition and the movement of the interpreter. The anticipation of meaning that governs our understanding of a text is not an act of subjectivity, but proceeds from the communality that binds us to the tradition. But this is contained in our relation to tradition, in the constant process of education. Tradition is not simply a precondition into which we come, but we produce it ourselves, inasmuch as we understand, participate in the evolution of tradition and hence further determine it ourselves.[22]

The trouble is that Gadamer's formula does not require or entail the classical, except (perhaps) in the purely formal sense that understanding or interpretation moves circularly between part and whole. *Nothing* he says shows: either that understanding anything entails universal substantive norms of practical life, or of intelligibility, or of rationality; or that *understanding* presupposes or entails a *shared tradition* in any sense that would yield discernibly inherent virtues or norms; or that whatever might plausibly be fitted to the practices of this or that tradition could plausibly be made to yield *normative invariances* that all cultural practices confirm. Certainly, one might fairly say to Gadamer: the Nietzschean tradition that you yourself respect—say, in the Heideggerian vein at least—has now managed to generate a whole family of doctrines that regard history as subject to discontinuities, incommensurabilities, constructive and artifactual variations, radical diversities, normative oppositions from age to age, uncertainties regarding internal coherence, prejudiced presumptions of uniformity and the like, with the result that we can no longer take at face value *any* affirmation of historicized invariances. *Traditionalism,* the supposition that viable practices central to any historical society, *yield,* through communal understanding, a sense of the "true" that organizes the "before and after" and "part and whole" of that culture, *and* that a similar idealization applied to every other society substantively converges on the classical, is simply false or unconfirmed or not even tested against the objections here adduced. (One might well say that traditionalism—of which, perhaps, Gadamer is the doyen—is simply a high form of modernism.) In any case, it cannot be ignored that traditionalism may well be conceptually bankrupt. There you have the harsh reality of applying our tally (1)–(3) to the two citations with which we began.

III

Our charge is, you will remember, that Gadamer does not resolve the puzzles of (1)–(3) and that, without doing so, he cannot make coherent sense either of the metaphysics of hermeneutic existence or the hermeneutics of understanding. We have just demonstrated that, on its face, Gadamer has not succeeded in reconciling historicality (or historicism) and universalism—which he requires for both the projects just mentioned. If it would not be misunderstood as proposing a disjunction, we might say that *wirkungsgeschichtliches Bewußtsein* is meant to provide, with regard to the analysis of hermeneutic existence, what *Horizontverschmelzung* provides for the hermeneutic understanding of texts. Of course, understanding is also the work of a creature itself *formed* and *transformed* by the preconditions of understanding and the conditions of its ongoing work; and, on the other hand, understanding affects the very nature or being of just those creatures who engage in relevant undertakings. But however that is done, Gadamer does not tell us how it could be counted on to recover the classical ideal.

Beyond that, he does not explain how it is that an "I and thou" *can* function as particular selves or effective agents subject to the forces of the "fusion of horizons" and the "effective history" of social existence. Presumably, I's and thou's are *subjects* capable of making cognitive and hermeneutic *claims*—hence, capable of making claims entitled to a measure of *objectivity*. (Objectivism, of the sort Gadamer wishes to oppose, is hardly implicated in merely admitting, under preformative conditions, some range of discursive, enunciative, or constative acts that address the thereupon discriminated "objects," appearances, *Erscheinungen,* or phenomena that, on the theory that *Gadamer* advances, are stable enough to support hermeneutic understanding.) Anything less would disallow Gadamer's entire project *ab initio.* But that shows that Gadamer has not met the requirements of (2). It is hardly enough, in providing for the distributed claims of cognitively apt subjects, merely to insist on the preformative, symbiotized order of "Being" (whether developed in Heidegger's way or in Gadamer's leaner way) *within which such* subjects gain and exercise their characteristic function. We must know what *they* are.

Finally, to solve the puzzles of (1) and (2) entails our being able to formulate an ontic adequation between the *nature* of the human self (hermeneutically construed) and the powers of understanding and interpretation predicable of it (according to a hermeneutic account). What, we may ask, is the ontic structure of the self in virtue of which: it first gathers the cognitive powers it possesses under the symbiotized conditions adduced; it exercises those powers as functions of a hermeneutically functioning community; it is itself altered by its own changing understanding of whatever it does understand; it retains its numerical identity under hermeneutically induced change; and it is capable of altering the shared tradition in which it lives by exercising its own hermeneutic competence? By "ontic adequation," here, we mean simply the conceptual congruity between what is assigned as the "nature" of a particular entity (substance or being) and what may be predicated of it consistent with its remaining the same particular.[23] Clearly, the answer to this question would go a great distance toward explaining how Gadamer supposes the historicism/universalism issue (1) can be satisfactorily resolved, and toward explaining how discursively functioning particular selves emerge and actually do function within the tradition in which they live (2). Without an answer, let it be said quite frankly, Gadamer cannot convincingly recover either the ideal of the classical or the validity of hermeneutic understanding. But to give up those claims would be to give up everything. So the questions must be met.

6

Caputo's Critique of Gadamer: Hermeneutics and the Metaphorics of the Person

Francis J. Ambrosio

The encounter of one person with another is the central arena of history.

—*Athol Fugard*

For one like myself who both feels at home with the philosophical hermeneutics of H.-G. Gadamer and also finds much to admire in John Caputo's recent book, *Radical Hermeneutics*,[1] it is initially quite disconcerting to find statements like the following two in the book's Introduction. Under the heading, "Restoring Life to Its Original Difficulty," Caputo first explains why Gadamer will play only a secondary role and have only a minor voice in the study that follows. He asserts that, "From the point of view of radical hermeneutics, Gadamer's 'philosophical hermeneutics' is a reactionary gesture, an attempt to block off the radicalization of hermeneutics and to turn it back to the fold of metaphysics" (*RH*, 5). He goes on to say that Gadamer pursues the more comforting doctrine of the fusion of horizons, the wedding of the epochs, the perpetuation of the life of the tradition which sees in Heidegger only a philosophy of appropriation, and which cuts off Heidegger's self-criticism in midstream.

But a second judgment, even more summary than the first, follows hard upon this one. Radical hermeneutics, which traces its authentic line of descent from Kierkegaard to Heidegger to Derrida, gives us the chance to clear up, Caputo argues, "some of the smoke metaphysics has been sending up for over two millennia, ever since Plato took it upon himself to answer all of Socrates' questions, whereas the hermeneutic point was to keep them open, to let them waver and tremble a bit . . . making things difficult" (*RH*, 6).

To make things difficult. Caputo begins with a notion of hermeneutics as uprooting, as rooting about to disturb the settled, stable, fixed quality of things. To him, radical hermeneutics is an attempt to stick with the original difficulty of life, to resist the tendency of life to stop moving, to put down roots and to get stuck. Its challenge is not to betray life by making it easy with a metaphysics of presence which "always makes a show of beginning with questions, but no sooner do things begin to waver a bit and look uncertain than the question is foreclosed. The disruptive force of the question is contained; the opening it created is closed; the wavering is stilled" (*RH*, 1). In all this, Caputo is, of course, following Heidegger, for whom the hermeneutics of facticity had assumed, in *Being and Time*, "the dimensions of a deconstruction of the metaphysics of presence and of a new raising of the question of Being; it had come to mean restoring the original difficulty in Being" (*RH*, 2).

The major strengths of Caputo's book, and they are very considerable strengths, are, first of all, the insightfulness with which he is able to argue, convincingly in my view, that Kierkegaard, Heidegger, and Derrida are bound together in this radical version of the hermeneutical enterprise, and secondly, the originality and philosophical imagination with which he develops the consequences of this project for the future development of hermeneutics—what he refers to as a postmetaphysical conception of rationality, an ethics of dissemination, and an openness to mystery. These strengths, and several others, merit our most serious attention, genuine respect and warm admiration. Yet, precisely for that reason, statements like the ones quoted above become a stumbling-block, a sort of scandal to one who is not ready to relegate Gadamer's version of hermeneutics to the philosophical backwaters of our age and who, more importantly, is not willing to acquiesce to the radical hermeneut's dogmatic anathema pronounced against the "metaphysics of presence" and the dismissal of all its proponents from Plato to Hegel, with the possible, ambiguous exception of Aristotle, as false friends of the flux.

To put the matter differently, it must be said that Caputo's book,

FRANCIS J. AMBROSIO

like the thought of Heidegger himself, is one-sided: that is both its strength and its limitation. To make itself understood, it must necessarily profile itself against those with whom it is engaged in dialogue. For from the hermeneutic perspective, such "one-sidedness" is the necessary character of *wirkungsgeschichtliches Bewußtsein,* and of the experience of understanding that always occurs in the midst of and in virtue of the *Vorurteile,* the prejudgments, that make any understanding at all possible from the beginning, and make any final or purely methodological understanding impossible to the end. But the decision not to change profiles so as to allow the other side to emerge is not a hermeneutical necessity. Rather it is a tactical choice which could be otherwise, with results to which this radical option is not open and therefore not competent to judge unilaterally. The first statement quoted above makes it clear not only that Caputo misunderstands what Gadamer has been saying about hermeneutics, but also that the reason he does so is because he is interested in what he takes Heidegger and Derrida to be doing, and he is not interested in what Gadamer is doing. Disinterest results in a lack of sympathetic attention, which in turn breeds misunderstanding, while genuine interest lights the way to understanding. The second thing that these quotations make clear is that the reason Caputo is not interested in Gadamer ultimately has to do with the fact that he is not interested in Plato either, and for that reason misunderstands Plato even more seriously than he misunderstands Gadamer.

I wish at this point to make it emphatically clear that I have no interest in either harping on what Caputo gets wrong about Gadamer or Plato, or beating him over the head with his own book on the grounds that his interest in Heidegger and Derrida in preference to Gadamer is illegitimate, that he should have written a different book than he did. The first is an important but prephilosophical concern; the second is spurious, indeed antiphilosophical. Rather, what does concern me in Caputo's criticism of Gadamer, precisely because I am interested in *both* Gadamer's philosophical hermeneutics and Caputo's radical hermeneutics, is what the difference between them really is and whether there is also something which is the same, a common root which justifies calling them both "hermeneutics"; indeed, whether there might not be something beyond both options which their difference invites us to consider. Is there really a relationship, in other words, between Caputo's radical hermeneutics and what he refers to as Gadamer's most liberal possible version of an essentially conservative metaphysics of presence and truth? To pursue this question, I want to examine the premise that Caputo misunderstands the dialogical character of Gadamer's philosophical hermeneutics and therefore misinterprets the nature and key elements of his relationship to each of his principal interlocutors, Hegel, Heidegger, Aristotle, and Plato, and therefore, that he misunderstands Gadamer's hermeneutics as a whole. Then I want to suggest that, recognizing the legitimacy and truthfulness of Gadamer's as well as Caputo's brand of hermeneutics, we have the opportunity to double-cross both strategies. The result will be the transformation of the metaphysics of presence into what I will call the metaphorics of the person.

I

Kierkegaard's doctrine of repetition and its opposition to the Greek notion of recollection serve to set the basic frame for Caputo's argument. Kierkegaard meant by repetition an existential version of *kinesis*, the Aristotelian counterpoint to Eleaticism, a movement which occurs in the existing individual (*RH*, 11). From Kierkegaard's version of the Christian perspective, the use by Plato of the recollection motif, coupled with the pervasive emphasis on body/soul dualism, constitute a theory of pseudomovement, of movement in reverse, where the goal lies behind and where growth means recovery. Being in the world of matter and time is a catastrophe for the soul, and the only good that can come of it is to get out of it as quickly as possible. Kierkegaard sees in this Eleatic/ Platonic escapism an image of the failure of Greek culture to comprehend the true nature of time, i.e., temporality, the openness of the future imaged as eternity or the world to come, which is the unique contribution of Christianity. The sole exception here is Aristotle, whose philosophy of motion as growth toward an immanent *telos* allowed him, in Kierkegaard's eyes, to confront change in the world and in the individual without flinching or apologizing, without resort to theories of imitation or stories of a fall to make excuses. Kierkegaardian repetition is an expression of Christian faith in the dynamics of existence, which ranges itself with Aristotle against the philosophers of pseudomovement, Plato and Hegel, indeed against all metaphysicians of presence, and anticipates those later friends of the flux, Heidegger and Derrida.

Caputo's battlelines are now clearly drawn, and for our purposes what is most apparent is the caricature opposition that has been set up between Plato and Aristotle. No doubt this is at least one plausible version of the standard received view of the relationship between these two thinkers, but as Gadamer has effectively shown, it is a hermeneutically naive one, based ultimately on a failure to understand the dialogical structure and dynamics of philosophical conversation.[2] So at the very beginning of Caputo's project we encounter the issue of how well he understands Plato, Gadamer, and indeed the very nature of the philosophical relationship between thinkers. We shall return to this issue in a enlarged context later on.

II

Caputo's critique of Gadamer arises as part of a triangulation technique which he employs to trace the lines of development that issue in what he is calling "radical hermeneutics." The central path in that development for him is the one taken by Heidegger. Two other paths swing off to the left and right. To the left, Derrida; to the right, Gadamer. So, for Caputo, Gadamer's version of hermeneutics is nothing more than a modification of Platonic and Hegelian metaphysics from a Heideggerian standpoint, but a standpoint which never develops the more radical side of Heidegger. In this sense, Caputo says that Gadamer's hermeneutics is "traditionalism and the philosophy of eternal truths pushed to its historical limits. He offers us the most liberal form of traditionalism possible. He introduces as much change as possible into the philosophy of unchanging truth, as much movement as possible into immobile verity" (*RH*, 111). In other words, according to Caputo, Gadamer retains the Hegelian Absolute with its characteristics of eternality and infinity, but denies to it real historical determinacy. "His [Gadamer's] is not a Hegelianism without the absolute, but Hegelianism where the absolute lacks absolute expression" (*RH*, 111). But what is this unchanging "truth" with which philosophical hermeneutics is concerned? Is it in some genuine sense unchanging and infinite, and if so, must not the Heideggerian modification of which Caputo speaks indeed be an external and ultimately incoherent one? How can one accommodate *both* Hegel and Heidegger on the question of truth?

A full response on Gadamer's behalf would require expanding the scope of our discussion to take into account, among other factors, the status of *Wahrheit und Methode* as a formalized, reflective account of Gadamer's hermeneutical practice such that what he says there cannot be reliably understood apart from the context of what he does in the many encounters he has had with the text of Hegel, for example; the development in his interpretive relationship to Hegel, which has changed over the years from profiling himself *against* Hegel in *Wahrheit und Methode* to identifying himself *with* Hegel, for example on the relation of truth and freedom in the much later essay "The Heritage of Hegel";[3] and finally the way in which the authentic participation of Hegel in Gadamer's development of philosophical hermeneutics must be understood in terms of its essentially dialogical, as opposed to methodological, character. All this would be ingredient to an adequate response to Caputo's criticism, but for the moment we must focus on the sense in which it could be said that Gadamer's conception of truth does include the characteristics of an unchanging and infinite element. If we take as a working characterization of the notion of truth operative in Gadamer's hermeneutics that truth means the emergence into language of the human relationship to the world as a virtual whole of meaning, then we are in a position to see just what Gadamer shares with Hegel and where he fundamentally departs from him. Gadamer, it seems to me, shares with Hegel both the conviction that "the true is the whole," and a commitment to the Greek view of the speculative structure of thought which unfolds itself dialectically according to the inner rule or logic of its subject matter. The difference between Hegel and Gadamer, a difference which it seems to me that Caputo fails to see, is that Gadamer has rethought the wholeness of truth and the speculative, dialectical, and logical elements of thought from out of *die Mitte der Sprache*, and in so doing has radically transformed those shared commitments, not merely modified them in an external fashion. First of all, the wholeness of truth for Gadamer is a virtual one, the wholeness that language possesses, a unity of meaning which goes on without limit and reaches out to include whatever comes to be real, but never in such a way that it reaches full determinacy or the absolute mastery of systematic comprehension. "Speaking," Gadamer says, "remains tied to language as a whole, the hermeneutic virtuality of discourse which surpasses at any moment that which has been said."[4] Here the metaphysical relation of finite to infinite is transformed into the hermeneutic relation of the said to the unsaid, and both are bound together in a unity of meaning which is a genuine though virtual whole.

Secondly, the "unchanging truths" to which Caputo refers recalls Hegel's realm of "*das Logische*" as the fulfillment of the speculative and dialectical movement of the subject matter of thought toward its final systematic determination in the concrete universality of the Concept. But for Gadamer, logical priority resides with the question, whose directed openness is determinative of understanding, rather than with knowledge, which depends on the scientific achievement of determination. If there is a sense in which Gadamer's hermeneutics might accurately be said to concern itself with the transmission of unchanging truths, then this must refer to those questions which are universal and most fundamental for all of us, and which, as such, are the essence of what is handed over in tradition. For Gadamer, these shared questions regarding the meaning of human existence are the unchanging truths with which hermeneutics is concerned and which rule all understanding by determining the direction of any interpretation that makes a truth-claim, because it has first been claimed by the prior, more original and fundamental truth at work in the question which initiates and centers any hermeneutical encounter. Gadamer chooses to articulate the event-structure of truth, which is part of his legacy from Heidegger, in Hegelian terms, while rethinking those terms from "the center of language," because he hears in Hegel's metaphysical language resonances of Greek thinking which are lost on Heidegger, who is intent on stepping back behind the metaphysics of presence. In this sense, Caputo is correct: Gadamer is attempting to conserve something of the truth of metaphysics, which does indeed have its origin in Plato, and he is trying to do this mindful of Heidegger's radical redirection of the questions that gave rise to that tradition. Whether and how such a fusion of horizons between Heidegger and the Greeks, with Hegel as intermediary, is possible is the challenge that Caputo's critique poses. Our next step is to assess Caputo's claim that Gadamer is willing to attend to only one side of Heidegger's project, and presents us with "a kind of Heideggerianism without the scandal of the *Ereignis* and the play of the epochs" (*RH*, 115).

III

An indication of the flavor of this "radical" side of Heidegger, for which Gadamer supposedly has no taste, can be gotten from a characterization such as the following one given by Caputo, which, allowing for a certain amount of caricature, is nonetheless basically accurate; Heidegger "thinks all the trouble started with Plato, culminated in Hegel, and is about to explode in our faces in the *Gestell*. He does not believe in ageless truths but in the historicity of the truth-event, of *a-letheia*, of its endless flux and transiency" (*RH*, 115). Caputo argues that in the refining fire of Derrida's critique, Heidegger's thought can be demythologized and liberated from what Caputo insightfully designates as the "eschatology of truth," and thus become fully radicalized in the direction in which it is already headed in the thinking of *das Ereignis*. In Caputo's hands this becomes an immensely fruitful thesis for thinking about the relationship of Derrida and Heidegger and the radical side of hermeneutics, but in its one-sided dismissal of Gadamer, it impoverishes its own potential by reducing itself to a profile, and an exaggerated, caricatured one at that. Gadamer had himself suggested the same sort of demythologizing of the eschatological Heidegger at least twenty-five years ago when he said,

> I do not wish to deny that I for my part have emphasized within the universal matrix of the elements of understanding its direction toward the appropriation of what is past and has been handed down. Heidegger, too, like many of my critics, may here feel the absence of an ultimate radicality in drawing out consequences. What does the end of metaphysics as a science mean? What is the significance of it ending in science? If science climaxes in a total technocracy and brings on with it the "cosmic night" of the forgetfulness of being, the nihilism foretold by Nietzsche, is one permitted to look back toward the last rays of dusk as the sun sets in the evening sky instead of turning to watch out for the first shimmer of its return? (*WM*, xxv; *TM*, xxxvii; my translation)

The difference between Gadamer and Heidegger is not the difference between night and day; there is too much genuinely shared between them for that, first and foremost the question of the way in which truth happens as an event in language. Furthermore, we should be suspicious of Caputo's charge that Gadamer is unwilling to follow Heidegger in this direction as far as "the scandal of the *Ereignis*." Gadamer has said that "it seems possible to me to bring to expression within hermeneutical consciousness itself Heidegger's statements concerning "Being" and the line of inquiry he developed out of the experience of the *Kehre*. I have carried out this attempt in [*Wahrheit und Methode*]."[5] We know that for Heidegger the experience of the *Kehre* led to the thinking of *Ereignis*. Where did it lead for Gadamer? Caputo would argue back into metaphysics. I have attempted in another context[6] to present an argument to the contrary, that it lead him to situate the dynamics of hermeneutical consciousness within an ontology of language, i.e., in *die Mitte der Sprache*, and that it is *die Virtualität des Sprechens*, the virtuality of living language, that marks Gadamer's arrival at the "same" destination for which Heidegger had set out, namely the structure of the event of truth as unconcealment occurring in the midst of prevailing concealment. For Gadamer, virtuality means the reverberation of whatever is said out without end into the penumbra of the unsaid, while remaining effectively bound together with it in the unity of a virtual whole of meaning that makes itself understood and lays claim to us as the truth-value of the questions that encounter us over and over again.

But to say, contra Caputo, that Gadamer and Heidegger arrive at the "same" destination, the "same" view of truth is itself one-sided. That one-sidedness is inevitable, because it has to do with the very nature of truth-as-event, as *a-letheia/Ereignis* or *Virtualität*, or rather, has to do with truth in its relation to freedom. The relationship of Gadamer to Heidegger cannot be fully understood in terms of the question of truth alone, but only in terms of the relation of truth to freedom. We hear the powerful (virtual) presencing of the question of freedom in Gadamer's words addressed to Heidegger, "is one then permitted to look back . . . instead of turning to watch out?" And we hear it even more clearly in the words that follow these,

> It seems to me, however, that the one-sidedness of hermeneutical universalism possesses the truth of a corrective. . . . What man needs is not only the unswerving posing of ultimate questions, but just as much the sense of what is doable, what is possible, what is appropriate here and now. . . . Hermeneutic consciousness . . . seeks to counterpose to the will of man, which more than ever is mounting in an utopian or eschatological consciousness a critique of what has gone before, something of the truth of remembrance: what still yet and ever again is real. (*WM*, xxv-xxvi; *TM*, xxxviii; my translation)

Here I think we come closer to seeing how Gadamer can genuinely listen to both Hegel *and* Heidegger concerning the question of truth, how he can recognize the difference between them, as well as the differences between himself and both of them, and still say something about truth which is the "same" as both of them say: *the question of truth and the question of freedom belong together from the beginning and to the end.* Hegel responds to the question of truth in terms of "concrete universality," Heidegger in terms of *a-letheia/Ereignis*, and Gadamer in terms of the "virtuality of living language." This sameness-amid-difference is as much a matter of freedom as it is of truth, and the willing capacity to hear it and allow it to make its claim in the universal play of conversation that in the tradition is what distinguishes Gadamer from both Heidegger and Hegel without deafening him to either.

IV

Of course it would still be one-sided to understand Gadamer's hermeneutics even in terms of his relation to both Heidegger and Hegel. There are still Aristotle and Plato to be heard. But Caputo goes too far in suggesting that the most important contribution that Gadamer makes is his treatment of the Aristotelian notion of *phronesis,* pointing out that it was Heidegger who first read Aristotle's theory of practical knowledge in terms of a hermeneutics of facticity. He argues that "Heidegger's interpretation of Aristotle thus goes to the heart of Gadamer's hermeneutics, providing it with its pivotal conception of 'application'" (*RH,* 110). Here the issue we first encountered in terms of the confrontation between Kierkegaardian repetition and Platonic recollection is rejoined. However pivotal the notion of *Anwendung* may be, it is not the heart of Gadamer's hermeneutics. Moreover, to suggest that it is his most important contribution indicates that what may well have been a legitimate decision in freedom on Caputo's part to direct his questioning away from the "truth of remembrance" and toward what is to come has here degenerated into misunderstanding born of inattention. It is certainly true that Aristotle's doctrine of *phronesis* provides Gadamer with a way of *explaining* how philosophical conversation is ruled by an open-ended principle of determination capable of reconciling the universality of truth as a virtual whole of meaning (Hegel) with the finite historical determinacy of its happening as an event of understanding in language (Heidegger). Nevertheless, while Aristotle is the source of the conceptual explanation, it is the Platonic Socrates who originally embodies its truth for Gadamer. Caputo comments blandly that Gadamer offers an "illuminating" account of the Platonic conception of the "dynamics of dialogue, of the expanding and essentially revisable nature of knowledge which grows only by exposure to the other" (*RH,* 109). But who could fail to recognize a portrait of Socrates in Aristotle's description of the man of practical wisdom, or in Gadamer's characterization of the "experienced" person who knows the wisdom of the Aeschylean *pathein mathein* and in whom the "truth-value" of experience is realized? The use Gadamer makes of the Aristotelian notion of *phronesis* is to conceptualize and explain the discipline of dialogue practiced by Socrates, the practice of philosophical conversation which is the flesh and blood reality of what it means to say that knowledge "grows only in exposure to the other."

This corrective to Caputo's overemphasis of Aristotle and underemphasis of Plato is much more in keeping with the view of the hermeneutic relationship between these two thinkers developed by Gadamer in *The Idea of the Good in Platonic-Aristotelian Philosophy,* a development which in my opinion could much better support the weight of a claim to be Gadamer's most important contribution than could the doctrine of application. What Gadamer has done in this study is to apply to the issue of the relationship of Plato and Aristotle what I take to be the governing principle of philosophical hermeneutics, namely, the logic of question and answer. In so doing he has given us a paradigm for how to think about any relationship between philosophers and, at the same time, the key to understanding how he is able to listen effectively not just to both Heidegger and Hegel, but to Aristotle and Plato as well. The logic of question and answer is the rule that governs philosophical dialogue, disciplining its movement into the open space of its freedom and standing warrant for its truth claims. *Philosophy is nothing other than disciplined dialogue about the few questions that we all share and which are most important to us all simply as persons.* The questions that we call philosophical have logical priority over every human response to them, indeed over even the free work of forming the question in one way rather than in another, thereby setting the direction for whatever response might come. In this sense, the logical priority of the question means that there is both more truth and more freedom in the question than in any possible response to it. Here too we can see the original meaning of virtuality, the "evermore" within which language as dialogue is always already underway.

Applying all this to the philosophical relationship of Plato and Aristotle means recognizing that the central point of Gadamer's essay is that what these two thinkers share takes virtually absolute precedence over the several important ways in which they differ. What they share most fundamentally is the question of the Good—that for the sake of which all things are what they are and do what they do. The question of the Good is the question of meaning, of the light that lets all things be for a while and lets them not be, the question of origin and destiny. The Aristotle of whom Kierkegaard, Heidegger, and Caputo approve is the Aristotle whose *response* to the question of the Good is cast in terms of the metaphysics of *physis* and *kinesis*, in the biological metaphors of organic growth, and in the cautious style of conceptual analysis which Gadamer identifies as being characteristic of him. But all this is how he differs from Plato, the Plato whose *response* to the question of the Good is cast in terms of the metaphysics of the soul and the theory of the *eide*, with its attendant doctrines of *methexis* and *anamnesis*, in the mathematical metaphors of the one and the indeterminate two, and in the mythic and poetic style to which Gadamer is so well attuned. This is the Plato of whom Kierkegaard, Heidegger, and Caputo so heartily and unqualifiedly disapprove.

But this is not Gadamer's Plato, the Plato with whom Aristotle was in harmony before and far beyond any disagreement, the dialogical and ironic Plato from whose name that of Socrates can never be separated, the Plato from whom Gadamer came to understand the logic of question and answer as the ruling principle of all dialogue and, as such, *die Mitte der Sprache*, the effective centering in language of all understanding as the ongoing event of tradition. Gadamer is able to listen effectively to Heidegger, Hegel, Aristotle, and the metaphysical Plato because, like Plato, he has learned the discipline of dialogue from its master, the one who is able to create another like himself and pass on the excellence that he himself possesses, Socrates.

As Gadamer has demonstrated so convincingly, for example in "The Proofs for Immortality in Plato's *Phaedo*,"[7] no doctrine, no argument, no theory or myth in Plato's dialogues can be understood or the effective power of its truth-claim experienced by hermeneutical consciousness, unless it is interpreted through the dramatic and ironic dynamics of Socratic dialogue. It may not be too much to say that all misinterpretation of Plato begins with the forgetting of this principle. Indeed, remembering what was said earlier about Gadamer's essay *The Idea of the Good* as a paradigm for thinking about the relationship between any philosophers, we might generalize this to say that all misinterpretation in philosophy occurs when we engage in the static comparison of positions, forgetting the necessity to restore them to the living dialogue from which they arose and to hear them as responses to shared questions so that they may be understood in terms of the dynamics of sameness-amid-difference that is the necessary structure of language as conversation and therefore of thinking. Socrates embodies for Platonic thought the dramatic and ironic truth of being-in-question. For Plato Socrates is philosophy, because philosophy is that way of living centered in the asking of the universal and fundamental questions that bond together the free citizens of a free community. Philosophy is the business of responding to Socrates's questions as Plato attempted to do in the dialogues. Here we see where Caputo goes wrong in the citation with which we began: Plato did not attempt to answer Socrates's questions in the sense of put an end to them, but rather he took responsibility for them by making them his own and responding to them, for this is the only way to go on questioning.

Now I have stressed the notion that I take the logic of question and answer to be the key to Gadamer's hermeneutics and that it reflects what Gadamer learned from Plato and Plato from Socrates, namely the discipline of dialogue, because that is the sense in which I would wish to be understood when I say that Gadamer's hermeneutics is essentially Platonic in character. It has at its center a living person whose soul is to be in question and whose care it is to bring that questioning home. In this sense Plato is the origin of the tradition, if not its beginning, and its destiny, if not its end. It is in this sense that philosophical thought is *both* recollection of what has already fulfilled itself and also repetition which must make itself new. Each must do for him or herself what Plato did for himself—respond to the questions which live in us, which we are, respond to Socrates's questions. Whether by telling stories of Socrates or not hardly matters. That belongs to the difference in truth and is free. The questioning is the same.

V

I said earlier that I thought Caputo's book to be an excellent one, however one-sided his interpretation of Gadamer may be. My concern here has been to correct some of that one-sidedness. But I also said that task is basically a technical and prephilosophical one; not unimportant but also not a matter of truth. The truth is to be looked for in what remains unsaid between Gadamer and Caputo, who is speaking for Kierkegaard, Heidegger and Derrida, as well as quite ably for himself. When all is said and done his critique of Gadamer is really quite tangential to his main project, the radicalizing of both Heidegger and Derrida by exposing each to the other's difference. The result is what Caputo refers to as a postmetaphysical theory of rationality, an ethics of dissemination, and an openness to mystery. This is of great value, and I wish to conclude this paper with a gesture of respect for Caputo's achievement by suggesting a way in which his strategy of "double-crossing" Heidegger and Derrida could be repeated. I want to suggest what might happen if we took the time and attention to expose Gadamer to Caputo's better side, and Caputo to the ungarbled Gadamer. The result as I envision it would no longer be hermeneutics properly speaking, radical or philosophical, but might better be referred to as the "metaphorics of the person." Let me try to explain briefly what I mean by this by saying something about each of the main terms. In doing so, I will be taking a leading idea of Gadamer's, crossing it with Caputo's main concern to restore the difficulty to life without making life impossible, and then arguing that in order to achieve his goal, Caputo will have to accept being double-crossed by Gadamer.

First, metaphor. I do not mean the everyday sense of metaphor, as in "*just* a metaphor," a sort of pleasant or convenient half truth/half lie. I mean rather something very much like Gadamer's notion of *Virtualität*, the silent *power* (*virtus*) of language to create relation. More fully said, I would mean metaphor as the power of language to reach out in response to the silence of mystery and draw it into the near familiarity of meaning. Metaphor conceived in this way is the universal structure of truth occurring as an event of relation, of belonging-together, sameness-amid-difference. The Greeks thought it as the paradox of the one and the many, the medievals as the generalized analogy of Being, the moderns as the identity of the subject, Heidegger as *a-letheia/Ereignis*. Metaphor is the bond of truth that makes it one. But here is where Caputo uses Derrida's stylus to cross out truth and to point out what hides behind it—power, and more specifically, the kind of power play in language that tries to establish the rule (logic) of a master name to which all others must reduce themselves. It is naive to think that language always plays by the rules, even its own, and that it plays the sort of game in which time will be called when the ball goes out of bounds. Deconstruction is the sort of reading that allows signifiers to escape the gravitational field of *die Mitte der Sprache* and to spin out of bounds where the play really is free. Of course, Gadamer knows about play and freedom too, but as he himself has said, he is interested in the play of language as dialogue according to the logic of question and answer and in the kind of freedom that recognizes itself as being at home. To this Caputo responds, with Derrida, by writing freedom as *différance* and play as the deconstruction of truth-logics down to their power-base. So while metaphor may be, from one point of view, the bond of truth that makes it one, viewed from the other side, it is the line that freedom draws as it crosses out of bounds, thereby allowing what is the same to differ. So this is what, in the end, I would mean by metaphor: the power of language to give meaning to human existence as the relation of truth and freedom. But the question remains, how does this relation happen?

Now for the double cross. This difference which crosses out the truth of dialogue and remembrance does, I believe, succeed in de-centering Gadamer's philosophical hermeneutics and properly locating it on one side of the cut that freedom makes. *Die Mitte der Sprache,* too, sustains a fissure. But if this powerful irruption of freedom into meaning is allowed to set things trembling for a while, its shock-wave eventually passes and sometimes something, or rather someone, remains who has absorbed the shock and been liberated and empowered by it. Structures rise and fall; they are by their nature more or less rigid. But people can move and change; people are free to respond to the power that comes over them.

I began with a quotation from Athol Fugard, the white, South African playwright. "The encounter of one individual person with another is the central arena of history." Persons in dialogue together mark out the ground they will share so that they can construct truths that will be effective enough to allow them to live together in the face of the deeper truths they always already share, the questions of life and death, the questions of meaning. *Die Mitte der Sprache* is a construct, an arena, the center-stage of meaning. Perhaps we have now sustained enough of the shock of the deconstruction of the metaphysics of presence to be able to use the word "person" again without fear of being understood to mean "subject." If so, we can say that the virtuality of living language resides *in* the individual persons who play metaphorically upon that stage. The virtual power of language comes into play through the human person, and, apart from the person, truth and freedom have no meaning whatever. The ongoing history of meaning as tradition is the giving over of the truth of the person in free response to the question that each one is.

It is only a small step from here to recognize that this is what it means to say that Gadamer's hermeneutics is essentially Platonic. Socrates is the root-metaphor; he is the *Virtualität des Sprechens* through whom the power of freedom cuts and makes itself effective as the truth-claim which his presence exerts. Truth and freedom come into presence together in the integrity of this person. In the *Phaedo*, when the arguments for immortality are themselves in danger of dying, it is the touch of Socrates's hand on Phaedo's curls and the familiar sound of his voice that keeps them in question. When Diotima's teaching on Beauty and love are put to the test, it is the power of Socrates's own beauty, evident in the attraction/repulsion it begets in Alcibiades, which stands warrant for the theory's truth. And it is Socrates who, at the close of the *Symposium*, explains to Agathon and Aristophanes that the same person can write tragedy and comedy, as he drinks them both under the table. Truth and freedom so clearly come into presence and belong together in this person that they shine forth with the unique beauty of integrity.

Such integrity always takes the shape of a double cross. The lines of power we call truth and freedom extend out, as language, beyond the person into the silence of mystery, but they center in the person whose integrity is always dramatic and ironic, whose identity is always ambiguous and in question. The task of hermeneutics, traditional or radical, has been to interpret what was really going on in the metaphysics of presence. Hermeneutics can now, perhaps, retrieve itself in the metaphorics of the person.

7

Hermeneutics of the Possible: On Finitude and Truth in Philosophical Hermeneutics

James Risser

ruth and Method announces the project of a *philosophical* hermeneutics, presenting the task of understanding the human sciences in relation to the more primordial experience of understanding that occurs beyond a methodological self-consciousness. From the outset, Gadamer acknowledges that this project depends on taking its starting point from the work of Heidegger. Accordingly, philosophical hermeneutics begins with the recognition that understanding cannot escape its finitude and historicity. At the same time, philosophical hermeneutics can distinguish its project from the hermeneutic ontology of *Being and Time* by inverting the procedural orientation: where Heidegger examines the problems of hermeneutics and historicity of understanding for the purposes of ontology, Gadamer wants to know how hermeneutics, once freed from the ontological obstructions of methodologism, can do justice to historicity of understanding.

But in making use of Heidegger in the way that he does for his project Gadamer has left himself open to a number of criticisms. On the one hand, there is the criticism of the traditionalist (understood in its Rortyan sense as the one who sees philosophy as the discipline that must secure truth and knowledge). It is the criticism that when the historicity of understanding is applied to the interpretation of texts, the question of truth vanishes. To be more precise, the traditionalist claims that without the measure of adequation we are no longer in a position to say of any particular interpretation of a text that it is false. If one counters this claim by saying that in philosophical hermeneutics truth is to be understood differently—that truth has the character of an event, of an occurrence of coming to light, rather than of correctness—this proves to be insufficient for the traditionalist who would argue that this is nothing more than a clever disguise for relativism. One finds this criticism, but I do not wish to limit it to this, in Hirsch.[1] On the other hand, there is the criticism of the so-called "left Heideggerian" who accuses Gadamer of drawing from Heidegger all the conservative elements such that, when coupled with its implicit Hegelianism, philosophical hermeneutics is nothing but a "closet essentialism."[2] This latter criticism is, of course, the more recent, and so it needs to be spelled out in more detail.

In a recent paper that extends the work of *Radical Hermeneutics*,[3] John Caputo claims that, in appearance, the notion of finitude sets Gadamer off from Hegel and situates philosophical hermeneutics within the line of criticism that Kierkegaard makes of Hegel; but, in fact, finitude functions in a profoundly Hegelian and metaphysical manner, and thus Gadamer's hermeneutics is to be understood within a metaphysics of infinity of the most classical sort. Finitude in philosophical hermeneutics is so fundamentally bound to its other, it is nothing but a cover for a "closet theory of essence, ideality, and infinity."

Specifically, Caputo argues that what Gadamer has gotten right about the notion of finitude is seen in the critique of Dilthey. The search for historical objectivity in Dilthey's project is essentially an effort at infinite understanding, an effort of an understanding that thinks it can cure itself, by means of methodological control, of its own situatedness in history. Gadamer wants to hold Dilthey to his own *Lebensphilosophie*, to the fact that the subject cannot disengage itself from the conditions of life so as to produce the distantiation required for objective historical reflection. Finitude, Gadamer recognizes, cannot be neutralized insofar as it is an ontological structure of Dasein. Here, according to Caputo, we find Gadamer's Heideggerian side, for it was Heidegger who first disclosed the ontological foundation of historical science: we do history (*Historie*) because we are in our very being historical (*geschichtlich*). But in this recognition of the limit of (historical) reflection, of the irreducibility of Being to thought, Gadamer's own thought gives way to a profoundly Hegelian posture: that which is understood, whether it be the historical event or the written text, is limited always in relation to the infinity present within the event or text. According to Caputo, the "inexhaustible depth" that Gadamer constantly refers to in the description of the hermeneutic event is a kind of infinite spirit that gradually keeps unfolding over the course of time. To take but one example from *Truth and Method* that would support Caputo's claim: in describing the mediation that takes place in linguistic tradition Gadamer writes, "all human speaking is finite in such a way that there is laid up within it an infinity of meaning to be explicated and laid out" (*WM*, 434; *TM*, 458). The hermeneutic event is not really the isolable (finite) historical entity but a whole history, "a continuity of movement made up of both the original and the history of its effects which follow after it like a comet's tail." The interpreter, situated within a history of wholeness, remains too finite to contain the fullness that sweeps over him or her.

It is interesting to note that the two criticisms (the one about truth, the other about infinity) come from the opposite ends of the spectrum—one accusing Gadamer of a failure to be essentialistic, the other accusing him of remaining essentialistic. However, despite this difference, the two criticisms are in fact united by their common misunderstanding of the ontological commitments of philosophical hermeneutics. Both critiques occur under the sway of a metaphysics of actuality, either by insisting that the question of truth is only possible within a metaphysics of actuality or by falsely accusing philosophical hermeneutics of holding to a metaphysics of actuality (Gadamer's limited Hegelianism). Both critiques fail to see that it is an ontology of possible being, which is ultimately traced back to Aristotle, that constitutes hermeneutic experience and mutatis mutandis frames the questions of truth and finitude.

Most provisionally, we can identify the general character of this ontology of possible being through the essential element in the *Existenzphilosophie* that, in its indebtedness to Heidegger's ontology of understanding, is incorporated into philosophical hermeneutics. Quite simply, that element pertains to the unique relation that holds between possibility and actuality in human existence. Here one must look to Kierkegaard (who in turn looks to Aristotle) as well as Hegel when one traces the lineage of a philosophical hermeneutics. In looking to Kierkegaard, what is decisive for our purposes is precisely what was decisive for Kierkegaard's attack on Hegelianism, namely, the movement intrinsic to existence that, according to Kierkegaard, was bastardized by the system. For Kierkegaard, the movement, *kinesis*, of existence disrupts the system precisely because for it possibility is higher than actuality. For philosophical hermeneutics the issue is likewise the movement, *kinesis*, of existence, albeit not of existence as such (for it is never a question of existentialism for philosophical hermeneutics), but of existence in language. As the medium of the event of understanding, language, for Gadamer, is always living language. Accordingly, the ontology of philosophical hermeneutics is an ontology of living being; and this is, with respect to the essential element in *Existenzphilosophie*, at once an ontology of possible being.

In order to establish the ontology of the possible at work in philosophical hermeneutics that, in turn, will allow us to address the questions of finitude and truth, we need to see, first of all, how the priority of possibility is itself established in an ontology of living being.

The Ontology of Living Being as an Ontology of the Possible

Let us recall that Kierkegaard's critique of Hegel was motivated by the fact that Hegel could not adequately incorporate an ontology of living being into his onto-logico system. From Kierkegaard's perspective the question of an ontology of living being was simply the question of movement, *kinesis*, properly understood, that is, of the transition from possibility to actuality in individual existence. Ironically, Hegel, of course, thought that the failure of previous philosophy, to which his own philosophy stands as a corrective, was that it did not adequately deal with movement. Seen from Hegel's perspective: whereas understanding (*Verstand*) separates possibility and actuality leaving the transition between the two concepts unexplained, reason (*Vernunft*) suffers no such incompleteness. The logic of dialectical reason can claim that actuality is possible, for were it not so it could not be actual, and conversely, the possible is actual in the sense that real possibility, in contrast to formal possibility, is the totality of conditions which is presupposed by a certain actuality. Necessity, as the third movement of the triadic structure, is the truth into which possibility and actuality withdraw. By virtue of the identity-within-difference of dialectical logic Hegel maintains that this necessity is freedom.[4]

Against this production of dialectical necessity, Kierkegaard insists that the transition occurring in human existence is in no way comparable to the transition occurring in dialectical development.[5] The speculative mediation of opposites does not apply to concrete existence, which of its nature gives priority to possibility (*Möglichkeit*). Hegelian movement actually renders becoming, as the transition from possibility to actuality, illusory by ignoring the temporality of existential becoming. The becoming of human existence is not effected by means of a necessary transition precisely because necessity characterizes purely atemporal relations of logical ideas.[6] Thus, in contrast to the Hegelian view, Kierkegaard argues that the becoming of human existence is marked by a fundamental creative repetition whereby existence which has been now becomes. This means that in repetition we return to *possibilities* that have already been there in existence: past possibilities become future possibilities in each moment of decision. All decisive changes in existence, the acts by which we become who we are, are brought about by the projection of imaginative possibilities which are actualized in the concrete. By virtue of the fact that existence is essentially a "qualitative dialectic," a self-projection of the individual toward the openness of the future in the movement from possibility to actuality in temporality, possibility, in this sense, is higher than actuality. The future is the condition for possibility for the freedom of possibility. Thus Kierkegaard would have us reorder the relation between necessity and possibility: the existing self is that which it has been (necessity) and becomes that which it is not yet (possibility qualified by futurity). This is precisely what freedom is for Kierkegaard: the *kinesis* through which the existing self realizes itself.

The question that can be posed to Kierkegaard, however, is whether he completely succeeds in separating his ontology of living being, where possibility has priority, from an essentialist metaphysics in which actuality stands higher than possibility. That is to say, despite his critique of Hegel's system, it may be the case that Kierkegaard remains too close to the Hegelianism he wants to reject. One could very well argue that dialectical thought is certainly compatible with Kierkegaard's emphasis on possibility, insofar as the real is initially conceived as contingency and the real contains within itself the negation of its possibility. If the question of this difference is simply a question of whether there is a law that determines the self-development, we are simply looking at two sides of the same coin.

We can account for this closeness by the fact that both Kierkegaard and Hegel are drawing from the same source for their philosophy of movement, viz., Aristotle. What Kierkegaard is specifically drawn to in Aristotle is the transition from possibility (*dynamis*) to actuality (*energeia*) that characterizes qualitative change, since this could be accommodated to historical freedom, to the capacity to act in accordance with a subjectively posited telos.[7] Hegel, on the other hand, seemingly incorporates Aristotle's analysis of movement into his system as a general law of Being, especially with respect to its teleological component. Moreover, and perhaps most decisively, he incorporates Aristotle's analysis into his system without any attempt to rethink that analysis.

Let us briefly recall that traditional reading of Aristotle. According to Aristotle, possibility is recognized as a fundamental mode of *ousia;* but in the interplay with actuality that expresses the inner movement of an essential being, there is always a priority of actuality. For Aristotle, actuality is prior to possibility logically, temporally, and with regard to *ousia.*[8] Moreover, this "ousiology" is inseparable from teleology: the movement to actuality is that for the sake of which a thing becomes, which of itself is a purposive structure. Every *dynamis* exists only for the sake of the telos which is the *energeia* of a being: "We do not see in order that we may have sight, but we have sight that we may see." In this teleological movement, the priority of actuality demands that the end be connected with its beginning; the movement, in other words, exhibits a circular structure: in the movement toward actualization "what is prefigured comes forth and out into the open in a circular form as the remaining-within-itself of the telos, as the teleological self-actualization in which the *ousia* returns to its beginning, the *arche.*"[9] When *energeia* is translated into Latin as *actus* or *actualitas,* Being is determined in such a way that the being of a being is only insofar as it is actual. Potentiality must be understood in terms of actuality. Hegel, standing at the end of the tradition, does nothing to overturn this formulation; the modality of possibility is oriented toward a kind of essence which appears.

Where we find that decisive rethinking of the analysis of movement is, of course, in Heidegger. The project of fundamental ontology defines itself in opposition to the metaphysics of essence that constitutes that history which stretches from Aristotle to Hegel. In particular, in the analytic of Dasein, Heidegger interprets the character of Dasein's transcendence ("the essence of Dasein lies in its to-be") in terms of possibility. Dasein is disclosed not as an actualization of its own potential but as primarily possibility, an ability to be. This existential possibility is to be distinguished from empty logical possibility (noncontradictoriness) as well as from the mere contingency of something *Vorhandenheit* (what is not yet actual and what is not at any time necessary). When Heidegger asserts that "higher than actuality stands possibility," possibility is understood as a mode which simply cannot come to actualization. Dasein is such that it is always "ahead of itself" within possibilities.

The most succinct explanation of this notion is found in *The Basic Problems of Phenomenology,* the text of a lecture course from the summer of 1927. In response to the question about how understanding belongs to Dasein's existence, Heidegger asserts that to exist is essentially to understand. This equivalence occurs because, as existing, Dasein is occupied with its own *ability to be,* with projecting itself upon possibility, and this is the meaning of the existential concept of understanding. Heidegger explains:

> A can-be, a possibility as possibility, is there only in projection, in project-
> ing oneself upon that can-be. If in contrast I merely reflect on some
> empty possibility into which I could enter, and, as it were, just gab
> [*beschwätze*] about it, then this possibility is not there, precisely as possibil-
> ity; instead for me it is, as we might say, actual. The character of possibili-
> ty becomes manifest and is manifest only in projection, so long as the
> possibility is held fast in the projection.[10]

Possibility is what it is only when it is left standing before us as impend-
ing, and not such that it becomes actualized in the traditional sense.
What Heidegger says here sounds very much like Kierkegaard: the projection upon possibility is the way in which I am the possibility and is the
way in which Dasein exists freely. Then, to underscore the fact that
understanding, in this context, is not a mode of cognition, Heidegger
asserts:

> Understanding as the Dasein's self-projection is the Dasein's fundamen-
> tal mode of happening [*Geschehen*]. As we may also say, it is the authentic
> meaning of action. It is by understanding that the Dasein's happening is
> characterized: its historicity [*Geschichtlichkeit*].[11]

The occurrence of Dasein *is* understanding which is at the same time,
with proper qualification, historicity. Clearly, the question concerning
the ontological status of philosophical hermeneutics must be placed in
this context.

What remains to be seen here is precisely how the attempt to
rethink the question of Being beyond the traditional concepts of substance and essence is rooted in a creative reading of Aristotle's *kinesis*.[12]
According to Heidegger, Aristotle always regards experience as the experience of beingness: the condition of being which at once stands in its
telos without having fully arrived there—"the state of being which is present in partial appearance, yet absent in relative non-appearance
(*energeia ateles*)."[13] The relative nonappearance is what Heidegger takes
Aristotle to mean by *dynamis*, the possibilizing condition for a moving
being's partial and negative appearance, whereby a play of presence and
absence is enacted. The play is such that the moving being's possibilizing
absence becomes present in a special way. The placing into the appearance—Heidegger's expression for *kinesis*, the change which in itself is

the breaking out of something—"always lets something become present in such a way that in the becoming-present a becoming-absent simultaneously becomes present."[14] In a growing natural being such as a flower, the relative nonappearance of the source of growth indirectly becomes present in allowing the flower to appear. Thus, in Heidegger's reading of Aristotle, *kinesis* is at bottom a play of presence and absence.

More importantly, with respect to living being as a being of movement, a being's *dynamis* must be preserved if it is to remain what it is; it must conserve its *dynamis* precisely as possibility. In suggesting that living being must constantly go back into its *dynamis* as it comes forth into appearance, Heidegger is able to say that there is a formal pattern of retrieve (*Wiederholung*) in *kinesis*, of becoming what one already is. The plant retrieves (*Wiederholung*) its *dynamis* in order to appear. Now, it is precisely this structure that one finds in the analytic of Dasein. Retrieval becomes the way in which any laying out (*Auslegung*)—hermeneutics—occurs for Heidegger. Such retrieval occurs not only at the methodological level in the function of the analysis of Dasein, but, quite appropriately, in the way to be of Dasein itself: "the act of resolve is the self-disclosive retrieval whereby existence accepts and understandingly becomes the most proper possibility it already is, its dying." In the stretching ahead of itself toward death, Dasein opens the realm of meaning as such.

Of course, one should not be misled to think that Heidegger's dramatic transformation of *kinesis* is simply an elevated form of biologism or *Lebensphilosophie* based on a notion of organic growth. Ultimately, for Heidegger the matter at the heart of the question of Being pertains very little to the idea of growth as such. At one place Heidegger writes: "all origination and genesis in the field of the ontological is not growth and unfolding, but degeneration, since everything arising arises, that is, in a certain way, runs *away*, removes itself from the superior force of the source."[15] What Heidegger later on calls *Ereignis* can be read as an extension of this notion of movement in Aristotle. For our purposes, what is most important here is the fact that Heidegger has taken the movement that is *physis* and transformed it into the basis of the structure of historicity. Historicity is nothing less than the pattern of retrieve with respect to the temporality of Dasein.

> The resoluteness in which Dasein comes back to itself, discloses current factical possibilities of authentic existing, and discloses them *in terms of the heritage* [*Erbe*] which that resoluteness, as thrown, takes over. In one's coming back resolutely to one's thrownness, there is hidden a *handing*

down [*Sichüberliefern*] to oneself of the possibilities that have come down to one, but not necessarily as having thus come down. (*SZ*, 383)

Historical retrieve does not hand down possibilities so much as it frees up possibilities. The *kinesis* of historical retrieve, in other words, does not cancel its *dynamis* whereby factical possibilities would be drawn into full present appearance, but brings *dynamis* into presence by leaving it possible.

Philosophical Hermeneutics and the Ontology of the Possible

Let us begin here by returning for a moment to Caputo's critique. He wants to insist that Gadamer has betrayed the subversiveness of Heideggerian facticity, that the finitude of understanding gives way to an Aristotelico-Hegelian metaphysics of infinity. Every understanding is an actualization of a potential (Aristotle's ousiology) carried out in a Hegelian process of historical unfolding. To extend the critique even further, Caputo draws on Gadamer's analysis of modern art as an illustration of a metaphysics of infinity, for even here, with modern art's seeming disruption of the idea of a deep unity, hermeneutics simply lets the infinity sink deeper into the artwork, and thus requires an even greater effort on the part of the interpreter. According to Caputo, the retrieval of the unity transpires in the special temporality of the artwork in which we become contemporaneous with a meaning and truth that transcends time. Human finitude is thus part of an argument for infinity, a broken *symbolon* that is made whole by the ideality and infinity of the artwork.

Against this reading, I want to suggest that the question of Gadamer's infinity (and ultimately the question of truth as well) must be interpreted along the lines of an ontology of living being outlined above in which possibility stands higher than actuality. Following this line of interpretation it will become apparent that finitude for Gadamer does not function in a Hegelian and metaphysical manner. Accordingly, it is not enough to say, as Gadamer himself has said, that philosophical hermeneutics is a matter of "saving the honor of the 'bad infinity'" (*GW*II, 505). Taken by itself this statement suggests that the dialectical *kinesis* of the hermeneutic event is simply the mediation of otherness, relative to infinity, in the absence of a grand teleological construction.

Clearly, in Gadamer's own mind, the project of philosophical hermeneutics defines itself in opposition to any metaphysics of infinity. In part 3 of *Truth and Method*, where the concern is with the problem of the relation between language and world, Gadamer points out that philosophical hermeneutics is not to be confused with the essentially theological answer to the problem that appears in Greek thought, and ultimately this means that philosophical hermeneutics is not to be confused with the Hegelian answer to the problem as well.

> In considering the being of beings, Greek metaphysics regarded it as a being that fulfilled itself in thought. This thought is the thought of nous, which is conceived as the highest and most perfect being, gathering within itself the being of all beings. The articulation of the logos brings the structure of being into language, and this coming into language [*Zursprachekommen*] is, for Greek thought, nothing other than the presencing [*Gegenwart*] of the being itself, its aletheia. Human thought regards the infinity of this presence as its fulfilled potential, its divinity. (*WM*, 432–33; *TM*, 456–57)

Gadamer is emphatic in saying that he cannot follow this way of thinking, for above all else the hermeneutic phenomenon is guided by the finitude of historical experience. The question, though, is just how decisively finitude sustains the structure of hermeneutic experience. For Gadamer, insofar as coming into language is the experience of finitude, the answer to the question lies in the analysis of language.

In general terms, Gadamer regards the experience of language as that which constitutes the order and structure of our experience of the world. Such experience is incapable of turning out of itself. Philosophical hermeneutics, in other words, cannot follow the logos philosophy that unites thought and Being, not because it rejects the possibility that language accomplishes the presencing of Being, but because language cannot be transcended. Language is the medium of our *whole* experience of the world.

How, then, is the being of language to be understood? To be sure, the being of language cannot be understood as a system of signs where what is, is simply reflected in language. Drawing on a distinction first emphasized by Heidegger, Gadamer insists that the being of language cannot be found in the act. of signifying (*actus signatus*), but is to be found in its lived execution (*actus exercitus*). The being of language is there in language in use where meaning comes forth in the doing, in the exercise: language is a communicative event having "its true being only in conversation, in coming to an understanding" (*WM*, 422; *TM*, 446). Language understood in this way is, accordingly, living language. As such it is the particular expression of the ontology of living being for philosophical hermeneutics. This means that here too there is *kinesis*, that every speaker is caught up in a version of the play of presence and absence.

This kinetic dimension of language can be seen in connection with Gadamer's description of language as the medium within which our relation to the world transpires. Language does indeed hold within itself a totality of meaning. However, this totality is not a presence waiting to be realized. It is rather that which withholds itself in being held in language. Gadamer calls this totality contained in language the "virtuality of speech." Every speaking contains a totality, as the holding within itself of possible being, in terms of which it is possible for there to be a new possibilities of meaning. Gadamer writes:

> Every word causes the whole of language to which it belongs to resonate and the whole world-view that underlies it to appear. Thus every word, as the event of the moment, carries with it the unsaid, to which it is related by responding and summoning. The occasionality of human speech is not a casual imperfection of its expressive power; it is, rather, the logical expression of the living virtuality of speech [*die Virtualität des Redens*] that brings a totality of meaning [*Sinn*] into play, without being able to express it totality. All human speaking is finite in such a way that there is laid up within it an infinity of meaning to be explicated and laid out. (*WM*, 434; *TM*, 458)[16]

The talk of infinity in this context of living language has nothing to do with an actualizing essence, an unfolding actualization, but describes the character of language as a center (*Mitte*) in which every word breaks forth. Language qua living is finite and as such it presses forth into possibilities.

But how so? In order to see precisely how Gadamer takes up an ontology of the possible let us look more closely at the reason why one cannot express the totality of meaning. The unsaid held within the center of language whereby there is a creative multiplication of the word is not a potential waiting to be realized, because the center (*Mitte*) of language is for Gadamer speculative. Ironically, the use of this term immediately puts Gadamer together again in close proximity to Hegel. But here the issue, as is often the case when Gadamer draws upon Hegel, is the retrieval of a notion that aids an ontology bent on overcoming a philosophy of subjectivity. Language is speculative in the sense that language does not re-present the *Sache*, but rather, what is at stake in language, in living language to be more precise, is the very formation of the intelligible with respect to the *Sache*. Gadamer writes:

> To be expressed in language does not mean that a second being is acquired. The way in which a thing presents itself is, rather, part of its own being. Thus everything that is language has a speculative unity: it contains a distinction, that between its being and the way it presents itself, but this is a distinction that is not really a distinction at all. (*WM*, 450; *TM*, 475)

The event of speech as the realization of meaning in language is for Gadamer speculative: "To say what one means . . . means to hold what is said together with an infinity of what is not said in the unity of the one meaning and to ensure that it be understood in this way" (*WM*, 444; *TM*, 469). In speaking speculatively, which is often found in an intensified way in the poetic word, we express a relation to the whole of Being.

But this hermeneutic situation as a speculative situation is fundamentally different from Hegel's dialectical self-unfolding of *Geist*, notwithstanding the fact that there is even a teleological component in hermeneutic experience. It is true that Gadamer sees a real correspondence between dialectic presentation in Hegel and the structure of hermeneutic interpretation that by virtue of a relative fulfillment conceives the unity of the *Sache* only in successiveness. However, Gadamer insists that this correspondence ultimately fails because of the radical finitude at the basis of hermeneutic experience. That difference in dialectical presentation for which finitude is responsible is essentially twofold: (1) the dialectical realization of sense in hermeneutic experience begins as a *response* and thus there is no problem of a beginning; (2) the dialectical realization of sense in hermeneutic experience is a completion that issues in a new creation of understanding in such a way that the conception of end is transformed.

Regarding the notion of response, Gadamer writes: "The apparently thetic beginning of interpretation is, in a fact, a response, and, like every response, the sense of an interpretation is determined by the question asked. Thus the dialectic of question and answer always precedes the dialectic of interpretation" (*WM*, 447; *TM*, 472). In reading a text, interpretation is first called for when the accord between reader and text is disrupted, but this means that the text poses a question to us. Notice what occurs by the question. It arises as a mark of finitude, of the negativity of not knowing. But more important, the mark of the question itself is that it opens up the being of the questioned and doing so is the holding open of possibilities. Questioning is not a positing, but a probing of possibilities that come out of and are taken up by the *Sache*. For Gadamer the point is not so much that questions then get answered, that possibilities are actualized—this of course occurs in interpretation in the very disappearance of interpretation[17]—but of being able to remain within the open against the inevitable closure of a question. The art of questioning is being able to go on asking questions which is at once the art of conducting a real conversation. Reading a text is ultimately a matter of allowing the text to speak to us like a partner in a conversation. Perhaps it is here that the ontology of the possible is most evident, for in no way is conversation a repetition in which something prefigured comes forth and out into the open in the manner of self-actualization. Tradition does not stand behind the partners in conversation prefiguring its possibilities, but is the standing within the possible as such as the source of the "always already" of the *Sache*. Every conversation occurs within the element of not knowing what one is talking about.

And yet, the text does speak, there is a communicative event that by its very constitution will say the same within the tradition; interpretation, as the movement of making that which is far near again, disappears in communication, in the "completion" of the interpretive act. What emerges as self-same, though, is not the reactualized original, but a common sphere of meaning. "It is not Being in itself that is increasingly revealed when Homer's *Iliad* or Alexander's *Indian Campaign* speaks to us in the new appropriation of tradition, but as in genuine conversation, something emerges that is contained in neither parties individually" (*WM*, 438; *TM*, 462). How then are we to understand this telos of hermeneutic experience? Unlike Hegel's objective teleology, and for that matter unlike Kierkegaard's subjective teleology, Gadamer's teleology is the teleology of language itself with respect to a state of openness (*Offenheit*). The completion can only be measured against the content of tradition itself, and, Gadamer insists, every assimilation of tradition is historically other. The hermeneutic standpoint has nothing to do with establishing correct meaning, as if this stood firm or possessed a firmness that could be reached. But at the same time, the difference that occurs in the way tradition speaks is not to be understood as an imperfect grasp (*getrübte Erfassung*) of it in the manner of a yet to be actualized. According to Gadamer "the paradox that is true of every content of tradition, namely of being one and the same and yet other, proves all interpretation to be, in fact, speculative" (*WM*, 448; *TM*, 473). Difference exists within identity, otherwise identity would not be identity. Thought contains deferral and distance, otherwise, thought would not be thought.[18] Thus we can say that in the play of presence and absence, in the play of language itself, every speaking is a pregnant speaking ready to give birth to a new creation of understanding.

Conversation is thus language on the move (*kinesis*), a movement of discourse in which word and idea first become what they are. Meaning emerges within the dialogue, within the *kinesis* of living language, in such a way that it inevitably transforms itself. The ensuing dialectic is an inexhaustible play of words, a self-propelled language game, which cannot be steered by the will of the one who wishes to understand. What occurs in language is "the play of language itself, which addresses us, proposes and withdraws, and fulfills itself in the answer" (*WM*, 464; *TM*, 490). When Caputo suggests that whenever the tradition comes to speak again we have simply the infinity of an unfolding *Geist* he fails to see that the wholeness of tradition is more regulative than constitutive of experience, for every speaking is a new voice. In the event of language something comes into being that had not existed before, in the sense that new possibilities of sense emerge from within the tradition itself. Like the *kinesis* of living being, the movement of tradition repeats its own *dynamis*, and more importantly, this unfolding of possibility does not come from a sphere of an already delineated essence. If such were the case, possibility would not be higher than actuality. If such were the case, the totality of meaning would be nothing other than a prescribed set of possibilities, and thus the merely indeterminate as such. The contemporaneousness of every interpretation, the repetition of its possibility, is imbedded in the multifarious mixture of past and future which opens up to a whole new field of possibilities. The inexhaustible depth found in every interpretation must be understood in this context: the infinite is a function of the finite and not vice versa.

But now we have to face the criticism from the other side. If we have been successful in arguing against an essentialism of wholeness as underpinning the movement in hermeneutic experience, have we not simply confirmed the suspicions of the essentialist regarding truth in hermeneutic experience? If every interpretation is without beginning and without end, truth would seem to be nothing more than a vanishing factor, a momentary halt that never really touches the world. How can one be mistaken in interpretation if every interpretation by its design gives way to its own future? In what sense could we ever say that an interpretation is erroneous when it is the case that every interpretation is simply a different understanding?

Here I am able to provide only a general sketch of an answer.[19] The most general observation that we can make about truth in hermeneutic experience is also the most obvious, namely that truth is not tied exclusively to methodological procedure. This claim seems to strengthen the connection between the notion of truth in hermeneutic experience and

Heidegger's use of the Greek *aletheia* for the eventing character of truth. But to establish such a connection does nothing to allay the suspicions of the traditionalist who would argue that without a notion of correspondence, especially as it regards determinate meaning, one has no truth at all. The question before us then concerns the specific way in which a philosophical hermeneutics incorporates the eventing character of truth within the structure of its own ontology of the possible. The answer to this question requires a preliminary analysis that can only be summarized at this point. That analysis concerns Gadamer's use of the metaphysics of the beautiful as a description for the self-asserting character of truth. In *Truth and Method* and elsewhere,[20] Gadamer has been able to show that the Greek conception of the beautiful must be understood in its ontological dimension of shining-forth. The beautiful in connection with the comprehension of the intelligible is *einleuchtend*. Literally a "shining-in," its meaning is conveyed in the expression "an enlightening experience." The enlightening refers to the fact that something has come to light in the sense that something becomes clear in coming upon us. One finds this notion of clarity in rhetoric. The connection to truth is evident: clarity is also the mark of truth, of true shining (*Wahrscheinliche*). The shining-in is a shining-forth (*aletheia*).

Now, what interests us here is the peculiar character of the shining-forth. Drawing from the texts of Plato, Gadamer argues that the beautiful in relation to Being is such that it collapses the distinction between illuminated and illuminating. The beautiful as shining-forth is the one *eidos* that presents *itself* in its shining. Gadamer further contends that this kind of shining-imaging where the image is not a duplicated original expresses the character of an image in its genuine sense. Moreover, the mimetic character of image-making has a corresponding genuine sense. *Mimesis* is genuinely an image-making in which something comes forth in sensuous abundance, a something which is not simply original or copy. In *Truth and Method* when Gadamer talks about how the intelligible is not simply copied in language, how the word is not simply a sign, but that in language the intelligible comes to show itself, we can understand the character of such words as images.

This means that in hermeneutic experience, as a coming to an understanding in language, we undergo an image-play, and in light of what we said earlier, it is an image-play that no longer subordinates the drive to presence to a telos of pure presence. Or, in different words, for philosophical hermeneutics it is not a matter of seeing truth itself instead of an image, but precisely the inverse: of getting entangled in the image which entangles us in truth. Accordingly, we can say that for philosophical hermeneutics, where we have neither the vision of a completed telos, nor the remembrance of an *arche*, there are only *thick images* in which the intelligible and the image are entangled. And also in light of what we said earlier, we can say that these thick images seep with possibility, which comes forth not from a possibilizing essence of wholeness, but in the rupturing and breaking forth that occurs in every image-play.

From this brief analysis it is possible to situate the question of truth within a metaphorics of surface and depth. The traditionalist confines the matter of truth to surface. Correspondence requires a certain kind of alignment, a linear correlation that becomes the measure of the thing. But this account of truth is insufficient to account for the dynamic of hermeneutic experience. In commenting on the development of his own thought Gadamer writes:

> Life experience and the study of Plato had led me quite early to the
> insight that the truth of a single proposition cannot be measured by its
> merely factual relationship to correctness and congruency; nor does it
> depend merely upon the context in which it stands. Ultimately it
> depends upon the genuineness of its enrootedness and bond with the
> person of the speaker in whom it wins its truth potential, for the meaning
> of the statement is not exhausted in what is stated.[21]

On this account it is not a matter of truth vanishing, but of seeing precisely how difficult the fixation of meaning and truth is, given the dynamic of hermeneutic experience. In the image-play we are already in the truth so to speak inasmuch as hermeneutic experience starts with a "deep common accord" (*tragendes Einverständnis*). Understanding, in other words, precedes misunderstanding:

> There is always a world already interpreted, already organized into its
> basic relations, into which experience steps as something new, upsetting
> what has led our expectations and undergoing reorganization itself in
> the upheaval. Misunderstanding and strangeness are not the first factors,
> so that avoiding misunderstanding can be regarded as the specific task of
> hermeneutics. Just the reverse is the case. Only the support of the famil-
> iar and common understanding makes possible the venture into the
> alien, and lifting up of something out of the alien, and thus the broaden-
> ing and enrichment of our own experience of the world.[22]

At the same time Gadamer does not wish to say that truth is simply identified with anything that makes sense, for such a claim does not take into
consideration the critical analysis that is part of the movement between

the strange and familiar. To the point, the matter of truth for philosophical hermeneutics is played out in unraveling the multiple layers of
thick images.

In light of what has now been said, we can give two determinations
to the moment of truth in hermeneutic experience. First of all, in the
moment of truth we find the occurrence of something fitting. In the
logic of question and answer, for example, we can speak of a fitting
response. In conversation we throw out statements along the way in a
double sense: we put statements forward, but we also discard, abandon
statements along the way for some statements are found to lead us
nowhere. Fitting, then, pertains to a certain disentanglement, a separating out in which something comes together, a moment of coherence not
of wholeness, but what forms a whole in coming together as it does. In
this context we can speak of falsifiability in hermeneutic experience in
the sense that the *Sache* breaks through in conversation to show itself as
other than it first presented itself. This same notion is what underlies
Gadamer's analysis of recognition in *mimesis* with respect to the work of
art. According to Gadamer, in *mimesis* there is the recognition of the represented in the representation. But this does not mean that we see something we have seen before; it means that "I now **recognize** something as
something that I have already seen." The **emphasis is** rightly placed on
the "as" and not on the matter of recollection, for "it is part of the
process of recognition that we see things in terms of what is permanent
and essential in them, unencumbered by the contingent circumstances
in which they were seen before and are seen again."[23]

This interpretation of *mimesis* brings us to the second determination of the moment of truth. The thick image suggests that we can speak
of truth within the continuum of empty and full. *Mimesis*, we should
recall, also pertains to an image-making in which something comes forth
in sensuous abundance. Inasmuch as the work of art does not simply
refer to something, because what it refers to is actually there, its productive character can be described as an "increase in being." The matter of
truth in the work of art, as well as in conversation, appears to be pointed
at this overflow; it has to do with the possibility of saying more. Similarly,
in the virtuality of living speech we are "full up" so to speak and yet always
able to say more. We can see more precisely what is meant here by what
would constitute error in our interpretive efforts. Error coincides with
the empty, when the interpretation comes to nothing. Of course what
constitutes being full—the moment of truth—is not determined by a
quantitative mark, but occurs whenever the *Sache* remains the same in
speaking in a new voice.

Thus the mark against which the traditionalist would have us measure all truth-claims is not to be found in philosophical hermeneutics. And yet, it is possible to speak of truth in hermeneutic experience. What I am suggesting is that in hermeneutic experience we come back to a richer notion of truth as *veritas*, to the notion of truth as making real. In "verification" it is not so much a matter of strict confirmation, but of making the matter itself real which is the achievement of language. In this context, any question of essentialism must be approached from its founding condition of living being. Essence thus means, to quote Heidegger, "to dwell and sojourn—that which from out of itself stands, the enduring as presence and absence."[24] Finitude and truth are caught up in an image-play which takes up the play of the upsurge of the possible.

PART   2

ON THE TRUTH OF
THE WORD

8

The Ontological Valence
of the Word: Introducing
"On the Truth of the Word"

Lawrence K. Schmidt

ans-Georg Gadamer's essay "On the Truth of the Word" marks an important development after *Truth and Method* concerning the ability of words to express hermeneutic truth. In the discussion of the truth of the work of art, Gadamer identified the ontological valence of a work of art (*WM*, 128ff.; *TM*, 134ff.). This increase in the being of a work of art is what permitted the truth of a work of art, throughout its effective history, to be able to call or to make a claim on the person involved with this work. In *Truth and Method* this concept in the example of art is only indirectly recovered in the later discussion of language. In the discussions of the ideality of the word and the poetic word, Gadamer hints at the concept of the ontological valence of the word that is developed in this essay. When a word achieves ideality in being written, it enters into another realm, detached from its original author and reader so that it is able to preserve itself through effective history (*WM*, 368–72; *TM*, 390–94). The poetic word is able to hold what is said in relation to what is not said (*WM*, 445; *TM*, 469–70). These two directions of thought are united in the concept of the ontological valence of the word. The clarification of this concept allows Gadamer to go further in characterizing the truth of the word. The true word is able to open a clearing within Being where the said and unsaid are held forth uncovering further possibilities of Being. The true word preserves this vicinity to Being.

"On the Truth of the Word" addresses the way truth comes to be in the word. The word is not a single word nor a symbol, but a statement. It lives among humans and has its own Dasein. As Heidegger has demonstrated, Gadamer continues, "the word and language have an existential relation to hearing and being silent."[1] The concealing and unconcealing of truth refers to humans being in the There, among others and at home in language. "The authentic word—the word as the true word—is to be determined from Being and as the word in which truth occurs." The authenticity of a word lies not in what it states but in its mode of being as saying: "it stands and one stands by it." Gadamer's purpose is to uncover this mode of being for the true word. For methodological reasons only, he restricts the investigation to texts; this does not imply a depreciation of what exists as living speech. Texts speak only in being read, interpreted, and understood. Gadamer identifies this "saying-being of the word [as] 'statement' [Aussage]."

Gadamer isolates three types of texts, the religious, the judicial, and the literary, correlated to the three basic forms of saying: the pledge (Zusage), the notification (Ansage), and the statement (Aussage), which in its narrow sense is a state-ment (Aus-Sage). His analysis concentrates on the text as statement in the narrower sense, specifically the poetic text, since the poem is best able to illustrate the being of the word as statement. Poetry is a work of art in words, where truth is put to work. Gadamer's first thesis is that "the word in a work of poetry is more saying than elsewhere." It is articulate in its resurrection by the reader, although the path through writing is essential and lends the word its "radiance." The speaking of the words in a poem is not a productive act of reproduction. The poem speaks and speaks better through a listener or reader than through the reciter. The reciter recognizes "the fortuitousness of a particular presentation" in relation to the speaking of the poem. This indicates the autonomy of the word or text as well as its claimed univocality. The poem raises its own voice "and speaks for no other," not even in the name of the nameless.

Gadamer's second thesis is that "the ideal speaker of such words is the ideal reader." The ability of the word to speak in this eminent sense is not primarily determined by the content of what is said, since such speaking may occur in all genre of literature. Also a comparison with modern, abstract art demonstrates that its beauty and meaning are independent of a depicted object. However, the other extreme, that the subject matter is completely unimportant, is also to be avoided. When a word speaks well it is not noticed in itself, but what is said, is there. The word of poetry becomes more articulate through neither what is said nor through what is not said. Instead of some concrete object, "self-presence, the being of the 'There'" comes forth in the saying.

To discover how this occurs, Gadamer examines lyric poetry, since it has a high degree of coherence. The whole is united by various connective tissues, including rhythm, rhyme, configurations of sounds, as well as meaning and logical relationships. Following Hölderlin, Gadamer calls this coherence "the *tone*" of a poem. It indicates what comes to stand and to preserve itself in the special unity of each poem. The saying power of poetic language is not derived from common usage but, quoting Hölderlin, "presupposes the dissolution of all positivities" so that the word may come forth with a new power. The more saying a word is, the more of the "There" is uncovered by it. Such an increase in being of the word Gadamer terms the "ontological valence of the word."

This is the major advance over *Truth and Method*. Analogous to the concept of the ontological valence in a work of art, Gadamer has now established this ontological structure for language. A word has meaning within the context of its language so that an increase in valence does not mean merely an increase in the objective content of that word but includes a coming forth or increase in the speaking of that language in its potentiality. The place where we are, is more clearly enacted in the saying of the word. "The universal 'There' of Being in the word is the wonder of language."

Therefore, the saying-being of the word is a "preservation of the vicinity," which does not refer to some stable content of speech but to the proximity of Being. This preservation occurs in all works of art. As Heidegger has shown, "The truth of the work of art is not the *logos* in its having been stated, but rather and at the same time, a That and a There." In poetry one has already presupposed "the being-in-language and the being-in of being in language." Only one who is at home in that language is able to experience "the self-preserving and self-determining statement of the poetic word, which secures another being-at-home in the primordially familiar." For this reason, Gadamer concludes, the poetic word differs from all other works of art—"it must and is able to preserve this vicinity, that means, to stop the withdrawing." In speaking it withdraws itself to further remembrance, thereby releasing possibilities. It overcomes itself as word to achieve its highest possibility and "enters into the thinking of the thinker."

Gadamer's essay has developed the ontological status of the word that enables the listener to hear the truth of the word. It should be noted that this event of hermeneutic truth is a dialogue between the word in its saying power and the listener. In *Truth and Method,* as well as afterwards (*GW*, 447, 465; *TM*, 443, 461), Gadamer insists on the importance of dialogue in the constitution of language and so the poetic word. This role of dialogue has not been part of this questioning, but has been presupposed by it.

9

On the Truth of the Word

Hans-Georg Gadamer

Translated by Lawrence K. Schmidt and Monika Reuss

To speak about the truth of the word today amounts to a provocation, since deception through language and the suspicion of implicit ideology or even metaphysics have become so common expressions.[1] Especially if one speaks of *the* word. For, if something appears
beyond discussion then it is that speaking about truth as *en synthesei aei*
has its application. And if—following the Greeks—one wants to use the
term *alethes* for perceptions that present specific sense data and the what-
ness of the intended, then it simply makes no sense to speak of the truth
of the word, where the word completely disappears in what the discourse
[*Rede*] means. It would no longer be a word if it could be false as a word.
A discourse formed of words can be false or true only if its expressed
opinion concerning a state of affairs is in question.

"Word" refers not only to the individual word, the singular of
"words" or of the words that together form a discourse, rather it more
importantly relates to a use of language, where "word" has a collective
meaning and implies a social relation.[2] The word that one is told, also
the word that one gives, or when one affirms a promise by saying, "That
is my word"—in all these cases it does not mean a single word and even
if it is only the word "yes." It says more, infinitely more, than one can
"mean." When Luther translated *logos* in the Prologue to John as "word,"
this rested upon a whole theology of the word that reached back at least
to Augustine's interpretation of the Trinity. Nevertheless, the ordinary
reader understands that Jesus Christ is, for the faithful, the living

promise that has become flesh. So when the truth of the word is sought in what follows, no particular word is to be considered with reference to its contents, not even the word of salvation. However, one must remember that the word "lives among humans" and that in all of its modes of appearance, where it is completely what it is, the word has its own reliably constant existence [*Dasein*]. In the end it is always the word that "stands," be it that one stands by one's word or warrants it, as the one who has said it or as the one who has taken another at his word. The word itself stands. In spite of its being uttered only once, it is continuously there: as the message of salvation, as a blessing or curse, as a prayer—or also as precept, law or pronounced judgment, or as the poet's myth or the philosopher's principle. It appears to be more than a superficial fact that one can say of such a word that it "stands written" and documents itself. With reference to these modes of being of the word, where, in accordance to their own meaning, they "do things" and are not merely communicating something true, the question can now be raised concerning what it can mean that they are true and are true as words. I am referring here to Austin's well-known investigations in order to make clear the poetic word in its rank of being.

In order to clarify this question it is necessary to first discuss what "truth" can mean in this context. It is evident that the traditional concept of truth, *adaequatio rei et intellectus*, cannot function here, where the word is not at all intended as a proposition about something, but rather where the word, in having its own Dasein, raises and fulfills a claim to being by itself. The excellent unity, the singular, which "the" word receives, certainly contains within itself an existential and logical inadequacy, insofar as that word points toward an inner infinity of possible responding words [*Ant-worten*], all of which—and so none of which—are "appropriate." One will, however, think of the Greek word, *aletheia*, whose fundamental meaning Heidegger has taught us to see. I do not mean only the negative sense of *a-letheia* as unconcealment or uncoveredness. As such, this was not that new a claim and one had for a long time already noticed that *aletheia* has the sense of unhiddenness with verbs of speaking (Humboldt): "Don't deceive me," (*me me lathes*) says Zeus to Hera. The Greeks' blooming imagination and the fine sense for language allowed *aletheia* to be characterized as not-concealed even in Homer. Heidegger's renewal of the insight into the negative sense of the word was important because it demonstrated that this Greek word is not limited to the context of discourse but can also be used in the sense of "genuine," as meaning the "unadulterated." So one can say in Greek: a true friend and true, that is genuine, gold, which does not produce the false appearance of being gold. In these contexts uncoveredness gains an ontological meaning, that is, it does not characterize an activity or self-expression of someone or something, but characterizes its being (as *aletheia* can also mean the character trait honesty). It is surprising enough that not only the essence, who can speak and disguise itself, and can even lie and may be characterized by *a-letheia*, but also entities as such can be true, like gold. What is it that there conceals, or keeps secret, or disguises so that non-concealment may be attributed—and not by our doing—to entities? How must Being "be," if entities "are" in such a manner that they can be false?

The answer must begin from the familiar experience: What is in it, comes forth. It is not fortuitous that Heidegger gave special attention to the Aristotelian concept of *physis*, which characterizes the ontological status of what grows forth by itself. But what does it mean that Being itself is such that entities, as what they are, must first come forth? And that they could be "false" like false gold? What type of concealment is it that belongs to entities in the same manner as does the uncoveredness with which they enter into presence? The unconcealment, attributed to entities and wherein they come forth, certainly appears to be an absolute There [*Da*], like the light in Aristotle's description of the *nous poietikos*, and like the "clearing" that unfolds in Being and as Being.

As long as Heidegger attempted to ask the question of Being from the position of an existential analysis of Dasein, it was hard to avoid the consequence that it is authentic Dasein that is its there and is "there" for the other. Clearly Heidegger was determined to contrast the historical nature of Dasein, i.e., its structure as a thrown projection, to the idealism of transcendental subjectivity and its lofty conceptions. Certainly the structure of care in Dasein wished to be fundamentally differentiated from the idealistic concept of "consciousness itself" or "absolute knowledge." One also does not wish to overlook that authenticity and inauthenticity belong "equiprimordially" to the structural whole of Dasein, and that therefore idle talk belongs to Dasein just as much as the word or silence. So, a sense of authenticity or genuineness, what the earlier Heidegger termed "anxiety producing resoluteness," attaches not only to being silent but to breaking the silence, the word. Furthermore, already in *Being and Time* the challenge had been fully accepted that the Greek concept of logos posed from the beginning to the "Christian theologian" Heidegger. (Heidegger still used this appellation as a private docent of philosophy when he began his life work.) Language is already being considered as an existential, namely as an attribute of Dasein, who is characterized by an understanding of Being. But just as the essence of truth, from the position of the restraint and insistence of Dasein, was still related to the "mystery" and its absolute concealment, as if to its other, so too could the word and language have an existential relation to hearing and being silent. However, what was "true" in this and what "came forth" there, was precisely existence, Dasein awaiting its being while facing nothingness. So the word was not the expression of the Aristotelian *apophansis*, which, when stated, is completely given (*en to deloun*) in what it says and points out. The word had rather the temporal character of uniqueness and of an event. What does event mean here? What occurs there? At that time Heidegger certainly saw how the word "entered idle talk" with an inner necessity and thereby deteriorated. He also saw that the fate of thinking was connected to this ambiguity between authenticity and fallenness, or between Being and appearing. Nevertheless, that the word as word is not only uncovering but also must be, and precisely for that reason, covering and concealing, was not to be understood from the position of the transcendental analysis of Dasein. In his famous Davoser confrontation with the author of the philosophy of symbolic forms, Heidegger still insisted on the self-understanding of Dasein as opposed to the intermediate world of forms.

If concealment and unconcealment are truly to be thought of as structural moments of "Being" and if temporality belongs to being and not merely to entities that hold the place for being, then it still remains the characteristic of humans "to be there," and equally so, to be not the only one at home in language, but also that "Being" is there in the language that we speak with one another. Further, all of this results not from an existential decision that one could also avoid, but because there-being [*Da-sein*] is a resoluteness, a continuous openness, for the "There." Therefore, we cannot commence our thinking from the human, in the sense that the authentic word would be the word of authenticity—and not the one of idle talk. It is rather the case that the authentic word—the word as the true word—is to be determined from Being and as the word in which truth occurs. In this way one can relate to Heidegger's later insight and ask the question concerning the truth of words. Perhaps in asking this question we may come closer, in a concrete manner, to Heidegger's insight and puzzling expressions such as "the clearing of Being."

What is an "authentic" word? This surely does not mean the word where something true, or even the highest truth, is expressed, but where the "word" is in the most authentic sense. To be a word means to be saying [*Wort sein heißt sagend sein*].[3] In order to find those words that are the most saying from among the infinite variety of possible words, we must remember what truly characterizes "a word": that it stands and that one stands by it. This clearly already implies that the word lays claim to an enduring validity through what it says or sayingly does. I already mentioned that the mystery of writing corroborates this claim. Therefore, it is neither as arbitrary nor as absurd as it first sounds when I define the word that authentically speaks to be "text." Clearly this is only a methodological move. This does not mean to deny the genuineness, primordiality, significance, or the power of determination that exists in living speech or in a prayer, sermon, blessing, curse, or in political speech. However, in this manner, the question concerning what the word as word is able to allow to be true, can be methodologically isolated. That texts also regain their character as words only in the living event of their understanding, oral presentation, or proclamation, does not at all alter the fact that the text's content, and nothing else, is being reawakened here, i.e., the potential word that says something. How the word is there, when it is a "text," clarifies what it is as something saying, i.e., what constitutes its saying-being.

I will term this so isolated saying-being of the word "statement" [*Aussage*]. For it is the case that the statement's essence is determinable, even if not irrevocably, in spite of all the problems in its use and abuse, e.g., in legal proceedings.[4] Its essence is determinable and so valid just until such a recall, which means for the time being. Its validity implies that what the statement alone says, and only this, is admissible. Here as well, the discussion about the univocal content of a statement and whether such a claim can be justified, indirectly confirms the claim to such univocality. It is clear, of course, that the witness's statement in court actually first acquires truth-value from the context of the proceedings. Especially in the hermeneutic context, e.g., in theological exegesis or in literary aesthetics, the word "statement" prevailed, because it is able to establish that it alone concerns what was said as such, without recourse to the occasionality of the author, and that nothing but the interpretation of the text as a whole can make the meaning clear. Therefore, it is completely mistaken to see the event character of the word undermined by such a concentration on the text, which as a whole is the statement— rather, by such means, the event character first achieves its full meaning.

Certainly there are written solidifications of the spoken without these constituting a text in the specific sense of the word that means it stands. So, for example, all private sketches, notes or reports of what was said, are used only to help remind us. Here it is evident that the written record comes alive only by recalling that fresh memory. Such a text does not express itself and if published by itself, it would not be something that spoke. Such a text is just the written spur of a living memory. In contrast to this, it will become apparent in what sense there are texts that actually have the character of a statement, i.e., that are a word in the sense discussed above: a word that is said (and not only the transmission of something). We may, therefore, further characterize the word as saying by adding that it, as a saying, is said. We ask ourselves again, which word, that is such a said word, is the most saying and, for that reason, can be termed "true"?

We may differentiate three categories of texts that are "statements" in this sense: the religious, the judicial, and the literary. In the last case it is perhaps necessary to differentiate further in order to encompass such different forms of statement as the poetic word, the speculative sentence of philosophers, and the logical and fundamental unity of predicative judgments. The latter also belongs here to the extent that it is the universal character of words to be saying, and so, no word is separable from the merely pointing letting-be-present that we call the judgment in the context of argumentation.

The differentiation of these categories of words should be exclusively based on the character of the word and not brought to it from outside, from the circumstances of its being said. This is the case in all the different modes where the word becomes "literature." For just this defines literature, that in being written down there is no depreciation of its primordial, living-oral being, but rather this is its genuine form of being, which itself permits and demands the secondary completion of reading or speaking. One can relate these three categories of texts to three basic forms of saying: the pledge [Zusage], the notification [Ansage], and the statement [Aussage]⁵ in the narrower sense, which in an eminent sense may be a state-ment [Aus-sage], i.e., that leads saying to its true end, and so is the most saying word.

This does not imply a limitation to the extent that, for example, religious texts or even legal texts are "statements" in the complete sense of our concept, i.e., that the specific character of their saying is contained in their linguistic-written mode of presentation. It is not the case that a statement that is not yet a pledge can only become a pledge when it is spoken to someone, for example as a consolation or a covenant. Rather, it is such a statement that it has in itself the character of a pledge and must be understood as a pledge. This means, however, that language steps beyond itself in the pledge. Whether in relation to an old or a new agreement, it does not complete itself in itself, as a poem completes itself. Therefore, the pledge, like a covenant, finds its completion in the acceptance of belief—as clearly every promise becomes binding only after it has been accepted. Similarly, a legal text that formulates a law or judgment is binding as soon as it is proclaimed; however, it completes itself as something proclaimed not in itself, but first in being carried out, i.e. in its execution. Also a mere "historical" report is different from a poetic one in that the latter completes itself. Take the example of the Gospels. The evangelist tells a story. A chronicler or historian could also tell such a story, or even a poet. However, the claim of the saying that is raised by the "reading" of this story—and every reading of this is essentially one reading—is evidently and immediately a particular saying, which I termed a pledge. For it is the Good News. One could certainly read this text in another way, e.g., with the interest of a historian who is critically examining its value as a source. However, if the historian would not understand the statement of the text in its pledging character, then an adequate and source-critical use of the text could not be developed. As hermeneutics states: the text has its scope according to which it must be understood. On the other hand, one can read the same text as literature, for example, to discover the artistic means that give its presentation life and color, or to discover the stylistic means of its composition, syntax, and semantics. There can be no question that especially in the Old Testament there is eloquent poetry whose artistic means are obvious. Nevertheless, even such a text as the Song of Solomon stands in the context of the Bible, i.e., it requires one to understand it as a pledge. Here it is clearly the context—but that is again a purely linguistic fact of the text—that lends a love song the character of a pledge. Also texts that are modest and unartistic in literary terms, such as the synoptic Gospels, are to be related to the same scope. One will have to derive the pledging character of such texts from the scope that the context indicates.

One may raise the critical question, whether the religious character, which itself speaks from such texts, already determines their character as a pledge, or whether it is the particular character of redemptive and revealed religions—which are really book-religions like the Jewish, Christian, and Islamic ones—that lend their writings the character of a pledge. In fact, the world of myths, i.e., all religious traditions that do not acknowledge something like canonic texts, opens up a completely different hermeneutic problematic. There exist, for example, the "statements" that one may discover behind the poetic texts of the Greeks in their myths and sagas. They certainly do not have of themselves already the structure of a text, i.e., of the word that stands. But they are nevertheless "sayings," i.e., a speaking through nothing but their being said. Could or would such worlds of religious traditions be recognizable at all if they did not, so to speak, enter into the literary forms of tradition? Recognizing the value of the methods of the structural analysis of myths, the hermeneutic interest starts, however, by questioning not so much what they reveal to one as what they say to one when encountered as poetry. What they say to one lies in the statement that they are and that necessarily moves toward fixation and perhaps even the cumulative fixation through myth-interpreting poetry. Therefore, the hermeneutic problem of interpreting myths will have its legitimate place among the forms of the literary word.[6]

A similar discussion could be conducted for the character of a notification [*Ansage*]. It seems to relate specifically to legal statements. It encompasses the broad range from orders, which are officially announced, proclaimed laws, to finally even law books, written constitutions, legal judgments, and so on. The range of texts encompassed here and the literary character adopted by the legal tradition clearly retain their particular character of saying. They say what is valid in the legal sense of the word and can only be understood under the scope of this claim to validity. Here it is quite clear that such a claim to the validity of a word is not first achieved through being written down. Although, on the other hand, the possibility of codification of such validities is neither incidental nor accidental. In such validities the meaning of the saying of such statements is first realized to any extent. That an order or general law in its complete verbal meaning can be established in writing, clearly depends upon its being unalterable and applicable to all. What stands *there* and what *stands* there, so long as it is not overturned, determines the essential character of the validity of the notifications inherent in such texts. Therefore, one speaks of the announcement or publication of a law as the time when it takes effect. That the interpretation of such words or texts is a particular creative task in jurisprudence, does not at all alter the fact that the statement wants to be univocal in itself, nor does it alter its legal binding force. The hermeneutic task, which is presented here, is a legal one and may have, in a secondary manner, a legal-historical and perhaps even a literary-historical side. Nevertheless, also in this form of the notification, the word remains a statement, i.e., it wants, as a word, to be true.

When we now turn to statements in the eminent sense of the word, which belong especially to the narrower sense of literature, the plethora of possible means of statement is bewildering. It appears to me to be methodologically justified to limit our question concerning the word to the so-called *belles-lettres*. It is evidently not by chance that the narrower sense of "literature" means *belles-lettres*, namely texts that are not categorized in any other context of meaning, i.e., where one can ignore all possible categories: for example, the cultic, judicial, scientific, yes and even the philosophical—although this would be the exceptional case. This was from the beginning the meaning of the beautiful, *kalon*, that it is something desirable in itself, i.e., it enlightens for no other reason than because of its own appearance, which unquestionably elicits approval. This in no way implies that the hermeneutic problem is to be transferred to the field of aesthetics. On the contrary, the question concerning the truth of the word is exactly proposed to the literary word, knowing that this question has not found a real home in traditional aesthetics. Certainly from time immemorial, the art of words, poetry, has been a specific object of reflection—at least long before the thematization of other art forms. Should one include someone like Vitruvius here or, in other areas, the theoreticians of music? In both cases these are practical disciplines and so basically all *ars poetica*. For philosophers, poetry above all was considered to be an object of contemplation, and not fortuitously. Poetry was the old rival of philosophy's own authority. Not only Plato's critique of poetry but also Aristotle's particular interest in poetry, demonstrate this point. One must also consider the close relationship between poetry and rhetoric, which had turned at an early date to reflect upon artistic communication.[7] This contemplation was productive in many respects and fundamentally determined the development of many concepts for the consideration of art. The concept of style alone, the *stilus scribendi*, is an eloquent case in point.

Nevertheless, one must ask oneself whether the role of poetry within aesthetics ever achieved its full potentiality. Consider the fundamental concept that has ruled aesthetics for two millennia: *mimesis, imitatio, Nachahmung* [imitation].[8] Originally it was closely connected with the transitory arts, such as dance, music, and poetry, and was particularly applied to the art of the theater. But Plato already introduces visual arts, such as sculpture and painting, as illustrations, and Aristotle did so as well. By means of the visual concept of the Form, Plato especially interprets the world of entities to be an imitation, and poetry as its imitation, so an imitation of an imitation. This completely removed the concept of *mimesis* from its origin. In Hegel's definition of the beautiful, as the sensuous shining of the idea, Plato's thought is still heard. All romantic proclamations about universal poetry have not removed the confusion that pins the art of words between rhetoric and aesthetics.

Therefore, the question concerning the truth of the word cannot be based on a broad preparation. In romanticism and especially in Hegel's system of the arts, only incomplete attempts can be found. Heidegger's rupturing of the traditional concepts of metaphysics and aesthetics first opened a new entrance by interpreting the work of art as a "putting the truth to work" and defending the sensuous-ethical unity of the work of art against all ontological dualisms.[9] In this way he brought to all art a new respect for the romantic insight into the key position of poeticizing. However, from Heidegger's position as well, it appears much easier to say how the true being of color arises in the painting or the true being of the stone arises in a building, than to say how the true word arises in poetry. Our question lies here.

What does the coming forth of the word in poetry mean? As the colors in a painting shine more brightly and the stone in a building carries more, so the word in a work of poetry is more saying than elsewhere. This is the thesis. If it can be made convincing, then the general question concerning the truth of words can be answered from this position of its perfection. But what does it mean that the word is "more saying"? Our methodological uniting of word and text prepares us well for this question. Clearly, the dead letter of the written cannot, but only the resurrected word (spoken or read) can be included in the being of the work of art. But, only the path through its downfall into writing gives the word its radiance, which can be termed its truth. In this investigation, the question of the historical or genetic meaning of writing can be completely ignored. The path through writing methodologically accomplishes just the exposure of the particular linguistic mode of being of words, especially the poetic statement. We will have to examine whether the path through writing may reveal more in the case of *belles-lettres* than what has been discovered in the other cases of actual texts.

At first what is common appears, e.g., the disappearance of the author or his transformation into the ideal figure of a speaker. In the case of religious canons this is often pushed to the fiction, God would be the speaker, and in the case of a judgment it expressly states: "In the Name of the Law." Understanding such texts can certainly not mean, as has been said since Schleiermacher: to reproduce the productive act. Therefore, one should draw the same conclusion for the literary text, that the psychological interpretation also does not have the hermeneutic adequacy that is attributed to it. In all these cases the statement of the text is not to be understood as a phenomenal expression of the soul's interior (and it is often not even reducible to a single creator). At the same time, there are evidently many different ideal speakers, who promise one a religious message of salvation or who speak in the name of the law or . . .—upon reaching this "or" one falters. Should one really say: Who as poets speak to one? Would it not be more appropriate here to say only that the poem speaks? And I would add: speaks better and more authentically through the listener, the spectator or even the reader, than through the one who literally says something, the reciter, actor, or lecturer. For there can be no doubt that such a speaker (even if it is the author himself who adopts the role of the lecturer or actor) is in a secondary position in relation to the text, inasmuch as the speaker forces the text into the fortuitousness of a particular presentation. It is a hopeless misunderstanding of what literature is, if one wishes to reduce the literary image to an act of intending to which the author gives expression. Here there exists a very convincing difference to the notes that one makes for oneself or to the messages one leaves for another. The literary text is not, while these texts are, secondary in relation to a first, originally meaningful speaking. It is rather the case that each later interpretation—even the author's own—is based on the text, but not in such a way, for example, that the author wishes to refresh a dim memory of something that he had wanted to say by returning to his preparatory versions. Returning to earlier variations is often required to produce a text. Each production of a text, however, presupposes an understanding of it. Facing these circumstances, those who fear for the objectivity of interpretation should rather worry about whether the reduction of a literary text to the expressed opinion of its creator does not destroy the artistic meaning of literature all together.

Of course, this is only a preliminary and negative differentiation by which the autonomy of the word or text is made compelling. But what is the basis for this? How can a word say so much and be so articulate [*vielsagend*] that even the author does not know, but must listen to the word? An initial sense of the saying-being of a literary text is clearly discovered through the negative determination of the autonomy of the word. It is truly unparalleled that a literary text raises its own voice, so to speak, of itself and speaks for no other, not even a God or a law. I now claim: the ideal speaker of such words is the ideal reader. Here one could develop the point that this sentence, as well, contains no historical limitation. Even in preliterary cultures, for example, in the oral tradition of epics, it remains true that there is such an ideal reader, i.e., listener, who is able to hear behind all recitations (or even a single one) what only the inner ear can perceive. Following this criterion he is even able to judge the rhapsodist—as we can see in the old motive of the minstrel's competition. Such an ideal listener is therefore like the ideal reader.[10] One could further discuss that and why reading, as opposed to reading aloud or reciting, is not the reproduction of the original, but rather directly shares the ideality of the original, since reading does not require a move into the contingency of reproduction. For this, the investigations of the

Polish phenomenologist Roman Ingarden on the schematic character of literary words establish the direction to be followed. It would be very illuminating to draw a parallel to the problem of absolute music and the musical score that presents its fixation. One would be able to demonstrate with the music scholar, Georgiades, the important difference between one score and another score, between a word here and a tone there, and therefore also between the literary work and the musical score. Without question, the example of music is special in that one must make music and that even the listener must participate in the making, almost like someone who, in the case of songs, sings along. The reader of a score is not like a reader of a text. That would be the case only if it were an inner making, by means of which one did not commit oneself but retained the freedom of the flowing imagination like a reader. In the case of music, however, the interpretation is preformed by the musician for the listener, no matter how much freedom may be exercised in this process. The musician, as performer and sometimes as director, is in an intermediate position between the composer and the listener, and has to be an interpreter in the truest sense of the word. It is the same as what we know from the theater: the performance is an interpretation standing between the poetic text and the audience. For the audience there is not the accomplishment similar to reading when one reads something aloud. Here it is oneself who "reproduces," who puts something of oneself into being. When one reads to oneself with one's own voice, which is always how one read in classical times and until the late middle ages, one accomplishes, in truth, only one's own reading and remains with oneself, understanding the text and not an other who reads to you and so has understood the text in his or her own manner. And even then such a reading aloud is not an actual reproducing, but a service to the sovereign who wishes to understand, as if he himself were reading. Therefore, it sounds completely different when one only reads aloud, or recites, or tries as an actor to bring forth the text in a truly new way. Here there are, of course, varying degrees of difference. A brilliant renderer like Ludwig Tieck, especially in reciting Shakespeare, appears to have attained so complete a command of the variations of language that it is like a one-person theater.

What is the situation in an actual theater, the literary theater, that performs a poetic text? There the actors play their parts and more or less follow the interpretation of the director. Only in the ideal case would the director make the whole of his own interpretation of the poem so known to the actors that it would condition the individual roles. Whether with or without the director, with or without the conductor, the play is always an interpretation in its performance, which is given to the audience as a particular accomplishment.

But all this must retreat before the more pressing question that is directed to the "saying" *word*: What permits it to be saying when it is saying in the eminent sense? We are smothered by the whole complexity of literary genera and stylistic differences: epic and drama and lyric and artful prose, naive story, lyric simplicity, mythical, fanciful, instructional, meditative, reflective, historical, and hermetic forms of statement, up to pure poetry. If everything can be literature, i.e., if the word as word speaks in them all with the autonomy described above, then the ideal speaker or reader, whom we were constructing, completely disintegrates and cannot help us with the question of how the word is saying. And we had entrusted him or her with the word's fulfillment. What causes us to hesitate here is certainly not just the multiplicity of what the literary word says nor the different ways it says its word. Rather, it appears above all to be convincing that the word that is able to speak from itself cannot just be characterized by the content to which it points. The same is true in the fine arts and for the same reasons. One who only sees the objects presented in a painting obviously looks right past what makes it a work of art. The "object-less" painters of today are able to make this plain to anyone. The amount of information that is contained, for example, in the reproduction of a flowering plant in a sales catalog, is certainly greater than that in the orgy of colors in a flower painted by Nolde. On the other hand, one can understand from this how a combination of colors that depicts no object can nevertheless be as convincing as a Flemish still-life of flowers. It appears as if hints of meaning, allusions, and possibilities of contact are still at play in our usual object-oriented seeing, but they do not attract attention to themselves, rather they turn our view to the new interconnected structures that make such combinations of colors into a picture, without it being an image. Goal-dominated practical life cannot offer something like that. With the poetic word it appears to be the same. Of course, such structures can never cease to be constituted by words or rudimentary words that have meaning and can never cease to form a unity of complete discourse and meaning, not even as pure poetry. But the interconnected structure, into which they have been molded, can no longer be discovered in the normal direction of meaning found in grammatical-syntactical speech, which dominates our forms of communication.

The extreme situation in modern fine arts appears to me also methodologically helpful in exposing the mistaken orientation toward communicative contents in the question concerning the truth of the work of art—and in our case, of the poetic word. It also preserves us from the opposite extreme of assuming that what one recognizes as presented and said is completely unimportant. For the word that says the most is certainly not a word that forces itself upon us and is conspicuous as a mere sound composition. Saying is not isolated in itself, but says something. If what is said in the saying is totally there, then the word is saying, without something ceasing to be, and yet the word has faded off and was not noticed as itself. If one's attention were primarily drawn to the manner of the saying, to its having been beautifully said, then, as in all grandiloquence, the power of Being in the word and the force of the subject matter in speaking are lost. And nevertheless, that a text speaks from itself must lie in the how of its being said as such, even if it is not the case that the interconnected whole could be the statement while ignoring the intended meaning of the discourse or (in pictures) of what is depicted. It is also precisely the concrete content that is elevated to such absolute presence by the art of the language or fine art, that all relations to a real being or a past being fade—yes, even all distractions concerning how it has been said fade along with it. It appears as if the how of what is said, which certainly still characterizes art before non-art, shows itself only in order to completely supersede itself—even if it is only for an interconnected structure of images or of meaning and sound elements that appear to "say nothing," although itself well composed, as in the modern hermetic lyric poem. The word of poetry is not "more saying" due to the anteriority of form and content: *Ars latet arte sua* [Art lies in its own artistry]. Science using its method can thematize much of a work of art, but not the essence and totality of its "statement."

Let us remain with the word of poetry: What is it that comes to be in everything that it says and when the statement is achieved? I contend: self-presence, the Being of the "There," and not what is expressed as its objective facts. There are no poetic objects, there is only a poetic presentation of objects (varying a well-known Nietzsche saying).

But this is just the first step in examining our problem. Since now the question arises, how does the poetically presented object become poetic through language? Aristotle states the convincing proposition: poetry is more philosophic than history is, and that means, it contains more actual knowledge, more truth, since it does not present things as they occurred but as they could have occurred. So the question is: How does poetry do this? By presenting the idealized instead of the concrete actual? But if so, that is just the puzzle: Why does the idealized appear in the poetic word like the concrete actual—indeed, more actual than the actual and not as the idealized usually does, sickled over with the pale cast of thoughts looking toward universality? And further, why is it that everything that shines forth in the poetic word participates in this transfiguration into the essential (so that one can hardly call it the "idealized")? For this question we need not be bothered by the various differences in poetic speech. Rather, they make the task more precise. What is sought is what transforms all these ways of speaking into texts, i.e. what gives them that "ideal" linguistic identity that permits them to become entirely "text." The broad spectrum of presentational modes, which have developed into literary genre with their own stylistic requirements, may be completely bypassed here. Common to them all is that they are "literature." There has hardly been anything written that is completely without linguistic coherence. There exists only one type of linguistic expression, set in writing, that barely satisfies this fundamental requirement for identity in language, which applies to texts, and that type is such a "text" that its linguistic form is arbitrarily interchangeable, as is sometimes the case in artless scientific prose. One could also say that this occurs where translation—even by a computer—is possible without loss, because the informative function of the text is the only part that matters. Such a case may be an ideal limiting case. It stands in the doorway to nonlanguage and artificial symbolisms, where the choice of symbols is just as arbitrary as its univocality is advantageous (and disadvantageous), inasmuch as there is a stable ordering to the referent. And so, for example, the publication of natural-scientific results occurs in English. But even as a limiting case, it is informative, namely as the zero point of that degree of coherence of the individual word that so admirably belongs to literary texts. In literary texts the word attains its highest coherence with the whole of the text. We will not further develop here the difficult problem of the various degrees of coherence within literature. Their range becomes clear in the nontranslatability that culminates in the lyric poem and especially in "pure poetry." The following remarks wish to reveal only the cohesive matter that binds texts together in their linguistic identity and to demonstrate the "being" of such texts, i.e., the "truth of the word."

It is always linguistic means that bind language back to its own or inner sounding, although they disappear in having given way [*Weggegebensein*] to what is said. And yet, they make possible that this having given way permits the unique evocative energy that characterizes literary texts. Rhythm, a pure embodiment of time, belongs to these means. It is also at home in music, but in language it underlies a specific enlivening relation to meaning and is therefore mostly not limited to exact forms of repetition. It is difficult to say exactly what articulates this poetic rhythm, so that one exactly feels when it has been missed in a recitation. Fundamentally, one can say that it concerns a sensitive balance that is to be maintained between the movement of meaning and the movement of sound. Both movements that always—often not without force—melt together into a single motion, have their own specific syntactical means. In the realm of sound these means extend from extreme forms of temporality (meter) and rhyme to configurations of sounds lying under any level of conscious awareness. In addition, they are more or less thickly permeated with more or less implicit and logically meaningful cohesive matter. What thereby comes to stand and wherein the created coherence of poetic language becomes clearly present, I wish to call, following Hölderlin, the *tone*. The tone is what preserves itself in the whole of the linguistic structure and especially demonstrates its complete power of determination in the disruptive case through a created dissonance. Dissonance is not just a false tone but a tone that infects the whole atmosphere. This is no different in literature than in the life of human society. On the other hand, the preserving tone is such that it holds together the unity of the structure [*Gebilde*] with all the differences and degrees of disruptive moods and thick coherences that are possible. This tone, which preserves itself, binds the elements of speech to one another. It unites the structure as a structure in such a manner that it distinguishes itself from other speech (so that, for example, one can recognize a quotation by its tone). This tone especially distinguishes the structure of literature from other forms of speech that are not "literature" and that do not contain within themselves a concordance [*Stimmigkeit*] but must seek or find it outside of themselves.

In critical questions limiting cases are always the most revealing. For example, the specific way Pindar weaves the victor's laudation into the context of his odes contains an occasional element. But the power and coherence of the linguistic structuring is proven by exactly the fact that this poetic form is able to successfully carry this laudation. It is the same in Hölderlin, who follows Pindar in his hymns. Even more revealing than such occasional parts in a text, are texts where the text itself, and as a whole, refers to a nonlinguistic reality, such as in a historical novel or drama. One cannot be of the opinion that true literary works of art make such references disappear completely. The claim to historical reality echoes unquestionably in the formed text. The subject matter is not simply imagined and this is confirmed by the appeal to poetic freedom, which one grants the poet, to alter the actual relations as they appear in historical sources. On the other hand, just because the poet may alter them—yes, he may imaginatively transgress any boundary set by true historical relationships—proves the degree to which true historical material, even when it is accurately portrayed, is superseded in the poetic creation. This clearly differentiates this case from the artistic elements that may be used in a historian's presentation.

In the same direction lies the important case concerning the extent to which the concepts of rhetoric are applicable at all to the cohesive means that we are characterizing. The artistic means of rhetoric are the artistic means of speech, which in themselves are not originally literature. The concept of the metaphor provides an example for the problematic of this subject matter. One has correctly challenged the poetic legitimacy of the concept of metaphor—of course, clearly not in the sense that one should not use metaphors in poetry (or any other form of speech within rhetoric). What is meant is that the essence of poetic language does not lie in the metaphor and use of metaphors. In fact, poetic language cannot be attained by making nonpoetic language poetic by using metaphors. When Gottfried Benn raises a storm against the poetic use of *as* in poems, he clearly did not misunderstand the exquisite and most expressive comparisons in Homer. Actually, in Homer the comparisons and metaphors are supported by the epic tone of the storyteller to such a degree that he is completely in the same world with them. The poetic irony that lives in the contrasting tension of Homeric comparisons illustrates exactly the perfection of their creation. Therefore, not only in the case of Kafka, where the fictional realism of the story especially motivates it, but in general, one can say that the poetic word has the character of an absolute metaphor (Allemann), i.e., completely opposed to everyday speech. Poetic speech, therefore, has the character of suspension and being supported that comes to be through the neutralization of all positing of being and that causes the transformation into structure [*Gebilde*]. When Husserl uses the expression "neutralizing modification" for this and states that the eidetic reduction "is spontaneously fulfilled" in the case of poetry, he is still describing the situation from the position of the intentionality of consciousness. This is primarily a positional analysis. Husserl thereby understands the language of poetry as a modification of the straightforward positing of being. The relation to the object is to be replaced by the self-relationship of the word, which one can also call self-reference. This is exactly the point that must be rethought. Here again Heidegger's critique of transcendental phenomenology and its concept of consciousness proves to be productive.

What language is as language and what we seek as the truth of the word is not graspable by proceeding from the so-called "natural" forms of linguistic communication. On the contrary, such forms of communication come to be understood in their own possibilities by looking at the poetic mode of speaking. The creation of poetic language presupposes the dissolution of all positivities (Hölderlin), i.e., conventions. This means, the creation of poetic language is the coming to be of language and not the rule-bound application of words and the construction of conventions. The poetic word endows meaning. How the word "comes forth" in a poem is by a new saying power that often lies concealed in its most common usage. To present an example: *Geräusch* in German is just as colorless and weak a word as *noise* is in English, and one does not at all hear along with it that it comes from *nausea,* seasickness. And yet, how it lives anew in George's verse: "Und das Geräusch der ungeheuren See" ["And the noise of the enormous sea"]. It is everything but a poeticizing use that an everyday word experiences here. It remains the everyday word. Here it is, however, so interwoven with relations of rhythm, meter, and vocalization, that it suddenly becomes more expressive and regains its original saying power. *Geräusch* is so strengthened by the word *ungeheuren* that it roars [*rauscht*] again, and by means of the consonance *r* in "*R*ausch" and "-heu*r*en" both become again woven together. These interweavings, at the same time, make the word responsible for itself and thereby frees it for itself. They permit the word to play itself out with other words anew, but clearly not without other relations of meaning coming into play—here, for example, the view of the Nordic coastline and its southern and opposite world.[11] Thereby the word becomes more saying, what is said is more essentially "there" than ever.

Just as I spoke of the ontological valence of the picture, in another context,[12] to mark the extent that what is presented in the picture increases in being by means of the picture, so I would also like to speak of the ontological valence of the word [*Seinsvalenz des Wortes*]. Of course there is difference. It is not so much what is stated, in the sense of the objective content, whose being increases, but being as a whole. Here there exists an essential difference between how the colorful world transforms itself into a pictured work of art and the way the word weighs itself and plays itself out. The word is not an element of the world that can be fitted together into a new order, as color or form are. Every word is itself rather already an element of a new order, and so potentially this order itself and complete. When a word resounds, a whole language is called forth and everything it is able to say—and it knows how to say everything. Therefore, in the "more saying" word, it is not so much the appearance of a single meaningful element of the world as rather the presencing of the whole established through language. Aristotle emphasized seeing because this sense could perceive the most differences; but clearly and still more accurately, hearing is able, by using the path of language, to perceive absolutely all that may be distinguished. The universal "There" of Being in the word is the wonder of language. And the utmost possibility of saying consists in binding its perishing and escaping, and securing the vicinity to Being. The poetic word is distinguished by this vicinity, this presence, not to this or that, but to the possibility of everything. It fulfills itself in itself since it is the "preservation of the vicinity" [*Halten der Nähe*]. And when it is reduced to its sign function, it empties itself becoming an empty word that then requires the communicative and mediating fulfillment. Therefore, one can understand from the self-fulfillment of the poetic word why language can be a means of information, but not the reverse.

The question raised above is to be reconsidered only in passing: Does the mythical word, the saga, and perhaps also the philosophical word, the speculative sentence, actually share the distinguishing characteristic of the poetic word—to be simply and purely saying? This consideration will carry us to the final stage of our presentation. The problem is clear: a saga is neither written nor a text, even when it speaks in a poem and receives the form of a text in the poem. As saga, it has not yet entered the determinacy of poetic-linguistic coherence, but floats here and there on a stream of wisdom of primordial origin, which feeds itself from cultic memory. Nevertheless, it appears sensible to claim "saga" is, in its most distinctive sense, "statement." Of course, the saga is not a statement due to the linguistic organization of its manner of telling a story, but it is statement in its heart, i.e., the calling names, whose secret power of naming encircles the telling of a saga. It appears that the saga, which comes forth in the telling, lies concealed in the names. This is corroborated by the fact that the *name* is always the zero point of translatability, i.e., the separation of saying from what is said. For what is a name other than the final consolidation in which Dasein listens to and heeds itself? Just this is the name, that one or another listens to it—and the proper name, as what one is and wherein one fulfills oneself.[13] So also the word of poetry is self-fulfilling—and stands so, as before its self-development in the discourse of the thinking word. To be "in the word" is the "syntax" of poetry. The word's degree of coherence determines the level of translatability (see I. A. Richards).

The extent to which the philosophical statement is such a "saga" will not be considered here in detail but just remarked upon with respect to the "speculative sentence." Its structure is analogous to the self-reference that actually belongs to the poetic word. Hegel, in fact, described the essence of the speculative sentence in a completely analogous manner. In this he was not primarily concerned with only his own dialectical method, but with the language of philosophy itself, inasmuch as it exists in its authentic possibilities. He demonstrated that in the speculative sentence, although speech naturally picks out the predicate that is attributed, as an other, to the subject, this act is disrupted at the same time and suffers a "reaction."[14] Thinking finds in the predicate nothing besides the actual subject itself. In this way the "statement" returns to itself and this constitutes, for Hegel, philosophical discourse: the exertion of the concept holds to its "statement" by dialectically developing the aspects within itself. This means, however, that it always advances only deeper into the "statement." That philosophy does not advance but seeks a return on all of it paths and detours, is true not only for Hegel and his dialectical method. The limit of translatability that characterizes the interwovenness of the saying with what is said, is also quickly reached here.

We termed the saying-being of the word the "preservation of the vicinity." We saw that neither this nor that determinate content of speech is near, but vicinity itself is. This is certainly not limited to the work of art in words, but is true for all art. "The silence of the Chinese vase," the stillness and perplexing peace that flows to one from any convincing artistic structure [*Gebilde*], says, to speak with Heidegger, that truth "is set to work" here. Heidegger has demonstrated to us that the truth of the work of art is not the logos in its having been stated, but rather and at the same time, a That and a There, that stands in the opposition to the revealing [*Entbergen*] and the sheltering [*Bergen*]. The question that guided us here was how this specifically occurs in the case of the work of art in words—where clearly the sheltering in the "structure" of art already presupposes the being-in-language and the being-in of being in language. The limit of translatability indicates exactly how far the sheltering in the word reaches. In its final concealment [*Verborgenheit*], it is the sheltering [*Bergende*]. Only one who is at home in a language is able to experience the self-preserving and self-determining statement of the poetic word, which secures another being-at-home in the primordially familiar. But, who is at home in a language? It appears that what modern research calls "linguistic competence" refers more to the not-being-at-home of the speaker, to the unlimited use of speech—and that is already its demise.

For that reason it appears to me that the poetic word has an additional characteristic, distinguishing it from all other works of art. Not only does the breathtaking vicinity of all art belong to it, but it must and is able to preserve this vicinity, that means, to stop the withdrawing. For speaking [*Reden*] is ex-pressing [*Sich-Äußern*] and escapes itself. The poetic word can also never cease becoming discourse (or stuttering) in order to continually and again play out its possibilities of meaning. How different the tone stands in the system of tones! How the picture or building occupies its place! In the poetic word's holding to itself and pre-serving itself, the word endures, I would say, and that means, it achieves its highest possibility. The word fulfills itself in the poetic word—and enters into the thinking of the thinker.

PART 3

ON DIALOGUE AND
PHRONESIS

10

Toward a Discursive Logic: Gadamer and Toulmin on Inquiry and Argument

P. Christopher Smith

My task in this paper will be to develop a logic of deliberative discourse by building upon the theory of question and answer that H.-G. Gadamer works out in his *Wahrheit und Methode*,[1] and upon the advances Stephen Toulmin has made in elaborating what he calls a practical logic, a logic, that is, which does not proceed *more geometrico*, as does traditional formal logic, but instead reflects schematically how we actually do argue in the various practical contexts in which we ordinarily have occasion to argue and think things through.[2] Both Gadamer and Toulmin respond to the fact that in reasoning about ethical, legal, and political matters the standard syllogistic inference or demonstration is for the most part inapplicable. I will contend here that in proposing alternatives to it Gadamer and Toulmin complement each other. Each explores dimensions of reasoning that the other had neglected.

For in his elaboration of the consequences of Heidegger's ontology (and anti-ontology) for a theory of interpretation, and in his careful expositions of Plato's and Aristotle's conceptions of how language works, Gadamer has given us indispensable pointers regarding the abstraction in traditional formal logic and its consequent inadequacy as a paradigm for practical reasoning. However, it was never Gadamer's purpose to put another logic of ordinary, concrete argument and dis-

P. CHRISTOPHER SMITH

cussion in its place. Toulmin, on the other hand, working out of the school of ordinary language analysis, has made an excellent start at providing just such a concrete practical logic, but, lacking any of Gadamer's familiarity with the questions Heidegger raises about the priority given to mathematic being and knowing in Western metaphysics, he falls short of the radical break with traditional logic that he wishes to effect.[3]

Put another way, one could say that in taking jurisprudence as his starting point and paradigm Toulmin does indeed succeed in moving logic from abstract mathematic reasoning back to the realm of concrete practical rhetoric. But Toulmin is not radical enough. Despite the introduction of challenges and questions by a second voice into his descriptive account of reasoning, in the end its logical form, even in his exemplary forum of law, remains that of standard monological demonstration, or what Aristotle calls an *apodeixis*. In Toulmin reasoning is never fully recognized as the dialogue of question and answer that any dialectical and rhetorical speaking, especially in law, in fact presupposes even when it appears to be reasoning syllogistically.

For Toulmin does not see that, as opposed to the mathematic beings and subject matters of apodictic logic, the beings and subject matters of jurisprudential reasoning are never formulable in secured, indubitable *statements* from which one might infer conclusive conclusions. He does not see that, on the contrary, jurisprudential reality or being is inevitably dubitable and hence inevitably to be formulated first in *questions*. He does not see that since jurisprundential reasoning is about things that "are" susceptible of being otherwise (Aristotle: *ta endechomena allos echein*), it always begins, not with an assertion or statement, "*X* is so," but with a question, "Is *X* so or not?" or "*X* is so, isn't it?"

But it is to Gadamer's credit that he makes just this point in giving hermeneutical priority to the question over the answer (see *WM*, 344 ff.). The key to Gadamer's deeper insights regarding the interrogative nature of practical reasoning is, I will contend here, to be found in his development of a theory of *Sich-Verständigen*, or reaching an understanding through discussion. In part, he develops this theory as an extension of Heidegger's explorations of a kind of thought prior to Plato's arithmetical and geometrical paradigm for reasoning. For Heidegger had recognized that the mathematic paradigm has as its object an abstracted, derivative being and reality, the timeless being of static presence, the *aei on*, or what always "is" necessarily and can never have been, nor ever be, otherwise. And he had seen that its methods of reasoning were developed in strict correlation with this abstracted, derivative being. Consequently, if we, with Heidegger, were to get behind mathematic being and reality to the original, prior being it has displaced, we would also, Gadamer maintains, inevitably uncover a different *method* of reasoning; we would uncover a different way (*hodos*) with which (*meth' hou*) to reason about the different truth of this other, prior being and reality. Following out this train of thought, Gadamer's *Truth and Method* proposes *Sich-Verständigen* as just this new, or better said, earlier and eclipsed paradigm for approaching the truths of an earlier premathematic being or reality.

But Gadamer's theory of *Sich-Verständigen* relies not only on Heidegger's recovery of earlier senses of being. In taking seriously the public discourse that Heidegger had tended to dismiss as the mere "idle talk" of the everyday world, he also goes beyond Heidegger and is able to appropriate two Greek ideas that Heidegger had to bypass: Plato's *dialegesthai* or "talking something through," from which the words dialogue and dialectic derive; and Aristotle's *bouleuesthai*, which, though usually translated as "deliberating," means more literally, "taking counsel (*boule*)." I wish to begin here with a consideration of Gadamer's appropriation of each of these Greek words in order to establish how he has enriched Heidegger with recourse to them. Then we can proceed to apply Gadamer's insights to Toulmin's schema of practical logic, thereby remedying at least some of its deficiencies.

I

To be sure, we can say, following Heidegger, that Plato only prefigures modern mathematic reasoning insofar as he seeks to lift our thinking beyond the ambiguity of ordinary words and names (*onomata*) and to raise it to pure, univocal concepts or ideas that are what they are in clear distinction from what they are not. And Gadamer himself says precisely this in his discussion of the *Cratylus* (*WM*, 383f.). However, he also points out that as much as Plato would seem to want to turn the mind's eye to a univocal mathematic idea that cannot ever be other than it is, to a "justice itself," for instance, that clearly and distinctly is not "injustice" and is never to be confused with "injustice," Plato acknowledges nonetheless that in actually talking something through we human beings never do attain to such perfectly clear and distinct ideas. In *our* reasoning, even in the "finest of human arguments" (*Phaedo* 85c), the confusion of what something is with what it is not is inevitable and insurmountable. (See *D*, 99ff. on the distortion in all the human "means" of our knowing something.) As opposed to a god, any understanding we reach is thus occluded and indistinct, and any felicitous outcome (*euporia*) of a discussion is at the same time also a dead-ending (*aporia*) in impenetrable perplexity and confusion (*D*, 119; *Philebus*, 15c). Hence in "fleeing" to the *logoi*, to what is said in arguments, and in turning away from *phainesthai* and *physis*, away from things fading in and out in nature (*Phaedo*, 99e), Plato, contrary to what Heidegger argues, does not leave behind the "more original" oscillation of concomitant being and not-being (see *IGPAP*, 15). For given the "weakness of our arguments" (*he atheneia ton logon*), grasping something and missing the point are inevitably simultaneous in any human understanding; in the realm of thought and reasoning, the simultaneity of a thing's presence to mind and its lapsing out of view remains as basic as it is in our experience of nature (see *D*, 104). Thus in Plato the "earlier" and "more inceptive" Aristotelian *physical* conjunction of *eidos* and *steresis*, of the form and the privation of it, is preserved *logically* in our reasoning and arguments, preserved, that is, in the *logoi* to which Plato flees in abandoning physical philosophy.

Granted, the paradigm for Plato still remains the insight of a geometrician who sees clearly what a circle per se is and is not, and who will, accordingly, no longer be misled by physical instances of circular things that appear to have something straight or square about them, e.g., Gorgias's drawings in the sand, into thinking that a square can be constructed equal in area to a given circle. But precisely as discussion in contrast to demonstration, as *dialegesthai* in contrast to *apodeixis*, all of Plato's dialogues make plain that arithmeticians and geometricians alone can perfect this project of establishing clear ideas in distinction from all that they are not, and perfect it only in regard to mathematic beings, which alone are the proper subject of mathematic thinking. In practical and ethical matters, which are the appropriate subject matter of dialectical discussion, no such wisdom is attainable. Here human *philosophia*, not divine *sophia*, is our lot, seeking and inquiring after wisdom, not attaining to it (*IGPAP*, 176).

We discover an insight correlative to this one in Aristotle's conception of *bouleuesthai*, which Gadamer translates as *Mitsichzurategehen* (see *WM*, 304f. on giving counsel [*boule*, *Rat*]). At the beginning of Book VI of the *Nicomachean Ethics* (1139a4f.) Aristotle distinguishes between two kinds of reasoning, one with which we "contemplate those things whose first principles are not susceptible of being otherwise than they are, and one with which we contemplate things that are susceptible of being otherwise." Aristotle concludes that we must distinguish, accordingly, between two different rational capacities, one to be called scientific and the other to be called both calculative and deliberative, insofar as *logizesthai,* calculating and reckoning discursively, and *bouleuesthai,* deliberating or taking counsel, amount to the same thing. And in the *Rhetoric* (1357a23f.) Aristotle points out that rhetorical reasoning—precisely because it is not science but *bouleuesthai,* taking counsel, about actions to be chosen or shunned—cannot be reasoning by science's demonstrations of necessary conclusions from necessary premises. Rather it will be reasoning by enthymemes, whose premises, unlike those in demonstration, will not be necessary but only likely, and whose conclusions will consequently also be "susceptible of being otherwise" and, hence, inconclusive. For the political, legal, and ethical subject matters under discussion in rhetoric, namely the good and the bad (*to sympheron* and *to blaberon*), the right and the wrong (*to dikaion* and *to adikon*), and the decent and the despicable (*to kalon* and *to aischron*) are always capable of "being" the other way, always capable of actually not being the way we reckon they are. *Bouleuesthai,* then, which by definition concerns just those things that can be otherwise than they appear to us to be, is the only kind of reasoning appropriate to our concrete affairs. Later on we will need to pursue just how this deliberative reasoning that proceeds from variable premises to inconclusive conclusions differs in its structure from demonstrative reasoning, for it is precisely the logic of the former that we are seeking here. Let us remark at this point only that Aristotle equates such "taking counsel" with *inquiry* (*skepsis*), and evidently, then, we will be looking for a logic of the dialogue of question and answer— even when this dialogue is the soliloquy of the soul taking counsel with itself.

Now if, following Gadamer, we combine Platonic "talking something through" with Aristotelian "taking counsel," we obtain these results: in the first place, monological mathematic demonstration (*apodeiksis*) emerges as a distortion of the original dialogical process of *dialegesthai* and *bouleuesthai* or, to use Gadamer's expression, of *Sich-Ver-ständigen,* of coming to an understanding of something in a verbal exchange. In original, premathematic reasoning the reckoning of any one person is limited by his or her perspective. For far from being a spectator's theoretical overview of the whole from some theoretical, "cartological" vantage point above it, his or her view in argumentative practice is from down among the things and along side them and is thus one-sided. People who engage in taking counsel have limited horizons beyond which they cannot see at first. Hence an advance in understanding presupposes that something is heard and learned from another who

P . C H R I S T O P H E R   S M I T H

sees things from a different angle, and that two or more perceptions come to augment each other in what Gadamer calls a fusion of their horizons (see *WM*, 289f. on *Horizontverschmelzung*). Put another way, originally in any reasoning about something *none of us yet has present in mind the answer to the open question, rather it is always absent and still to be reached in conjoint inquiry.* (Again, see *WM*, 344f. on the priority of the question over the answer.)

To see why this is so we need only return to Heidegger and to consider the different being or reality of the different things we talk about in our different kinds of discourse. In the discourse of mathematic demonstration what is, is tenselessly and statically, is with no is-not attaching to it. A mathematic circle, the circle of a geometrician, is what it is; and it is not getting to be a circle from a time when it *was not* a circle and is not ceasing to be a circle at a time when it will *not be* a circle any longer. A geometrician's circle can never not be a circle; it is self-identical and the law of noncontradiction holds for it.

But in our premathematic, original experience of reality and being, what is and what is not are indissociable; hence anything we can say about something is bound to be contradictory. Poets, Shakespeare for one, know something about this:

> O brawling love! O loving hate!
> O anything of nothing first create!
> O heavy lightness, serious vanity!
> Misshapen chaos of well-seeming forms!
> Feather of lead, bright smoke, cold fire, sick health!
> Still-waking sleep, that is not what it is!
> (*Romeo and Juliet*, I, i)

Shakespeare has hold of an original oxymoronic truth of things here that geometricians, arithmeticians, and mathematic logicians systematically seek to suppress and escape.

It follows that original being in which being and not being are concomitant can only have its appropriate logos, not in a statement or proposition that asserts that something is so, but in a question that asks whether something is so or is not. *Ultimately original, premathematic being is expressible interrogatively and not declaratively.* To declare or, with Toulmin, to "claim" that something simply *is* the case is to falsify its reality, for in original, premathematic experience, whatever something is, is never sufficiently established for any one of us to state certainly and definitively what it is. Rather it is always still so opaque, so withheld from our knowledge of it and absent, that we must somehow say that it might not be what it seemingly displays itself to be. And this we do by *asking* one another in *dialegesthai* and *bouleuesthai* what the case is. The truth here can be expressed only in the *question*, "Is it or isn't it?"

I point this out because, as noted previously, Toulmin, by turning to legal argument as the paradigm instead of reasoning *more geometrico*, does succeed in returning logic and argument from the theoretical and mathematic to the practical and rhetorical. What he fails to see, however, is that in so doing he has in fact gotten only part way back to the origins of our reasoning in *dialegesthai* and *bouleuesthai*. As we will see momentarily, the pattern of analysis he proposes does include questions, but, significantly, these do not come first. First in his analysis of the logic of reasoning is the "claim" an advocate makes, and only second are the questions that it engenders like "What reasons do you have for saying that?" Hence, in the end, rather than looking behind rhetoric, as Plato does, to its origins in the question and answer of *dialegesthai*, he faces the other way, and while continuing to look to the canons of demonstrative logic as the ultimate standard, he adapts legal rhetoric in such a way as to keep it a form of *apodeixis* or demonstration.

Our task and question thus comes down to this: What sort of logical structure can we find for successful *dialegesthai* and *bouleuesthai*? What would an interrogative dialogical logic look like as opposed to the monological logic of demonstration? Let us turn now to Gadamer for the general answers he gives to these questions concerning the procedure of successful discursive reasoning. And after that let us examine the specific pattern of reasoning Toulmin proposes to see how close it actually comes to the structure of inquiry and interrogative argument Gadamer has indicated and, given the things we have learned from Gadamer, what modifications it might require.

II

Rather than beginning with a statement for which grounds are to be adduced or from which consequences are to be inferred, in the procedure of reasoning as inquiry and reaching an understanding (*Sich-Verständigen*), Gadamer tells us, a question must first be opened up—a real question, that is, and not a rhetorical one that presupposes its answer and thus already concludes a discussion, already closes it off, before it has begun (*WM*, 346). This is not to say that an interrogative argument will begin as argument does in Descartes, by placing *all* things in question (. . . *omnia dubitandum est*). The initial open question cannot be universal and unfocused in this way. Rather, while leaving tacit background assumptions in place and *un*questioned, it must delimit the horizons of a "determinate indeterminacy," of a particular and definite question that has come up (*WM*, 346).

The inevitability of this requirement is made clear by two kinds of misplaced questions that fail to meet it, the senseless question and the skewed question (*WM*, 346; *HD*, 52, fn. 13). The first cannot be pursued at all, for it lacks all direction and definition. Hence it disrupts the discussion and plunges us back into the void of sheer indeterminacy and confusion. Here the only response can be, "I don't see what you are getting at," which might prompt the interlocutor to give the question direction by narrowing and defining it. The skewed question, on the other hand, could be pursued, but if it were, it would lead the discussion astray and take the discussants outside the horizons of the actual issue that a well-put question would delimit. The senseless question is pointless, not to any point at all, and the skewed question is not to *the* point but to another. So first in any argumentative procedure a question must be opened up and properly delimited.

In the next "logical" step, says Gadamer, a felicitous argument proceeds to *decide* the open question. Deciding a question, Gadamer tells us, "is the way to knowledge" (*WM*, 346). The model here is jurisprudence, which, Gadamer says, decides an open question that hangs in the balance between yes and no (*WM*, 346). Of course, jurisprudence, *dikaste phronesis*, is only a special case of prudence or *phronesis* in general, which is to say, of "taking counsel" under the guidance of practical reason about something that can be one way or the other, and then coming to a decision about it. In legal matters that decision has the form of a *krisis* or judgment; in ethical and political matters it has the form of a *pro-hairesis* or choice in which one of the two contrary answers, "Yes, we should do this" and "No, we should not do this," is to be "taken over" the other (*pro-haireton estin*) (see *WM*, 300; *IGPAP*, 109–10, 122; and *EN*, 1113a 10ff.).[4] Either kind of decision will result from the grounds (*Grunde*) for one side outweighing the grounds for the other (*WM*, 347; *IGPAP*, 109). Hence the proper way to reach a decision will be by advancing of grounds both for and against each of the conflicting proposals advocated.

As his example of this procedure Gadamer takes scholastic argument by *pro* and *contra*, which, he says, displays the original "connection of scientific knowledge with dialectic, i.e., with answer and question"

(*WM*, 347). For knowing, he contends, always means entertaining contrary possibilities: "knowledge can only be had by one who has questions, but questions contain within themselves the contrary yes and no, this way or otherwise" (*WM*, 347). As in a court of law, any decision or judgment reached must result from hearing both sides of the question, both the *pro* and *contra*, the "Yes it is" and "No it isn't." Far from being stated as a "claim" at the beginning, the answer is always still to be arrived at, and the question cannot be begged by the ones who are to judge presuming to have answered it already.[5]

Now in a remarkably similar way Toulmin too rejects any mathematic logic as a paradigm and takes jurisprudence instead for his paradigm (*UA*, 43). For, he says, as opposed to abstract mathematic logic, actual logic

> is concerned with the soundness of the claims we make—with the solidity of the grounds we produce to support them, the firmness of the backing we provide for them—or, to change this metaphor, with the sort of case we present in defence of our claims. . . . Logic (we may say) is generalised jurisprudence. (*UA*, 7)

And "our subject," Toulmin adds, "will be the *prudentia*, not simply of *jus*, but more generally of *ratio*" (*UA*, 8). Here too, then, we are in the realm of that special kind of reasoned argument, of *ratio* or of logos, that Aristotle calls deliberation, argument guided by *prudentia* or *phronesis* and leading to a *decisio*, i.e., to either a *krisis* or *prohairesis*. And unlike mathematic arguments, the arguments that concern Toulmin start with an as yet indeterminate matter, an issue still contested. They do not start, that is to say, with what is already settled; rather, as Aristotle had put it, and Gadamer following him, they start with what could either be this way or that. For unlike axioms and the indubitable *archai* or *principia* of mathematic reasoning, "claims," the starting point in Toulmin's schema, may *or may not* stand up under cross-examination. Whether they do or do not, depends on the grounds that can be advanced for and against them. Hence, even though Toulmin's proposed procedure would start with a claim, which prima facie has the form of a statement or answer, it is clear that behind and before the claim lies a question that is still open. After all, if the claim were as settled as it claims to be, no case would need to be made for it.

Furthermore, and significantly for our concerns here, Toulmin points out that if we were to seek a universal logical form for all kinds of actual arguments, the sort of form, that is, which mathematic logic seeks and which would correspond to actual arguments in the way that plane figures in geometry correspond to the actual practice of surveying, we will inevitably be disappointed (*UA*, 186). Instead, arguing much as Aristotle does in criticizing the Platonic ideas, Toulmin asserts that there is no universal form of argument, rather there are only particular arguments relative to their particular fields. And these have only a *structural analogy* to each other. Just as Aristotle replaces Plato's idea of being with a structural *analogia entis*, or analogy of particular beings in their development from potentiality to actuality (see *IGPAP*, 152–55; *AM*, 49), and just as he replaces Plato's idea of the Good with the structural analogy of the virtues insofar as they are parallel in maintaining the mean between the extremes of deficiency and excess in a feeling, Toulmin replaces the supposedly universal logical form of valid argument with *analogous procedural rules* (*UA*, 14–15, 255–56). Keeping in mind, then, that each "forum" of reasoning, as Toulmin calls it, will have its own due process and goals, let us turn to Toulmin's analogical schema of the proper "stages" of reasoning, the "layout," as he calls it.

III

To begin with, he says, (1) a *claim* is to be advanced (*UA*, 11f.; *IR*, 29f.). But a claim turns out to be a claim only if a particular language game is being played with its special rules or procedures. For one thing, a claim is a claim only if it speaks to a contested issue. For as we have just observed, one does not bother to claim something that is already settled and no longer open to question. The statement, for instance, that "Socrates is mortal" turns out to be simply a description and not a claim at all if nobody would contest it. Indeed, like this one, most of the examples used in standard propositional logic fail as claims and fall flat because they are either so patently true that nobody would contest them or so patently false that nobody would make them, and herein lies the key to why propositional logic seems so contrived and irrelevant as a theory of actual argument: propositions are declarative statements that in the very way they are put forward foreclose on any questionability. But in order to function effectively in the language game of actual argument, a claim, in contrast to a proposition, must be open to question. It must provoke (2) a question, namely, "What do you have to go on?" or "What reasons do you have for saying that?" and it fails as a claim if it does not (see *IR*, 5f.). Next this question draws the answer that, by the rules of the language game of argument, says Toulmin, any claimant must be prepared to give, namely (3) a *ground* or reason in support of his or her claim: "Because Socrates is a man"—to take this usefully inappropriate example a step further (see *IR*, 37f. on "grounds"; and *UA*, 13, 98–99 on "data").

In the next "stage" in Toulmin's analogical schema or "layout" the ground advanced may now draw (4) yet another question: "What does that have to do with it?" (see *UA*, 17, 94f.). In answer to this question the claimant must then provide (5) a general principle, a rule, or law, which Toulmin calls a *warrant*, e.g., "All men are mortal" (see *UA*, 98–99; *IR*, 45ff.). But this too can always provoke (6) yet another question concerning its validity or force: "Why do you think that?" In answer to this we provide (7) what Toulmin calls the *backing* (*UA*, 102; *IR*, 61f.), i.e., some authority or source, in this case presumably a piece of collective wisdom like "We all know that everybody dies." We see, then, that given a real example concerning something that really could be this way or that, for instance, the claim, "General Motors will show a profit next quarter," not only the claim, but each of the links in the chain of argument supporting it are, with the exception of whatever happens to be the last, still in question, and even the last could always be called in question if the parties did not tacitly agree to let it stand. (Though Toulmin himself seems not to acknowledge it, one could always demand backing for the backing for the backing, ad infinitum.)

However, when Toulmin finally provides his schematization of these "stages" (1–7), he deletes the questions (2,4,6), and, in my view, with this omission he begins to forfeit much of the new ground he has won. For example, on page 64 of *An Introduction to Reasoning* we find only:

Facts about the enactment and
judicial history of the relevant
statutes and rulings

(the Backing)

provide the foundation of

facts about the present case	The statue or precedent operative in this case	Verdict in this case
(*Ground*)	(in accordance with the *Warrant*)	(supports *Claim*)

To Toulmin's credit we should note that despite his failure to maintain the priority of the questionable in practical reasoning there are still some important ways in which he has indeed gotten behind demon-strative logic by putting things the way he does. For in ordering the answers as he has, the emphasis, quite in contrast to Aristotle's theory of *apodeixis* in the *Analytics*, is not at all on intuitively certain *archai, princip-ia* or general principles from which to rigorously demonstrate equally certain conclusions (compare *Posterior Analytics*, II, 19). Indeed, the war-rant, or what would be the major premise of a proper syllogism, e.g., "All men are mortal," is largely incidental and may in fact never be intro-duced at all since, as Toulmin shows, any argument in ordinary discourse need proceed no further than giving a ground when that ground pro-vokes no further question. In this case we would have precisely what Aris-totle calls the enthymeme, which is distinguished, on the one hand, by the frequent omission of what would have been the major premise in a full syllogism and, on the other, by the mere likelihood of its one premise and consequent inconclusiveness of its conclusion. For his part, Toulmin speaks of the continuing "questionability" of the claim even after acceptable grounds are advanced for it. Toulmin, accordingly, has taken us into the realm of what Aristotle calls the *eikos logos* or probable argument. For in effect the open question that occasions the claim always remains open, not closed off, not con-cluded. Even apparently final decisions for the claim, "Yes, it is so" or "No, it is not so," are in fact subject to appeal and revision: the "case" is never really closed and can always be reopened. (That this is so is further underscored by Toulmin's introduction of modal qualifiers, "possibly," "probably," "perhaps," "quite likely," and possible rebuttals, "unless," "barring," "save," and the like, that as a rule must be attached to any conclusion drawn [see *IR*, 85ff., 95 ff.; *UA*, 101].)

Having said this, however, we must also note that Toulmin slips back into the patterns of demonstration (*apodeixis*) after all. For in delet-ing the questions from his schematization he has failed to penetrate the monological facade of argument and to uncover behind it the interrog-ative, dialogical structure of "talking something through." We must now ask what Toulmin's "layout" would look like if he had not abandoned his initial insight that argument is fundamentally interrogative. How would it have to be modified? For the answer we can return to Gadamer.

For Gadamer has suggested that we might best look to the struc-ture of scholastic argument, say in Aquinas, for our paradigm. And indeed, if we examine any of the arguments in the *Summa Theologica*, for example, the first thing we see is that Aquinas starts precisely not from a claim but from a *questio*, a delimited question that focuses subsequent questions in such a way as to keep them from being irrelevant or skewed but that remains an open question nonetheless; in other words he starts from a question whose answer, like the subjects of Aristotle's *bouleuesthai*, could be this way or that and is not necessarily one way or the other.

Consequently, in response to this question and in sharp contrast with any *apodeixis*, we have not one but two opposite answers simultaneously put into play: "Yes, *p* is the case," *and* "No, *p* is not the case." After all, any real question, say Hamlet's "To be or not to be?" leads to entertaining *both* of the contradictory answers to it. Aquinas thus shows us that Toulmin's "claim" not only starts too far along but, what is more important, cuts the argument in half. The jurisprudential model, which is Aquinas's too, is in fact abridged by Toulmin, who in his schema does not succeed in maintaining the structure of *dialogical* advocacy of the two contradictory claims leading ultimately to an always provisional decision for one or the other.

If we were to start not with a claim but, as Aquinas actually does, with an open question, and were to continue with not one but both answers to it, we would get the modifications of Toulmin's analogical "layout" of an argument:

We begin with (1) a delimited *open question*: "Is p the case or isn't it?"
This draws in answer to it two contrary *hypotheses* (not "claims"):
(2a) from party *A*, "No, *p* is not the case, right?"
and
(2b) from party *B*, "Yes, *p* is the case, is it not?"
The first *hypothesis* (2a) now draws (3) the question from party B in response to party *A*'s hypothesis:
"What reason do you have for saying that?"
which draws from party *A* (4) the *ground*:
"Because *x*," and, then,
(5) the *claim*, "Therefore, *p* is not the case."
(This argument leading to *A*'s *claim* may have also addressed:
(6) the question from *B* for a *warrant*, "What has *x* to do with *p*?"
with (7), a general principle, "Whenever *x* then *p*,"
and
(8) the question from *B* for *authority* (not "backing"), "Who says so?"
with
(9) "So and so says so."
In response to (5), party *A*'s *claim*, we now get:
(10) party *B*'s *refutation*, "I answer: 'No, not *x*,'"
and
(11) party *B*'s *counterclaim*: "Therefore, *p* is the case."

P. CHRISTOPHER SMITH

This counterclaim now draws from party *A* the question,

(12) "What reason of your own do you have for saying that *p* is the case?"

which draws in response:

(13) party *B*'s own *ground*,

"U," and

(14) the reassertion of party *B*'s *counterclaim*: "Therefore, p is the case."

What might this reformulation of the stages of argument have accomplished? To begin with, let us note that by extending Toulmin's application of ordinary language analysis to the steps of *dialogical* argument I have, like Toulmin, not tried to identify some fixed formal structure. Instead I have tried to clarify what each of these stages actually "does," i.e., how each functions as a proper move in the language game of argument that is being played here. Hence the initial response to the open question is to be distinguished, as a tentative *hypothesis*, from the same assertion later, which only *after* its defense, is reasserted as a *claim*. Furthermore, the concluding claim of the argument must, in accordance with the dialogical structure of the process, be recognized as a response to the opposed claim and hence as a *counterclaim*. For, on the whole, the dialogical origins of argument are suppressed in Toulmin's schema, which fails to make explicit that not just grounds, warrants and backing, but claims too are offered in *response*. Furthermore, Toulmin's schema fails to make explicit that, whereas grounds, warrants, and backing are offered in response to challenges, a claim is made in response to something more than a challenge, in response, namely, to the contradictory claim.

It needs to be emphasized in this regard how much of any argument is in refutation of the opposed point of view. In this, traditional jurisprudential rhetoric, which includes a *refutatio* in its standard order (see Quintilian, *Institutio Oratoria* III, 9), represents the origins of argument in dialogue more clearly and accurately than Toulmin's schema does. To be sure, traces of what is traditionally called refutation can be found where Toulmin introduces "possible rebuttals" in his schema (*UA*, 101–2; *IR*, 95ff.). Significantly, however, Toulmin interprets these "rebuttals" precisely not as counterarguments, precisely not as objections from another party in a bipartite argument, but as eventual *circumstances* that could undercut the single monological argument being made and that must be allowed for within it: "*P unless q.*" This reduction of the *refutatio* is another instance of Toulmin's characteristic tendency to absorb the dialogical in the monological.

Finally, I would note that what Toulmin calls "backing," since it is not itself supported, functions as authority and might better be called that. Not that the authority here must be a person, rather authority refers to whatever premise in the argument must be taken for granted. (Compare Aristotle on dialectical argument from *endoxa* or received opinions, as opposed to apodictic argument from *archai* or intuited first principles [*Topics*, 100a26f.].) Despite his return to the jurisprudential model of argument Toulmin, unlike Gadamer, remains committed enough to the ideals of the "enlightened" reason and "critical" thought that he overlooks, or at least downplays, the inevitable acceptance of inherently questionable things which, as the underpinning and basis for any questioning, are themselves left unquestioned. Any interrogative argument, however critical, must presuppose uncritically what Gadamer calls a *vorläufige Übereinstimmung*, a provisional consensus that itself is not placed in question. (Compare Gadamer's discussion of the necessity of prejudgments and "rehabilitation of authority and tradition" [*WM*, 261f.] and of the "sensus communis" or communal consensus [*WM*, 16f.].) Toulmin does not tell us why, in founding our train of thought, we must stop at the backing, and he does not address its supposed difference in this regard from the other elements of argument, each of which must be contestable and at least potentially in question if it is not to fail at what it is supposed to do.

IV

What, then, have we accomplished? Not everything we set out to, certainly. For even the schema of scholastic argument that I have elaborated here, though truer to the origins of argument in the dialogue of question and answer than Toulmin's schema, still falls short of fully accommodating Gadamer's insights into dialogical, deliberative logic. Indeed, to be completely true to its source in question and answer an argument would have to be viewed, not as *advocacy*, as it is in Toulmin and ultimately in Aquinas as well, but as what Gadamer calls *Gespräch*, namely conversation and discussion. Only in this way could argument and reasoning be explicated as the cooperative process of *Sich-Verständigen*, of reaching an understanding. And for a *Gespräch* to occur, the goal of one "claim" emerging victorious over its contradictory "rival" would have to be abandoned. In its place there would have to be the very different goal of merging the horizons of only seemingly opposed viewpoints in a clarified consensus that neither party had wholly in view to begin with.[6] Here, then, we would have to go behind even scholastic argument, which, though closer to dialogue than mathematic demonstration, is itself still derivative. We would have to abandon the jurisprudential form of "making a case." And we would have to return, as Gadamer ultimately does, to Platonic conjoint dialogical inquiry.

There are indications that Toulmin too feels the need to reconstrue argument and reasoning as dialogical discussion and inquiry issuing in an understanding. For instance, in the second edition of *An Introduction to Reasoning* a new paragraph entitled "Claims and discoveries" is inserted. Here we find,

> Often, one person uses an argument to convince another person about something he himself was clearly convinced of in advance. In these cases, as we put it, the first person makes a *claim* which he then uses the argument to justify or establish. On other occasions, people start off with questions to which they have at first no clear answers, and use argumentation as a way of arriving at answers. . . . Here we shall distinguish between *inquiry*, the kind of reasoning designed to lead to a novel discovery, and *advocacy*, the kind of reasoning designed to support a previous claim. (*IR*, 7).

However, the notions of "inquiry" and "discovery" are quickly dropped in Toulmin's exposition, for the chief concern remains advocacy and the model, consequently, of jurisprudential rhetoric rather than any sort of dialogue. Indeed, the chapter "Claims and Discoveries" (*IR*, 29-35) contains absolutely nothing on discoveries. And when he comes to distinguish among arguments according to the different ways they proceed (*IR*, 271f.), Toulmin again disappoints any hopes that he might provide a true alternative to argument by advocacy. For in proposing argument by "consensus" as such an alternative, he has in mind not a difference in procedure but only in result: whereas arguments by advocacy end in the winner taking all, in arguments by consensus, he tells us, a compromise is negotiated that both contestants "can live with" (*IR*, 274).

There is a fundamental oversight in Toulmin which, I think, accounts for his inability to see the inevitable distortion of discourse in the legal model of argument. If we compare his account of psychiatrists' discomfort in the courtroom (*IR*, 275) with Gadamer's account of everyone's discomfort there (*WM*, 444), we see that what concerns Toulmin is the forced displacement of what the speaker says into a language game and "forum" foreign to it, the displacement, for instance, of something the psychiatrist seeks only to diagnose as healthy or sick, into the framework of judging what is legally right or wrong. What concerns Gadamer, on the other hand, is the much wider and more fundamental suppression of "the whole of language" in which and out of which any speaking takes place, and from which anything anyone ever says is uprooted when it is reduced to testimony. The real problem for Gadamer is not at all that the speaker was unable to say what he or she intended to say. To put things this way gets them wrong from the beginning, for on Gadamer's understanding of argument we cannot start with a supposed agent speaker whose spontaneous "speech acts" might be inhibited by the conventional rules of the particular argument game being played. Rather we must start with the "condition of the possibility" of all speaking in the first place, the shared medium and center (Gadamer: *Mitte*) of speech and language itself. For in the strict sense, individuals do not do the speaking, rather it is the language itself that speaks in what we say. Consequently, the problem with the courtroom is that insofar as the witness's words are uprooted there from the generative "whole of language," from which alone they derive their full sense, these words can no longer say what they mean.

If we grant Gadamer's reversal of agent and patient in the speech event—grant that we do not speak, rather things either get said or fail to get said—it follows that it is not enough to have added into the analysis of what happens here a second "agent speaker" in response to whose individual "speech acts" the argument is then said to have been generated. Rather somehow in our schematization of argument it must be acknowledged that speakers do what they do and say what they say not as individual agents engaging in speech acts but as participants in a language community in which they live, and by virtue of which alone they can come to an understanding about something. As "talking something through," our "taking counsel," is more than a "transaction" between two indivdual agents trying to strike a deal in the interest of each (cf. *IR*, 10f., "Reasoning as a Critical Transaction"). In fact, it is not bipartite but tripartite: it is the interplay of two in the community of the ongoing language event taking place between them. Argument, original argument, is, as Gadamer shows us, "Sich-Verständigen *in einer Sache*," reaching understanding in a matter, and from within the language in which this matter comes to be clear for us. In truth neither you nor I are the agent here, rather this third, the shared speech itself, is the agent, what is said and what is meant. To be true to the nature of argument and our experience of it, Gadamer thus recurs to Plato's characterization of the dialogical experience as *to pathos ton logon*, the happening of arguments to us, our undergoing them. (See also *WM*, 306 on our *Zugehörigkeit* or our "belonging-to" any deliberation with a friend.)

It is precisely this dimension of argument and discourse that even the jurisprudential paradigm covers up, insofar as it construes argument in terms of claim and counterclaim each advocated by the individual party as the community-less Hobbesian adversary of the other. Indeed, one of the principal ways in which argument is in fact corrupted is precisely by one or both of the participants in it falling into defense of a "claim" as turf that she or he has staked out against another who would contest it. We should note in this regard page 30 of *An Introduction to Reasoning*, where precisely this adversarial background of the word "claim" is uncritically acknowledged. (On this point Gadamer is far more perspicacious; see his analysis in *D*, 99f. of the ways that insight can be blocked and well-intentioned inquiry devolve into contentiousness and self-assertion.)

Hence, in the end even the emendations I would make in Toulmin's schema of the procedure of deliberative argument are not enough to display the communal, participatory structure of "taking counsel" in "talking something through," not enough to show clearly that the essence of an argument lies, not in our making it as individual agents in competition with each other, but in our following it together where *it* would lead us. Whatever the uses of a logical schema, we must recognize that any attempt to construct a "logic" or schematization of argument, since it requires getting an overview of something that did not lie before each of us and at our disposal but at whose disposal we both are, will have to create a false appearance. In the end, as participants in the language game of argument we simply do not have the overview of it that schematization of it makes it seem that we have (see *WM*, 98 ff., 468 on *Spiel*). Thus *any* "layout"—of a Platonic dialogue, for instance—and not just those that traditional logicians have constructed is bound to be a petrification that falsifies what has actually happened. It will be like the historical reconstruction of a battle after it is over and once all the indeterminacies for those who were caught up in it at the time, have, in retrospect, become determinate and mappable for each.

For only in retrospect is something like an overview possible that would establish some logical sequence of steps in the strategies that apparent individual agents, in pursuing their self-interest, appear to have employed. But for those actually undergoing the experience, and who in reality were lost to themselves, it was not like that. As Plato's *pathos ton logon* makes clear, the truth of any genuine *dialegesthai* and *bouleuesthai* never lies in proving oneself to have been right and convicting the other of having been wrong. A good argument is never won. Rather it ends in the "Oh, now I understand!" said by both of the participants at the provisional close of the language event that was shared between them. For at that time they knew that in reaching an understanding they had both been given something to understand.

11

"You Don't Know What I'm Talking About": Alterity and the Hermeneutical Ideal

Robert Bernasconi

G adamer developed his hermeneutic theory to meet the challenge of the question of how understanding is possible across historical distance. He found the solution in the very place where his predecessors located the problem. On Gadamer's account, temporal distance is not something to be overcome. It does not form a yawning abyss, but, viewed in terms of the continuity of tradition, provides the positive condition of understanding (*TM*, 297; *GW1*, 302). At the time that he was framing his hermeneutic theory, Gadamer rarely posed the parallel question of how understanding is possible across cultural divisions. However, more recently, when looking back on his life's work, Gadamer has judged his account of hermeneutics to be suitable also to this broader task. Typical of such comments are the following remarks made in the course of an interview from July 1986:

> That is the essence, the soul of my hermeneutics: To understand someone else is to see the justice, the truth, of their position. And this is what transforms us. And if we then have to become part of a new worldcivilization, if this is our task, then we shall need a philosophy which is similar to my hermeneutics, a philosophy which teaches us to see the justification for the other's point of view and which thus makes us doubt our own.[1]

Gadamer is no doubt aware of the complex ramifications of any such extension of hermeneutics from the theory of the human sciences to "the human situation in the world in its entirety." His own example of the need for tolerance on the part of the West to the Soviet Union at least has the benefit of showing the kind of issue that is at stake: "Always insisting on human rights, insisting that they must accept parliamentary democracy in order to industrialize fully, that reveals only our own pre-occupations, which do not reflect their history."[2] The purpose of the present paper is not to expose the pitfalls to which such statements seem inevitably to fall prey, and of which Gadamer is, as a philosopher of *phronesis,* most certainly aware: it is never easy to gauge when to speak out and when to keep silent. I shall be concerned for the most part with Gadamer's self-presentation of his hermeneutical theory. Is it the case that Gadamer's theory describes the understanding of alterity as a yielding "in certain limits" to the truth of the other? And, to the extent that he gives such an account, does he succeed in providing a theory that develops the intellectual resources to account for such a phenomenon? When a philosopher gives an account of something, it still does not always mean that he or she can account *for* it. Has this happened here in Gadamer's own bold retrospective evaluation of his work, where, late in the day, he claims that his hermeneutic theory, which was largely developed as a description of how historical distance is bridged within the tradition, becomes an ethical demand in the face of cultural difference?

Conventionally, hermeneutics has represented alterity as a problem to be overcome. Only if one enters the author's world can one understand that author's meaning. Such a hermeneutics has on occasion even imposed the seemingly impossible task of becoming like the author as the way to comprehend his or her words. Gadamer challenges this approach by appealing to the model of dialogue.[3] According to him, in this most familiar experience of daily life, understanding takes place without any such requirements having been met. Understanding is not a matter of reliving the other's experiences or of "getting inside" someone else as if one had to transpose oneself into another person (*TM,* 383; *GWI,* 387). In a profound observation, Gadamer explicitly warns against the case where one's claim to know the Other serves to deprive the Other of his or her legitimacy, just as one can when helping or caring for someone end up simply dominating them (*TM,* 360; *GWI,* 366). Nevertheless, both dialogue and the interpretation of texts are concerned with reaching agreement about the matter at hand: "Just as each interlocutor is trying to reach agreement on some subject with his partner, so also the interpreter is trying to understand what the text is saying" (*TM,* 378;

GWI, 384). Understanding (*Verstehen*) is therefore still conceived by Gadamer as a kind of agreement (*Einverständnis*). It may not be necessary to be of one mind with the other, but the goal is accord concerning the object. In this way it is far from clear whether Gadamer succeeds in freeing himself from the prejudice of representing difference or otherness as a problem to be resolved. This is reflected in his frequent recourse to the concepts of self-recognition and of assimilation in his explication of understanding, at the same time that he acknowledges a positive sense of alterity in the form of the claim that the text makes on its reader. Are these two treatments of alterity two moments of a dialectic? Or do they mark an unresolved conflict at the heart of Gadamer's theory?

I will proceed by exploring Gadamer's attempt to address the puzzles of hermeneutic understanding by appealing to the model of dialogue. Or, more precisely, I shall examine three of the models of dialogue that he uses, arguably the three main ones.[4] That Gadamer favors certain ideas of dialogue and neglects others cannot of itself constitute an objection, as it would if he had set out to classify different ideas of dialogue within an exhaustive theory of dialogue. However, the conceptions of dialogue that he does select tend to have the common feature of diminishing alterity.

It should be said at the outset that dialogue is more than a model for Gadamerian hermeneutics. Gadamer attempts to show that certain characteristics of dialogue, which had hitherto been thought not to apply to our relation to written texts, are indeed present there. This is not new. As he himself reminds us, Schleiermacher already understood hermeneutics to include conversation (*PH*, 23; *GWII*, 236; *TM*, 392; *GWI*, 396).[5] By presenting hermeneutics always with reference to dialogue, Gadamer tries to show that the alleged deficiencies of written texts are illusory. Hermeneutics takes the written tradition from its alienation and restores it to the living present of dialogue (*TM*, 368; *GWI*, 374). Even if the art of dialogue is that of forming concepts and working out a common meaning, whereas hermeneutics is confronted with the rigidity and alienation of writing, the differences between speech and writing are less pronounced in Gadamer than they are traditionally thought to be. In fact, Gadamer's characterization of dialogue is as determined by his conception of writing as the reverse. Most importantly, the written text is exemplary for the restriction of the role of intentions in the analysis of dialogue. Just as in the understanding of written texts we move in a dimension of meaning that bears its own intelligibility in itself, so too in conversation there is no need to go back to the subjectivity of the author (*TM*, 292; *GWI*, 297).

This is apparent from Gadamer's treatment of Plato's dialectic, the most prominent of the three models of dialogue with which I shall be concerned. What Gadamer takes from Plato is not his reference to "the mind of the learner," but his appeal to the word "that can defend itself, and knows to whom it should speak and to whom it should say nothing."[6] When Gadamer construes the task of hermeneutics as returning what is written from its alienation, it must be understood that it is being returned not to the living present of the author or speaker, but to the living present of the interplay between question and answer. As if to emphasize the proximity of hermeneutics and dialogue, Gadamer in one place calls the interplay of question and answer "the hermeneutic character of speech."[7] Gadamer explores this structure in most detail in a section of *Truth and Method* entitled "The Model [*Vorbild*] of Platonic Dialectic." He adopts from Plato's Socrates the idea that the art of asking questions lies not in winning arguments but in persisting with one's questioning in such a way as to preserve one's orientation toward openness (*TM*, 367; *GWI*, 372). One attempts with one's questions to bring something into the open (*TM*, 363; *GWI*, 368–69). The task is not to expose weaknesses in what the other person is saying, but to recognize what is to be said for it, which may involve strengthening the case (*TM*, 367–68; *GWI*, 373). Nevertheless, the openness of the question has its limits. Without a horizon, the question is simply empty. A properly formed question "implies the explicit establishing of presuppositions" (*TM*, 363; *GWI*, 369). It is contrasted with the slanted (*schief*) question, which is a question posed in a misleading way or without any sense of direction, even though there may be a genuine question lurking in the vicinity (*TM*, 364; *GWI*, 370).

The second conception of dialogue that I shall consider attempts to systematize the focus on the question found in the Platonic model. Gadamer identifies R. G. Collingwood as his predecessor in this enterprise. According to Gadamer, Collingwood recognized that "We can understand a text only when we have understood the question to which it is an answer" (*TM*, 370; *GWI*, 376). Here Gadamer insists that it is not so much the interpreter who brings a question to the text, as the text that puts a question to the interpreter. In consequence one's questions to the text should be directed toward finding the question that lies behind what it says directly. Not that this is the end of the matter. "Reconstructing the question, to which the meaning of a text is understood as an answer, merges with our own questioning. For the text must be understood as an answer to a real question" (*TM*, 374; *GWI*, 380). Clearly this introduces the danger of imposing an alien question on a text, but it is better than supposing that understanding is a question of discovering what the author had in mind in writing the text, because at least understanding remains fixed on an issue rather than a person. The meaning of a text cannot be identified with the intentions of its author (*TM*, 292; *GWI*, 297): "Not just occasionally but always, the meaning of a text goes beyond its author" (*TM*, 296; *GWI*, 301). This is the positive meaning Gadamer gives to the claim that one can understand an author better than that author understood him- or herself (*TM*, 192–97; *GWI*, 195–201). Instead of trying to fathom what was in the author's mind, one should engage with the topic being addressed, just as in a conversation one does not so much try to understand the person one is speaking with, but what he or she is saying. When two or more people are engrossed in a conversation, they are bound together by the common subject matter (*TM*, 388; *GWI*, 391).[8] But, of course, insofar as Gadamer believes that the task of hermeneutics is to change the written marks back into meaning, the situation is that "one partner in the hermeneutical conversation, the text, speaks only through the other partner, the interpreter" (*TM*, 387; *GWI*, 391). This is why Gadamer does not understand the hermeneutic conversation as binding interpreter and author together, but as binding interpreter and text (*TM*, 388; *GWI*, 391).

If these two conceptions of dialogue draw attention away from the other human being, whether author or speaker, to the topic being addressed, a third model that derives from the I-Thou relation seems to offer itself as a corrective.[9] Gadamer contrasts three modes of experience of the Thou and in each case considers the corresponding form of hermeneutic experience. The first mode is that where one relates to one's fellow human beings as subjects of inquiry, perhaps under the rubric of a human nature. It is no surprise that Gadamer finds this model inadequate (*TM*, 358; *GWI*, 364). The second way is also ultimately a form of self-relatedness, even though the Thou is acknowledged as a person and not an object that can be taken up within a predictive science. Nevertheless, the Thou is still understood reflectively from the standpoint of the "I," such that it is always the Thou of an "I." It is to this mode of the experience of the Thou that Gadamer assimilates the hermeneutic ideal of understanding the other better than the other understands him- or herself. In an important discussion, Gadamer introduces a third mode where relations to the Thou are marked by openness. Indeed, such openness is said to be the condition for the possibility of any genuine relationship. "I" and Thou belong together in such a way that in the to and fro of dialogue I may find myself accepting things that are against myself. Gadamer writes, "Openness to the other, then, involves recognizing that I myself must accept some things that are against me, even though no one else forces me to do so" (*TM*, 361; *GW1*, 367). In the context of *Truth and Method* this is a strong statement, even if as an account of the alterity of the other it is limited: I admit (*gelten lassen*) something against myself, even if there is no other who urges it (*geltend machen*) against me.

This discussion of openness is especially important because it provides the occasion for Gadamer to relate the idea of openness developed in the context of dialogue to his description of hermeneutic experience. He does so by appealing to the notion of tradition.

> I must allow the tradition's claim to validity, not in the sense of simply
> acknowledging the past in its otherness, but in such a way that it has
> something to say to me. This too calls for a fundamental sort of open-
> ness. Someone who is open to tradition in this way sees that historical
> consciousness is not really open at all, but rather, when it reads its texts
> "historically," it has always thoroughly smoothed them out beforehand,
> so that the criteria of the historian's own knowledge can never be called
> into question by tradition. (*TM*, 361; *GW1*, 367)

It seems that Gadamer allows for some alterity, whether it be that of the claim of the other in dialogue or of the text, but that in both cases the alterity is always, as it were, contained within language as what makes it possible. Gadamer can even write that, as language, the tradition "expresses itself like a 'Thou'" (*TM*, 358; *GW1*, 364). Admittedly, a few pages later, he says the contrary: "a text does not speak to us in the same way as does a Thou" (*TM*, 377; *GW1*, 383). However, the contrast between these two statements is not as sharp as might first appear to be the case. Restored to its context the second serves simply as a reminder that the interpreter must make the text speak. This is accomplished, not arbitrarily, but by posing questions that the text is expected to answer. These expectations are formed by the tradition. "Anticipating an answer itself presupposes that the questioner is part of the tradition and regards himself as addressed by it" (*TM*, 377; *GW1*, 383). It is in this way that the hermeneutics of the text appeals to tradition to render understanding possible without resorting to the model of an alterity that has to be overcome.

The notions of agreement (*Einverständnis*) and, more simply, understanding (*Verständnis*) play a parallel role in the analysis of dialogue that tradition plays in hermeneutics. The language in which specific agreements or disagreements are formulated itself constitutes a form of agreement at a deeper level. The creation of a common language is both the precondition of dialogue and its ultimate fulfillment. "Every conversation presupposes a common language, or better, creates a common language" (*TM*, 378; *GWI*, 384). Common accord is more than openness, and that makes it all the harder to understand what is meant by a common language, which is both the presupposition and the goal of dialogue. A similar tension is found in a formulation arrived at twelve years later in the essay "The Incapacity for Dialogue:" "It is true that understanding is difficult where a common language is lacking. But one already has understanding where a common language is sought and finally found" (*GWII*, 215). The precise meaning of these sentences is unclear, but Gadamer seems to be saying that being agreed on wanting to understand one another is more than a commitment. It is already an understanding and, insofar as it is shared, constitutes a kind of common language.

Nevertheless, the concept of tradition is required to do even more work in the hermeneutic realm than the concept of agreement has to do in the realm of dialogue. Tradition is introduced to explain how it is possible to bridge historical distance insofar as the latter presents an obstacle to understanding. The notion of tradition functions monolithically in such a way as to diminish alterity, as when, for example, in discussing historical research, Gadamer refers to "the unity of the total tradition" (*TM*, 339; *GWI*, 345). Indeed, the problem is more pervasive and it can be traced back to the fact that Gadamer tends to employ the concept of tradition in what is largely a Hegelian manner.[10] I can recognize myself in what appears to be other only insofar as that other is a reflected other, the other of myself. The ambiguity to which this gives rise is reflected in a passage from the essay "On the Circle of Understanding" where one notion of historical research is contrasted with another which Gadamer here identifies as *Wirkungsgeschichte*, a term which is variously translated as "effective history," "operant history," and "history of influence."

> A truly historical way of thinking has also to keep in mind its own historicity. Only then will it give up pursuing the phantom of a historical object, the topic of linearly advancing research, learning instead to recognize in the object the Other of its Own, therewith bringing to recognition the One and the Other. The true historical object is not an object, but rather the unity of the One and Other, a relationship in which the reality of history consists just as much as the reality of historical understanding.[11]

Is the notion of otherness in the phrase "the unity of the One and the Other" sufficiently other to put me radically in question? Or does the phrase "Other of its Own" suggest, on the contrary, that the other is being understood reflectively from the standpoint of the "I"? In *Truth and Method* Gadamer had correlated *Wirkungsgeschichte* with the third of the three kinds of I-Thou relations (*TM*, 361; *GWI*, 367), but it is far from clear whether in this instance it should not be associated with the second mode of the I-Thou.

The indications are, therefore, that Gadamer employs the parallel between dialogue and the hermeneutic text in order to diminish the sense of alterity and thereby maintain his resolution of the problem of historical distance. So, for example, in one complex passage in *Truth and Method* Gadamer introduces the hypothesis that unless we place ourselves within the historical horizon from which tradition speaks, historical understanding will be defeated in its attempt to grasp the significance of what we are seeking to understand. But Gadamer then issues the warning that this attempt to avoid misunderstanding merely courts another danger. This is the point at which he reintroduces the model of dialogue. The parallel danger in respect of dialogue is when one poses questions and listens to someone simply in order to judge their standpoint or horizon. Gadamer offers the examples of the oral examination and the interview that a doctor holds with a patient. He concludes that these are not examples of true dialogue because they are not attempts to reach agreement about the object. To withdraw from the attempt to attain agreement is to exclude the possibility of a meeting or an encounter. It is to exclude the possibility of one's own standpoint being challenged. The corresponding hermeneutical danger arises therefore when, in an attempt to understand a text historically, one excludes the possibility of discovering in that text a valid and intelligible truth. "Acknowledging the otherness of the other in this way, making him the object of objective knowledge, involves the fundamental suspension of his claim to truth" (*TM*, 303–4; *GWI*, 309). However, at this point Gadamer pauses to ask whether the initial characterization of historical understanding was correct. Does it attempt to place itself within an alien horizon? Does the model not assume that horizons are closed? Historical consciousness does not have the task of passing between discreet alien worlds. "Everything contained in historical consciousness is in fact embraced by a single [historical] horizon" (*TM*, 304; *GWI*, 309).[12] In this context Gadamer writes of a "moving horizon," a term which is perhaps less confusing than the more frequently used "fusion of horizons." The fusion of horizons in its primary sense is not to be understood as one horizon, that of the interpreter, coming into contact with another, that of the author of the text, and somehow being fused in an interpretive act. "Understanding is always the fusion of these horizons supposedly existing by themselves" (*TM*, 306; *GW1*, 311). The horizons have no sep-arate existence and Gadamer only talks of a fusion because of the ten-sion that can exist between the historical text and the present.[13]

The conclusion that Gadamer encapsulates in the notion of the fusion of horizons is that it makes no sense to attempt to acquire a spe-cific historical horizon by transposing oneself into that historical situa-tion. One puts oneself in the situation of another by elevating oneself to a higher universality through which one overcomes not only one's own particularity, but also that of the other. Gadamer understands this over-coming of the interpreter's particularity as an important moment in inhibiting the overhasty assimilation of the past to our own expectations of meaning (*TM*, 305; *GW1*, 310). However, by the same token, the oth-erness of the past is at best only an initial appearance which subsequent-ly gives way to familiarity.

> At any rate, our usual relationship to the past is not characterized by dis-tancing and freeing of ourselves from tradition. Rather, we are always sit-uated within traditions, and this is no objectifying process—i.e. we do not conceive of what tradition says as something other, something alien. It is always part of us, a model or exemplar, a kind of cognizance that our later historical judgment would hardly regard as a kind of knowledge, but as the most ingenuous affinity with tradition. (*TM*, 282; *GW1*, 286–87)

The concept of tradition which sustains the hermeneutical process here has the function of reducing the strange or foreign to a moment that is to be overcome.

It is this way of addressing alterity that has led to the charge that Gadamer's dialogue is monological. The same objection has also been leveled at both Hegel and Heidegger for whom the history of philosophy is allegedly reduced to a monologue of reason or of Being, respectively. Indeed, Gadamer himself understands Hegel's dialectic, on which he relies so heavily, as a monologue of thinking (*TM*, 369; *GW1*, 375). The evidence that Gadamer's account of dialogue is itself monological can be found, for example, in his reliance on the idea of assimilation in his explication of the encounter with alterity. So openness always includes "our situating the other meaning in relation to the whole of our own meanings or situating ourselves in relation to it" (*TM*, 268; *GW1*, 273). For Gadamer, the alternative to relating the other person's opinions to that person is relating them to our own opinions and beliefs, as if these were somehow set in advance (*TM*, 385; *GW1*, 391). It is striking in this regard that Gadamer includes thinking, the dialogue one has with oneself, in the art of dialogue (*PA*, 186; *GW*II, 502). More generally, the notion of the fusion of horizons seems fundamentally antagonistic to alterity. But even if Gadamer in his *theory* seems to diminish the moment of alterity, this is possibly because the hermeneutic *experience* from which he starts, and to which he frequently gives testimony, is that of alterity. Perhaps the theory focuses on proximity because it is designed to compensate for alterity, or rather to show how understanding is possible on its basis. There are times when Gadamer's descriptions bring this to the fore:

> Hermeneutics bridges the distance between minds and reveals the foreignness of the other mind. But revealing what is unfamiliar does not mean merely reconstructing historically the "world" in which the work had its original meaning and function. It also means apprehending what is said to us, which is always more than the declared and comprehended meaning. Whatever says something to us is like a person who says something. It is alien in the sense that it transcends us.[14]

So the model Gadamer describes is not exactly monological, because it describes an openness that is ready for the text to say something (*TM*, 269; *GW*I, 273). The text makes a claim and the claim makes a demand (*TM*, 127; *GW*I, 132). No doubt that is why Gadamer considers himself in a position to evoke the philosophical critics of monological thinking, such as Rosenzweig, Buber, Gogarten, and Ebner (*GW*II, 211). However, the question must be posed, especially now that Gadamer has announced this alliance, as to how far he can go in this direction without sacrificing some of the fundamental tenets of *Truth and Method*.

In 1977, in a text that was his contribution to the series *Philosophie in Selbstdarstellungen*, Gadamer goes a considerable way in acknowledging the radical alterity of the partner in dialogue. Openness in conversation means recognizing "in advance the possible correctness, even the superiority of one's conversation partner" (*PA*, 189; *GW*II, 505. Trans. modified). This claim is not unproblematic insofar as the very word Gadamer uses here, *Überlegenheit*, is the same one he employs elsewhere to describe what he means by authority as a dogmatic acceptance: "One concedes superiority in knowledge and insight to the authority, and for this reason one believes that authority is right" (*PH*, 33; *GW*II, 244). It is apparent, therefore, that we are moving into a difficult area, made all the more so by the appeal to the hermeneutic notion of the authority of tradition (*TM*, 280; *GW*I, 285). It is clear from the context that Gadamer is setting himself against those who, for example, do not set out to philosophize with Plato, but only to criticize him. They are so convinced of the superiority of their own logical tools that they fail to see the irony by which Plato tries to strip his reader of his supposed superiority (*PA*, 184, 191; *GW*II, 501, 507). This might sound parallel to the suggestion in *Truth and Method* that the text makes its claim on me in the moment of exposure without my being in control of what is happening and without my being able to submit it to the neutral authority of reason: "It [the text] has asserted itself and captivated us before we can come to ourselves and be in a position to test the claim to meaning that it makes" (*TM*, 490; *GW*, 494). In this regard one inevitably recalls Gadamer's reminder that "It is part of the elementary experience of philosophy that when we try to understand the classics of philosophical thought, they of themselves make a claim to truth that the consciousness of later times can neither reject nor transcend" (*TM*, xxii; *GW*, 2). This description mirrors the anecdotes Gadamer tells of how he discovered the power of philosophy through Heidegger's teaching of Aristotle in Marburg in the 1920s. When Gadamer writes of the possibility that a text might say something that transcends us, he is appealing to an experience that had been decisive for him in his own philosophical development. However, the defense of the hermeneutical notion of authority is usually made on the grounds that it is purely descriptive. The 1977 formula is clearly ethical. Why this shift?

In *Truth and Method* the appeal to the superiority of the philosophical classics is justified by the centrality given there to the concept of tradition as the condition of understanding. One of the main theses of *Truth and Method* is that practitioners of the human sciences have been misled in their understanding of what they are doing by employing a false idea of science: Gadamer does not set out to tell us what we ought to do, but rather "what happens to us over and above our wanting and doing" (*TM*, xxviii; *GW*II, 438).[15] In *Truth and Method*, one might say, therefore, that the Platonic texts, among others, make understanding possible. The status of those texts, their "superiority," is never in question within the context of the tradition as a given in the sense of a presupposition. This is why the emphasis lies on focusing on what is spoken about, rather than dwelling on Plato's standpoint, which might only serve to bring the discussion within the orbit of historical consciousness and possibly relativism. This, of course, is not to say that Plato's texts cannot be criticized. The difficulty arises when one is confronted by a text that stands outside the tradition as constituted. It is simply not the case that such texts are accorded a parallel status "over and above our wanting and doing." They are, as likely as not, to be dismissed as incomprehensible, obfuscating, primitive and so on.

Another passage shows very clearly the problem Gadamer faced in accounting for dialogue across the limits of tradition. In an essay on Plato within the context of Heidegger's presentation of the pervasive unity of metaphysics as founded by the Greeks, Gadamer acknowledged that Heidegger had made it possible for the modern world (*Weltzivilisation*) to experience the limits of Greek thinking. In the German version of this essay, Gadamer commented, "These limits may not be evaded" (*GW*III, 248). However, when another version of the same essay was published in a volume devoted to comparative philosophy, *The Question of Being: East-West Perspectives*, Gadamer changed the reference to *Weltzivilisation* simply to "civilization" and he altered the last sentence to read: "It may be that by virtue of this a dialogue has become possible with philosophical traditions which have developed outside these limits, if they learn to free themselves from any tendency to parallel Western thought."[16] The tentative nature of this statement is an indication of the problem posed by different traditions within this framework. It is to Gadamer's credit that he did not, at least on this occasion, simply ignore it.

In *Truth and Method* Gadamer addresses a parallel problem insofar as it relates to a succession of historical "worlds" across a single tradition by appealing to a common world.

> It is true that the historical "worlds" that succeed one another in the course of history are different from one another and from the world of today; but in whatever tradition we consider it, it is always a human—i.e., verbally constituted—world that presents itself to us. As verbally constituted, every such world is of itself always open to every possible insight and hence to every expansion of its own world picture, and is accordingly available to others. (*TM*, 447; *GW*I, 451)

It seems likely that Gadamer favors a similar solution to the problem of understanding across cultures and traditions.[17] However, his appreciation of the difficulty of translation seems perhaps to lead him to the conclusion that the problem can be addressed only with the arrival of a world-civilization.[18] One must not forget that in his discussion of translation, Gadamer posits a gap (*Abstand*) that can never be closed (*TM*, 384; *GW*I, 388). The normal case is for one of the two languages to take the upper hand. This is why attempts to conduct a dialogue in two different languages, with each person speaking in their own tongue, always lead to one of the languages taking over. It would be naive not to recognize a certain violence here, just as there is a much more obvious violence behind the establishment of what is called *Weltzivilisation*. But to what extent can it be said that, within the context of the task of becoming part of this "new world civilization," Gadamerian hermeneutics offers itself as a philosophy that "teaches us to see the justification for the other's point of view and which thus makes us doubt our own"?[19] To what extent does Gadamerian hermeneutics resist the assimilation of alterity? To what extent is alterity treated simply as a limit case? Is Gadamer's presentation of the superiority of one's conversation partner as an ethical demand a radical reformation of his earlier position? These questions are best pursued by returning to Gadamer's discussion of dialogue.

Gadamer guards against the other becoming a theme, and repeats the classic formula that in speech not only is something said, but that someone says something to someone else.[20] He insists that where one has the other in view and attempts to get to know him or her, it is not a case of genuine dialogue. Dialogue partners should be directed to what is being spoken about so as not to be at cross purposes with each other (*TM*, 367; *GWI*, 372–73). The 1971 essay "On the Contribution of Poetry to the Search for Truth" argues not that openness gives access to alterity: openness forms a bond. "There must be a readiness to allow something to be said to us. It is only in this way that the word becomes binding, as it were: it binds one human being with another."[21] Gadamer tends to treat it as a deficient case of dialogue if I direct myself to the other rather than to the object. This is because all the examples he cites are cases in which I make the other into a theme, as when I am trying to transpose myself into the author's mind (*TM*, 292; *GWI*, 297) or focus on the text as an expression of the life of a Thou (*TM*, 358; *GWI*, 364). One wonders if Gadamer is still under the impact of Heidegger's analysis of *Gerede*. Philosophers have a habit of discounting dialogue unless it is clearly about something, whereas it seems that it is often when talking about nothing in particular that one makes contact with someone, particularly that crucial initial contact. In most cases, if somebody remarks on the weather, it is not important to correct the description or try and improve on its accuracy. Of course, the example is a trivial one, but it suggests that the crucial category is not so much those cases of language where the discussants are directed to a topic, as those cases in which one person is directed to another (*DD*, 106; *GWII*, 364–65).

Gadamer's prejudice in favor of the topic or subject matter is displayed when he employs the example of the letter. The letter is for Gadamer a kind of written conversation and so serves as an intermediate phenomenon for the purposes of his analysis (*TM*, 368; *GWI*, 374; *DD*, 33–34; *GWII*, 343). Gadamer tells us that the recipient of a letter does not look for the singular viewpoint of the correspondent, but considers what is written for true and sees things through his or her eyes (*TM*, 394;

GWI, 299).[22] According to Gadamer, it is only when one finds oneself unable to take what is said as true that one refers the text to the meaning of the author, whether in historical or psychological terms. But one suspects that Gadamer is here treating letters like historical or scientific documents in the same way that he tends to assimilate conversation to philosophical discussion. He has neglected those personal letters, the letters which perhaps touch us most deeply and mean the most to us, where what matters is that we are put in touch with the correspondent, irrespective of what is said. To someone else, and particularly someone who does not know the person writing, such letters seem to be quite banal and about nothing at all. Nevertheless, such examples are not so far distant from Gadamer's concerns because they do not appear to challenge the idea that language is a bonding operation in which distances are bridged. In Gadamer the changes that are brought about through dialogue almost invariably bring us closer together. To attain an understanding through conversation is to submit to "being transformed into a communion in which we do not remain what we were" (*TM*, 379; *GWI*, 384).

The question arises therefore as to whether Gadamer could insist on the importance of attending to the saying of the other without shifting his focus from the object of discourse. Would it not amount to returning to what he would regard as a false understanding of the fusion of horizons? One recent text—and it seems that all of the texts that emphasize alterity are recent, suggesting a change of mind on Gadamer's part—seems to suggest otherwise. In "Text and Interpretation," Gadamer insists on the mere presence of the other as already provoking doubt in one's own view even prior to the other saying something.

> The mere presence of the other before whom we stand helps us to break up our own bias and narrowness, even before he opens his mouth to make a reply. That which becomes a dialogical experience for us here is not limited to the sphere of arguments and counter-arguments the exchange and unification of which may be the end meaning of every confrontation. Rather, as the experiences that have been described indicate, there is something else in this experience, namely, a potentiality for being other [*Anderssein*] that lies beyond every coming to agreement [*Verständigung*] about what is common. (*DD*, 26; *GWII*, 336).

This is a departure from the models Gadamer employed earlier, leading to the question as to whether he succeeds in integrating this experience into his theory. Elsewhere Gadamer attempts a resolution by claiming that through the other I myself become other so that being in conversation is being beyond oneself, thinking with the other and returning to oneself as to another (*DD*, 110; *GWII*, 369). But there is a question as to whether it is only our bias and limitation that are put in question by the other, and not also the presumption with which I approach the other with the idea of convincing him or her of something. And what of the still more decisive instance where I find not just my opinions but my self-assurance shattered to the point whereby I am reduced to silence or incoherence? Even though I subsequently take a grip on myself and may indeed find myself changed, can one say that the other in his or her alterity has been assimilated? Am I not still perhaps haunted by the enigmatic other which shows itself occasionally in the pain of disorientation?

Gadamer acknowledges the way in which one can be changed through dialogue, but his account attributes to the other human being nothing like the power that he attributes to the work of art. In "Aesthetics and Hermeneutics" he refers to the enigmatic impact of the work of art as it shatters and demolishes the familiar in these terms: "It is not only the 'This art thou!' disclosed in a joyous and frightening shock; it also says to us; 'Thou must alter thy life!'"[23] In another essay Gadamer establishes a parallel between the experience of art and religious experience, specifically, the call to conversion as it takes place in the sermon.[24] Gadamer is quite explicit that his own hermeneutics is far removed from the dimension of poetical and religious speaking. He draws on Collingwood's dialogical model of question and answer and not the preacher's call to his congregation, pronounced as a call to change one's life.[25]

Even if the preacher employs the familiar formula, "You don't know what I'm talking about," the preacher anticipates mutual understanding and is directed toward it. To this extent it does not run contrary to Gadamer's hermeneutic framework. However, the same phrase can be used in another context where the possibility of understanding is refused. Then the phrase says, "You cannot be yourself and understand me." It not only says "this is you"; it also implies "you ought to change," and yet at the same time acknowledges that the change won't—in a sense, can't—take place. Women say it to men; the poor say it to the rich; the victim says it to the oppressor; the target of racism says it to the racist. At least Gadamer would not make the mistake of responding "I do understand." However, Gadamer would still be committed to anticipating an agreement that is being refused. Furthermore, what would the agreement be about? To suppose that there is a position to be appropriated, or even a common theme or topic to be addressed, is to impose a hermeneutic model without listening to what is being said. It might seem that Gadamer can better accommodate the case where there is no agreement on language because the idioms and grammatical forms of so-called standard discourse have been rejected. Such an example at least shows what weight must be attached to such an agreement. Nevertheless one has an entirely different experience with, for example, standard English, if it is the only form one knows, than if it is associated with selling out. If Gadamer rarely says very much about the cases where the conditions he prescribes for understanding do not prevail, that can be explained in part by the fact that in many cases the obstacles to understanding cannot be overcome or circumvented by hermeneutic strategies. They belong to the sociopolitical framework that Gadamer prefers to ignore.

If there is an appropriate response to the person who challenges me by refusing me the possibility of understanding, it lies in my finding myself judged and finding myself in this judgment, even if I may be unable to sustain myself in this stance for any time. But this response is appropriate not because it amounts to an agreement, as if I have understood that I do not understand. Misunderstanding is not a contingent phenomenon that occasionally threatens the possibility of genuine understanding and can be corrected. That "you do not know what I'm talking about" reveals a more fundamental sense of misunderstanding, the misunderstanding that pervades all understanding and that compromises the Gadamerian picture.

It might be possible to dismiss these observations as irrelevant to Gadamer's hermeneutics and to see them as the result of a failure to understand the scope and limits of Gadamer's theory.[26] Or, rather, that would have been possible had Gadamer not in recent years acknowledged in his descriptions the encounter with the other who puts me in question. Now that he has done so, it is incumbent on him to account for what is set out in those descriptions. The moment of genuine alterity in Gadamer's hermeneutical theory, which that theory can neither control nor erase completely, is the experience of the other as a radical challenge. I find myself addressed and put in question, prior to my assimilating what has been said to me. This moment cannot readily be reconciled with the theory into which it is interposed, because that theory works to deprive alterity of its otherness prior to its appearance within the system: the other is always *my* other, *my* Thou;[27] the text always belongs to the tradition to which I too belong; if it speaks to me at all it is in a language which has been established in advance in a common accord which unites us from the outset; and if we lack even that level of agreement, we are at least united in our openness to find or await agreement. And yet Gadamer now seems inclined to intersperse his presentation of this theory with testimony that shows that he also recognizes an alterity that has the form of a claim to truth, and that has the structure of a question insofar as it suspends my judgments and prejudices.

Does this represent a failure in the theory, such that it needs to be reformulated to encapsulate what it seems to have left out of account? Does the experience of what Gadamer calls "the claim" put his own model of dialogue in question, just as he appeals to dialogue in his attempt to put in question the inappropriate way in which methodological ideals drawn from the exact sciences have been subsequently imposed on human sciences? Or is it perhaps possible that an event which takes place as an interruption of the ordinary receives its proper articulation only when it interrupts the theory that denies it? In that case Gadamer would be obliged to call "slanted" the questions to which his hermeneutical theory is an answer—such questions as "How do the communality of meaning, which is built up in conversation, and the impenetrability of the otherness of the other *mediate* each other? And is linguisticality in the final analysis a bridge or a barrier?" (*DD*, 27; *GWII*, 336. Translation modified. My italics). The decisive question would rather be the one that Gadamer posed to himself in an essay especially written in 1985 for the publication of his complete works, and which appeared under the title "Between Phenomenology and Dialectic—Attempt at Self-criticism." Gadamer asked, "how far did I succeed in presenting the hermeneutic dimension as beyond self-consciousness, that is to say, in preserving and not simply sublating the Otherness of the Other in understanding?" (*GWII*, 5). This paper is inclined to answer that question negatively, if what is sought is a theory. Starting from a recognition of how difficult that task might be within the confines of a tradition that has tended to approach the other only to assimilate him or her, I have found the preservation of alterity in Gadamer's writings less in his hermeneutic theory as such, as in his occasional testimony to experiences that no theory can readily accommodate. Is it the task of hermeneutic philosophy to relieve theory of its alienation from experience by translating experience into theory? Or can it accomplish this only by allowing the experience of alterity to interrupt theory?[28]

12

Understanding and Willing

Kees Vuyk

Translated by Lawrence K. Schmidt

would like to reconsider the question that Derrida posed to Gadamer a few years ago in a colloquium in Paris and that prompted a small discussion between them.[1] A consensus was, however, never achieved. Derrida's question concerned the role of the will in Gadamer's explication of hermeneutic understanding. Is not understanding, in the final analysis, an act of the will? This is how I would pose Derrida's question here. And therefore, is not hermeneutics an enterprise that belongs to the project of modern metaphysics, which Heidegger, following Nietzsche, has exposed as a metaphysics of the will?

Gadamer adamantly responded to this question in the negative. The good will, which he sometimes mentions as a presupposition for understanding—namely, that one must take pains to understand another, that one must want to understand another (*GW*II, 343; *DD*, 33)—has nothing to do, in his opinion, with the will of modern metaphysics. If it were otherwise, it would also be incomprehensible that Gadamer continually opposes important developments of this metaphysics, such as modern science and technology and their cult of experts, and proposes his own hermeneutics as the alternative to them. Nevertheless, the question to be posed is: What is the relationship between the good will and the will to power (or to will), between hermeneutics and metaphysics?

I will not primarily discuss this question in relation to Gadamer's works, but will consider how the philosopher, Martin Heidegger, whom both Gadamer and Derrida acknowledged as their teacher, was occupied with this question in a specific period of his investigations.[2] Heidegger sometimes refers to a willing that he equates with resoluteness [*Entschlossenheit*] in his works that were written after the publication of *Sein und Zeit* in 1927 and up to the first Nietzsche lecture in the winter semester of 1936/37. This resoluteness is, as one knows, the name for authentic understanding in *Being and Time*, an understanding that understands more primordially than modern metaphysics. What is Heidegger thinking when he connects the will and resoluteness? And why did he later reject this relationship in order to reserve the expression *will* after 1937 for representational thinking of metaphysics, which he attempts to overcome? To answer this question requires that one recall what was meant by the will. In the examination of these opinions lies the key, I believe, to the response to the above mentioned question of Derrida. This discussion builds the first step to such an examination.

In *Being and Time* Heidegger differentiates between authentic and inauthentic understanding.

> Understanding *can* devote itself primarily to the disclosedness of the world; that is, Dasein can, proximately and for the most part, understand itself in terms of its world. Or else understanding throws itself primarily into the "for-the-sake-of-which"; that is, Dasein exists as itself. Understanding is either authentic, arising out of one's own Self as such, or inauthentic. (*BT*, 186; *SZ*, 146).

In order to "understand" this difference we must remember that in *Being and Time* understanding is an existential of Dasein, i.e. a primordial way of Being of that entity, the human, whose distinctive characteristic is self-understanding. Authentic understanding is an understanding that knows this, its own existentiality. It is an understanding where Dasein has particularly made its understanding its own.[3] It is an understanding of understanding as a mode of being. Inauthentic understanding is the understanding of the various entities in the midst of which Dasein is, without understanding in this understanding that understanding is a mode of Being. In inauthenticity Dasein is absorbed in the understanding of entities. It understands equipment in its readiness-to-hand. It can use it, the hammer to hammer, the pen to write. It understands the present-at-hand in its presence-at-hand. But what understanding is, it does not understand. It just does not ask itself this. In everyday life Dasein usually understands in the inauthentic mode. Not only when it is simply acting, as in hammering and writing, but also when it attempts more complex processes as, for example, in management and technology, or in understanding in the narrower sense of understanding a foreign expression—in all these cases humans understand usually in an inauthentic manner. One understands oneself through the entities to be understood, through what one makes understandable, and so does not understand what understanding is, i.e., a mode of one's own Being. Only in rare cases does Dasein, while understanding, abandon the entities and understand Being.

Heidegger discusses two such cases in *Being and Time*: the understanding of death and the understanding of the call of conscience. When Dasein attempts to understand these "things" then it can happen—*nota bene*: it can but must not—that understanding turns from the entities and toward an understanding of Being.

Death is a possibility for Dasein. However, it is a very particular possibility. Concerning usual possibilities it is the case that understanding means attempting to realize them. Death one tries exactly not to realize. To understand death means to let it alone, if possible. In understanding death the accent is removed from the entity that is to be understood and placed on the Being of understanding itself. This understanding lends itself to be understood as a potentiality-for-Being, a possible-Being. The understanding of death, which Heidegger also terms anticipation, is primarily an understanding of understanding as a mode of Being of Dasein. "Being-towards-death is the anticipation of a potentiality-for-Being of that entity whose kind of Being is anticipation itself. In the anticipatory revealing of this potentiality-for-Being, Dasein discloses itself to itself as regards its uttermost possibility" (*BT*, 307; *SZ*, 262). What understanding becomes is not the entity, death, but the Being of Dasein as potentiality-for-Being, a possible-Being and as such a Being-towards-death. For Heidegger this possible-Being is authentic understanding. Understanding as an existential of Dasein is the possible-Being of Dasein.

The analysis of conscience, which I will not develop here, leads to the same conclusion.

Hearing the appeal [of conscience] correctly is thus tantamount to having an understanding of oneself in one's ownmost potentiality-for-Being. (*BT*, 333; *SZ*, 287)

Thus conscience manifests itself as an *attestation* which belongs to Dasein's Being—an attestation in which conscience calls Dasein itself face to face with its ownmost potentiality-for-Being. (*BT*, 334; *SZ*, 288)

For the question concerning the relation between understanding and willing, it is important that Heidegger uses the word *resoluteness* to refer not only to anticipation, the Being-toward-death, but to the hearing of the call of conscience, which is also termed the willing-to-have-conscience. Resoluteness is authentic understanding, understanding as self-understanding, understanding as a mode of existing, and so understanding that Dasein *is*. A relation between resoluteness and willing does not really appear yet in *Being and Time*. A relation is only indirectly suggested in the definition of resoluteness as willing-to-have-conscience. In several texts that were written in the ten years following the publication of *Being and Time*, in the first half of the thirties, such a relationship is expressed. Although not often stated, this relationship is expressed often enough to be able to conclude that it is not an oversight (if there are any oversights at all in Heidegger's thought!).

The texts where resoluteness and willing are explicitly related are: "The Self-Assertion of the German University" ("Die Selbstbehauptung der Universität," 1933), *An Introduction to Metaphysics* (*Einführung in die Metaphysik*, 1935), "The Origin of the Work of Art" ("Der Ursprung des Kunstwerks," 1935) and the first Nietzsche lectures *The Will to Power as Art* (*Wille zur Macht als Kunst*, 1936).[4] In these texts Heidegger continually attempts to think a well-known, traditional philosophical subject matter in the sense of its authenticity. Willing appears then in relation to the "turn" to the dimension of authenticity. I will now examine these texts more closely.

In the rectoral address, "The Self-Assertion of the German University," a type of knowledge is elaborated upon, genuine knowledge, that is, the "Spirit" (*Geist*) of science. This "Spirit" is not "empty analysis nor the noncommittal game of wits, nor the boundless activity of producing rational analysis, nor world reason. Spirit is originally in tune with a knowing resoluteness regarding the essence of Being" (SdU, 14; SGU, 474). This resoluteness is also called "willing the essence of science" and Spirit is also termed "willing the essence." If science is to be more than just a "harmless engagement promoting a mere step forwards in knowledge" (SdU, 13; SGU, 474) and university studies are to be something other than "lackluster and expedient training that leads to a 'distinguished' profession" (SdU, 16; SGU, 477), that is if knowledge is not mere knowledge of entities, but knowledge of Being, then knowledge is a will to knowledge or resoluteness. Science that is carried by this will is "a questioning steadfastness in the middle of the continually concealing entities as a totality" (SdU, 12; SGU, 473).

We find a comparable relationship between knowledge and will in the book, *An Introduction to Metaphysics*. In the first part of this text, Heidegger tries to explicate authentic philosophizing. This philosophizing is a questioning, "inquiry into the extra-ordinary." That means this questioning "gratifies no urgent or prevailing need" (*EM*, 10; *IM*, 12). Questioning is, Heidegger states, willing to know.

> Willing—that is no mere wishing or striving. Those who wish to know also seem to question; but they do not go beyond the stating of the question, they stop precisely where the question begins. . . . He who wills, he who puts his whole Dasein into a will, is resolute. . . . Willing is being resolute. (*EM*, 16; *IM*, 20–21).

The will to know can also be defined as: "The resoluteness to be able to stand in the openness of entities" (*EM*, 17; *IM*, 22). Entities are not the object of true knowledge, but the openness of entities or truth is. In a remark inserted later into this text, Heidegger terms this openness of entities, "the clearing of Being." Willing is then related to Being. Of this he states, "the relation to Being is one of letting-be." And he adds: "That all willing should be grounded in letting-be, offends the understanding." Therefore, in this text as well, willing is the name for a knowledge that not only includes entities but also is open for Being. This willing is resoluteness and resoluteness must not be interpreted as "a storing up of energy for 'action'" (*EM*, 16; *IM*, 21) but as letting-be.

Precisely this relationship among willing, knowing, resoluteness, and an authentic understanding of Being is presented in a passage from "The Origin of the Work of Art."

> Knowing that remains a willing and willing that remains a knowing, is the ecstatic self-involvement of the existing human in the unconcealedness of Being. The resoluteness intended in *Being and Time* is not the deliberate action of a subject, but the opening of Dasein out from the captivity of entities into the openness of Being. . . . Willing is the sober re-soluteness of existing self-transcendence that exposes itself to the openness of entities as it is set into the work (UKW, 76; OWA, 67).

Just as in the text discussed above, here also, willing to know is an indication for a mode of existing in which Dasein does not understand entities in the normal way. In the essay on the work of art Heidegger gives an example: art as "produced form" or as created by an artist.[5] Rather, Dasein understands understanding itself and so understands itself in its Being. To understand something in its Being is authentic understanding. Authentic understanding is understanding as a mode of Being of Dasein.

A final example of the relationship between resoluteness and will in Heidegger's writings is taken from the first lecture on Nietzsche, which is entitled "The Will to Power as Art." In this lecture Heidegger does not yet see Nietzsche—as he later does—as the one who carried metaphysics to its end. Also at this time, he does not yet experience his own thinking as constituting a definitive break with the tradition of metaphysics, but he experiences it more as a radicalization of this tradition. Therefore in this lecture he can still discover in Nietzsche a companion in his attempt to radicalize metaphysics. His interpretation of the will to power as art is connected with this attempt. For this reason he can see an agreement between Nietzsche's will and what he himself terms resoluteness. "Will is," we read (and what is meant is the will of the will to power) "resoluteness, in which he who wills stations himself abroad among entities in order to keep them firmly within his field of action" (*NI*, 59; *N*, 48). And where Nietzsche calls willing a "feeling" and even a "very agreeable one," Heidegger interprets: "What opens up in the will— willing itself as resoluteness—is agreeable to the one for whom it is so opened, the one who wills. In willing we come toward ourselves, as the one we properly are" (*NI*, 64; *N*, 52).

In many of his later works, namely in the later lectures on Nietzsche and those texts on the history of metaphysics that were inspired by the Nietzsche interpretation, Heidegger describes modern thinking as a metaphysics of the will, which is to be overcome by a new thinking.[6] This interpretation of metaphysics builds the background for Derrida's question to Gadamer, with which I began. However, one can now see that Heidegger in his earlier works mentions the will in connection with the attempt to think metaphysics more primordially, i.e., from Being and not from entities. Evidently there was a change in Heidegger's thinking concerning the will. This change is related to the one known as the "turn." Just as the turn—according to Heidegger's own words—so too the change in his thinking about the will—in my opinion—concerns not the subject matter but just his strategy and terminology. This implies that what Heidegger in the earlier texts thought of as resoluteness, authenticity, authentic understanding, and—sometimes—willing, is later no longer emphasized for strategic reasons, and so he preferred not to refer to it with the term *willing*. For me the terminological is the most important. If it is only a matter of terminology that Heidegger earlier used *willing* and later did not use this term, then it remains to ask what subject matter Heidegger intended with *willing* and whether it would be correct to characterize this subject matter with *willing*.[7] I will now turn to this question. This will also lead me back to Gadamer's good will.

So far I have only attempted to demonstrate that, in certain texts from the thirties, Heidegger sometimes refers to authentic understanding and resoluteness as willing. What willing means here has not been systematically discussed, although some indications have come forth. It is now time to develop a systematic view of this willing. What is willing as authentic understanding? It is a mode of Being of Dasein. How is Dasein when it wills?

Generally in the quoted passages of willing as resoluteness, there is an openness, an openness where entities become open in their Being. "The Origin of the Work of Art" states:

> The resoluteness . . . is not the deliberate action of a subject, but the opening of Dasein out from the captivity of entities into the openness of Being. . . . Willing is the sober re-soluteness of existing self-transcendence that exposes itself to the openness of entities. (UK, 76; OWA, 67)

Two other important elements of willing may be seen in this text. Willing is not a "decided action of a subject" (UK, 76; OWA, 67). In *An Introduction to Metaphysics* we read that all "willing is grounded in letting-be"— something that "offends the understanding" (*EM*, 16; *IM*, 21). In the essay on the work of art willing is a way of preserving the work of art, and preservation means "letting the work be a work" (UK, 75; OWA, 66). And in the rector's address it is said of science as essentially will to knowledge that it "knows its impotence facing fate" (SdU, 12; SGU, 473). Willing that is exposed to openness, is therefore not the effect of a subject, not imagination and not production, all machinations of the modern will to will.

The second point to be taken from the quoted passage is that the willing of openness goes together with escaping "the captivity of entities." In "The Origin of the Work of Art" we also hear of a "displacement" that changes "the accustomed ties to world and to earth" (UK, 75; OWA, 66). In *An Introduction to Metaphysics* this dis-interestedness is the presupposition for the question as willing to know, the question that is "'out of order'" (*EM*, 10; *IM*, 12). The rector's address speaks in this context of the "danger of world-uncertainty" (SdU, 14; SGU, 475), which accompanies the willing of the true science. Willing is, therefore, not only not an action of a subject, but it is also not something that creates something in the usual sense; it aims nowhere—except toward openness, in order to take its stand there.

This view of willing as authentic understanding is most clearly seen if we return to Heidegger's analysis of authentic understanding in *Being and Time.* As has been stated, authentic understanding is understanding the understanding to be a mode of Being of Dasein itself. It is not understanding of entities, alongside which Dasein is, but the understanding of the authentic *Being* of Dasein as understanding. The emphasis on ownmostness and Being-one's-self as understanding might lead one to think that in authentic understanding Dasein is, with itself, at home, and that authentic understanding is an understanding of familiarity, a familiarity that is lost when Dasein gives itself over to entities. However, that is exactly not the case. Precisely when it understands authentically, Dasein is "not-at-home" [*unheimlich*]. "*The not-at-home,*" Heidegger writes, "[is] *the more primordial phenomenon.*" "That kind of Being-in-the-world that is tranquilized and familiar is a mode of Dasein's uncanniness, not the reverse" (*SZ*, 189; *BT*, 234).[8] The caller of the call of conscience who calls Dasein to authentic Being-one's-self, is therefore also "Dasein that finds itself in the very depths of its uncanniness" (*SZ*, 276; *BT*, 321). Listening to the call of conscience in resoluteness, Dasein understands his own "authentic" uncanniness, from which it had fled into inauthenticity. So authentic understanding is not an understanding where the world becomes more meaningful than it was in inauthenticity. Exactly the opposite occurs: the world sinks into meaninglessness in authentic Being (*SZ*, 343; *BT*, 393). When Dasein understands itself as understanding, then it understands that its everyday understanding of the world is not self-evident. When it has come to this understanding, then it understands understanding authentically, i.e., as a mode of Being. Understanding is not an entity, not an ability that Dasein possesses, nor is it instinct or reason. Dasein is in the world (thrown) but there is nothing—*animalitas* nor *rationalitas*—that unites Dasein with the world, *and nevertheless or perhaps especially for this reason Dasein is understanding*—and this is essential for this investigation. This understanding is possible-Being, potentiality-for-Being in the openness. Although Heidegger more often terms this understanding "projection," it has nothing to do with the planned activities of an engineer or—philosophically stated—the activities of a subject. Projection as the Being of Dasein is not the production of a human environment. Rather such production is only possible on the basis of the more primordial projecting Being, where Dasein understands itself as possible-Being.

All understanding of entities rests upon this foundation that is not a foundation but an abyss.[9] Dasein understands in uncanniness, not in order to escape from it but in order to take its stand there. In its everydayness, existence gladly forgets this abyss of its understanding and makes itself at home. When it authentically understands, it holds itself open for this abyss. This openness, which distinguishes authentic under-standing, is also termed by Heidegger willing.

In nonorthodox Heideggerian terminology—for example as used by Richard Rorty[10]—one could say: what Heidegger describes in the pre-vious discussion is the radical contingency of human existence. But if one's whole life is by chance—to put it another way—and one recognizes this indeterminacy, what can this recognition be other than an affirma-tion of contingency? What can this affirmation be other than a willing? Since everything could be different, does that not imply that, what is as it is, is this way only for the one who so wills it? Therefore, to understand something "authentically" is to will to understand it in that manner?[11] In this context Heidegger also discloses that willing can never be a founda-tion, in which the understood may find its stability—although a whole tradition of modern metaphysics has sought such a will. Understanding as willing can only mean that one places the understood in the openness and acknowledges it as a possibility without permitting it to disappear so that it would soon no longer be. This last possibility is the ever-present temptation of nihilism (what Nietzsche calls "the uncanniest of all guests"!).

From what has been disclosed, I believe now—following good hermeneutic tradition—to be able to understand Gadamer better than he understood himself, when interpreting his emphasis on the good will as a presupposition for understanding. In *Truth and Method* one often reads that understanding is a willing to understand, especially when speaking of the otherness of the language to be understood. For Gadamer understanding is more than just the appropriation of some-thing foreign, one must experience the foreign in its otherness (*GWI*, 305 fn. 230). To understand, one should be able to suspend one's own opinions and prejudices. To will to understand means also "to be recep-tive to otherness" (*GWI*, 273; *TM*, 269). "*The true place of hermeneutics*" is therefore located in a "*between*," which lies "between the foreign and the familiar" (*GWI*, 300; *TM*, 295). This situation establishes the priority of the question as it is discussed in Gadamer's hermeneutics. Following Socrates and Plato (but here, as well, Heidegger could be his teacher), Gadamer argues that questioning implies "a desire to know and that means knowing that one does not know" (*GWI*, 369; *TM*, 362). "All ques-tioning and the desire to know presuppose a knowledge that one does not know" (*GWI*, 371; *TM*, 365–66). And sounding like Heidegger: "Questioning means bringing into the open" (*GWI*, 369; *TM*, 363).

When Gadamer says that understanding presupposes a good will, this does not mean that understanding is an act of the will, as Derrida suggests, nor is it an act by the subject as understood in modern meta-physics, nor an act, according to Heidegger, that finally leads to Niet-zsche's will to power, nor an act of will as an act of force, willing as will-ing-to-be-ruler. That a willing exists within understanding means only that the person capable of correct understanding is one who is aware of the finitude of his present understandings, and so is open for what is pre-sented in understanding as foreign. This willing is closer to the willing of the good, which Aristotle called *prohairesis* in his practical philosophy, than to the will of modern metaphysics.[12] However, I believe that it is also different from the authentic will that I have discussed in Heidegger's ear-lier works.

Heidegger's will is more radical, because his concept of finitude is more radical. The gulf that separates the familiar from the foreign goes much deeper in Heidegger's thought than in the hermeneutics of Gadamer. In Gadamer this gulf opens up a between, which is between man and world, especially between man and man, a between that is therefore primarily conversation. In Heidegger, however, this gulf goes all the way through Dasein itself as an entity that understands Being. One is removed to a between where one "belongs to Being and yet is a foreigner among entities."[13] When Gadamer speaks of otherness, the other is the other of what I am [*Eigene*], even when what I am under-stands itself as the other of the other. The other in Heidegger's thought is the other who *is* one's own self—the uncanniness that lives within. The willing that accompanies understanding in Gadamer is, therefore, a willed placing oneself in the open for the other. Gadamer explicates his good will as that behavior where "one attempts to make the other as strong as possible, so that its statement becomes something enlighten-ing."[14] The purpose of this willing is an understanding in which what I am and the other come together. "One surrenders oneself, in order to find oneself," although one does not know what one will find oneself to be.[15] For Heidegger willing is authentic understanding, i.e., an under-standing that understands itself as a mode of Being of Dasein, as it pri-mordially *is*. Here Dasein is, however, exposed to be primordially with-out foundation—or as I have also stated: contingent. And because the origin of Dasein is actually an abyss, all understanding, as the under-standing of entities in the light of Being, can also be called willing. This willing is primarily a mode of Being. In Gadamer's hermeneutics willing is especially a relation among entities. From this perspective, hermeneu-tics lacks a dimension. One could perhaps also say—in order to prob-lematize this lack—that hermeneutics has an illusion too many: the illu-sion of truth, which is still hidden, for example, in Gadamer's thesis concerning the universality of *phronesis,* practical wisdom.[16] If, as Heidegger claims, all understanding is a willing because every understanding begins with the uncanniness of the Being of man in the world—his radical contingency—then there is no other universality of understanding other than the universality of exactly this uncanniness.[17]

It is well known that Heidegger firmly connects willing to modern metaphysics in his later writings where he investigates the history of metaphysics. He has demonstrated how modern philosophers—Leibniz, Schelling, Hegel, Nietzsche—in their search for a final foundation have made the will into the highest entity, which, as subject, underlies every entity. These philosophers sensed the importance of the will, but were astounded by its levity and attempted to add importance to it. Heidegger's thinking concerning Being, could be read as the attempt to give the will back its levity. But because the will had received such a determinate meaning in the history of metaphysics, Heidegger preferred later to no longer refer to his questioning concerning Being as a willing or the will. Nevertheless, I contend that an investigation of the will would still be a possible means to shed light on the dimension of Being beyond metaphysics.[18] That this investigation, which I have conducted on only a single element of Gadamer's philosophy, should conclude by exposing a difficulty in Gadamer's philosophy, does not dispute the facility of his whole thought. That in Gadamer understanding presupposes a will, is certainly connected to the tradition of metaphysics—one must credit Derrida with this much. But I hope to have especially demonstrated that Gadamer also offers the possibility of overcoming this tradition.

13

Play and Ethics in
Culturus Interruptus: Gadamer's
Hermeneutics in Postmodernity

Marc J. LaFountain

Opening: Toward a Tragic Silence?

Are there ways of perceiving and experiencing that exceed, or are outside of, or fracture the transport of understanding such that *phronesis* is ruptured, or is *phronesis* to be taken as the embrace that gathers any and all events such that "the" tradition into which they are appropriated always remains unified and impervious to transgression? If such rupture were to occur (or is occurring), what would its scenario be? Would its duration and intensity be such that its consequences would be tolerable and sufferable by those who would wait for the moment of understanding that would "overcome" what happened in that space? Would the realities of those spaces be dismissed as "only" ontic? If Gadamer speaks of the significance of the "here and now," then what becomes of ontological hermeneutics as they descend into the world, into the flesh of the quotidian?

Is it appropriate to appeal to Gadamer's hermeneutics when seeking what is ethical? Agreeing with his stance that truth and understanding come to us above and beyond our wanting and our methods, it is both possible and necessary to make this appeal. To not do so, to not ask hermeneutics to face the here and now, is to do hermeneutics "just for the fun of it." While particulars do eventually pale in the light of infinite time, to do hermeneutics "just for the fun of it" would indeed be a travesty, as Gadamer himself recognizes in speaking of "playing with life" (*TM*, 106). For in the still shimmering grief of the Zeitgeist Lyotard (*PE*, 78), following Adorno, named "Auschwitz," we now press against limits (e.g., the extinction of species and ecosystems, ethnic wars and genocide, nuclear and toxic waste contamination, excessively tragic scarcity, AIDS) where infinite time is no acceptable relief.[1] Indeed there can be within an historically continuous tradition interruptions, silences, and confusions, which can be subsumed into the infinite process of dialectical recuperation and becoming. But there can also be interruptions and silences that inscribe exteriorities and alterities, things that are dangerous and "unbecoming."

Presented here is a commentary on the "play" and "game" now framing the contemporary hermeneutic situation. The intent is not simply, however, to pit the postmodernist against the hermeneuticist. Nor is it a whimsical effort to locate what is exorbitant (rather than just complex) and what cannot be coopted into a totality. This commentary then forms a critique of contemporary culture which, when set against a philosophical stance such as ontological hermeneutics, problematizes that stance when it inquires about its destiny in the world. That the very problem of locating what is questionable about hermeneutics coincides with hermeneutic activity itself (i.e., the significance of finding what is alien or questionable) is purely coincidental.

What will become problematic in all this is that it is difficult to discern whether this commentary is a critique of Gadamer's hermeneutics or an implicit agreement with his stance. Precisely this makes the "postmodern situation" poignant. The positive productivity of this ambiguity is that "the question" is revitalized. Not just a question about whether or not a particular hermeneutics is valid, but a question about what our current cultural configuration is about and what it means for "ethics," and for silence. Though Vattimo's (*TS*) "postmodernist hermeneutics" will be mentioned only briefly, its reformulation and defense of Gadamer's position will likewise be questioned.

Hermeneutics and "The Call"

The task of Gadamer's hermeneutics is to articulate what happens when we claim to arrive at an understanding of self, other, and/or world. Its task, vis-à-vis that of positivism, subjectivism, historicism, relativism, and other vagaries of modernity, is to resituate consciousness and intersubjectivity in such a way that universals, historically transformed as tradition-becoming, can be applied in particular, concrete situations. As such Gadamer's hermeneutics can be taken as a clue to the problem of ethics, that problem being: What are "ethics" and how do we know we are being ethical? In his words, "What man needs is not only a persistent asking of ultimate questions, but the sense of what is feasible, what is possible, what is correct, here and now" (*TM*, xxxviii).

Central to both understanding and a sense of what is correct is the notion of "play." Play is essential as it is the "to and fro motion" of self-presentation and self-renewal that are the very mode of being-in-motion that individuals and communities already are and that hermeneutics seeks to bring to language (*TM*, xxx, 103–4). Play is without goal or purpose or effort, and what it presents and reveals is "truth." Truth for Gadamer does not refer to an absolute, totalized, metaphysical ultimate, but rather to what happens when a fusion of horizons occurs. This event of fusion is a transformative event in which "truth" emerges from a "hermeneutic circle" (*TM*, 266, 291)—a mingling of tradition and interpretation where a disclosure of possibilities for being and doing generates enhanced self-realization and coherent continuity of intersubjectivity and community.

In an effort to arrive at a postrationalist, decentered, nonfoundational subjectivity and community that lie somewhere between those senses implicated in Descartes's excessive humanism and Heidegger's antihumanism, Gadamer's hermeneutics suggests that play is not an activity or creation of an agent, though subjects do in fact participate. For play "happens, as it were, by itself," and "all playing is being-played" (*TM*, 104, 105). Herein are clues to what he means when he allows that truth comes to us "behind our backs" (*PH*, 38) . . . "over and above our wanting and doing" (*TM*, xxviii). We "belong" to history, and self-awareness is but a "flickering in the closed circuits of historical life" (*TM*, 276). This flickering too often assumes a hasty authority over the genesis of meaning and truth, for we are always "more being than consciousness" (*PH*, 38).

In this light, one of the particular tasks of Gadamer's work is to rethink the place of reason in contemporary life. It was the Enlightenment, Gadamer reminds us, that subordinated "prejudices" to the demands of reason. Ironically, this effort turned the prejudices of authority into objectivism and historicism, and those of overhastiness into subjectivism, radical individualism, and relativism. To rehabilitate the relationship of reason and prejudice is to overcome the severance of reason from tradition and the body politic, and hence from morality. Such rehabilitation restores prejudices to their rightful place as our historical being, a horizon from which we are productively projected toward a possible future that is transformative in the sense that is an expectation of truth. The play that bears us forth locates us in encounters which are the possibility of a fusion of horizons, i.e., understanding. For this understanding to transpire there inevitably and necessarily are resistances that occur between the call of tradition and the call of the present, resistances that are resolved in fusion.

It is in resistance that the living voice of tradition and the current situation (including the subject) conspire to produce the unthought and the unasked. What these questions are or what their answers can be cannot be decided ahead of time. Rather we must be courageously and patiently open to the mutual interrogation of tradition and present, accepting the risk it carries. As the "miracle" of understanding unfolds, the productive force of the moving forth of "effective history" and "effective historical consciousness" (*TM*, 300–307, 341–79) produces questions and answers that, in dialogue, become a fusion of horizons where a "new" tradition emerges, preserving yet transforming the "old" tradition as well as altering the self-understanding of those who live it out. This living out of tradition as a moment of interpretation and application, and as an openness to the fusions that are our lives, are the "methods" by which we rummage through our beliefs and fallen resistances and discover those understandings that have valid "truth" claims.

That such understanding is miraculous is indeed miraculous! For the source of every understanding is an immanent call-waiting that continues to overcome its finitude and historical rootedness and to achieve a new presence. It is not though a primordial or originary call. It is not a call from a Platonic essence, nor is it a Hegelian *Bildung*. What is interesting is not the triumph of the truth of understanding, but rather Gadamer's suggestion that "Inasmuch as the tradition is newly expressed in language, something comes into being that had not existed before and that exists from now on" (*TM*, 462). It is this that makes for understanding or misunderstanding, and it is this that is becoming problematic these days: the trouble that arises when the persistent "hermeneutical experience" finds itself interrupted, delayed, dislocated, and deferred by things it cannot rehabilitate and incorporate. For many, e.g., Mark Poster (*MI*), the later condition is synonymous with poststructuralism, or postmodernism.

As an instance of this interruption and deferral the seemingly innocuous example of "call-waiting" can be considered. Call-waiting is a recent feature of telephone communication made possible by advanced technology in response to a desire/demand for information, self-expression, expediency (of efficiency and productivity), and omnipresence and omniscience (and their relations to omnipotence). Call-waiting can be taken, in a weak sense, to be emblematic of the communicative process common in a hypercapitalistic, ultraindustrial society such as America. Call-waiting yields insights for discussing the nature of this contemporary cultural configuration and what is questionable and problematic about it. Further, though, call-waiting has implications for hermeneutics and ethical formation in the "here and now."

Call-waiting alerts the one who has made it part of his/her telephone system that another person is on the line and waiting to speak. For instance, call-waiting permits me to interrupt our conversation, put you on "hold," and speak with another. There is no limit to the time I may spend with this other caller, and the number of interruptions our conversation might suffer is open, varying only with the number of times others might telephone me (or you if you too possess it). Of course, I may choose not to respond to the auditory signal that alerts me to a call waiting, but our conversation is nonetheless interrupted and chances are that if I don't answer it I will at least be distracted thinking about who and what it is. In this case our conversation will be disrupted and it may even be hastened or deferred to a later time. While many who possess call-waiting report it is a desirable feature, at home or at work, they also indicate it is annoying, distracting, and a source of disruption. But so it is with those to whom information and time are so crucial. (While we will not discuss it at length, there is also another feature known as "call-for-warding."[2] It permits me to program my telephone to relay an incoming message to me at another site. Thus, I may be visiting you at your residence and still we can be interrupted. We see here that the future can be manipulated and deferred as can be the present.) Let us consider the consequences.

From *Phronesis* to *Phrenesis*, Fusion to Fission

An initial, crucial move in Gadamer's effort to establish his hermeneutics was to rehabilitate prejudices so as to align them with "effective history." Noting that "the fundamental prejudice of the Enlightenment is the prejudice against prejudice itself which denies tradition of its power"

(*TM*, 270), he argues that prejudices are fore-structures or "fore-meanings" (*TM*, 267) that, as part of the hermeneutic circle, have the consequence of lending themselves to the "fore-conception of *completion*" (*TM*, 294, emphasis mine). One of the foundational problems of leaning on prejudice, however, is that of treating it as "authority," which induces one not to use one's powers of reason. Perhaps as great a problem is "overhastiness," where one indeed employs reason, but generates errors in so doing. For Gadamer, both authority and overhastiness are problematic; it is either the "authority [of others] that leads us into error, or else it is an overhastiness in ourselves" (*TM*, 271). It is the "or" in the later statement that I take to be highly problematic.

My concern, given the times in which we presently dwell, is that the "or" that forges a distinction between the non-use of reason and excessive or erroneous use no longer holds. I suggest in these times the mistaken uses of reason are *con-fused*, and as such, their *con-fusion* constitutes another problematic. By this I mean that the authority of reason, here in the form of a technology of communication aimed at expediency, has the force of a moral norm (akin to Weber's descriptions of capitalism and rationality as moral systems). That is to say, "if you are this type of person, who values these things, then it is appropriate and desirable for you to deploy these devices as an indication of your participation in and homage to/support of them. Your use of them is a statement about who and what you are." Not following the norms of this code is conterminous with rupturing a social bond. I also mean that in actually deploying such devices we fall prey to overhastiness in that our desire for self-expression and omnipresence, i.e., our radical individualism, dislodges us from our embeddedness in history. That is, in relying on the logic of our own self-interest and self-directedness, and the assumption it will enhance our self-knowledge and growth, we in effect cut ourselves off from the traditions that promise such enhancement. For according to Gadamer, to be historical means that one is not absorbed in self-knowledge.

This collusion of authority and overhastiness is not contradictory, but is a parodic and ironic condition that oppositional thinking cannot embrace or diminish. But what are its consequences, and what does it make of us, particularly in relation to the issue of ethics? As an opening, let us consider the "game" and its relation to play. It will be remembered that Gadamer has suggested that the game is a space where the to-an-fro movement that is "play" is arranged in a peculiar fashion that is always "for someone" (*TM*, 106–10). This is as true for the "game" of ethics as for any other game. For here, as elsewhere, the real subject of playing is the game itself, the game being a medial space in which to-and-fro motion signals a continuous eventing of possibilities and meanings that transcend a particular goal. The aim of the game of ethics then is the renewal of the dialectical process that makes of ethics an effort to set out, for the time being, the order or boundaries within which the activity that realizes the to-and-fro motion of the becoming-of-understanding transpires. That is to say that ethics, however foundational they may appear to be, are a *medial* space, a "language" through which understanding is "concretized" (*TM*, 389). As this mode of understanding is interpretation, it operates, like conversation, as a "closed circle within the dialectic of question and answer" (*TM*, 389).

Of concern here is the eventing nature of this to-and-fro motion as well as the status of "the question." Perhaps most significant though is the problem of asserting and maintaining a coherent sense of what "uninterrupted listening" (*TM*, 465) might be. For Gadamer it refers to an ongoing encounter with a "thing" where "being played" moves toward understanding. Apparent now, however, is that this sense of "play" and "game" have been overwhelmed by postmodernity's code of speed. Part of this code may be summarized here as: *speed requires interruption.* While it is true that to be totally effective speed must overcome and transcend interruption, postmodernity is that space of cultural acceleration where speed demands interruption (*culturus interruptus*). For interruptions make in-site-tations possible, circuits along which information and desire, as well as being-played, flow.[3] What is to be interrupted, of course, is the "conversation of humanity" that is both an obstacle to real speed *and* that which speed is for. Ironically, hyperactive societal organization asserts itself in a manner where the "self cancellation" (*TM*, 465) of interruption defers understanding rather than unfolding it. Here "uninterrupted listening" becomes an absorption into the environment of being-played. This poses a problem that even the most sincere, seeking to avoid overhastiness, fall prey to.

We have already learned well from modernity that success comes from gaining speed. In our current use-it-and-throw-it-away cultural configuration, expenditure, excess, and waste are the signs of a sprinting, overdetermined lifestyle; they appear wherever in-site-tations appear. In such a situation, conversation is dissipated and becomes expendable. The sublime ecstacy of speed thrives on conditions of cultural aphasia and countermemory. In that shopping malls, soap operas, television game shows, news programs, and advertising constantly speed up and overwhelm critical reflection on consumption and desire, interruption appears as a new cultural necessity. In such a reality, anything can be juxtaposed to anything else. Tensionless juxtaposition (eclecticism), howev-

er, con-fuses meaning, rendering it hyperactively irrelevant and inconsequential. It matters little as long as it is quick and efficient, consumable
and expendable. In the hyperreality that is our "present," speed *simulates*
cohesion and solidarity. Messages and codes move so rapidly as to blur
and conceal that things are the same, thus simulating the sense that they
are different. We assume we are different, but we are tied together in a
game where the "one who has the most when he dies, wins." Thus, even
though we disdain them, we come to accept and expect discontinuity,
fragmentation, breaches of attention, intrusions, rapid cut-aways, and
sound bytes as ways of indulging the fetish of speed. Is it any wonder
hyperactivity and "attention deficit disorders" (ADD) now afflict both
children and adults?

Postmodernity names a problematic time where the Gadamerian
game has been disrupted and delayed, if not dislocated or even suspended. Ironically enough this occurs precisely when we have been led
to believe that we have just entered the golden age of gamesmanship. (I
refer here to the post-Machiavellian, strategic culture alluded to by Goff-
man, Burke, Oliver Stone's *Wall Street*, Star Wars, lotteries, the mediatization of politics, symbolic, nuclear warfare, "Wheel of Fortune," and the
like.) Instead of a to-and-fro motion, movement is now hither-thither
and helter-skelter. The game, a simulacrum of the dialectic of oppositions, has become a space of speedy con-fusion, of hysteria—a space of
rupture and conflict. It is a space of exorbitance and alterity, where
absence is not the other side of presence and where negativity is not the
other side of a movement of self-understanding that is broadening and
illuminating. It is something other than the "peculiar restlessness and
dispersion" that is the negativity at the ground of Becoming referred to
by Hegel in the preface to the second edition of the *Science of Logic.* Such
space is a space of *phrenesis*, not *phronesis*—not a historical time, but a hysterical time where uninterrupted and interrupted listening are no
longer distinguishable.

So what becomes of hermeneutics in such a period? In an effort to
find a mediating point between critical theory and hermeneutics, Bernstein chided Gadamer for attempting to apply the notion of *phronesis* to
a contemporary time where the conditions necessary for its exercise
(shared acceptance and stability of universal principles and laws) are
breaking down or absent (*BO*, 157). In defense of Gadamer, a breakdown of normative consensus does not mean there are no traditions that
can sustain *phronesis* and praxis. Indeed there are; that is the issue! I
should like then to radicalize Bernstein's critique by returning to call-
waiting and considering it the light of the "primary hermeneutical con-

dition" and the "postmodern hermeneutical situation." Here I am following Poster's advice that to "discern 'new events' . . . one must problematize the nature of communications in modern society by retheorizing the relation between action and language, behavior and belief, material reality and culture" (*MI*, 5).

In a reminder crucial to the analysis unfolding here, Linge has carefully observed that hermeneutics has its origins in silence: in breaches in intersubjectivity and in alienation from meaning (*PH*, xii). Hermeneutical activity arises in those situations that require bridging a gap between what is familiar and what is alien or strange. In such a situation Gadamer tells us we bring to an encounter with the alien what is most familiar, and when open to the risk of new possibilities, we are transported to new understandings. In fact, "It is enough to say that we understand in a different way, if we understand at all" (*TM*, 297). This is so because there is a "productivity" to the tradition that inheres in the excess of the unsaid in that tradition that comes to life as a new understanding in the event of linguisticality. But where Linge observes that Gadamer's formulation of the mediation of the alien and the traditional modifies what is said "so that it can remain the same" (*PH*, xxvi), I suggest the contemporary postmodern hermeneutical situation desiccates this dialectic of identity and difference.

In the postmodern hermeneutical situation there is a fundamental distortion and displacement of what Gadamer names the "first condition of hermeneutics" (*TM*, 299). The primary hermeneutical situation is that episode in which we begin to isolate particular prejudices so we can be aware of them and begin to assess the validity of their current claims to meaning and truth. It is here that understanding begins—where we are addressed or faced by a question—for it is the question that raises what is silent to the possibility of being cognizantly voiced in a given situation. Yet because of our contemporary existence and the destabilization of the to-and-fro of play, we are not absorbed into the game. We cannot lose ourselves in the game and give ourselves over to it to be played by it, to become selfless and open to new understandings. Unreleased from ourselves, we become singularities that subvert dialogue, spoilsports who stand outside the game and yet are cynically absorbed into it.

A consequence of this displacement comes to light by returning to the telephone conversation and call-waiting. Let us say our conversation was interrupted or suspended by call-waiting. It would not be unusual for me (or you) to ask: Where are you? What did you want? When will you return? What is the meaning of this communication? What is my part in it? That one is open to being questioned and provoked, a precondition for understanding, is rendered irrelevant. That one might imaginatively seek what is questionable, is moot (mute) in that what offers resistance for such questions is delayed and/or displaced. Call-waiting then becomes a simulacrum of "the call" hermeneutics attempts to illuminate. The call that emerges from the meeting of tradition and the present is suspended. With the primary hermeneutical situation being undercut, the possibility of understanding collapses.

If indeed "the world [is] 'world' only insofar as it comes into language, but language, too, has its real being only in the fact that the world is presented in it" (*TM*, 443), and if conversation is always the sharing of a common meaning (*TM*, 290), then certainly the eventing of the world and common meaning are made difficult by their interruption and delay. In fact, such a problematic inscribes a distortion in the assertion by Gadamer that one who speaks a language no one else understands does not speak (*PH*, 65). Of course, the disrupted conversation does not result in a private language per se. But it does result in an isolation and privatization of language in that the other who would help sustain communication is systematically deferred. As such, monologue displaces dialogue, and an interruption of linguisticality occurs that has the consequence of postponing and displacing (the) world. Call-waiting in-sites a silence in linguisticality that exceeds the productive silence recuperable by dialectic embrace. The consequence of this "other silence" is the in-site-tation of another language, that of the circuit's code(s) of speed and interruption.

The infinity of meaning that comes with the "occasionality of human speech" (*TM*, 458) is thus drastically reduced and made even more radically finite. Without a world, or with a fractured or simulated world at best, the issue of ethics is seriously confounded. But then again, the absence of conversation, understanding, and meaning is not complete absence. For the code and circuitry that continue to push information about now simulates a community, simulates meaning, always pushing dialogue closer to monologue, for what is said is said again and again and remains the same. We have become a community of conversationalists who talk much but say little. From this great chatter comes a deafening silence upon which ultraindustrial, hyperinformational society thrives.

In such a condition we have become decentered in a way not envisioned by Gadamer's hermeneutic decentering of subjectivity and community. History has become "ineffective history," and the fracture of dialogue has lead to "ineffective historical consciousness." History has become histories. As singularities, these histories lend themselves to self-knowledge first and foremost, and result in a "fission of horizons." The fusion of horizons that attains the "higher universality that overcomes, not only our own particularity, but also that of the other" (*TM*, 305) is, for the time being, pushed aside. Fission prevails, for the linguisticality that "concretizes" effective historical consciousness—and "effective reflection" (*PH*, 35)—does not occur. The self-renewing, self-transcending capacity of language, which yields the fluidity of horizons, is dislocated and silenced. It is exceeded by an effluence of interrupted singularities whose ecstacy and exorbitance overdetermine the embrace of dialectical eventing. That is, the excess of meanings of the infinity of the unsaid occasioned by each individual, whose fusion with others is deferred, truly becomes excessive, positing questions that get no answers (in the form of too many answers), leaving them open, running sores in the dialectic. Call-waiting.

Here we return again to the issues of authority and overhastiness. In the postmodern hermeneutical situation the double problems of subjectivism and objectivism reassert themselves together as a *con-fused*, duplicitous solicitation. It is already evident that our current condition lends itself to ineffective historical consciousness and to a fission of horizons. But that is not all, as ineffective history is not at all simply ineffective. Its ineffectivity is not unproductive, just as Foucault noted that the negativity of power is not unproductive. The singularities that render history ineffective do so by being-played-as, that is, constituted as a precession of singularities that in effect operate as intensities, making selves and others relays in an indeterminate roundabout.

Standing outside Gadamerian history, these histories become *hysteries*. In their ecstacy they form together a nontotalized, open circuit through which flicker the codes of advanced technosociety. Relays in a semiotic flow, these *hysteries*, as excessive individual self-expressions, are also the repetitious expressions of this code. In that these multiple expressions are driven by their own overhastiness, which is embedded in their code-induced lack of horizon and subsequent affinity to what is "nearest" them, they are eclecticized, suppressed, and lose their effectivity. As noted though they lose their effectivity only with regard to their ability to overcome their subjectivism. They do not lose it with regard to being dominated by the authority of the code and its mythologies. These histories then take on an ecstatic, hyperactive character somewhat akin to what the Krokers and Kroker and Cook have referred to as "panic" states (*PS, BI*).

Under the seductive, entropic signs of excess and panic, the postmodern hermeneutical situation *in-sites* an ignorance and forgetting (speed as countermemory) of both our history and our *difference* from our history. Born of a *con-fusion* of overhastiness *and* authority, this ineffective historical consciousness instigates a double refusal of identity *and* difference. Here the paradoxical modification of history that permits it to be transformed, yet remain the same, collapses in the overheated intensity of the circulation and recirculation of information, leading to a parodic carrying on of tradition where a simulation of the same is exceeded by overwhelming differences. Identity is thus dislocated. Yet at the same time real transformative difference is itself refused by the simulation of difference that is incessantly packaged and repackaged in the media and commodity markets. So it is that many now wear blue jeans that are tattered and torn at the factory prior to sale so as to invoke the resistance and defiance that characterized the 1960s. But the memory that attaches to such garb is more faded than the cloth itself, and is refused. So too is the difference that these people are from those of the 1960s, and even from their own commodified, prefabricated identities.

Incessant decontextualization, random reinscription, and ready juxtaposition of almost any cultural product prevail. The collapse of a distinction between identity and difference (as well as between lack and excess) incarnates an "artificial intelligence." Artificial intelligence is no longer able to be distinguished from that which mimics intelligent, sentient beings, or that which is fake or fiction, or that which is "real." Hypercapitalistic society thrives on such intelligence, and this simulated intelligence defines the logic and desire by which bodies and minds are colonized by the coded realities of whatever is produced in the media and commodity markets. Artificial intelligence moves toward what is nearest, without memory, without question. It is a derivative and duplicitous intelligence that willingly promotes the relay of environmental input while taking itself to be the author of that very information/meaning. Artificial intelligence intensifies ineffective historical consciousness, producing "ineffective hysterical consciousness." Ineffective hysterical consciousness is the hermeneutic analogue of artificial intelligence, and is capable of moving only at high speed and only within the circuits that prejudice it. The countermemory of artificial intelligence promotes cultural aphasia and dyslexia, for traditions are con-fused with the circuit's code, are misread and are rendered voiceless.

Gianni Vattimo's counterreading of the postmodern hermeneutic situation also identifies "disorientation," "oscillation," and "confusion," but sites them as opportunities for emancipation grounded in difference and multiplicity (*TS*, 7–11). What is relevant about Vattimo's argument here is its focus on media, communication, and the ethical possibilities of hermeneutics. In particular his concern is with electronically mediated communication and how it permits a diverse array of local "dialects" (or "calls") to present themselves and "get into shape for recognition" (*TS*, 9).

The larger grid of multi-mediated particularities discussed here, however, takes disorientation-as-liberation as a possibility, but underscores instead a cultural configuration where disorientation and confusion only *simulate* liberation. Thus, mediatization, in the narrow sense of electronic communication devices, must be seen as being subsumed by a mediatization that inserts itself into the communicative process in a way that defers and delays. It is this deferral and delay of the call of a "confusion of dialects" that simulates emancipation by creating a number of local, particular sites that simulate opportunities for fusions of horizons. (It is important not to mistake the latter with Adorno's claims about the homogenization of society. While there may be similarities, understanding how such homogenization occurs is crucial. This also is the basis for Baudrillard's claim that we must "forget Foucault" in that even Foucault's understanding of power/knowledge overlooks the reality of simulation.)

What is troubling or "unbecoming" about all this is the speed with which these interruptions are occurring. This very speed, though in-citing local dialects, also in-sites them as relays in the circuitry of delay whose accomplice is the spread of a larger code of consumption, evacuation, and waste which masquerades as identity *and* difference, that is, as individuation *and* liberation. Thus, while there may be occasions for a sense of identity and uniqueness within particular sites, it is questionable whether or not this radical subjectivity is eclipsed by the pure speed of the code. It is further a question as to whether or not this undercuts the fusion of horizons.

Tradition thus is not only parodic, but also predatory and cynical. History is wasted. Identity and self-understanding are canceled, rendered vacant and vacuous, ready for the inscription of simulated reality, for spectatorial inertia—ready for a world where television and movies are reality and where everything goes better with Coke. The speedy, hysterical code of ultratechnocapitalism thrives on excessive noise and chatter, and on silence. Not only is conversation that generates understanding blunted by ineffective history, but individuals become blank and indifferent: noisily silent spectators and voyeurs. As suggested by Kroker and Cook, in such a situation

> Words are no longer necessary; but merely the seductive pose which
> entices the eye of the tourist. Codes are no longer required, as long as

silence is eliminated. . . . We have the information and the theory. We have the experience; we know that aspartame is bad even in Diet Coke. We don't have to wonder; we just know for the "fun of it." We write just for the fun of it, just as we think, make love, parody, and praise. (*PS*, 27)

We seem to make ethics too "just for the fun of it."

Ethics in *Culturus Interruptus*

What is at stake in Gadamer's notion of play is our very being, our individual self-understanding and our self-understanding as a community capable of a coherent realization of meaning and truth. As Gadamer notes, "The dialectic of experience has its proper fulfillment not in definitive knowledge but in the openness that is made possible by experience itself" (*TM*, 355). This "openness to experience" is mediated by tradition—the "highest type" of hermeneutical experience (*TM*, 361)—and this tradition informs the moral and ethical bonds we share with others in the living present. The "ethics" we establish, however finite and temporary they may be, thus have a source in an *ethos* from which they take their force, and this force, molded for the present, gives a sense of what is right and correct.

But here is where the postmodern hermeneutical situation positions itself to give postmetaphysical culture a character quite different than that imagined by Gadamer. The "play" emerging in postmodernity is not one of "definitive knowledge" (which Gadamer eschews), nor is it one of "openness" (which he espouses). Rather it is one where there is an ironic limitation of possibilities for understanding that stems from an excessive overdetermination of absence and openness.

Ethics thus become what we do and speak when we attempt to coexist *with* others and *in spite* of each other. Ethics are what we invoke to guide us when we don't know what to do. They are what we do to accommodate ourselves to our alienated being. Ethics do not now appear to be that which is transported in the phronetic to-and-fro of Aristotelian/Hegelian inspired Gadamerian hermeneutic movement. Instead they seem to be the pathetic, phrenetic grasping and wandering of a nomadic life. For code-induced speed and con-fusion are now a cultural lifestyle, a way of being and experiencing. Seduction, hyperactivity, hysteria, consumption, simulation, expenditure, and waste form the ethics we live by. We hold others (e.g., public officials) accountable to standards we ourselves do not live by. When we do hold ourselves accountable, it is only when scrutiny is turned on us, or "just for the fun of it," as in *Scruples* (a game of ethics) or in films such as *Indecent Proposal*. We are ethical only when we absolutely have to be, and we judge this by precise statements of law. It is not uncommon to hear our legislative, corporate, and scientific leaders tell us, "I haven't broken a law or violated any ethics." They never say whether or not they have acted morally or immorally, or they leave morals out of their statements so as to suggest that because they haven't transgressed law or ethics that they are moral. Ethics are *not* synonymous with morals, although the positivistic equation of law, ethics, and morals suggests they are. In postmodernity we have deflated any difference in favor of a simulated difference. Simulated difference thus permits an enormous variety of acts to be juxtaposed and tolerated. Not because of rampant relativism, but because no one knows the real difference anymore!

Indeed we are transforming ethics into law and rule in order to have them at our disposal. And dispose of them is precisely what happens, for we have made of ethics a game. In Gadamer's sense a game "has no goal that brings it to an end; rather it renews itself in constant repetition" (*TM*, 103). The irony of the postmodern hermeneutic situation is that there is no "end." There is no end, and that endlessness is constantly repeated. Indeed, this is a cruel inversion of Gadamer's notion that in game-play individuals surrender their particular stances so as to be absorbed in the "productive" transformation of the game. It is also a cruel inversion of the notion that when interpretation is "right" it disappears in the name of furthering the communicative process. What is "right" for artificial intelligence is to consume and expand what is made available by the circuit's code, and what disappears or recedes is the ethos of ethics.

Noisily silent voyeurs in the spectator sport/game of ethics, we count the flaws of the other(s) and exercise damage control on our own failures and absences. Ethics and understanding here become little other than a homeless field on which to hold power, status, and image, or on which to try to disrupt or wrest from others their manipulation of these commodities. The score is what counts. The aesthetics of the staging of simulated differences is what counts (what Adorno or Benjamin might have called an "applied aestheticization" of ethics?). In the agitated age of endless statistics and trivia that shape the aesthetic dimensions of these differences, which tell us who is ethical and who isn't, we, in our speed, skip over what Gadamer termed the "application" of understanding (*TM*, 307). As such ethics are not for someone, but are for *anyone, and no one*. Like trite facades on shopping strip stores, ethics are so much banal decoration necessary for propriety's appearance—surfaces to be willingly consumed, but anxiously and cynically disdained and denied. So it is the call waits.

But perhaps this is how "we" establish ethics in postmodernity. We play in the nomos. Our play is perhaps more slippage and wandering than it is dialectical eventing. This play is somewhat akin to what Americans refer to when they say there is "play" in an automobile steering wheel, meaning that before the steering mechanism actually engages and turns the auto in the desired direction, there is a certain ineffective, inconsequential free movement to be dispensed with. Postmodernity makes of the primary hermeneutic situation a space of slippage and indeterminate, ungrounded commotion.

A consequence of this motion is that ethics do not seem to lie now in the polis of the ethos. That history has become histories has effectively fractured the temporal flow of tradition that yields the continuity necessary for sustenance of ethos and polis. Indeed ethos and polis do not mean now what they meant earlier. But the difference that characterizes this present is not subsumable by invoking the notion of a transformative-becoming-of-a-tradition, for the radical separation of ethos and polis exceeds the embrace of identity. History, and tradition, interrupted and transfigured by the raw speed that *in-sites hysteries,* are unable to sustain the moral sensibilities required to meaningfully ground ethics. Ethics thus becomes a free signifier capable of attaching itself to any signified, upon demand. It is this very detachment of morality from ethics that is problematic. The estrangement of ethics from a mooring in morality permits both the schizoid possibility of moral sentiment without ethical sensitivity and the cynical possibility of con-fusing morality and ethics such that propriety and appropriateness are open to manipulation and can mean anything. As such, ethics are something at our disposal for whatever purposes are deemed necessary. And as such, ethics reside more in the nomos than in ethos or polis. What is fitting and proper (e.g., *kathakonta*) and what is practiced to achieve and display them (e.g., *askesis*) have receded into the nomos where they are undifferentiated and irrelevant to each other. Postmodernity marks a siting of ethos and polis in the "primordial" *miasma* ("forestructurelessness") of meaning and understanding.

Such a siting would make it a mistake to assume that nomos refers only to a particular set of usages or rules, for nomos, like nomad, is rooted in *nemo,* referring to a spreading out and distribution of things in space. Whereas *nomos* does refer to customary or conventional usage, it also carries with it the sense that a particular usage (i.e., polis) is always exceeded by something radically beyond it. Nomad (*nomas*), on the other hand, refers to a dwelling place, a pasturage, a range of dwelling. It also more specifically refers to a movement in this space, a searching for and wandering about it. Thus, to seek what is ethical in the contemporary polis is to be thrust into the nomos. Postmodernity is the current cultural configuration in which we are thrust into the wandering and nomadism where nomos exceeds and transgresses ethos and polis all the while feigning their interconnectedness. Postmodernity ironically is the space of the nomos, the space of the problem of the "origin" that is opened to confound the very structures and meanings it grounds.

(The present discussion of the nomadic wandering in the postmodern hermeneutic situation is, against Gadamer's discourse, a delay or undoing of ethics, resistance, and political action, as well as more fundamentally an undercutting of communicative interaction. To say Gadamer only maintains the status quo is to say meaning wanders within its own space and never gets outside it. In another discourse, though, this very nomadic action forms the basis of Deleuze's notion of "deterritorialization" which is an ethics of resistance and action against the Same.)

In this light Vattimo's reconstruction of hermeneutics, based in part on a rejection of Gadamer's version, is perhaps promising. He proposes that postmodernity ("post-history") is a postapocalyptic utopia where history has a future when that history is understood in an "ironic-hermeneutico-distortive" fashion. That is to say, hermeneutics, following Nietzsche and Heidegger, must recognize a nonreactive nihilism as the only hope for creating ethics. This positive hermeneutics is articulated by Vattimo in the light of Heidegger's *Verwindung* and Nietzsche's "disenchantment." The resulting positive nihilism Vattimo equates with "ethics" (*EM*, 102).

Although I agree with Vattimo on the latter, and with his depiction of Gadamer as an apologist "for what already exists" (*EM*, 143), the crucial problem is knowing whether or not we are now able to know if passive or reactive nihilism simulates active nihilism. To pose this is not to endorse reactive nihilism or *ressentiment*. Rather it is to recognize that the speed with which we are confronted with "reality" and "knowledge" has set us adrift in search of ethics. We are no longer able to determine if our very movement is "ethics," as Vattimo suggests, or whether we must find something which we can grasp, objectify, and know as ethics. Ineffective hysterical consciousness is precisely a lack of a fusion of horizons that could possibly answer this. Vattimo's rehabilitation of Gadamer is thus commendable, but we are still stuck not knowing, and while we wonder, we acknowledge and participate in the "unbecoming" events of daily life alluded to at the outset of this essay. If indeed the horizon of ethics is ethos, the shared customs and culture of a society and epoch, and if the postmodern hermeneutic situation is one of dissociation, ecstacy, and hysteria, then can we but wander? The possibility of a "logos-common consciousness" (*EM*, 107), a living historical community, is rendered moot and mute in the postmodern hermeneutic situation.

I have not aimed here to return Gadamer forever to the tragic pessimism of *Kulturkritik* he so valiantly sought to overcome. Rather, I have asked a perplexing question whose answer offers no refuge or comfort, unless one is willing to wrap it in the warmth of an ontology devoid of praxis. Because Gadamer himself, however, did not eschew praxis, while at the same time embracing an ontological destiny for his hermeneutics, we are forced to reckon *now* with what very much appears to be a very cruel irony beyond the eventing he so cherished and promoted in his hermeneutics. I do not advocate what has happened to Gadamer's hermeneutics anymore than I advocate a Baudrillardian "fatal strategy" (see *FS*). I seek only to call attention to one of the ways that social criticism is disabled and how *culturus interruptus* seduces its bearers into an insidious silence. It is absolutely imperative to comprehend how such silencing irrupts and establishes itself. The trick, however, is to differentiate the possibility of a critique of that silencing from a complicitous expression and denial of it.

Gadamer's hermeneutics have thus articulated a pleasing way to present the "call" resident in the nomos. The postmodern moment, however, appears to have interrupted that call and con-fused the medial spaces and sites by which it events. While we play in the nomos, hoping to understand each other, we continue to see signs of private languages, unbecoming silences, terrible misunderstandings, and unovercome suffering.

The call waits.

And "we" wait.

14

Gadamer, Foucault, and Habermas on Ethical Critique

Michael Kelly

s Foucault's genealogical-archeological method compatible with Gadamer's philosophical hermeneutics, at least in ethics? Given Foucault's criticisms of hermeneutics in *The Birth of the Clinic*,[1] his rejection of the text as the center of linguistic and historical meaning, and his concern for the roles of power and nondiscursive practices in the formation of knowledge, the answer to this question seems clear enough, at least from Foucault's perspective. The answer seems equally negative from Gadamer's side, since, following Heidegger, he rejects Nietzsche's genealogy centered on the will to power as part of the last stage of the history of the metaphysics of presence. Furthermore, the Foucaultian emphasis on discontinuity in history contradicts Gadamer's stress on historical continuity; under Foucault, Gadamer's "fusion of horizons" becomes a seething diffusion of horizons within a network of power/ knowledge configurations. It thus seems that this question about the compatibility of Gadamer's and Foucault's philosophies is hardly worth asking.

I shall argue, however, that hermeneutics and genealogy are complementary in certain important respects in ethics, especially if they are unified to answer Jürgen Habermas's unrelenting objections. Habermas has long criticized hermeneutics and has more recently turned his critical pen on Foucault. I hope to show that a combined hermeneutic-genealogical mode of ethical critique is a more effective response than either mode alone to Habermas's objections. My discussion will have two sections: after arguing that Gadamer's and Foucault's philosophies are not incompatible, in principle, I shall respond to Habermas's criticisms that neither philosophy is capable of sustaining philosophical critique; then I shall discuss Gadamer's and Foucault's conceptions of philosophical ethics and particularly their notions of ethical critique.

I

First of all, I do not think it is accurate to say that Foucault's genealogy is, by definition, antihermeneutics. The kind of hermeneutics that Foucault criticizes in his early *The Birth of the Clinic* is depth hermeneutics, a hermeneutics of suspicion, an attempt to uncover hidden truths obscured by ideology or other devices of distortion.[2] But this is not the kind of hermeneutics that Gadamer has ever advocated,[3] so Foucault's early critique does not apply to him. In fact, it is more of a self-critique of the method Foucault himself used in *Madness and Civilization*. Moreover, Foucault claims in one of his last interviews[4] that the hermeneutics of the subject, marked by the poles of subjectivity and truth, was always a major concern in his writings. He thus has no principled objection to hermeneutics, at least certain forms of it.[5]

Furthermore, the apparent radical difference between Gadamer and Foucault because of their respective concepts of tradition and discontinuity has been exaggerated. Hermeneutics does not ignore discontinuities and conflicts within traditions; rather, it claims that some continuity is a condition for understanding in general; it is even, one could add, a condition for understanding discontinuity itself. And genealogy does not ignore the evident continuities and harmonies within and between traditions; rather, it analyzes the discursive and nondiscursive practices which generate discontinuities and which underlie whatever continuities there may be.[6] Gadamer's and Foucault's philosophies are thus not mutually exclusive, at least so long as the hermeneutic emphasis on tradition—the effectivity of history in the present—does not make us conceptually blind to discontinuities, and the genealogical stress on discontinuity—the history of the present with origins in history—does not imply the wholesale rejection of tradition.

At the same time, there is a major source of solidarity between Gadamer and Foucault, which is that both have been subject to Habermas's critique that each is uncritical, in principle. Habermas argues that, for somewhat different reasons, neither Gadamer nor Foucault can account for the critical stance that they claim for their respective philosophies.[7]

II

Habermas's critique of Gadamer has two, somewhat incompatible dimensions: he claims both that hermeneutic reflection is naively universal, because it overlooks the many forms of distortion lying within language and its uses; and that it is not universal enough, because it excludes the possibility of a truly universal reference system, a normative basis of social theory free from such distortions. Habermas thus charges that philosophical hermeneutics both exaggerates and underestimates the power of reflection.

The first objection is that Gadamer makes a false move from his correct insight into the *Vorurteilsstruktur* of understanding to the rehabilitation of prejudices and authority, and he thereby undermines critical reflection: "Gadamer's prejudice for the rights of prejudices certified by tradition denies the power of reflection. The latter proves itself, however, in being able to reject the claim of tradition."[8] The hermeneutic, ontological link between understanding and tradition does not imply an epistemological priority of tradition over critique and reflection. If Gadamer's hermeneutics does have this implication, then it cannot take account of the distortions for which language itself is responsible, which means that it cannot distinguish a true, noncoerced fusion of horizons from a false, coerced one. According to Habermas, when hermeneutics becomes self-reflective and recognizes the need for normative criteria with which such a distinction can be made, it is thereby transformed into the critique of ideology.

Habermas's second objection is that, even if he were to grant Gadamer his ontological claim about the historicity of understanding, there remains the epistemological problem of how to establish a universal normative basis, especially in moral and social theory, to distinguish critically between rational and irrational aspects of tradition. Habermas's claim, in short, is that Gadamer's overemphasis on historicity undermines any such normative basis, without which moral and social theory are impossible.

Gadamer's persistent response to Habermas has been to argue that he misunderstands the hermeneutic claims about the relationship between reason and tradition:

the thing which hermeneutics teaches us is to see through the dogmatism of asserting an opposition between the ongoing natural "tradition" and the reflective appropriation of it. For behind the assertion stands a dogmatic objectivism that distorts the very concept of hermeneutic reflection itself.[9]

Instead of this dogmatic opposition, Gadamer sees a dialectical relationship between reason and tradition as a consequence of "the effectivity of history in understanding." He also argues that it is Habermas who overestimates the competence of reason: "Inasmuch as it [reason] seeks to penetrate the masked interests which reflect public opinion, it implies its own freedom from any ideology, and that means that it enthrones its own norms and ideals as self-evident and absolute."[10] The critique of ideology is not a substitute for hermeneutics, because it is itself always subject to hermeneutic reflection.

III

Whereas Gadamer ignores power, according to Habermas, Foucault brings power into the philosophical picture, although not in the way Habermas had hoped.[11] Habermas accuses Foucault of stressing the relationship between knowledge and power to such an extent that he undermines the epistemological distinction between knowledge distorted by power and knowledge which, though still linked to power, can nevertheless claim to be true. Once again, ideology is the problem, though it is different here than in Gadamer's case. Habermas insists that Foucault's seemingly total critique of ideology must be tempered by a critical social theory which acknowledges the influence of power, but which is able to provide a normative basis for making distinctions between good and evil uses of power.[12] Thus, Habermas again invokes the need for a universal, normative social theory to provide a critical dimension to the otherwise uncritical genealogy.[13]

Foucault responds to Habermas by claiming that the critique of ideology is subject to the very same power dynamics that it is introduced to criticize.[14] This does not mean that power now becomes total or is allowed to exercise its influences without normative restraints; nor does it mean that reason is impotent so long as it fails to purify itself of power relations:

The problem is not of trying to dissolve them [relations of power] in the utopia of a perfectly transparent communication, but to give one's self the rules of law, the techniques of management, and also the ethics, the *ethos*, the practice of self, which would allow these games of power to be played with a minimum of domination.[15]

Foucault is thus concerned both to understand and to limit the domination that results from the games of power; it is just that, like Gadamer and in sharp contrast to Habermas, he is more modest about how much reason can do for us in these respects. In the end, his response to Habermas is similar to Gadamer's. Moreover, it is one concrete, significant instance where genealogy complements hermeneutics; for Foucault undercuts the critique of ideology into which Habermas has tried to transform hermeneutics.

IV

Nevertheless, there is a serious philosophical problem raised by Habermas's objections to Gadamer's and Foucault's philosophies: Is philosophical critique still possible once we acknowledge the pervasive presence of tradition and power within the very structure of reflection itself? Do the dialectics between reason/tradition and knowledge/power undermine critique? Although Gadamer, Foucault, and Habermas have been at odds on the answer to this question, it is not because they disagree about the need for philosophical critique. Their disagreement is rather about how this critique is possible, what form it should take, and how it can be most effective in practical terms. These issues are related, of course, because the conditions that make critique possible—whether they are grounded in tradition, practices of the self, or the universal presuppositions of rational speech—are what determine its form and efficacy.

So how is critique possible, first, according to Gadamer and then according to Foucault, in each case in the field of ethics? The basic task of philosophical ethics today, according to Gadamer, is to synthesize Aristotle's notions of *phronesis* and ethos with Kant's formalism and his notion of the "natural dialectic" in ethical reflection.[16] The mere suggestion of such a synthesis seems problematic, for how can these two ethical theories be unified when they are based on what seem to be two opposing notions of practical reason? Aristotle's *phronesis* is conditioned by its ethos (the customs, habits, laws, etc., of its polis), and Kant's practical reason is pure, i.e., unconditioned by any empirical factors definitive of a particular, concrete ethos. Gadamer argues that the synthesis is indeed possible because, although the idea of the purity of practical reason represents "the unconditionality of our duty against the plea of our desires," it does not "determine the whole of our ethical being":[17]

> The autonomy of ethical reason certainly has the character of intelligible self-determination. But that does not exclude the empirical conditionedness of all human actions and decisions. . . . The recognition of human conditionedness is compatible with the sublime unconditionality of ethical law.[18]

But, still, how can the conditionedness and unconditionedness of practical reason be reconciled in ethical reflection?

Gadamer argues that the conflict between conditionedness and unconditionedness is not a conflict between two conceptions of practical reason; rather, it is a dialectic within practical reason itself. More precisely, the dialectic is between the laws that practical reason gives to itself and the context of ethical deliberation and action from which these laws emerge and to which they must then be applied. As expressions of practical reason's self-determination, the laws are unconditional with respect to their intended universal applicability; but deliberation and action are conditioned by the restraints on this self-determination which are embodied in practical reason's ethos. So the relevant attributes here are not "conditioned" and "unconditioned" (as applied to practical reason), but "conditioned" (as applied to practical reason) and "unconditional" (as applied to the laws articulated by conditioned practical reason).

This same dialectic helps to render Gadamer's proposed synthesis of Aristotelian and Kantian ethics much less paradoxical than it seemed to be at first; for it is similar both to the "natural dialectic" in practical reason which Kant discusses in the *Groundwork for the Metaphysics of Morals*[19] and to Aristotle's dialectic between *phronesis* and ethos. In all three cases, the dialectic is, to use Kant's language, a manifestation within practical reason of a conflict between our ordinary moral consciousness (our recognition of our moral duties, laws, rights, etc.) and the empirical (moral and immoral) forces in our ethos which lead this moral consciousness astray. Philosophical ethics is introduced to clarify and strengthen moral consciousness so that it might offset these forces and also distinguish the moral from the immoral aspects of its ethos.

Gadamer refers to the natural dialectic within practical reason as a mixture of the "substance of ethical life" and the "watchful conscience." Aristotle represents the substance of ethical life by showing us that "the necessary limitation [of conditionedness] that underlies our insight into what is ethically right or just does not necessarily lead us to a corrupt mixture of motives";[20] the dichotomy between completely pure and completely corrupt (corrupt because empirical) practical reason is too extreme and untenable. And Kant represents the watchful conscience that cautions us about the limits of Aristotle's "all-encompassing concepts," such as "what is appropriate," because they are often powerless against the counterweight of natural, nonmoral inclinations that lead us toward evil. Thus, whereas Kant makes us aware of the limitations of an empirically conditioned practical reason, Aristotle demonstrates how we can best develop and utilize this, our only type of practical reason, whose purity is relative to its conditionedness. This synthesis of Aristotelian and Kantian ethics, characterized by the dialectic between *phronesis* and ethos, unconditionedness and conditionedness, and duty and inclination, is, according to Gadamer, what determines the possibility of philosophical ethics.

But Habermas's question still lingers. For how is ethical critique possible in the face of these dialectics? In Gadamer's proposed synthesis, critique is made possible primarily by the Kantian contribution—the categorical imperative, the procedural test of whether moral laws are unconditional. Kant provides a normative criterion for deciding whether the moral (social, political, economic, or legal) norms or substantive principles of a particular ethos are valid: they are valid only if they satisfy the categorical imperative, that is, if they can show themselves to be universal. Although practical reason remains situated in a single ethos at any given time, the validity of its laws may have a broader, even universal extension if they pass the test of the categorical imperative.

What Gadamer's hermeneutics makes clear, as I have interpreted it here and elsewhere, is that Kant's moral law is not incompatible with the recognition of the conditionedness of practical reason. One convenient, if unexpected, example of such an unconditional law that is possible despite the conditionedness of practical reason is Habermas's own universalization principle, which he formulates as follows:

> Every valid norm must satisfy the condition that the consequences and side-effects which probably follow from its general compliance can, for the satisfaction of the interests of every individual, be accepted without force by all those affected.[21]

The validity of the laws articulated by practical reason can still be universally valid, even though practical reason itself is historically conditioned (as Habermas himself acknowledges it is), if they satisfy the conditions of this principle. In fact, laws are valid only if they satisfy this principle; if they do, they are universal, which is really just another way of saying that valid moral laws are, by definition, universal.

The substantive difference in ethics between Gadamer and Habermas concerns the issue of the grounding or justification of Kant's categorical imperative or, for my purposes here, Habermas's universalization principle. If by "to ground" is understood "to give rationally defensible reasons," Gadamer argues that the reasons, like practical reason itself, are bound to a particular tradition, whereas Habermas argues they can be derived from the universal, structural features of the competence for communicative action which distinguishes modernity from its predecessors and postmodern rivals alike.[22] Gadamer argues that the structural feature of practical reason—the natural dialectic—cannot be overcome; whereas Habermas continues to insist it must be if ethics is ever to be critical. Foucault, for his part, provides a model of ethical critique which, I shall try to show, complements Gadamer's model and thereby strengthens Gadamer's position on this key issue of how moral laws can be justified.

V

Ethics is, for Foucault, one of three domains of genealogical or historical ontology: the first domain is truth—how we constitute ourselves as subjects of knowledge; the second is power—how we constitute ourselves as subjects acting on others; and the third is ethics—how we constitute ourselves as moral agents.[23] The constitution of the self as a moral agent has four aspects: (1) ethical substance—"the way in which the individual has to constitute this or that part of himself as the prime material of his moral conduct"; (2) mode of subjection—"the way in which the individual establishes his relation to the rule and recognizes himself as obliged to put it into practice"; (3) the forms of elaboration of ethical work that one performs on oneself; and (4) the telos of the ethical subject.[24] What Foucault analyzes through these four aspects is the "process in which the individual delimits that part of himself that will form the object of his moral practice, defines his position relative to the precept he will follow, and decides on a certain mode of being that will serve as his moral goal."[25]

Now, what is critique in this model of philosophical ethics? In answering this question, Foucault associates himself, to the surprise of many, especially Habermas, with modernity and the Enlightenment and, in particular, with Kant. What he links himself to is "not faithfulness to doctrinal elements, but rather the permanent reactivation of an attitude—that is, of a philosophical *ethos* that could be described as a permanent critique of our historical era."[26] Kant is credited with introducing this ethos, which is continued by Foucault through a form of ethical critique which has two sides: one is oriented toward what he calls the "'contemporary limits of the necessary,' that is, toward what is not or is no longer indispensable for the constitution of ourselves as autonomous subjects";[27] while the other, which he characterizes as being more positive, is introduced with the following question:

> in what is given to us as universal, necessary, obligatory, what place is occupied by whatever is singular, contingent, and the product of arbitrary constraints? The point, in brief, is to transform the critique conducted in the form of necessary limitation into a practical critique that takes the form of possible transgression.[28]

Critique thus incorporates both an analysis of the limits of the necessary, of what is presented to us as universal when it may not be, and an exploration of possible transgressions of these same limits.[29] A perfect object for Foucault's critique is Habermas's claim to have established a universal basis for philosophical ethics in the structural features of communication. Another object, of course, is the claim that moral laws must be universal to be valid.

The design or purpose of Foucault's proposed new form of critique is *genealogical*: "it will separate out, from the contingency that has made us what we are, the possibility of no longer being, doing, or thinking what we are, do, or think."[30] And its method is *archaeological*: "[it] will seek to treat the instances of discourse that articulate what we think, say, and do as so many historical events."[31] This genealogical-archaeological critique becomes more concrete when it is translated into analyses of ethical problematizations structured according to the four aspects outlined above. By "problematization," Foucault means the following: "It is the totality of discursive or non-discursive practices that introduces something into the play of true and false and constitutes it as an object for thought (whether in the form of moral reflection, scientific knowledge, political analysis, etc.)."[32]

These analyses are tied to historical ethical practices of the self, and are as much part of an attitude or ethos as of an abstract theory.[33] Again, a perfect example for Foucault is Habermas's "practice" of grounding the universalization principle and discourse ethics in general in the allegedly universal presuppositions of rational speech. After arguing that this principle does not have a universal ground, a Foucaultian would either have to argue that such a universalization principle is impossible, or have to demonstrate, as a Gadamerian pursuing the proposed synthesis of Aristotelian and Kantian ethics would have to do, that a universalization principle might indeed be possible without itself being universal, i.e., without having the universal ground on which Habermas insists. And, again, the Foucaultian would have to continue to challenge any claim that a particular moral law is universal and the more basic claim that moral laws must be universal, in principle.

Finally, the coherence of the analyses that make up Foucault's ethical critique is ensured on three levels: methodologically, the analyses are based on the combined archaeological and genealogical study of practices as both a technological mode of rationality and as a strategic game of liberties; theoretically, they have their coherence "in the definition of the historically unique forms in which the generalities of our relations to things [knowledge], to others [power], to ourselves [ethics], have been problematized"; and, practically, their coherence consists in "the care brought to the process of putting historico-critical reflection to the test of concrete practices."[34]

Now, to understand whether Foucault's ethics is viable, it is important to ask the Habermasian question of what it presupposes; for such presuppositions are, Habermas would insist, what determine whether ethics can be critical. If Foucault's ethical critique does not assume a neutral standpoint and does not deny that it can have practical efficacy, how can it account for its standpoint and for the efficacy it promises? Or does Foucault leave us, as Habermas claims, with, at worst, a deeply entrenched pessimism about the prospects of freedom and, at best, a decisionistic or actionistic basis for engaging in activities to advance freedom?[35]

First of all, despite Habermas's claim to the contrary, Foucault never abandoned the Enlightenment ideal of freedom qua autonomy. As he makes clear, the design of ethics is "the undefined work of freedom," for the ontological condition of ethics is freedom.[36] As early as *The Birth of the Clinic*, Foucault's purpose was critical with an eye on freedom, in the sense that the analysis of the emergence of the discourse of medicine was intended to open the task of transforming the practice of medicine. If Foucault is asked, "transforming it for whom and for what purpose?" he would answer that archeology is diagnostic and, to continue the medical reference, the answer depends on the patients; the participants in the relevant practices are the ones to decide what the cure might be.[37] Because they have not attained freedom yet, neither in medicine nor in any other practice, Foucault introduces the historical ontology of the present both to identify the limits on freedom and, once this is done, to explore actions that might eliminate them. He begins with the action of disturbing "what was previously considered immobile," of fragmenting "what was thought unified," of showing "the heterogeneity of what was imagined consistent with itself."[38] Such identification and action are constant pursuits within the ethos of the Enlightenment.

In his effort to perpetuate this ethos, Foucault does of course presuppose that those who undertake or listen to the critique, as well as those who initiate or participate in any political action to follow up on its practical effects, must also be committed to freedom; otherwise, the critique would be unintelligible and the action impossible. But he need not presuppose, as Habermas does, that this commitment is universal; he focuses instead on local rather than global critique and opposition. And he does not think it is necessary, let alone possible, to justify the form of critique or action he has proposed. The shared commitment to freedom is grounded in itself,[39] for modernity creates its normativity out of itself.[40] Against Habermas, he argues that, because of the fallibilism of the method of rational reconstruction used in discourse ethics, Habermas himself can defend the universality of the competence for discourse only as a hypothesis to be confirmed or not by further empirical evidence. As a result, Habermas's own ground of critique is as tenuous as he claims the hermeneutic and genealogical grounds of critiques are.

VI

In the end, perhaps Gadamer and Foucault's best possible response to the Habermasian critique that it is not possible to criticize tradition or power without presupposing certain universal criteria is to retort, as William Connolly suggests, that Habermas cannot make good on his critique unless he can first defend the universality of the criteria that his own form of ethical critique presupposes.[41] So far, he has been unable to convince his Gadamerian and Foucaultian opponents on this score.

Thus, the dialogue between the ethical theories of Gadamer, Foucault, and Habermas consists in a plurality of conflicting options concerning the modern moral point of view and how it can be justified. These issues are, in turn, part of the larger question of how to understand modernity. What unifies this plurality and quells the conflict to some degree, however, is the solidarity on the Enlightenment ideal of moral freedom, which Gadamer calls the highest principle of reason.[42] Freedom can only be enhanced by this dialogue; for Gadamer, Foucault, and Habermas have all devoted their philosophical work to the "patient labor giving form to our impatience for liberty."

15

Phronesis as Understanding: Situating Philosophical Hermeneutics

Günter Figal

Translated by Lawrence K. Schmidt

A characteristic of philosophical hermeneutics is always also to be hermeneutic in itself. This means that the development of a theory of understanding is itself already an understanding. Therefore, the development of such a theory in the sense of a philosophical hermeneutics has neither the status of an "art" of understanding (see *GW*II, 254) nor does it relate to everyday understanding as the philosophy of science relates to science. Philosophical hermeneutics does not aim to raise everyday understanding to the level of a conscious use of rules (*GW*II, 254). Nor can one appease everyday understanding by claiming that philosophical hermeneutics does not concern its clarification.

The assertion that philosophical hermeneutics is itself an understanding can be well justified in Hans-Georg Gadamer's book *Truth and Method*. The wealth of theories, which are developed and related to one another in this book so that the "Fundamentals of a Philosophical Hermeneutics" may be envisioned, must first be understood and made present in their intelligibility before one is able to form that concept of philosophical hermeneutics that these theories by themselves do not simply offer. So philosophical hermeneutics is subject to that "circular structure" of understanding that it itself develops (see *GW*I, 270ff., 296ff.). This means that it moves among the various individual theories it has selected in such a manner that the whole of philosophical hermeneutics has always already been anticipated. And it develops this whole by considering carefully the individually selected theories.

Among the theories that philosophical hermeneutics presents in their intelligibility, one theory is surely primary: the practical philosophy of Aristotle. In saying this one challenges the primacy of another theory for philosophical hermeneutics: namely Heidegger's analysis of Dasein as developed in *Being and Time*. Despite the unquestionable significance of Heidegger's analysis of Dasein for *Truth and Method*, one is justified to draw this conclusion for two reasons. First, and this is the more important of the two reasons, the recourse to the practical philosophy of Aristotle establishes the philosophical situation of hermeneutics. Second, Heidegger's analysis of Dasein is relevant to philosophical hermeneutics especially because it is itself influenced by Aristotle.

Allow me to briefly expand upon these two reasons. Concerning the first: the analysis of *phronesis* (practical wisdom or practical knowledge) is referred to in order to explicate the structure of understanding in the discussions on "The hermeneutic actuality of Aristotle," which are central to the theory of *Truth and Method*. As *phronesis*, understanding is also "not separable from a created being, but determined by it and determining for it" (*GWI*, 317; *TM*, 312). As in *phronesis*, so understanding is also concerned to bring to bear in the particular a mode of being in which one always already is. And this is neither an application in the sense of technical knowledge nor is it a pure observation of the unchanging (*GWI*, 219, 321). In the interpretation of Aristotle's practical philosophy, philosophical hermeneutics involves itself in a very specific manner: hermeneutic reflection, in interpreting Aristotle, operates not only in relation to a tradition from which it can alone receive clarification of its present siltation; in addition it reveals in Aristotle what is to be accomplished in interpretation. But there is more. In the interpretation of Aristotle, philosophical hermeneutics attains clarity concerning how it is to continue the inherited philosophy. *Truth and Method* is clearly also a contribution to the justification of the humanities—a contribution that is concerned to free the humanities from the problematic analogy to the natural sciences and to make it intelligible as a form of understanding. Although in *Truth and Method* the humanities are mentioned together with "ways of experiencing" like philosophy, art, and history—and only these—in Gadamer's later works the relation of the humanities to "ethical" or "practical" knowledge, in Aristotle's sense, is emphasized more and more. So one reads in the essay "Ethos und Logos" of 1989:

> The humanities are not only a section of the sciences. In spite of all their "inexactness," they are the authentic transporters of the great weight of tradition, which found its language in Hegel's concept of the absolute spirit and its forms and which continues in other languages as the "humanities" or as the "*lettres.*"[1]

In the humanities, in the "moral sciences," the spirit of practical philosophy lives. Today it is important to establish the vitality of the spirit of practical philosophy in the humanities. This can be accomplished only if the humanities do not strive to attain the ideal of a "method" inappropriate for them and are able to make themselves intelligible as effective forms of understanding related to "truth." Such intelligibility can be found in hermeneutic reflection and so philosophical hermeneutics, in the end, carries the weight of the tradition of what Aristotle called political knowledge (1094a27). Clearly, only because philosophical hermeneutics bears the weight of this tradition on its shoulders can it claim universality for itself. It justifies this claim "because understanding and communication . . . are the effective forms of human social life, which is, in the final analysis, a community of conversation" (*GW*II, 255).

Therefore, the practical philosophy of Aristotle has a unique priority for philosophical hermeneutics and so Heidegger's analysis of Dasein does not have this priority. When the theory of *Truth and Method* does refer to Heidegger's analysis of Dasein, this analysis chiefly appears as a clarifying radicalization of what Aristotle considered *phronesis* to be. The belongingness of understanding to its "object"—which one may write only in quotation marks—is emphasized especially in relation to Heidegger's characterization of understanding. More exactly stated, it is emphasized in relation to Heidegger's idea that understanding in its projective character must always be considered along with the thrownness of one's own Dasein. If the possibilities of being are experienced in understanding in such a manner that one can interpret them as being in them, then they must always be those possibilities in which one already "finds" oneself. But in this, the particular structure of "practical knowledge" (*GW*V, 230ff.; *GW*I, 237; *TM*, 233) is recognizable as it was developed by Aristotle and is "actualized" by philosophical hermeneutics. And finally, it is well-known that Heidegger oriented himself on Aristotle's discussion of *phronesis* when he was concerned to assert the structure of Dasein in opposition to an "ontology of the present-to-hand" (*GW*V, 244).

However, as clear as the priority of Aristotle's practical philosophy in philosophical hermeneutics may be, an attentive reader will not find it easy to subsume all the aspects developed in *Truth and Method* under a concept of understanding that refers back to Aristotle's discussion of *phronesis*. Therefore, one cannot state without misunderstanding that philosophical hermeneutics bears the weight of practical philosophy on its shoulders. In a more careful examination, the idea that the "horizon" of hermeneutic ontology is language proves itself to be completely independent from the Aristotelian perspective. Language, as it is discussed in *Truth and Method*, is not merely the form of the articulation of practical knowledge; it is not merely the form of the articulation of an understanding that in itself has the character of practical knowledge. Language is rather an "event" that can still best be conceived following the "guiding image" of the game and explicated by the unique experience of the classical. It is "the game of language itself" (*GWI*, 494; *TM*, 490) within which one, in understanding, is always already embedded. And therefore, understanding can only be accomplished if the game of language has always already occurred. Since this is the case, philosophical hermeneutics cannot be just an unselfish bearer of the tradition of practical philosophy. It must necessarily be more, since its means of continuing the tradition of practical philosophy cause this tradition to be modified. Since the accomplishment of understanding is always already embedded in the event of language, one must express the relation of hermeneutics to practical philosophy thusly: what is called "practical philosophy" with reference to Aristotle, is not simply continued in philosophical hermeneutics, but it finds a new place in a new context.

If philosophical hermeneutics reinterprets practical philosophy in such a manner in continuing it, then practical philosophy may retain its priority for the theory of philosophical hermeneutics only in a very specific respect: philosophical hermeneutics orients itself interpretively toward practical philosophy. But this is just one aspect, for in order to initiate the reinterpretation of practical philosophy at all, philosophical hermeneutics must already find itself in a horizon. And this implies that it cannot be identical with practical philosophy. This thought may be summarized in this way: just because philosophical hermeneutics bears the weight of the tradition of practical philosophy on its shoulders, it cannot itself be a practical philosophy. In this sense philosophical hermeneutics makes reference to Heidegger not only or primarily where Heidegger's theory contains Aristotelian influences. For this reason, in looking back, the author of *Truth and Method* could also say that philosophical hermeneutics specifically attempted "to follow the direction of the questioning of the later Heidegger and to make it available in a new manner" (*GWII*, 10). The new availability of the later Heidegger and his path toward language consists, however, in the fact that by following this path, the weight of the tradition of practical philosophy can be interpretively received by philosophical hermeneutics.

I will now attempt to explicate these thoughts more thoroughly. For this I will first discuss in greater detail than previously the theory of practical knowledge as it was proposed by Aristotle and actualized by philosophical hermeneutics. Following and related to this, I wish to demonstrate more exactly how the reinterpretation of practical philosophy relates to the hermeneutic theory of language.

As concerns Aristotle, the form of knowledge called *phronesis* is unique in that it not only relates to acting, but that it is effective in acting itself and only in acting. Alternatively, one can formulate Aristotle's thought to be that acting truly deserves to be called acting only when acting itself can be conceived of as knowledge, as the completion of knowledge. This thought is more clearly expressed by Aristotle where he reveals a noetic element—or as one should more exactly state: an element comparable to *nous*—in *phronesis* itself, than in his discussion of the so-called practical syllogism. As is stated in the passage of the *Nicomachean Ethics* relevant to this point, *phronesis* conforms to *nous* in that *phronesis*, so to speak, "lies opposite" *nous*. This is the case since *nous* is the direct apprehension of limitations, i.e., the simple definiteness that cannot be expressed in language but only can be "touched and said," as one may state following *Metaphysics* (Book IX, sec. 10). *Phronesis* aims at a comparable end about which there can be no knowledge but only "perception" and, although not the perception of individual objects, it is rather of the type like when we "perceive" that the triangle is the final geometric figure, therefore, a figure that is not further separable into other figures (1142a25–29). And it is not a mistake to interpret what is apprehended in *phronesis* to be acting itself, more specifically, that action which is recognized as correct by means of deliberations in a particular situation and for which one deliberatively decides. Seen in this light, what is apprehended in *phronesis* is "what is to be done" (*das Tunliche*, *GW*, 244). And one has to understand this "what is to be done" as having been apprehended, insofar as the deliberations of practical knowledge have presupposed it from the first. It is just because "what is to be done" has always already been apprehended in this sense, that the specific deliberations are at all elements of practical knowledge. What is apprehended in practical knowledge is clearly not this or that specific possible action alone. Rather the good itself, the good in the form of the good life, is always already and primarily apprehended. Every deliberate action, therefore every action that truly deserves this name, always already answers the question whether a possible action conforms to the completion of life in such a manner that this life in its totality can be an ordered one incorporating all the particular actions. To live well one is required to accomplish a coordinating activity with reference to one's life, which with reference to a particular area of life is comparable to the accomplishment of an architect or general (1094a13f.). Therefore, "what is to be done" is directly apprehended since each considered possible action must then be recognized as "something good" if it is chosen. But it can be something good only if it agrees with the good itself, the good life. The good itself, in the sense of the good life, is for Aristotle an *arche*, the principle of acting: knowledge of an *arche* can only be, as is stated in *Metaphysics* (Book I, sec. 2), a beholding, an apprehending knowledge. And the good is also an *arche* (982b9f.).

Aristotle's point will become clearer when one considers that the referenced place from the *Metaphysics* does not occur in the discussion of *phronesis* but in the discussion of wisdom, knowledge in its primary sense, the knowledge of philosophy. Aristotle discovered in *phronesis* a unique knowledge of acting, precisely a practical knowledge. Yet he wanted to make clear, at the same time, the parallel between this knowledge and knowledge in its primary sense. That one is nevertheless only concerned with a parallel is in itself already reflected in Aristotle's choice of words. Since practical knowledge is an apprehending it is not termed *nous* but *aisthesis*, "perception." The vision of an end that is unique to this knowledge is, as such, only possible in the process of acting, for it first constitutes the action as such.

In relation to this idea, one is able to better understand the "hermeneutic actuality" of Aristotle. Although "hermeneutic consciousness," and so the accomplishment of understanding, does not concern an "ethical knowledge," as is explicitly stated in *Truth and Method*, nevertheless the accomplishment of understanding does contain in itself, just as ethical knowledge does, the "task of application" (*GWI*, 320; *TM*, 315). This idea can also be formulated as: understanding is always of such a type that it is completed in the development of an understanding [*Verständnis*]. Understanding is always something other than mere contemplation. What is understood is clearly always something that already determines one's own being, and the task of understanding is to bring this forth. But what always and already determines one's being and what is to be brought forth, is tradition [*Überlieferung*]. As is stated in *Truth and Method*:

> The interpreter who is concerned with tradition, seeks to apply this. But also here [as with reference to *phronesis*—G.F.] that does not mean that the inherited text is present and understood by the interpreter as a uni-

versal and must therefore first be brought into use for particular applica-
tions. The interpreter wants to understand nothing other than this universal—the text—, i.e. to understand what tradition says, what constitutes
the meaning and significance of the text. In order to understand this, he
cannot ignore himself and the concrete hermeneutic situation in which
he finds himself. He must relate the text to the situation if he wants to
understand at all. (*GWI*, 329; *TM*, 324)

If one takes the hermeneutic actuality of *phronesis* seriously, as it is explicated in this quotation, then one could more pointedly state that only in
tradition can there exist something like a hermeneutic situation. The
interpreter does not apply the inherited text to a situation that he has
already experienced. Rather the text opens up a situation for understanding wherein one must ask how one can conform to [*entsprechen*] the
text in the development of an understanding. Therefore, tradition is the
good itself for the interpreter. And with reference to the always already
apprehended tradition, the interpreter has to ask whether his momentary understanding is "something good."

If one would only say this, then one would clearly not go beyond a
mere analogy between ethical knowledge and understanding. Ethical
knowledge would remain, as it is explicitly stated in the context of *Truth
and Method*, "a model for the problems that occur in the hermeneutic
task" (*GWI*, 329; *TM*, 324). Philosophical hermeneutics can accept the
weight of the tradition of practical philosophy only when the understanding of tradition is not only an isolated understanding of texts but
when it develops the life of the whole in the understanding of tradition
to such a degree that it may be called "good." And the practical relevance
of philosophical hermeneutics appears to be implied in this sense, when
Gadamer states that the "tremendous destructive power that has been
placed in human hands thanks to science" may only "be controlled by
superior reasonableness, a *phronesis* in the old Aristotelian sense."[2] However, such a superior reasonableness develops, in no small part, in the
understanding of tradition, which itself is primarily found in texts—the
texts of Aristotle, for example, where the unique condition of practical
knowledge, its superior reasonableness, is clarified.

But can the understanding of tradition be the accomplishment of
a good life in the Aristotelian sense and is understanding therefore
phronesis? If this were the case, tradition as well as understanding, which
continually applies it, would have to be comprehended as the completion of life. The relationship among particular understandings would be
nothing other than a unified life, whose unity would be due to the

enduring prudence in which the life is fulfilled. Understanding would be a linguistic accomplishment that has always already been fulfilled. To use an expression of Aristotle, it would be a *psyches energeia kata logon*: the living activity of thinking, which essentially articulates itself in speech and is concerned to unify the multiple relations and moments of life. Insofar as understanding in its accomplishment would do justice to the tradition, it would even be a *psyches energeia kat' areten*: this activity in its best form (1098a7, 1098a16f.).

Although understanding, just as the understood tradition, is certainly linguistic in character, understanding as it is conceived in philosophical hermeneutics has also at least the character of a linguistic activity, which Aristotle specified to be only a capability and not an actuality of practical knowledge. Understanding is at least always a trusting in what is spoken. It is constituted by following what is said (1098a4).

The importance of this idea for philosophical hermeneutics can be made clear in three points. (1) If philosophical hermeneutics were completely oriented toward the Aristotelian discussion of *phronesis*, then it could accept without any problem Humboldt's determination of language, which is that "true language occurs in the act of its actual utterance" and therefore is "not a work (*ergon*) but an activity (*energeia*)."[3] Humboldt's theory of language, however, is criticized by Gadamer as "an abstraction that we must reverse for our purposes" (*GWI*, 445; *TM*, 441). There is more, and so (2) the game, which guides the discussion of the linguistic tradition, has, as is explicitly stated, "the character of a work, of an *ergon*, and not only of an *energeia*" (*GWI*, 116; *TM*, 110). Although it is also stated the game is "always retrieving, pure fulfillment, *energeia*, which has its *telos* in itself" (*GWI*, 118; *TM*, 113), this does not mean that the complete presence of a game would actually be achieved through its being played. The completion of a game can always only be "fulfilled" when all possible individual playings belong to a unitary space of a playing [*Spielraum*] and so the individual playings are not negatively affected by the underdetermination of a questionable meaning. In the space of play, in the "world of a work of art" (*GWI*, 118; *TM*, 113) and in relation to the whole tradition, each particular, completed understanding is meaningful without it having to incorporate the whole playing field of meaning. If it were otherwise and understanding were pure completion, then philosophical hermeneutics could not (3) refer to the foreignness of tradition, which essentially characterizes every understanding. The understanding of tradition occurs "between foreignness and familiarity," and "the true situation of hermeneutics is in this between" (*GWI*, 300; *TM*, 295; see also *GWII*, 63). Due to such foreignness, understanding, as discussed in philosophical hermeneutics, is never just the completion of what had been already and continued to be at work, but it is always also the experience of an event. On the other hand, the experience of this event has the character of an apprehension [*Vernehmen*]. It is an apprehension that differs from Aristotle's *aisthesis* in that it is not identical to the completion of understanding. There exists a difference between the apprehension of tradition and the completion of understanding. This difference is the situation of philosophical hermeneutics. Although philosophical hermeneutics clearly belongs in this situation, it is not a practical philosophy. Since it bears the burden of the tradition of practical philosophy on its shoulders, philosophical hermeneutics reinterprets practical philosophy. What remains is to clarify how this reinterpretation is to be understood in detail.

For such a clarification one need only pursue the question of exactly how tradition is experienced as an event. For this I believe one must consider two aspects. First, tradition "happens" in such a way that what is inherited in its linguistic form must not first be completed or even reconstructed in its meaning, but captivates by itself just because it is meaningful. When we understand a text, what is meaningful therein "asserts itself and has always already captivated us before one, so to speak, comes to oneself and is able to test the meaning claim which one has received" (*GW*, 494; *TM*, 490). What has been directly experienced as meaningful, presents itself directly as familiar. Seen in this manner, the experience of understanding could now again appear as the experience of a completion of what had been already and continued to be at work. However, since it is the case that after the experience of the meaningful one must "come to oneself," then this experience cannot be the experience of a completion of understanding in the sense of *energeia*. The experience of the meaningful is rather such that it prohibits an unquestioning understanding. The reason for this lies in the inherited character of the meaningful itself: the inherited is not just simply meaningful, but is always also of a "historically meant and stale objectivity" (*GW*, 300; *TM*, 295). This means it is also always encountered as something foreign. This foreignness presents itself most clearly where the inherited is encountered in the form of a work, the work of art. But one must also say that everything inherited must also always have the form of a work, in a more or less developed manner, since it could otherwise only be experienced in its foreignness and not as also meaningful. The inherited work is foreign and captivating at the same time. The understanding of tradition shows itself, therefore, to be an event since something is experienced as meaningful and at the same time it remains independent—since something is experienced as meaningful, inasmuch as a claim issues from it in its indestructible independence. This claim is itself not a completion, but when understanding is a completion, it first emerges out of this claim.

Understanding in philosophical hermeneutics is, therefore, first of all always a listening and following, and then, a speaking. In other words, understanding is never simply just a linguistic completion, but always a completion that has the character of an agreement. The completion of understanding remains embedded in the context of tradition. Understanding can truly and adequately only be completed when it is supported by the experience of its embeddedness and thereby limited in its character of completion. One would clearly not do justice to the idea of such embeddedness if one were to conceive its meaning to be obedient subordination. One who understands the inherited must in no way be of the opinion that the "embodied knowledge" in the inherited is "fundamentally superior to the interpreter's,"[4] so that we, in understanding, could only learn from tradition and not that tradition could learn, just as well, from us.[5] This objection raised by Jürgen Habermas is only then convincing if the relationship between tradition and understanding is, in truth, symmetrical, but where philosophical hermeneutics, in a finally untenable predetermination of it, is interpreted to hold an asymmetry of superiority and inferiority. In the text of *Truth and Method,* Habermas's objection may be indicated inasmuch as the relationship between tradition and understanding is characterized as "an interchange, like a conversation" (*GWI,* 383; *TM,* 377). So, if one maintains that conversations, in their proper sense, only occur between equal partners, then it would also follow that one should judge as one-sided an asymmetry in the relation between tradition and understanding, which is emphasized in philosophical hermeneutics.[6] However, the conversation among persons is no more than a "model" (*GWI,* 383; *TM,* 378) for philosophical hermeneutics. And as a model, the conversation should only demonstrate that, as in understanding tradition so also in a conversation among persons, one is concerned with a "subject matter . . . with which one is confronted" (*GWI,* 384; *TM,* 378). Tradition, for example in the form of a text, confronts one first with such a "subject matter" and therein alone lies its supposed superiority. Tradition has an unconcealing character. For example, a conversation with Aristotle where we, who attempt to understand, wish to suggest to him that his theory be reformulated or relativized in this or that point, is only possible if we are in the space of a playing [*Spielraum*] of those texts that have been inherited by us under the name of Aristotle. A text can be unconcealing in relation to the subject matter only if it has the form of a work—because, on the one hand, it is not clearly understandable to us from the beginning. On the other hand, a text can be unconcealing in relation to a subject matter, only because something from the text appeals to us as meaningful or "is enlightening" (*GWI*, 489; *TM*, 485), without it—now again due to its "stale objectivity"—being able to be completely conveyed in the completion of an understanding, i.e., in the development of an understanding. Conversations are often enough only possible in the space of a playing of texts; that this is the case will soon be clear to anyone who, as a reader, can actually enter into a conversation with the author of a text.

In stating that conversations are often enough only possible in the space of a playing of texts, one is clearly not stating that they are *only* possible in the space of a playing of texts—or more explicitly formulated—one is not claiming that only the space of a playing of texts is able to open something like a conversation. Rather, clearly, an other must be already directly apprehended as a possible conversant if one is to be able to join him or her in the process of a conversation. Seen in this manner, a philosophical situating of conversations will not be able to be just a theory of communicative *action*. As far as philosophical hermeneutics is concerned, this idea has been taken into consideration when it is stated that language exists in the form of a conversation (*GWII*, 152). Language as such has the character of a space of a playing that is finally always concerned to be actualized in the completion of conversation without ever exhausting itself in such actuality. Inherited texts are then, however, nothing other than representations of the space of a playing of language itself. We can be guided by these representations in the process of understanding since they are not simply copies of the space of a playing of language that have become independent, but because their openness has shined forth out of the texts (see *GWI*, 486ff; *TM*, 482ff.).

Since philosophical hermeneutics itself brings into language the space of a playing of language and its representation in the inherited texts, it is different from and more than just a completion of understanding. To an equal extent, it does not have the character of "political knowledge" [*politike episteme*] that is concerned to be incorporated into acting and to be fulfilled in such an incorporation. Inasmuch as philosophical hermeneutics brings into language the space of a playing of language, it transcends the completions of understanding to such an extent that, by means of its transcending of the space of a playing of language, it is experienced as what is utterly not reachable in the completions of understanding. So viewed, philosophical hermeneutics is not practical philosophy but is the attempt, which must always be undertaken anew, to make evident to acting, and so also to the process of understanding, its embeddedness in the space of a playing. In reference to the process of understanding it is not "useful" in the way that political knowledge is. Rather it exposes the space of a playing for the completions of understanding and is therefore a "situating" of understanding. If one characterizes this space of a playing as the free space, wherein communicating action can occur at all, then one can say of philosophical hermeneutics that it is a contribution to a phenomenology of freedom. The phenomenology of freedom, however, incorporates practical philosophy into itself. And so, in philosophical hermeneutics this incorporation occurs in such a way that practical knowledge, *phronesis*, is conceived as understanding in the space of a playing of language. In particular this occurs in that the space of a playing of tradition, which is unconcealed in the works, is made understandable as the present situation of understanding. In this way philosophical hermeneutics makes clear that practical philosophy, in its essence, is always "effective historical consciousness." And effective historical consciousness is more than a completed action guided by knowledge. If one wished to conceive the relation to tradition to be only a completion of acting, then either this relation would be viewed as merely a prudence that continues without interruption and is applicable in the presently doable, or it would be the "repetition of a past possibility of existing" (*SZ*, 385) in the choice of a hero. The relation to tradition as it is conceived by philosophical hermeneutics is, however, neither *phronesis* nor historicality in the sense of *Being and Time*. Neither Aristotle's concept of *phronesis* nor Heidegger's concept of historicality does justice to the foreignness that is involved in the accessibility of tradition. And because of this foreignness, philosophical hermeneutics can conceive of its own situation as only a "between." For practical knowledge that is not clearly aware of its situation, the possibility also remains concealed for it to care for the explicit preservation of its own space of a playing and to rediscover itself therein as a practical knowledge. And the choice of a hero alone cannot make a conversation possible. In contrast, philosophical hermeneutics is hermeneutic in itself. That means not just and not primarily, as I hope to have demonstrated, that the inherited concepts must first be understood so that they may be made productive in relation to a theory of understanding. It means primarily that philosophical hermeneutics, as such, is clarity concerning its own situation, and therefore also is able to situate the presently inherited in the play between foreignness and accessibility.

Notes

Introduction

1. For a discussion of the relationship between hermeneutics and the developments in the philosophy of science, see Weinsheimer's introductory essay in Joel C. Weinsheimer, *Gadamer's Hermeneutics* (New Haven: Yale University Press, 1985), 1–59.

2. Emilio Betti, *Die Hermeneutik als Allgemeinen Methodik der Geisteswissenschaften* (Tübingen: J. C. B. Mohr, 1962), 49. An English translation is in Josef Bleicher, *Contemporary Hermeneutics* (London: Routledge and Kegan Paul, 1980), 51ff. For a discussion of Betti and Gadamer see Jean Grondin, *Einführung in die philosophische Hermeneutik* (Darmstadt: Wissenschaftliche Buchgesellschaft, 1991), 162ff.

3. E. D. Hirsch, Jr., *Validity in Interpretation* (New Haven: Yale University Press, 1967), 254–55. See the discussion of Hirsch in David C. Hoy, *The Critical Circle* (Berkeley: University of California Press, 1978), 11–40.

4. Hirsch, *Validity in Interpretation*, 249 and 251, respectively.

5. Jürgen Habermas, "Zu Gadamers 'Wahrheit und Methode'" in *Hermeneutik und Ideologiekritik* (Frankfurt am Main: Suhrkamp Verlag, 1971), 48f.

6. See also Jürgen Habermas, *Theorie des kommunikativen Handelns*, vol. 1 (Frankfurt: Suhrkamp Verlag, 1981), 192ff. See the discussion of Habermas and Apel in Georgia Warnke's *Gadamer: Hermeneutics, Tradition and Reason* (Stanford: Stanford University Press, 1987), 107ff.

7. Karl Otto Apel, *Transformation der Philosophie*, vol. 1 (Frankfurt: Suhrkamp Verlag, 1973), 47.

8. Apel, *Transformation der Philosophie*, vol. 2, 216–17.

9. Ibid., 19–20.

10. Richard Rorty, *Consequences of Pragmatism* (Minneapolis: University of Minnesota Press, 1982), 152.

11. Richard Rorty, *Contingency, Irony, and Solidarity* (Cambridge: Cambridge University Press, 1989), 11.

12. John D. Caputo, *Radical Hermeneutics* (Bloomington: Indiana University Press, 1987), 110.

13. Ibid., 111.

14. Ibid., 115.

15. Ibid., 116.

Jean Grondin, On the Composition of *Truth and Method*

1. At this point I would like to thank Professor Gadamer for his willingness to discuss my questions concerning the composition of *TM*.

2. It is available to researchers in the manuscript section (*Handschriften-abteilung*) of the University of Heidelberg Library.

3. A trace of this insertion of the three named sections is preserved in the published work of 1960. If one moves from the end of the chapter entitled "The Principle of Effective History" (*WM*, in *GWI*, 316) to the beginning of the chapter entitled "On the Limitations of the Philosophy of Reflexivity" (*GWI*, 346), the continuity of the flow of thought and questioning is evident. The incompletability of effective historical reflection, which Gadamer advocates, constitutes the main thread. From this idea the classical (and modern) philosophy of reflexivity may be overturned.

4. See *GWI*, 11–14 (the beginning of the work), 47 (end and summary of the first section), and 90 (transition to the critique of aesthetics). In addition, Helmholtz is present in the published preliminary studies for *TM*. See the 1953 essay "Truth in the Humanities," in *GWII*, 39.

5. Original draft, 44 (the end of the quotation is identical to *GWI*, 13).

6. See *GWI*, 170: "Today's task could be to escape the dominating influence of Dilthey's formulation of the question and the prejudices concerning intellectual history that he justified." Ignoring Dilthey?

7. This is the title of a section, *GWI*, 94. A preliminary study for *TM* was the Venice lecture of 1958, "The Questionability of Aesthetic Consciousness" (in *Theorien der Kunst*, ed. D. Hendrik and W. Iser [Frankfurt, 1982], 59–69), to which *GWI*, 100 and *TM*, 94 refer.

8. *GWI*, 177 (first line of the second part). Ignoring Schleiermacher?

9. Original draft, 13. See also *GWI*, 171.

10. Original draft, 13.

11. Original draft, after 13.

12. See also *GWI*, 264, 286, 314, 316, 319, 330, 464. *GWI*, 286 is quoted as exemplary: "These considerations lead to the question whether, in the hermeneutics of the humanities, the moment of tradition must not be fundamentally recognized in its right" (where Gadamer is referring to his own philosophical project in the second part).

13. This was in part correctly grasped by Leo Strauss (see his correspondence with Gadamer in *Unabhängige Zeitschrift für Philosophie* 2 [1978]: 5–12) as the legitimation of the hermeneutic problematic in opposition to Heidegger, although Strauss overemphasized the fixation on Dilthey (see *GWI*, 170; note 6 above). Gadamer later recognized a shortcoming in his original intuitions for which he was responsible. For this, see the self-critique at the beginning of the second volume of *GW*.

14. *GWI*, 306 (same as original draft, 37a).

15. Recently, Manfred Riedel has explored this "acroamatic" (i.e., depending

upon an understanding reception) character of hermeneutic experience. See his study, "Zwischen Platon und Aristoteles: Heideggers doppelte Exposition der Seinsfrage und der Ansatz von Gadamers hermeneutischer Gesprächsdialektik," *Allgemeine Zeitschrift für Philosophie* 11 (1986), 1–28; "Die akroamatische Dimension der Hermeneutik," in *Philosophie und Poesie: Otto Pöggeler zum 60. Geburtstag,* ed. A. Gethmann-Siefert (Stuttgart, 1988), 107–19, reprinted in M. Riedel, *Hören auf die Sprache: Die akroamatische Dimension der Hermeneutik* (Frankfurt: Suhrkamp, 1990). See also the essays in the collection of the same author, *Für eine zweite Philosophie* (Frankfurt, 1988).

16. See Gadamer's reference to Heidegger's use of "actus exercitus" in his lectures, in Gadamer, "Erinnerung an Heideggers Anfänge," *Dilthey Jahrbuch* 4 (1986/87), 21.

17. "Die Universalität des hermeneutischen Problems" (1960), in *GW*II, 219.

18. Original draft, after 13.

19. "Die Universalität des hermeneutischen Problems," in *GW*II, 226.

20. *GW*I, 478 (last line before the concluding chapter of *TM*). See also *GW*I, 479: "Hermeneutics is, as we have seen, to that extent *a universal aspect of philosophy* and not merely the methodological basis of the so-called humanities" (Gadamer's emphasis).

21. As expressed on 6 December 1988.

22. Between 1936 and 1959 Gadamer often held lectures under the title or subtitle "Introduction to the Humanities" (SS 1936, SS 1939, WS 1941/42, WS 1944/45, WS 1948/49, SS 1951, SS 1955). Clearly the first sketches for *TM* refer back to these lectures.

23. H.-G. Gadamer, *Philosophische Lehrjahre* (Frankfurt, 1977), 182.

24. One should also consider the additional references in the third part to the supplementary material in volume 2, introduced in the fifth edition of 1986. See especially the addition (of 1986) to footnote 102 in *GW*I, 465: "Concerning the priority of the conversation before all propositions see the requisite supplementary material in vol. 2 of the *Collected Works*, p. 121–217" (similarly, the addition to *GW*I, 447). Also the propositions of *TM* are not to be reduced to their predicative character. Who thinks along hermeneutically, must also consider what lies behind them and what has happened to them in the further development of hermeneutics.

Tom Nenon, Hermeneutical Truth and the Structure of Human Experience

1. An earlier version of this essay appeared in *Dilthey Jahrbuch* 8 (1992–93), 75–92.

2. For example David Hoy, in *The Critical Circle* (Berkeley: University of California Press, 1978), places Dilthey in the lineage of "traditional hermeneutics," aligning him among others with E. D. Hirsch and Schleiermacher on the side of

a hermeneutics oriented on the author's intention and opposed to Gadamer's "abandoning the foundationalist enterprise that looks for a presuppositionless starting point in the self-certainty of subjectivity" (5). In particular, he sees Dilthey as one of the leading proponents of the "psychological reconstruction" that Gadamer effectively overcomes (11–12). Others who follow Gadamer's critique of Dilthey's "psychological orientation" include Anthony Giddens, "Hermeneutics and Social Theory," in *Hermeneutics: Questions and Prospects*, ed. Gary Shapiro and Alan Sica (Amherst: University of Massachusetts Press, 1984), 225; and Josef Bleicher, *Contemporary Hermeneutics: Hermeneutics as Method, Philosophy and Critique* (London: Routledge and Kegan Paul, 1980). The latter expressly repeats Gadamer's critique on 23–24, showing how Dilthey's psychological orientation at the same time leads to the scientistic tendencies that Habermas criticizes as well. See also in this vein: Rüdiger Bubner, *Essays in Hermeneutics and Critical Theory*, trans. Eric Matthews (New York: Columbia University Press, 1988), 99 ff.; and Joel Weinsheimer, *Gadamer's Hermeneutics* (New Haven: Yale University Press, 1985), who develops basically the same critique for the most part without explicit reference to Gadamer (see especially 148ff.).

A further list of scholars who have followed almost unquestioningly Gadamer's depiction of Dilthey is provided by Frithjof Rodi, "Hermeneutics and the Meaning of Life: A Critique of Gadamer's Interpretation of Dilthey," in *Hermeneutics and Deconstruction*, ed. H. Silverman and D. Ihde (Albany: State University of New York Press, 1985), 82–90. Rodi's article represents an important departure from the standard view; however, in this article the author intends "merely to indicate the direction which a meta-critique of the Gadamerian critique might take" (87) and not to provide a detailed exposition of Gadamer's critique and the limits of its legitimacy. In particular, Rodi indicates how Dilthey's insights into the "*Unergründlichkeit*" of life are not sacrificed at the altar of science as Gadamer seems to imply.

3. Notice for instance the way that Dilthey speaks of objectivity in his *Ideen über eine beschreibende und zergliedernde Psychologie*: "But precisely these works [i.e., those of Grote, Buckle, and Tain] prove that the historian's objectivities are better maintained when he relies on his feeling of life instead of trying to employ the one-sided theories advanced by explanatory psychologists" (V, 191). To equate Dilthey's procedures with the kind of induction modelled upon the natural sciences would be to identify him with just the kind of "*erklärende Psychologie*" from which he is at pains to distance himself in this major work and all subsequent works as well.

4. On the role of the inductive method in Dilthey, see Nenon, "Dilthey's Inductive Method and the Role of Philosophy," *Southwest Philosophy Review* 5 (1989), 121–34.

5. For example, *WM*, 240, 245, 343, 422.

6. Cf., e.g., *WM*, 211: "It is the problem of the transition from the psychological to the hermeneutic foundation of the human sciences that is the decisive point here. In this project Dilthey never achieved anything more than mere out-

lines"; or the essay "Hermeneutik und Historismus" in the "Anhang" to *WM* (476 ff.): "Thus he [Betti] never advances beyond the ambivalence that kept Dilthey between psychology and hermeneutics" (*WM*, 484).

7. See especially on this point, *WM*, 260.

8. This is why Hoy's (*The Critical Circle*) identification of Dilthey's thinking with a theory of psychological reconstruction such as Hirsch's is—at least with regard to the later stages of Dilthey's development—problematic.

9. Cf. the following passage where Gadamer sees himself following Heidegger: "To the extent that what is meant is not individuality and what it means, the text is not comprehended as a mere expression of life, but is rather taken seriously in its claim to truth." Noteworthy here is Gadamer's identification of individuality and life expression, his assumption that life here is first of all and inevitably the particular life of one individual.

10. Lawrence Schmidt, *The Epistemology of Hans-Georg Gadamer* (Frankfurt: Peter Lang Verlag, 1985).

11. Rodi points out that this does not necessarily imply that the possibility of understanding the other and his or her historical horizon is immediately present or even necessarily ever complete. In fact, the recognition of the *Unergründlichkeit* of life is a fundamental insight accompanying all encounters with the other and his or her expressions—even in the human sciences. Cf. especially "Hermeneutics and the Meaning of Life," 88-91, on this point.

Tom Rockmore, Gadamer's Hermeneutics and the Overcoming of Epistemology

1. On one reading, it remains throughout his later effort to go beyond philosophy, which is still concerned to reveal in apodictic fashion the future history of Being.

2. See Tom Rockmore, *Hegel's Circular Theory of Knowledge* (Bloomington: Indiana University Press, 1986).

3. For Dilthey's analysis of the circularity of the relation of whole and part, see "Die Entstehung der Hermeneutik," in *Gesammelte Schriften*, vol. 5: "Hier macht sich nun die zentrale Schwierigkeit aller Interpretationskunst geltend. Aus den einzelnen Worten und deren Verbindungen soll das Ganze eines Werkes verstanden werden, und doch setzt das volle Verständnis des einzelnen schon das volle Verständnis des Ganzen voraus."

4. For Fichte's view of circularity, which influences Hegel, see the *Grundlage der gesamten Wissenschaftslehre* and especially "Über den Begriff der Wissenschaftslehre," where he discusses the idea, proximally derived from Kant, that philosophy must be a scientific system which he interprets to mean that it can have no more than one premise that, however, cannot be demonstrated.

5. See *Grundlinien der Grammatik, Hermeneutik und Kritik* (Landshut, 1808), sec. 78, for a discussion of the circularity in the relation of whole and part, in

Hans-Georg Gadamer and Gottfried Boehm, *Seminar: Philosophische Hermeneutik* (Frankfurt: Suhrkamp, 1976), 119.

Lawrence K. Schmidt, Uncovering Hermeneutic Truth

1. For Gadamer's further explication of this central thesis, see *WM*, xxiii; *TM*, xxxv; *GWII*, 334, 496–97; *DD*, 25, and his "Replik" in *Hermeneutik und Ideologiekritik* (Frankfurt: Suhrkamp, 1971), 291.

2. After the composition of this essay, P. Christopher Smith, in *Hermeneutics and Human Finitude: Towards a Theory of Ethical Understanding* (New York: Fordham, 1991), has also argued that there is a criterion of truth in Gadamer's theory of interpretation. Referring to Gadamer's unpublished lectures, "Heidelberg Lectures on Aesthetics" (summer semester 1979), Smith claims this criterion to be "the appropriateness or propriety (*Anständigkeit*)" (200) of an interpretation. This concept is also related to *Sich-Bewähren* as a "kind of being borne out, or self-confirmation" (201).

3. Jean Grondin, *Hermeneutische Wahrheit?* (Konigstein: Forum Academicum, 1982). Hereafter cited as *HW*.

4. See Martin Heidegger, *Einführung in die Metaphysik* (Tübingen: Max Niemeyer: 1987), 130. *An Introduction to Metaphysics* (New Haven: Yale, 1959), 170f.

5. Edmund Husserl, *Logical Investigations*, vol. 1, trans. J. N. Findlay (New York: Humanitites Press, 1970), 194–95. *Logische Untersuchungen*, in *Husserliana*, vol. 18 (The Hague: Martinus Nijhoff, 1975), 192–93.

6. See Ernst Tugendhat, *Der Wahrheitsbegriff bei Husserl und Heidegger* (Berlin: Walter de Gruyter, 1970), 101ff., 230ff.

7. Edmund Husserl, *Logical Investigations*, vol. 2, trans. J. N. Findlay (New York: Humanitites Press, 1970), 762. *Logische Untersuchungen*, in *Husserliana*, vol. 19/2 (The Hague: Martinus Nijhoff: 1984), 647.

8. Ibid., 765; 651.

Joseph Margolis, Three Puzzles for Gadamer's Hermeneutics

1. Hans-Georg Gadamer, *Truth and Method*, 2d ed., trans. Garrett Barden and John Cumming (New York: Seabury Press, 1975), 235. Ensuing references are to this translation.

2. Hans-Georg Gadamer, "On the Scope and Function of Hermeneutical Reflection," trans. G. B. Hess and R. E. Palmer, in *Philosophical Hermeneutics*, trans. and ed. David E. Linge (Berkeley: University of California Press, 1976), 19. Cf. Jürgen Habermas, "A Review of Gadamer's *Truth and Method*," trans. Fred

Dallmayr and Thomas McCarthy, in *Understanding and Social Inquiry*, ed. Fred Dallmayr and Thomas McCarthy (Notre Dame: University of Notre Dame Press, 1977).

3. A promising beginning is suggested in a recent unpublished paper by Joel C. Weinsheimer, "A Word Is Not a Sign: Hermeneutic Semiotics and Peirce's 'Ethics of Terminology,'" presented at the Symposium: "Hermeneutische Gespräche," in honor of Hans-Georg Gadamer, at the University of Heidelberg, July 1989.

4. Hans-Georg Gadamer, "The Universality of the Hermeneutical Problem," in *Philosophical Hermeneutics*, 7.

5. Gadamer, *Truth and Method*, 256.

6. Gadamer, "The Universality of the Hermeneutical Problem," 8, 11.

7. Hans-Georg Gadamer, *The Idea of the Good in Platonic-Aristotelian Philosophy*, trans. P. Christopher Smith (New Haven: Yale University Press, 1986).

8. See, for instance, ibid., 131, 152.

9. Martin Heidegger, "Letter on Humanism," trans. Frank A. Capuzzi and J. Glenn Gray, in *Martin Heidegger: Basic Writings*, ed. David Farrell Krell (New York: Harper and Row, 1977), 213.

10. Ibid., 206.

11. See, for instance, "Truth, Power, Self: An Interview with Michel Foucault, October 25, 1982" (conducted by Rux Martin), in *Technologies of the Self*, ed. Luther H. Martin, et al. (Amherst: University of Massachusetts Press, 1988), particularly 11, where Foucault says: "All my analyses are against the idea of universal necessities in human existence."

12. The question is broached in Joseph Margolis, *Pragmatism without Foundations: Reconciling Realism and Relativism* (Oxford: Basil Blackwell, 1986); and part of a resolution is provided in *Texts without Referents: Reconciling Science and Narrative* (Oxford: Basil Blackwell, 1989).

13. See Gadamer, *Truth and Method*, 394.

14. Hans-Georg Gadamer, "Hermeneutics as Practical Philosophy," in *Reason in the Age of Science*, trans. Frederick G. Lawrence (Cambridge: MIT Press, 1981), 93–97.

15. Gadamer, "The Heritage of Hegel," in *Reason in the Age of Science*, 60–61.

16. I have introduced the term "traditionalism" as a term of art, in *Pragmatism without Foundations*, chapter 2. In the Anglo-American tradition, either influenced by Gadamer or remarkably in accord with his views, the closest author to the Gadamerian approach is surely Charles Taylor. See, for instance, Charles Taylor, "Philosophy and Its History," in *Philosophy in History*, ed. Richard Rorty, et al. (Cambridge: Cambridge University Press, 1984).

17. Gadamer, *Truth and Method*, 257.

18. Ibid., 257.

19. Ibid.

20. Alasdair MacIntyre, *After Virtue* (Notre Dame: Notre Dame University Press, 1981). (It has been somewhat revised in a second edition.)

21. Gadamer, *Truth and Method*, 259.

22. Ibid., 261.

23. I introduce "ontic adequation" as a term of art, in *Texts without Referents*, chapter 6. It is a distinction absolutely essential to the prevailing disputes about the analysis of cultural phenomena.

Francis J. Ambrosio, Caputo's Critique of Gadamer

1. John D. Caputo, *Radical Hermeneutics: Repetition, Deconstruction, and the Hermeneutic Project* (Bloomington: Indiana University Press, 1987); hereafter cited as *RH*.

2. Cf. Hans-Georg Gadamer, *The Idea of the Good in Platonic-Aristotelian Philosophy*, trans. P. Christopher Smith (New Haven: Yale University Press, 1986).

3. Hans-Georg Gadamer, "The Heritage of Hegel," in *Reason in the Age of Science*, trans. Frederick G. Lawrence (Cambridge: MIT Press, 1981).

4. Hans-Georg Gadamer, *Hegel's Dialectic*, trans. P. Christopher Smith (New Haven: Yale University Press, 1976), 115.

5. Hans-Georg Gadamer, "On the Problem of Self-Understanding," in *Philosophical Hermeneutics*, trans. David E. Linge (Berkeley: University of California Press, 1976), 50.

6. Cf. Francis J. Ambrosio, "Dawn and Dusk: Gadamer and Heidegger on Truth," *Man and World*, 19 (1986), 21–53.

7. Hans-Georg Gadamer, "The Proofs of Immortality in Plato's *Phaedo*," in *Dialogue and Dialectic*, trans. P. Christopher Smith (New Haven: Yale University Press, 1980), 21–38.

James Risser, Hermeneutics of the Possible

1. See, for example, *Validity in Interpretation* (New Haven: Yale University Press, 1967).

2. See Joseph Margolis, *Pragmatism without Foundations: Reconciling Realism and Relativism* (Oxford: Basil Blackwell, 1986), 76. A further treatment of this phrase is given by John D. Caputo. See "Gadamer's Closet Essentialism: A Derridian Critique," in *Dialogue and Deconstruction: The Gadamer-Derrida Encounter*, ed. D. Michelfelder and R. Palmer (Albany: State University of New York Press, 1989).

3. See John Caputo, "Finitude and Difference," in *Philosophy and Translation*, ed. David Wood (Bloomington: Indiana University Press, forthcoming).

4. See Hegel, *Wissenschaft der Logik*, vol. 2 (Frankfurt: Suhrkamp Verlag, 1969), 200ff.

5. "The importance of the logical consists in the transition of logic into becoming, where existence and actuality come forth. . . . Every moment, if for the moment one wishes to use this expression, is an immanent movement, which in a profound sense is no movement at all. One can easily convince oneself of this by considering that the concept of movement is itself a transcendence that has no place in logic." Kierkegaard, *The Concept of Anxiety*, ed. and trans. R. Thomte in collaboration with A. Anderson (Princeton: Princeton University Press, 1980), 13.

6. In *Journey to Selfhood: Hegel and Kierkegaard* (Berkeley: University of California Press, 1980), Mark Taylor points out that Kierkegaard's argument attributes a more necessitarian position to Hegel than Hegel intended to affirm, thus contributing greatly to the widespread misinterpretation of Hegel as a determinist. See 126.

7. This point is made by George Stack in *Kierkegaard's Existential Ethics* (Birmingham: University of Alabama Press, 1977). See 44ff.

8. See Aristotle's *Metaphysics*, 1049b5ff.

9. Werner Marx, *Heidegger and the Tradition*, trans. Theodore Kisiel and Murray Greene (Evanston: Northwestern University Press, 1971), 111.

10. Martin Heidegger, *The Basic Problems of Phenomenology*, trans. Albert Hofstadter (Bloomington: Indiana University Press, 1982), 277. This is the translation of *Die Grundprobleme der Phänomenologie*, in *Gesamtausgabe*, vol. 24 (Frankfurt: Klostermann, 1975).

11. Ibid., 277.

12. The following remarks are drawn primarily from Thomas Sheehan's work on Heidegger that explores the Aristotelian roots of Heidegger's thought. See especially "Getting to the Topic: The New Edition of *Wegmarken*," *Research in Phenomenology* 7 (1977). This is not to say that the issue of possibility in Heidegger is exhausted by the turn back to Aristotle. There is yet another figure that ultimately must be brought into consideration, namely, Nicholas of Cusa. For an excellent treatment of this connection to Cusanus, see Peter J. Casarella, "Nicholas of Cusa and the Power of the Possible," *American Catholic Philosophical Quarterly* 64 (Winter 1990), 7–34.

13. See Aristotle's *Physics*, III 2, 201b32.

14. Heidegger, "On the Being and Conception of *Physis*," trans. Thomas Sheehan, *Man and World* 9 (1976), 266. This essay is a translation of "Vom Wesen und der Begriff der *physis*: Aristotles Physik B 1 (1939)," in *Wegmarken*, 2d ed. (Frankfurt: Klostermann, 1978).

15. Heidegger, *Basic Problems*, 308.

16. In "Dawn and Dusk: Gadamer and Heidegger on Truth," *Man and World* 19 (1986), 21–53, Francis Ambrosio points out that Heidegger's notion of *Ereignis* and Gadamer's notion of *Virtualität des Sprechens* parallel each other with respect to the question of truth. I would agree that there is a parallel, but for a different reason. What enables us to speak of both is the common framework of an ontology of living being.

17. This idea that interpretation ceases in the completion of meaning is conveyed in passing in several of Gadamer's texts. See, for example, his essay "Are the Poets Falling Silent?": "Interpretative words should, however, disappear after they have evoked what they mean." *Hans-Georg Gadamer on Education, Poetry, and History*, ed. Dieter Misgeld and Graeme Nicholson, trans. Lawrence Schmidt and Monika Reuss (Albany: State University of New York Press, 1992), 76.

18. See Gadamer, "Hermeneutics and Logocentrism," in *Dialogue and Deconstruction*, 114–25.

19. For a detailed analysis of Gadamer's notion of truth, see my "The Imaging of Truth in Philosophical Hermeneutics," in *Selected Studies in Phenomenology and Existential Philosophy*, vol. 19 (Albany: State University of New York Press, 1994).

20. See *WM*, 455–65; *TM*, 481–91. See also *The Relevance of the Beautiful and Other Essays*, trans. Nicholas Walker (Cambridge: Cambridge University Press, 1986).

21. Gadamer, *Reason in the Age of Science*, trans. Frederick Lawrence (Cambridge: MIT Press, 1981), 44.

22. Gadamer, *Philosophical Hermeneutics*, trans. David E. Linge (Berkeley: University of California Press, 1976), 15. The German text of the essay quoted from *Philosophical Hermeneutics*, "Die Universalität des hermeneutischen Problems," appears in *GWII*, 230.

23. Gadamer, *The Relevance of the Beautiful*, 99.

24. Martin Heidegger, *An Introduction to Metaphysics*, trans. Ralph Manheim (New York: Anchor Books, 1961), 59.

Lawrence K. Schmidt, The Ontological Valence of the Word

1. All citations are from "On the Truth of the Word."

Hans-Georg Gadamer, On the Truth of the Word

1. Hans-Georg Gadamer, *Gesammelte Werke*, vol. 8: *Ästhetik und Poetik I: Kunst als Aussage* (Tübingen: J. C. B. Mohr, 1993), 37–58. An earlier version of this essay was delivered to a faculty colloquium at the University of Toronto in 1971.—*Trans.*

2. *Das Wort* has two declensions in German that are distinguished in the plural. *Die Wörter* refers to the smallest independent parts of speech, the many individual words as in a dictionary (*Wörterbuch*); *Die Worte* is used in all other cases and may refer to the collective sense of word as expression, sentence, or one's thought, as in the English expressions "you took the words right out of my

mouth," "words mean little when action is needed," "he had the last word," or "she gave her word."—*Trans.*

3. Throughout, the (albeit awkward) English expression *saying* has been used to preserve the German sense of *sagend.*—*Trans.*

4. The German word *Aussage* also means testimony.—*Trans.*

5. *Zusage* is literally a saying-to, here especially in the sense of a saying to another, in the senses of agreement, assent, approval, pledge and promise. *Ansage* is literally a saying-on/about in the senses of a notification or announcement. *Aussage* is literally a saying-out in the senses of statement, expression, assertion or testimony in court. *Ausage* is used in two senses, first as the broader classification and then as one of the three types of classified texts. *Aus-sage* does not appear again in the text, although it is discussed.—*Trans.*

6. The meaning that the religious tradition has for poetic style is now generally acknowledged due to Northop Frye's *Anatomy of Criticism.* To compare is also Paul Ricoeur's critical limitation of the structuralist "geometry."

7. Consider Aristotle's *synagoge technon.*

8. Concerning the concept of *mimesis* see the previous essay ["Kunst und Nachahmung"] in this volume [*Gesammelte Werke*, vol. 8] as well as the following ones: "Dichtung und Mimesis" (no. 8) and "Das Spiel der Kunst" (no. 9).

9. On this see "Die Wahrheit des Kunstwerkes," in *Gesammelte Werke*, vol. 3, 249–61. To what follows compare in this volume [*Gesammelte Werke*, vol. 8] also "Philosophie und Poesie" (no. 20).

10. For a more complete discussion of this, see "Stimme und Sprache" (no. 22) and "Hören—Sehen—Lesen" (no. 23) [in *Gesammelte Werke*, vol. 8].

11. For an interpretation of George's poem, see "Ich und du die selbe seele," in *Gesammelte Werke*, vol. 9, 245ff.

12. See *Wahrheit und Methode* (*Gesammelte Werke*, vol. 1), 139ff. [*TM*, 134ff.].

13. See Max Warburg, "Zwei Fragen zum Krytylos," *Neue Philologische Untersuchungen*, vol. 5 (Berlin, 1929).

14. See also the essay "Philosophie und Poesie," in *Gesammelte Werke* , vol. 8, 237ff.

P. Christopher Smith, Toward a Discursive Logic

1. Translations of *Wahrheit und Methode* (henceforth, *WM*) are my own. There is no single work that we may turn to in order to put together a Gadamerian theory of argument. In my exposition I have extrapolated principally from his treatments of dialogue, of deliberation, of reaching an understanding (*Sich-Verständigen*) in the medium of speech (*Mitte der Sprache*), and of jurisprudential interpretation, as these figure not only in *WM* but in *Hegel's Dialectic* (New Haven, 1976) (henceforth, *HD*), *Dialogue and Dialectic* (New Haven, 1980) (henceforth, *D*), and *The Idea of the Good in Platonic-Aristotelian Philosophy* (New Haven, 1986)

(henceforth, *IGPAP*). Many of the ideas for this study came from my encounter with these smaller works as their translator. (See *IGPAP*, Translator's Introduction, xxxi, n. 10.)

2. I will rely here on Stephen Toulmin, *The Uses of Argument* (Cambridge, 1958) (henceforth, *UA*) and on the later elaboration of this work in the textbook *An Introduction to Reasoning*, 2d. ed. (New York, 1984) (henceforth *IR*). Richard Rieke and Allan Janik have joined Toulmin as coauthors of this book and no indication is given concerning which contributions are theirs. I have taken *IR* to be part of what Gadamer might call a "unitary history of effect" (*einheitliche Wirkungsgeschichte*) and not concerned myself with who wrote which particular passage in it.

3. I am using the word "mathematic" here to denote a specific, restricted area of the mathematical, namely the paradigms for Plato of number theory and Euclidean geometry. Hence I am making no claims about modern mathematics in what follows, but only about the Platonic-Aristotelian apodictic reasoning to necessary conclusions from an insight (*mathesis*), which we do not just believe but have learned (*memathekamen*) and seen to be necessarily so (see *Gorgias*, 454Cf.). For instance, if we have seen that no odd numbers are doubles and four is double two, we can reason apodictically and necessarily that four is not odd. Or if we have seen that all squares are straight-sided figures and that a circle has no straight sides, we can reason that no circles are squares. The point is that such mathematic reasoning depends on our having in mind (*nous*) clearly and distinctly the universal ideas (*eide*) of "what it is" (*ti estin*) that we are reasoning about. But with Aristotle and against Plato, I want to argue that this paradigm is of limited use and does not fit practical reasoning, which is not demonstration (*apodeixis*), but dialectic and deliberation (see *Rhetoric*, 1357a1ff.), and which is not about mathematic beings such as "even number" or "square" but about the good, the just, and the decent, of which there is precisely no idea to be learned. See in this regard the *Nicomachean Ethics*, Book I, sec. vi for Aristotle's criticism of Plato's idea of the Good, and my own *Hermeneutics and Human Finitude* (Bronx, 1991), 209f. on "The Nature of Ethical Reasoning."

4. The boundary between *krisis* and *prohairesis* is fluid. The *Nicomachean Ethics* establishes that *prohairesis* or choice results from deliberation concerning one's own actions to be taken in the future (*EN*, III, iii) and that in this case *phronesis* is the intellectual faculty that guides one's deliberations (*EN*, VI, v). A *krisis* or judgment, on the other hand, results from deliberations about someone else's actions taken in the past, deliberations guided by *synesis* or the "understanding" one shows for that other person (*EN*, VI, x). In the *Rhetoric*, however, a *krisis* is said to result both from *dikanikon*, or judicial deliberation, and from *symbouleutikon*, or advisory deliberation. And whereas the *krisis* concerns somebody else's interests in the first case, it concerns one's own in the second (1354b30ff.).

5. In legal proceedings there are, of course, presumption and burden of proof (see *IR*, 291), and as Toulmin points out, these are required to insure due process. For instance, since it is to be presumed that the defendant is innocent

until proven guilty, the burden of proof falls to the prosecution, which must show, "Yes, he is guilty." The claim advocated by the defense, "No, he is not guilty," stands until disproven. One would think that presumption and burden of proof would have sufficed to make clear to Toulmin the dialogical structure of argument, to make clear, that is, that not one but two contradictory claims in opposition to each other are always in question. As we will see, it did not.

6. Though he has done a great deal to display the dialogical nature of argument, A. McIntyre's failure, it seems to me, lies in precisely his own inability to think of reasoning as anything but the contest of "rival" positions. In particular I have in mind his *Whose Justice? Which Rationality?* (Notre Dame, 1988). As a counter to Toulmin's and McIntyre's tendency to see argument as competitive and individualistic, see my "Sichberatenlassen, Nachgiebigkeit, Verständnis (*Bouleuesthai, Epiekeia, Synesis*)," *Heidelberger Jahrbücher* 34 (1990), 197–205.

Robert Bernasconi, "You Don't Know What I'm Talking About"

1. *Hans-Georg Gadamer on Education, Poetry and History*, ed. Dieter Misgeld and Graeme Nicholson, trans. Lawrence Schmidt and Monika Reuss (Albany: State University of New York Press, 1992), 152.

2. Ibid.

3. *Gespräch* does not translate readily as either "dialogue" or "conversation," which inevitably are the terms most often favored by translators. I shall most often use the first, although, it is in many respects misleading.

4. Among the other models of dialogue to be found in Gadamer that I do not take up in the main body of this paper, there are, for example, the dialogue between thinkers and the dialogue of the thinker with the poet, both borrowed from Heidegger. The idea that in genuine dialogue "something emerges that is contained in neither of the partners" (*TM*, 462; *GW*, 466) is an idea which, although now widespread, receives its philosophical justification from Heidegger. However, as I shall suggest later, even more decisive for Gadamer than any doctrine Heidegger taught about dialogue was his experience as a student in Heidegger's seminars about Aristotle. See, for example, *Philosophische Lehrjahre* (Frankfurt: Klostermann, 1977), 36, 216; *Philosophical Apprenticeships*, trans. Robert R. Sullivan (Cambridge: MIT Press, 1985), 38, 49. Henceforth *PA*.

5. See further W. Hamacher, "Hermeneutic Ellipses: Writing the Hermeneutical Circle in Schleiermacher," in *Transforming the Hermeneutic Context*, ed. Gayle Ormiston and Alan Schrift (Albany: State University of New York Press, 1990), 181–82.

6. Plato, *Phaedrus*, trans. R. Hackforth (Cambridge: Cambridge University Press, 1972), 276A, 159.

7. Hans-Georg Gadamer, *The Relevance of the Beautiful and Other Essays*, trans. N. Walker (Cambridge: Cambridge University Press, 1986), 106; *Kleine Schriften,*

vol. 4: *Variationen* (Tübingen: J. C. B. Mohr, 1977), 219. The phrase is already in keeping with Gadamer's earlier exposition in *Truth and Method*. Whereas in part 2, Gadamer concludes that the hermeneutic phenomenon implies the originality or primacy of dialogue and of the question-answer structure (*TM*, 369; *GWI*, 375), it is equally true that in part 3 he identifies the linguistic element of dialogue as a hermeneutic moment (*TM*, 378; *GWI*, 384).

8. I have written "two or more people" although Gadamer clearly specifies "zwei Personen," because it is not clear what in his model might lead him to impose this restriction beyond a certain tendency within the Western tradition to privilege the society of the couple. It is perhaps a certain idea of love which has led to the tendency to think in terms of two, but Gadamer's focus on what is being spoken about works less well in such a context.

9. The use of the phrase "I-Thou" should not be understood as evoking Buber. The difference is made clear when Gadamer defines understanding as "not a mysterious communion of souls, but sharing in a common meaning" (*TM*, 292; *GWI*, 297).

10. I have explored Gadamer's debt to Hegel in more detail in "Bridging the Abyss: Heidegger and Gadamer," *Research in Phenomenology* 16 (1986), 1–24, especially 18ff. Reprinted in *Heidegger in Question* (Atlantic Highlands: Humanities Press, 1993), 170–89, especially 186ff.

11. Hans-Georg Gadamer, "On the Circle of Understanding," in *Hermeneutics Versus Science?*, trans. and ed. John M. Connolly and Thomas Keutner (Notre Dame: University of Notre Dame Press, 1988), 70; *GWII*, 64–65.

12. See Paul Ricoeur, *Hermeneutics and the Human Sciences*, trans. John B. Thompson (Cambridge: Cambridge University Press, 1981), 75.

13. See Jan Edward Garrett, "Hans-Georg Gadamer on 'Fusion of Horizons,'" *Man and World* II (1978), 392–400.

14. *PH*, 100–101; *Kleine Schriften*, vol. 2: *Interpretationen* (Tübingen: J. C. B. Mohr, 1967), 5.

15. On this specific issue see Lawrence Hinman, "Quid Facti or Quid Juris? The Fundamental Ambiguity of Gadamer's Understanding of Hermeneutics," *Philosophy and Phenomenological Research* 40 (1980), 512–35.

16. , *The Question of Being: East-West Perspectives*, ed. Mervyn Sprung (University Park: Pennsylvania State University Press, 1978), 53.

17. Robert J. Dostal, "Philosophical Discourse and the Ethics of Hermeneutics," in *Festivals of Interpretation*, ed. Kathleen Wright (Albany: State University of New York Press, 1990), 67–68.

18. This, as I understand it, was Gadamer's reply to this question when I put it to him on the occasion of a conference at Heidelberg in July 1989, when the first version of the present paper was delivered.

19. See note 1 above.

20. *PH*, 101; *Kleine Schriften*, vol. 2, 5.

21. Gadamer, *The Relevance of the Beautiful*, 106; *Kleine Schriften*, vol. 4, 219.

22. See also "On the Circle of Understanding," 74-75; *GWII*, 62.

23. *PH*, 104; *Kleine Schriften*, vol. 2, 104. The reference is to Rilke's "Archaischer Torso Apollos."

24. Hans-Georg Gadamer, "Religious and Poetical Speaking," in *Myth, Symbol, and Reality*, ed. Alan Olson (Notre Dame: University of Notre Dame Press, 1980), 86–98. This is not to say that Gadamer does not acknowledge the differences between the two kinds of experience. These are more closely marked in another text, although Gadamer there draws the distinction solely in terms of the "This art thou" (*Das bist Du*). "Aesthetic and Religious Experience," in *The Relevance of the Beautiful*, 140–53; "Ästhetische und religiöse Erfahrung," *Nederlands Theologisch Tijdschrift* 32 (1978), 218–30.

25. Gadamer, "Religious and Poetical Speaking," 87–88.

26. Another way of making this point might be to say that I am charging Gadamer for not being Levinas, even though I would hasten to add that the account being proposed here, while indebted to Levinas, is not exactly Levinas's. For a contrast between Gadamer and Levinas, see Steven Crowell, "Dialogue and Text: Remarking the Difference," in *The Interpretation of Dialogue*, ed. Tullio Maranhao (Chicago: University of Chicago Press, 1990), 338–60.

27. On the difficulties of the other ever being other than myself, see Jacques Derrida, "Violence et métaphysique," in *L'écriture et la différence* (Paris: Seuil, 1967), 185; trans. Alan Bass, "Violence and Metaphysics," in *Writing and Difference* (Chicago: University of Chicago Press, 1978), 126.

28. This paper has undergone a number of revisions since it was originally delivered in 1989. I would like to thank James Hanas for his help in revising it for its publication here.

Kees Vuyk, Understanding and Willing

1. Jacques Derrida, "Guter Wille zur Macht," and Hans-Georg Gadamer, "Und dennoch: Macht des guten Willens," in *Text und Interpretation*, ed. Philippe Forget (München, 1984). [English trans. in *DD*.]

2. The works of Heidegger primarily referred to are listed below with the abbreviations that will be used in this essay.

> *Sein und Zeit* (*SZ*); *Being and Time* (*BT*).
> "Die Selbstbehauptung der deutschen Universität" (SdU). Frankfurt: Klostermann, 1983; "The Self-Assertion of the German University" (SGU). Trans. Karsten Harries, *Review of Metaphysics* 38 (March 1985), 467–502.
> *Einführung in die Metaphysik* (*EM*). Tübingen: Niemeyer, 1987; *An Introduction to Metaphysics* (*IM*). Trans. Ralph Manheim. New Haven: Yale University Press, 1959.
> "Der Ursprung des Kunstwerks" (UK). Stuttgart: Reclam, 1960; "The Ori-

gin of the Work of Art" (OWA), in *Poetry, Language, Thought.* Trans. Albert Hofstadter. New York: Harper and Row, 1971. *Nietzsche,* vol. 1 (*NI*). Pfullingen: Neske, 1961; *Nietzsche,* vol. 1: *The Will to Power as Art* (*N*). Trans. David Krell. San Francisco: Harper and Row, 1979.

3. *Authentic* is known to be a word that echoes two ways of speaking to be particularly (*eigens sein*) and to be one's own (*zu eigen sein*).

4. There are still other titles that I will not discuss here where the will is discussed. They are "Vom Wesen des Grundes" (in *Wegmarken,* 58), *Schellings Abhandlung über das Wesen der menschlichen Freiheit,* and the newly published *Beiträge zur Philosophie* (e.g., 15).

5. See Hans-Georg Gadamer, "Die Wahrheit des Kunstwerkes," in *Heideggers Wege: Studien zum Spätwerk* (Tübingen, 1983). (Also published under the title "Zur Einführung" in *UK.*

6. See, for example, "Überwindung der Metaphysik," in *Vorträge und Aufsätze,* "Nietzsches Wort 'Gott ist tot,'" in *Holzwege;* and "Der europäische Nihilismus," "Die Metaphysik als Geschichte des Seins," and "Entwürfe zur Geschichte des Seins als Metaphysik," all in *NII.*

7. That this concerns a terminological problem can also explain that Heidegger, in the works after the "turn," uses just once the word *will* or *willing* as an interpretation of thinking being, e.g., in "Wozu Dichter?" (in *Holzwege,* 294, where one reads of a "willing willing" and a "ready will" of the poet's language) and also in the *Beiträge zur Philosophie* (*GA,* 63), 15.

8. *Uncanniness* is the usual translation of *Unheimlichkeit* but one should hear its literal sense, not-at-homeness; I have continued the usual translation throughout.—*Trans.*

9. See "Von Wesen des Grundes," in *Wegmarken,* 69f.

10. See Richard Rorty, *Contingency, Irony and Solidarity* (Cambridge: Cambridge University Press, 1989). Similar thoughts on contingency and hermeneutics can be found in O. Marquard, *Abschied vom Prinzipiellen* (Stuttgart: Reclam, 1981), especially in the essay "Frage nach der Frage auf die die Hermeneutik die Antwort ist."

11. See also Rorty, ibid., 40, 97.

12. See Hans-Georg Gadamer, "Hermeneutik als praktische Philosophie," in *Vernunft im Zeitalter der Wissenschaft* (Frankfurt: Suhrkamp, 1976), 81.

13. Heidegger, "Die Zeit des Weltbildes," in *Holzwege,* 81.

14. Gadamer, "Und dennoch: Macht des guten Willens," 59 (*DD,* 55). See also *GWI,* 373.

15. Ibid.

16. A comparable critique of Gadamer is found in Thomas W. Oudemans, "Gadamers wijsgerige interpretatieleer," in Thomas de Boer, et al., *Hermeneutiek: Filosofische grondslagen van de mens- en cultuurwetenschappen,* 84ff. (especially in relation to practical wisdom), and Richard J. Bernstein, *Philosophical Profiles,* 105ff. (on truth in Gadamer).

17. Julia Kristeva places her hopes in this universality in her book *Etrangers à nous-mêms* (Paris, 1988), in that she analyzes an uncanniness of humans, following Freud, that agrees in many points with the uncanniness of Dasein in *Being and Time*.

18. I believe the work of Gianni Vattimo can be read as the attempt to continue Heidegger's thinking in this direction. See in relation to willing "La volonté de puissance en tant qu'art," in Vattimo, *Les aventures de la différence* (Paris, 1985). See in the same book "Andenken. La pensée et le fondement."

Marc J. LaFountain, Play and Ethics in *Culturus Interruptus*

1. The following references will be used:

FS   Jean Baudrillard. *Les Stratégies fatales.* Paris: Bernard Grasset, 1983.

BO   Richard J. Bernstein. *Beyond Objectivism and Relativism: Science, Hermeneutics, and Praxis.* Philadelphia: University of Pennsylvania Press, 1983.

PH   Hans-Georg Gadamer. *Philosophical Hermeneutics.* Trans. David E. Linge. Berkeley: University of California Press, 1976.

PS   Arthur Kroker and David Cook. *The Postmodern Scene: Excremental Culture and Hyper-Aesthetics.* New York: St. Martin's Press, 1986.

BI   Arthur Kroker and Marilouise Kroker, eds. *Body Invaders: Panic Sex in America.* New York: St. Martin's Press, 1987.

PE   Jean-François Lyotard. *The Postmodern Explained: Correspondence 1982–85.* Translation edited by Julian Pefanis and M. Thomas, trans. Don Barry, et al. Minneapolis: University of Minnesota Press, 1992.

MI   Mark Poster. *The Mode of Information: Poststructuralism and Context.* Chicago: University of Chicago Press, 1990.

TS   Gianni Vattimo. *The Transparent Society.* Trans. D. Webb. Baltimore: The Johns Hopkins University Press, 1989.

EM   Gianni Vattimo. *The End of Modernity: Nihilism and Hermeneutics in Postmodern Culture.* Trans. J. R. Snyder. Baltimore: The Johns Hopkins University Press., 1985.

2. For another interpretation of the theme of "call-waiting," see Avital Ronell's *The Telephone Book: Technology—Schizophrenia—Electric Speech* (Lincoln: University of Nebraska Press, 1989), especially chapter 1, "Delay Call Forwarding."

3. See Paul Virilio, *Vitesse et politique* (Paris: Galilee, 1977) for an analysis of the management of movement and speed by the State. Also see Deleuze and Guattari's commentaries on Virilio in *Nomadology: The War Machine* (New York: Semiotext(e), 1986).

Michael Kelly, Gadamer, Foucault, and Habermas on Ethical Critique

1. Michel Foucault, *The Birth of the Clinic*, trans. Alan M. Sheridan Smith (New York: Vintage, 1975).

2. Ibid., xvi–xvii.

3. Cf. Hans-Georg Gadamer's "The Hermeneutics of Suspicion," in *Hermeneutics: Questions and Prospects*, ed. Gary Shapiro and Alan Sica (Amherst: Massachusetts University Press, 1984), 54–65.

4. "The Ethic of Care for the Self As a Practice of Freedom: An Interview," in *The Final Foucault*, ed. James Bernauer and David Rasmussen (Cambridge: MIT Press, 1988), 18. Cf. also *The History of Sexuality*, vol. 2: *The Use of Pleasure*, trans. Robert Hurley (New York: Vintage, 1986), 5, where Foucault discusses the "hermeneutics of desire."

5. In *Michel Foucault: Beyond Structuralism and Hermeneutics* (Chicago: University Press, 1982), Hubert Dreyfus and Paul Rabinow call Foucault's general method beginning with *Discipline and Punishment* "interpretive analytics," and he accepted this label. Although they insist that Foucault goes beyond hermeneutics, interpretive analytics is, I think, a kind of hermeneutics.

6. Cf. "On the Genealogy of Ethics: An Overview of Work in Progress," in *Michel Foucault: Beyond Structuralism and Hermeneutics*, 231, where Foucault claims that the reason for engaging in the genealogy of Greek ethics is to show that our conception of ethics is historical and thus not necessary, and that it has some roots in the Greek alternative. At the same time, his interest is clearly in the ethics of the present rather than in that of the past.

7. For a recent critical discussion of Habermas's critique of Foucault, see *Critique and Power: Recasting the Foucault/Habermas Debate*, ed. Michael Kelly (Cambridge: MIT Press, 1994); it includes essays by Foucault and Habermas, plus eight essays by contemporary Foucaultians and Habermasians.

8. Jürgen Habermas, "A Review of Gadamer's *Truth and Method*," in *Understanding and Social Inquiry*, ed. Fred R. Dallmayr and Thomas A. McCarthy (Notre Dame: Notre Dame University Press, 1977), 358.

9. Hans-Georg Gadamer, "On the Scope and Function of Hermeneutical Reflection," in *Philosophical Hermeneutics*, trans. David E. Linge (Berkeley: University of California Press, 1976), 28.

10. Hans-Georg Gadamer, "Hermeneutics and the Social Sciences," *Cultural Hermeneutics* 2, no. 4 (February 1975), 315.

11. It may, in the end, be difficult to reconcile Foucault's notion of power with Gadamer's hermeneutics; but I shall leave this problem open for the time being. An equally difficult problem for Foucault is to reconcile his notion of power with his conception of ethics, which I shall discuss below.

12. In accusing Foucault of a form of total critique, Habermas mistakenly identifies his notion of power with the Frankfurt School's critique of the dialectic of enlightenment, and especially with Adorno's negative dialectics; cf. *The Philosophical Discourse of Modernity: Twelve Lectures*, trans. Frederick G. Lawrence

(Cambridge: MIT Press, 1987), chapters 9 and 10; and "Taking Aim at the Heart of the Present," in *Foucault: A Critical Reader*, ed. David Couzens Hoy (New York: Blackwell, 1986), 103–8, especially 106. On Foucault's own account of his relationship to Critical Theory, cf. *Politics, Philosophy, Culture: Interviews and other Writings of Michel Foucault, 1977–1984*, ed. Lawrence D. Kritzman (New York: Routledge, 1988), 25, 27, 59ff., 95. Cf. also the "Introduction" to *Foucault: A Critical Reader*, ed. David Couzens Hoy (New York: Blackwell, 1986), 14, where Hoy makes the point that Foucault could not have a total critique unless he were to accept some form of holism, which he rejects.

13. In *The Philosophical Discourse of Modernity*, 56–59, 97, Habermas argues that, after Hegel, there were three possible paths for modernity to pursue: Left Hegelianism, Right Hegelianism, and Nietzschean nihilism. He claims that Foucault chose the third path.

14. It is important to point out, as many commentators on the recent Habermas/Foucault debate have done, that Habermas's critique of Foucault in *The Philosophical Discourse of Modernity* is directed at Foucault's writings up through the late 1970s, whereas Foucault's response to Habermas, and especially the response that many others have given on his behalf, is from the perspective of Foucault's writings of the 1980s, most of which concern ethics. I shall not address the problem of how to interpret the relationship—is there a continuity or a discontinuity? or at least a shift in self-interpretation?—between Foucault's writings in these different periods, although this problem obviously bears on the debate. Elsewhere, however, I have argued that there is indeed a continuity between Foucault's early and late writings, in particular between *The Birth of the Clinic* and his writings on ethics in the 1980s; cf. Michael Kelly and Ricardo Sanchez, "The Emergence of Norms in the Emerging Space of the Emergency Room," in *Science in Context* (Cambridge: MIT Press, 1982).

15. Foucault, "The Ethic of Care for the Self," 18.

16. Hans-Georg Gadamer, "Über die Möglichkeit einer philosophischen Ethik," in *Kleine Schriften*, vol. 1 (Tübingen: J. C. B. Mohr, 1967), 179–91, especially 181, 191. ["On the Possibility of a Philosophical Ethics," trans. Michael Kelly, in *Kant and Political Philosophy: The Contemporary Legacy*, ed. R. S. Beiner and W. J. Booth (New Haven: Yale University Press, 1993), 361–73]. See also Gadamer, *Platos dialektische Ethik* (Hamburg: Meiner, 1931), especially 5; and *The Idea of the Good in Platonic-Aristotelian Philosophy*, trans. P. Christopher Smith (New Haven: Yale University Press, 1986).

17. Gadamer, "Über die Möglichkeit einer philosophischen Ethik," 188.

18. Ibid., 184.

19. Prussian Academy Edition, 405.

20. Gadamer, "Über die Möglichkeit einer philosophischen Ethik," 190.

21. Jürgen Habermas, "Über Moralität und Sittlichkeit—Was macht eine Lebensform 'rational'," in *Rationalität: Philosophische Beiträge*, ed. Hans Schnädelbach (Frankfurt: Suhrkamp, 1984), 219; and "Diskursethik—Notizen zu einem Begrundungsprogramm" and "Moralbewußtsein und kommunikatives Han-

deln," in *Moralbewußtsein und kommunikatives Handeln* (Frankfurt: Suhrkamp, 1983), 75, 103. This principle forms Habermas's minimal ethics, cf. *Habermas: Autonomy and Solidarity*, ed. Peter Dews (London: Verso, 1986), 170–71; also, cf. 160, 207.

22. Cf. Jürgen Habermas's *Theory of Communicative Action*, 2 vols., trans. Thomas A. McCarthy (Boston: Beacon, 1984, 1987), as well as *The Philosophical Discourse of Modernity*.

23. Foucault, "On the Genealogy of Ethics," 237.

24. The structure of part 1 of volume 2 of *The History of Sexuality* ("The Moral Problematization of Pleasures," 35–93) follows these four aspects: (1) *Aphrodisia* (pleasure—the ethical substance; the ontology of the moral experience of sexual conduct); (2) *Chresis* (use—the mode of subjection; or the deontology of the moral experience of sexual conduct); (3) *Enkrateia* (self-mastery—form of work on oneself; ascetics of the moral experience of sexual conduct); and (4) *Freedom and Truth* (and moderation—the telos; the teleology of the moral experience of sexual conduct).

25. Ibid., 28. Cf. Arnold I. Davidson, "Archaeology, Genealogy, Ethics," in *Foucault: A Critical Reader*, 221–33, where he offers a concise account of Foucault's ethics: "Foucault wanted to shift the focus [in ethics] to 'how the individual is supposed to constitute himself as a moral subject of his own actions,' without, however, denying the importance of either the moral code [what moral philosophers focus on] or the actual behaviour of people [what sociologists focus on]" (228; cf. his diagram on 229).

26. "What Is Enlightenment?" in *Interpretive Social Science: A Second Look*, ed. Paul Rabinow and William M. Sullivan (Berkeley: University of California Press, 1987), 167.

27. Ibid., 168.

28. Ibid., 170.

29. Cf. "Truth, Power, Self: An Interview with Michel Foucault, October 25, 1982," in *Technologies of the Self: A Seminar with Michel Foucault*, ed. Luther H. Martin, Huck Gutman, and Patrick Hutton (Amherst: University of Massachusetts Press, 1988), 11: "All my analyses are against the idea of universal necessities in human existence. They show the arbitrariness of institutions and show which space of freedom we can still enjoy and how many changes can still be made."

30. Foucault, "What Is Enlightenment?" 170. And cf. "Two Lectures," in *Power/Knowledge: Selected Interviews and Other Writings: 1972–77*, ed. Colin Gordon (New York: Pantheon, 1980), 83: "Let us give the term *genealogy* to the union of erudite knowledge and local memories which allows us to establish a historical knowledge of struggles and to make use of the knowledge tactically today."

31. Foucault, "What Is Enlightenment?" 170.

32. Foucault, "The Concern for Truth," in *Politics, Philosophy, Culture*, 257.

33. Cf. Foucault, "Politics and Reason," in *Politics, Philosophy, Culture*, 83: "But experience has taught me that the history of various forms of rationality is sometimes more effective in unsettling our certitudes and dogmatism than is abstract

criticism." At the same time, this focus on problematization provides Foucault's ethical critique with a level of generality of which Habermas has claimed it is incapable.

34. Foucault, "What Is Enlightenment?" 174.

35. Foucault calls himself a hyper- and pessimistic-activist in "On the Genealogy of Ethics," 232.

36. "What Is Enlightenment?" 170; and cf. "The Ethic of Care for the Self," 4.

37. In one of his last interviews ("Critical Theory/Intellectual History," in *Politics, Philosophy, Culture*, 36–37), Foucault makes a clear statement about the relationship between his historical genealogies, the design of freedom, his reluctance to propose utopias, and the link between the history of reason and forms of irrationality. In talking about the space of concrete freedom, he says: "it is fruitful . . . to describe that-which-is by making it appear as something that might not be, or that might not be as it is. Which is why this designation or description of the real never has a prescriptive value of the kind, 'because this is, that will be.' . . . history serves to show how that-which-is has not always been. . . . What reason perceives as *its* necessity, or rather, what different forms of rationality offer as their necessary being, can perfectly well be shown to have a history. . . . Which is not to say, however, that these forms of rationality were irrational. It means that they reside on a base of human practice and human history; and that since these things have been made, they can be unmade, as long as we know how it is that they were made."

38. "Nietzsche, Genealogy, History," in *Language, Counter-Memory, Practice: Selected Essays and Interviews*, ed. Donald F. Bouchard (Ithaca: Cornell University Press, 1977), 147.

39. Cf. Hubert Dreyfus and Paul Rabinow, "What is Maturity: Habermas and Foucault on 'What is Enlightenment?'" in *Foucault: A Critical Reader*, 118–20, for their defense of Foucault on this issue of "grounding" critique.

40. This is Habermas's own phrase in *The Philosophical Discourse of Modernity*, 7.

41. Cf. William Connolly, "Taylor, Foucault, and Otherness," in *Political Theory* 13, no. 3 (August 1985), 365–76, especially 372. If Foucault's texts presuppose a theory of truth and subjectivity while calling them into question, this predicament inverts that facing his critics—for they affirm conceptions of truth called into question by Foucault's critique of the modern age. Cf. Taylor's response to Connolly, in the same issue of *Political Theory*, 377–85; and his original article, "Foucault on Freedom and Truth," 69–102.

42. Hans-Georg Gadamer, "On the Philosophic Element in the Sciences and the Scientific Character of Philosophy," in *Reason in the Age of Science*, trans. Frederick G. Lawrence (Cambridge: MIT Press, 1981), 9.

Günter Figal, *Phronesis* as Understanding

1. Hans-Georg Gadamer, "Ethos und Logos," in *ANODOS: Festschrift für Helmut Kuhn*, ed. R. Hofmann, J. Jantzen, and H. Ottmann (Weinheim, 1989), 24.

2. Ibid., 33.

3. Wilhelm von Humboldt, *Schriften zur Sprachphilosophie*, in *Werke in fünf Bänden*, vol. 3), ed. A. Flitner and K. Giel (Darmstadt, 1963), 418.

4. Jürgen Habermas, *Theorie des kommunikativen Handelns*, vol. 1 (Frankfurt: Suhrkamp, 1981), 194.

5. Ibid., 193.

6. Ibid., 193.

Bibliography

Albrecht, Erhard. *Beiträge zur Erkenntnistheorie und das Verhältnis von Sprache und Denken.* Halle: Neimeyer, 1959.

Ambrosio, Francis. "Gadamer and the Ontology of Language: What Remains Unsaid." *Journal of the British Society for Phenomenology* 17 (1986), 124–42.

———. "Dawn and Dusk: Gadamer and Heidegger on Truth." *Man and World* 19 (1986), 21–53.

———. "Gadamer: On Making Oneself at Home with Hegel." *Owl of Minerva* 19 (1987), 23–40.

———. "Gadamer, Plato, and the Discipline of Dialogue." *International Philosophical Quarterly* 27 (1987), 17–32.

Apel, Karl Otto. "Das Verstehen." *Archiv für Begriffsgeschichte* 1 (1955), 142–99.

———. *Transformation der Philosophie.* 2 vols. Frankfurt: Suhrkamp, 1973. *Towards a Transformation of Philosophy.* Trans. Glyn Adey and David Frisby. London: Routledge and Kegan Paul, 1980.

———. "The Common Presuppositions of Hermeneutics and Ethics." *Research in Phenomenology* 9 (1979), 35–53.

———. *Understanding and Explanation: A Transcendental Pragmatic Perspective.* Trans. by Georgia Warnke. Cambridge: MIT Press, 1985.

Arthur, Christopher E. "Gadamer and Hirsch: The Canonical Work and the Interpreter's Intention." *Cultural Hermeneutics* 4 (1977), 183–97.

Bar-Hillel, Y. "Critique of Habermas' Hermeneutic Philosophy of Language." *Iyyon* (1973), 276–88.

Baudrillard, Jean. *Les stratégies fatales.* Paris: Bernard Grasset, 1983.

Baumann, Zygmunt. *Hermeneutics and Social Science: Approaches to Understanding.* London: Hutchinson, 1978.

Baynes, Kenneth, J. Bohman, and T. McCarthy, eds. *After Philosophy: End or Transformation?* Cambridge: MIT Press, 1987.

Becker, J. *Begegnung: Gadamer und Levinas.* Frankfurt, 1981.

Becker, Oskar. "Die Fragwürdigkeit der Transzendierung der ästhetischen Dimension der Kunst." *Philosophische Rundschau* 10 (1962), 225–38.

Behler, Ernst. "Deconstruction versus Hermeneutics: Derrida and Gadamer on Text and Interpretation." *Southern Humanities Review* 21 (1987), 201–23.

———. *Confrontations: Derrida/Heidegger/Nietzsche.* Trans. Steven Taubeneck. Stanford: Stanford University Press, 1991.

Beiner, R. S., and W. J. Booth, eds. *Kant and Political Philosophy: The Contemporary Legacy*. New Haven: Yale University Press, 1993.

Bernasconi, Robert. *The Question of Language in Heidegger's History of Being*. Atlantic Highlands: Humanities Press, 1985.

———. "Bridging the Abyss: Heidegger and Gadamer." *Research in Phenomenology* 16 (1986), 1–24.

———. *Heidegger in Question: The Art of Existing*. Atlantic Highlands: Humanities Press, 1993.

———, and D. Wood, eds. *Derrida and "Différance"*. Evanston: Northwestern University Press, 1988.

Bernstein, Richard J. "Philosophy in the Conversation of Mankind." *Review of Metaphysics* 33 (1980), 745–76.

———. "From Hermeneutics to Praxis." *Review of Metaphysics* 35 (1982), 823–45.

———. "What Is the Difference That Makes a Difference? Gadamer, Habermas, and Rorty." In *PSA 1982*. Vol. 2. Proceedings of the 1982 Biennial Meeting of the Philosophy of Science Association. Ed. P. D. Asquith and T. Nickles. East Lansing: Philosophy of Science Association, 1983.

———. *Beyond Objectivism and Relativism: Science, Hermeneutics, and Praxis*. Philadelphia: University of Pennsylvania Press, 1983.

———. *Philosophical Profiles*. Philadelphia: University of Pennsylvania Press, 1986.

Betti, Emilio. *Zur Grundlegung einer allgemeinen Auslegungslehre*. Reprinted from *Festschrift für Ernst Rabel*. Tübingen: J. C. B. Mohr, 1954. 79–168.

———. *Die Hermeneutik als allgemeine Methodik der Geisteswissenschaften*. Tübingen: J. C. B. Mohr, 1962.

———. *Teoria generale della interpretazione*. 2 vols. Milan: Giuffre, 1965.

Bleicher, Josef. *Contemporary Hermeneutics: Hermeneutics as Method, Philosophy and Critique*. London: Routledge and Kegan Paul, 1980.

———. *The Hermeneutic Imagination: Outline of a Positive Critique of Scientism and Sociology*. Boston: Routledge and Kegan Paul, 1982.

Boeckh, A. *Enzyklopädie und Methodenlehre der philologischen Wissenschaften*. (Edited by Bratuscheck, 1877). Darmstadt: Wissenschaftliche Verlagsanstalt, 1966.

Boehler, Dietrich. "Das Dialogische Prinzip Als Hermeneutische Maxime." *Man and World* 11 (1978), 131–64.

Bollnow, Otto Friedrich. *Das Verstehen: Drei Aufsätze zur Theorie der Geisteswissenschaften*. Mainz: Kirchheim, 1949.

———. *Die Methode der Geisteswissenschaften*. Mainz: Gutenberg, 1950.

———. "What Does it Mean to Understand a Writer Better Than He Understood Himself?" *Philosophy Today* 23 (1979), 16–28.

Bontekoe, Ron. "A Fusion of Horizons: Gadamer and Schleiermacher." *International Philosophical Quarterly* 27 (1987), 3–16.

Bourgeois, Patrick. "Paul Ricoeur's Hermeneutical Phenomenology." *Philosophy Today* 16 (1972), 20–27.

Bruns, Gerald. L. "On the Tragedy of Hermeneutical Experience." *Research in Phenomenology* 18 (1988), 191–204.

————. *Hermeneutics: Ancient and Modern.* New Haven: Yale University Press, 1992.

Bruzina, R., and B. Wilshire, eds. *Phenomenology: Dialogues and Bridges.* Albany: State University of New York Press, 1982.

Bubner, Rüdiger. *Theorie und Praxis: eine nachhegelsche Abstraktion.* Frankfurt: Klostermann, 1971.

————. "Theory and Practice in the Light of the Hermeneutic-Criticism Controversy." *Cultural Hermeneutics* 2 (1975), 337—52.

————. *Modern German Philosophy.* Trans. Eric Mathews. Cambridge: Cambridge University Press, 1981.

————. *Essays in Hermeneutics and Critical Theory.* Trans. Eric Mathews. New York: Columbia University Press, 1988.

————. Cramer, K., and R. Wiehl, eds. *Hermeneutik und Dialektik.* Vols. 1 and 2. Tübingen: J. C. B. Mohr, 1970.

Buck, Günter. "Hermeneutics of Texts and Hermeneutics of Action." *New Literary History* 12 (1980), 87–96.

————. *Hermeneutik und Bildung: Elemente einer verstehenden Bildungstheorie.* München, 1981.

Buker, Eloise. "Feminist Social Theory and Hermeneutics: An Empowering Dialectic?" *Social Epistemology* 4 (1990), 23–39.

Byrum, Charles S. "Philosophy as Play." *Man and World* 8 (1975), 315–26.

Caputo, John D. "Hermeneutics as the Recovery of Man." *Man and World* 15 (1982), 343–67.

————. "Husserl, Heidegger, and the Question of a 'Hermeneutic' Phenomenology." *Husserl Studies* 1 (1984), 157–78.

————. *Radical Hermeneutics: Repetition, Deconstruction, and the Hermeneutic Project.* Bloomington: Indiana University Press, 1987.

————. "From the Deconstruction of Hermeneutics to the Hermeneutics of Deconstruction." In *The Horizons of Continental Philosophy: Essays on Husserl, Heidegger, and Merleau-Ponty.* Ed. H. J. Silverman et al. Dordrecht: Kluwer Academic, 1988. 190–204.

————. *Against Ethics.* Bloomington: Indiana University Press, 1993.

Carr, David. *Phenomenology and the Problem of History.* Evanston: Northwestern University Press, 1974.

————. "Interpretation and Self-Evidence." *Analecta Husserliana* 11 (1980), 133–48.

Carrington, Robert S. "A Comparison of Royce's Key Notion of the Community of Interpretation with the Hermeneutics of Gadamer and Heidegger." *Transactions of the Charles S. Peirce Society* 20 (1984), 279–302.

Casarella, Peter J. "Nicholas of Cusa and the Power of the Possible." *American Catholic Philosophical Quarterly* 64 (1990), 7–34.

Cockhorn, Klaus. "Hans-Georg Gadamer's *Truth and Method.*" *Philosophy and Rhetoric* 13 (1980), 160–80.

Code, Lorraine. *What Can She Know? Feminist Theory and the Construction of Knowledge.* Ithaca: Cornell University Press, 1991.

Connolly, John M. "Gadamer and the Author's Authority: A Language-Game Approach." *The Journal of Aesthetics and Art Criticism* 44 (1986), 271–78.

Cook, Deborah. "Reflections on Gadamer's Notion of 'Sprachlichkeit.'" *Philosophy and Literature* 10 (1986), 84–92.

Coreth, Emrich. *Grundfragen der Hermeneutik*. Freiburg: Herder, 1969.

Dallmayr, Fred R. *Polis and Praxis: Exercises in Contemporary Political Theory*. Cambridge: MIT Press, 1985.

———. *Critical Encounters: Between Philosophy and Politics*. Notre Dame: University of Notre Dame, 1987.

———. *Between Freiburg and Frankfurt: Towards a Critical Ontology*. Amherst: University of Massachusetts Press, 1991.

———, ed. *Materialien zu Habermas' "Erkenntnis und Interesse."* Frankfurt: Suhrkamp, 1974.

———, and Thomas A. McCarthy, eds. *Understanding and Social Inquiry*. Notre Dame: University of Notre Dame Press, 1977.

Dascal, Marcelo. "Hermeneutical Interpretation and Pragmatic Interpretation." *Philosophy and Rhetoric* 22 (1989), 239–59.

Davey, Nicholas. "Baumgarten's Aesthetics: A Post-Gadamerian Reflection." *The British Journal of Aesthetics* 29 (1989), 101–15.

———. "A World of Hope and Optimism Despite Present Difficulties: Gadamer's Critique of Perspectivism." *Man and World* 23 (1990), 273–94.

———. "Hermeneutics, Language and Science: Gadamer's Distinction between Discursive and Propositional Language." *Journal of the British Society for Phenomenology* 24 (1993), 250–64.

Davidson, Donald. "On the Very Idea of a Conceptual Scheme." *Proceedings and Addresses of the American Philosophical Association* 47 (1973–74), 5–20.

———. *Inquiries into Truth and Interpretation*. Oxford: Oxford University Press, 1984.

Davies, Paul. "Derrida's Other Conversation." *Research in Phenomenology* 20 (1990), 67–84.

Derrida, Jacques. *Speech and Phenomena*. Trans. David B. Allison. Evanston: Northwestern University Press, 1973.

———. *Of Grammatology*. Trans. Gayatri Chakravorty Spivak. Baltimore: The Johns Hopkins University Press, 1974.

———. *Writing and Difference*. Trans. Alan Bass. Chicago: University of Chicago Press, 1978.

———. *Spurs/Eperons*. Trans. Barbara Harlow. Chicago: University of Chicago Press, 1979.

Detsch, Richard. "A Non-Subjectivist Concept of Play—Gadamer and Heidegger versus Rilke and Nietzsche." *Philosophy Today* 29 (1985), 156–72.

Devereaux, Mary. "Can Art Save Us? A Meditiation on Gadamer." *Philosophy and Literature* (1991), 59–73.

Dews, Peter, ed. *Habermas: Autonomy and Solidarity*. London: Verso, 1986.

Dilthey, Wilhelm. *Gesammelte Schriften*. 18 vols. Stuttgart: B. G. Teubener; Göttingen: Vandenhoeck and Ruprecht, 1914–77.

——. *Selected Writings*. Trans., ed. H. P. Rickman. Cambridge: Cambridge University Press, 1976.

Dockhorn, Klaus. "Hans-Georg Gadamer, *Wahrheit und Methode*." *Göttinsche Gelehrte Anzeigen* 218 (1966), 169–206. "Hans-Georg Gadamer's *Truth and Method*." *Philosophy and Rhetoric* 13 (1980), 160–80.

Dostal, Robert J. "The World Never Lost: The Hermeneutics of Trust." *Philosophy and Phenomenological Research* 47 (1987), 413–34.

Dreyfus, Hubert. "Holism and Hermeneutics." *Review of Metaphysics* 34 (1980), 3–24.

Dunne, Joseph. "Aristotle After Gadamer: An Analysis of the Distinction Between the Concepts of Phronesis and Techne." *Irish Philosophical Journal* 2 (1985), 105–23.

Echeverria, E. J. *Criticism and Commitment: Major Themes in Contemporary Post-Critical Philosophy*. Atlantic Highlands: Humanities Press, 1981.

Edie, James. *Speaking and Meaning: The Phenomenology of Language*. Bloomington: Indiana University Press, 1976.

Ermarth, Michael. "The Transformation of Hermeneutics." *Monist* 64 (1981), 175–94.

——. *Wilhelm Dilthey: The Critique of Historical Reason*. Chicago: University of Chicago Press, 1982.

Fairfield, Paul. "Truth without Methodologism: Gadamer and James." *American Catholic Quarterly* 67 (1993), 285–98.

Fekete, John. ed. *Life after Postmodernism: Essays on Value and Culture*. New York: St. Martin's Press, 1987.

Feyerabend, Paul. *Against Method: Outline of an Anarchistic Theory of Knowledge*. London: New Left Books, 1975.

Figal, Günter. *Martin Heidegger: Phänomenologie der Freiheit*. Frankfurt: Athenäum, 1988.

——. *Heidegger zur Einführung*. Hamburg: Junius Verlag, 1992.

——. *Für eine Philosophie von Freiheit und Streit: Politik—Ästhetik—Metaphysik*. Stuttgart, 1994.

——. "The Practical Reason of the Good Life and the Freedom of Understanding—The Hermeneutic Vision of the Idea of that which is Good with Reference to Gadamer, Hans-Georg." *Antike und Abendland* 38 (1992), 67–81.

Fish, Stanley. *Is There a Text in This Class?* Cambridge: Harvard University Press, 1980.

Fisher, Linda. "Circularity and Philosophical Reflection: a Methodological Investigation into Hermeneutics, Gadamer and Kant." Ann Arbor: University Microfilms International, 1992.

Follesdal, Dagfinn. "Hermeneutics and the Hypothetico-Deductive Method." *Dialectica* 33 (1979), 319–36.

Forget, Philippe, ed. *Text und Interpretation*. München: Fink Verlag, 1948.

Foster, Matthew. *Gadamer and Practical Philosophy: The Hermeneutics of Moral Confidence*. Atlanta: Scholars Press, 1991.

Foucault, Michel. *The Birth of the Clinic: An Archaeology of Medical Perception.* Trans. A. M. Sheridan Smith. New York: Vintage, 1975.

———. *The Archaeology of Knowledge.* Trans. A. M. Sheridan Smith. New York: Harper and Row, 1976.

———. *Language, Counter-Memory, Practice: Selected Essays and Interviews.* Ed. Donald F. Bouchard. Ithaca: Cornell, 1977.

———. *The History of Sexuality.* Vol. 2: *The Use of Pleasure.* Trans. Robert Hurley. New York: Vintage, 1986.

———. *The Final Foucault.* Ed. James Bernauer and David Rasmussen. Cambridge: MIT Press, 1988.

———. *Politics, Philosophy, Culture: Interviews and other Writings of Michel Foucault, 1977–1984.* Ed. Lawrence D. Kritzman. New York: Routledge, 1988.

Frank, Manfred. *Das Sagbare und das Unsagbare: Studien zur neuesten fanzösischen Hermeneutik und Texttheorie.* Frankfurt: Suhrkamp, 1980.

———. *Die Grenzen der Verständigung. Ein Geistergespräch zwischen Lyotard und Habermas.* Frankfurt, 1988.

Fruchon, Pierre. *Herméneutique, language et ontologie: Un disiernment du Platonisme chez H.-G. Gadamer.* Paris: Éditions du Seuil, 1975.

———. "Pour une herméneutique philosophique." *Revue de Métaphysique et de Morale* 82 (1977), 550–66.

Funke, Gerhard. "Problem und Theorie der Hermeneutik." *Zeitschrift für Philosophische Forschung* 14, no. 2.

Gadamer, Hans-Georg. *Gesammelte Werke.* Tübingen: J. C. B. Mohr, 1985–1995.

Bd. 1: *Hermeneutik I: Wahrheit und Methode. Grundzüge einer philosophischen Hermeneutik* (1960). 1986.

Bd. 2: *Hermeneutik II: Wahrheit und Methode. Ergänzungen, Register.* 1986.

Bd. 3: *Neuere Philosophie I: Hegel—Husserl—Heidegger.* 1987.

Bd. 4: *Neuere Philosophie II: Probleme—Gestalten.* 1987.

Bd. 5: *Griechische Philosophie I.* 1985.

Bd. 6: *Griechische Philosophie II.* 1985.

Bd. 7: *Griechische Philosophie III.* 1990.

Bd. 8: *Ästhetik und Poetik I: Kunst als Aussage.* 1993.

Bd. 9: *Ästhetik und Poetik II: Hermeneutik im Vollzug.* 1993.

Bd. 10: *Hermeneutik im Rückblick.* 1995.

———. *Platos dialektische Ethik: Phänomenologische Interpretationen zur "Philebos."* Habilitation Lectures. Leipzig: Meiner, 1931.

———. *Plato und die Dichter.* Frankfurt: Klostermann, 1934.

———. *Wahrheit und Methode.* Tübingen: J. C. B. Mohr, 1960. *Truth and Method.* Trans. from 2d ed. Garrett Barden and John Cumming. New York: Seabury Press, 1975. *Truth and Method.* 2d revised edition. Trans. J. Weinsheimer and D. Marshall. New York: Crossroad, 1989.

———. *Le problème de la conscience historique.* Paris/Louvain, 1963.

———. *Kleine Schriften.* Tübingen: J. C. B. Mohr.

Bd. 1: *Philosophische Hermeneutik.* 1967.

Bd. 2: *Interpretationen.* 1967.

Bd. 3: *Idee und Sprache. Platon, Husserl, Heidegger.* 1972.

Bd. 4: *Variationen.* 1977.

————. *Vernunft im Zeitalter der Wissenschaft.* Frankfurt: Suhrkamp, 1976.

————. *Rhetorik und Hermeneutik.* Göttingen: Vandenhoeck and Ruprecht, 1976.

————. *Philosophical Hermeneutics.* Ed., trans. David E. Linge. Berkeley: University of California Press, 1976.

————. *Hegel's Dialectic.* Trans. P. Christopher Smith. New Haven: Yale University Press, 1976.

————. *Philosophische Lehrjahre.* Frankfurt: Vittorio Klosterman, 1977.

————. *Poetica.* Frankfurt: Suhrkamp, 1977.

————. *Die Aktualität des Schönen.* Stuttgart: Reclam, 1977.

————. *Die Idee des Guten zwischen Platon und Aristoteles.* Heidelberg: C. Winter Universitätsverlag, 1978.

————. *Dialogue and Dialectic.* Trans. P. Christopher Smith. New Haven: Yale University Press, 1980.

————. *Reason in the Age of Science.* Trans. Fredrick G. Lawrence. Cambridge: MIT Press, 1981.

————. *Lob der Theorie.* Frankfurt: Suhrkamp, 1983.

————. *Heideggers Wege.* Tübingen: J. C. B. Mohr, 1983.

————. *Philosophical Apprenticeships.* Trans. Robert R. Sullivan. Cambridge: MIT Press, 1985.

————. *The Relevance of the Beautiful and Other Essays.* Trans. N. Walker. Ed. Robert Bernasconi. Cambridge: Cambridge University Press, 1986.

————. *The Idea of the Good in Platonic-Aristotelian Philosophy.* Trans. P. Christopher Smith. New Haven: Yale University Press, 1986.

————. "Erinnerung an Heideggers Anfänge." *Dilthey Jahrbuch* 4 (1986/87), 13–26.

————. *Das Erbe Europas: Beiträge.* Frankfurt: Suhrkamp, 1989.

————. "Ethos und Logos," in *ANODOS:Festschrift für Helmut Kuhn.* Ed. R. Hofmann, J. Jantzen, and H. Ottmann. Weinheim, 1989.

————. *Hans-Georg Gadamer on Education, Poetry, and History: Applied Hermeneutics.* Trans. L. Schmidt and M. Reuss. Ed. Dieter Misgeld and Graeme Nicholson. Albany: State University of New York Press, 1992.

————. *Hans-Georg Gadamer im Gespräch.* Ed. Carsten Dutt. Heidelberg: Universitätsverlag C. Winter, 1993.

————. and Gottfried Boehm, eds. *Seminar: Philosophische Hermeneutik.* Frankfurt: Suhrkamp, 1976.

Garrett, Jan Edward. "Hans-Georg Gadamer On 'Fusion of Horizons.'" *Man and World* 11 (1978), 392–400.

Gasché, Rodolphe. *The Tain of the Mirror: Derrida and the Philosophy of Reflection.* Cambridge: Harvard University Press, 1986.

Gilmour, John C. "Dewey and Gadamer on the Ontology of Art." *Man and World* 20 (1987), 205–19.

Gneser, A. "Über 'Sinn' und 'Bedeutung' bei Gadamer." *Zeitschrift für philosophische Forschung* 38 (1984), 436–45.

Gram, Moltke S. "Gadamer on Hegel's Dialectic: A Review Article." *Thomist* 43 (1979), 332–30.

Griswald, Charles. "Gadamer and the Interpretation of Plato." *Ancient Philosophy* 2 (1981), 121–28.

Grondin, Jean. "La conscience du travail de l'histoire et le problème la vérité en herméneutique." *Archives de Philosophie* 44 (1981), 435–54.

———. *Hermeneutische Wahrheit? Zum Wahrheitsbegriff Hans-Georg Gadamers.* Königstein: Athenäum, 1982.

———. "Herméneutique et relativisme." *Communio* 12 (1987), 101–20.

———. "Zur Entfaltung eines hermeneutischen Wahrheitsbegriffs." *Philosophisches Jahrbuch* 90 (1983), 145–53.

———. *Einführung in die philosophische Hermeneutik.* Darmstadt: Wissenschaftliche Buchergesellschaft, 1991.

———. *L'universalité de l'herméneutique.* Paris: Presses Universitaires de France, 1993.

Gründer, K. R. "Hermeneutik und Wissenschaftstheorie." *Philosophisches Jahrbuch der Görres-Gesellschaft* 75, 152–65.

Gutting, Gary. "Paradigms and Hermeneutics: A Dialogue on Kuhn, Rorty and the Social Sciences." *American Philosophical Quarterly* 21 (1984), 1–16.

Haase, U. "The Providence of Language in Gadamer's *Truth and Method.*" *Journal of the British Society for Phenomenology* 22 (1991), 170–84.

Habermas, Jürgen. "A Review of Gadamer's *Truth and Method.*" In Dallmayr and McCarthy, *Understanding and Social Inquiry.* 335–63.

———. *Theorie und Praxis.* Frankfurt: Suhrkamp, 1967 (4th rev. ed., 1971). *Theory and Practice.* Boston: Beacon Press, 1973.

———. *Erkenntnis und Interesse.* Frankfurt: Suhrkamp, 1968. *Knowledge and Human Interest.* Trans. Jeremy J. Shapiro. Boston: Beacon Press, 1971.

———. *Zur Logik der Sozialwissenschaften.* Frankfurt: Suhrkamp, 1970.

———. *Communicaton and the Evolution of Society.* Trans. Thomas McCarthy. Boston: Beacon Press, 1979.

———. *Theorie des Kommunikatiuen Handelns.* 2 vols. Frankfurt: Suhrkamp, 1981. *Theory of Communicative Action.* Boston: Beacon Press, 1984.

———. *The Philosophical Discourse of Modernity: Twelve Lectures.* Trans. Frederick G. Lawrence. Cambridge: MIT Press, 1987.

———, Henrich, Luhman, and Taubes, eds. *Hermeneutik und Ideologiekritik.* Mit Beitragen von Karl-Otto Apel, Calus v. Bormann, Rüdiger Bubner, Hans-Georg Gadamer, Hans Joachim Giegel, Jürgen Habermas. Framkfurt: Suhrkamp Verlag, 1971.

Hamburger, Käte. *Wahrheit und Ästhetische Wahrheit.* Stuttgart: Klett-Cotta, 1979.

Haney, D. P. "Viewing the Viewless-Wings-of-Poesy: Gadamer, Keats, and Historicity." *CLIO* 19 (1989), 130–22.

Hans, James S. "Hans-Georg Gadamer and Hermeneutic Phenomenology." *Philosophy Today* 22 (1978), 3–19.

———. "Hermeneutics, Play, Deconstruction." *Philosophy Today* 24 (1980), 299–317.

Heelan, Patrick A. "Horizon, Objectivity and Reality in the Physical Sciences." *International Philosophical Quarterly* 7 (1967), 375–412.

———. "The Logic of Framework Transpositions." *International Philosophical Quarterly 11* (1971), 314–34.

———. "Towards a Hermeneutics of Science." *Main Currents* 28 (1971), 85–93.

———. "Natural Science as a Hermeneutic of Instrumentation." *The Philosophy of Science* 50 (1983).

———. "Perception as a Hermeneutical Art." *Review of Metaphysics* 37 (1983), 61–76.

———. *Space Perception and the Philosophy of Science.* Berkeley: University of California Press, 1983.

Hegel, G. W. F. *Wissenschaft der Logik II.* Frankfurt: Suhrkamp Verlag, 1969.

Heidegger, Martin. *Gesamtausgabe.* Frankfurt: Klostermann, 1975–present.

———. *Sein und Zeit.* Tübingen: Niemeyer, 1927, 14th ed., 1977. *Being and Time.* Trans. John Macquarrie and Edward Robinson. New York: Harper and Row, 1962.

———. *Vorträge und Aufsätze.* Pfüllingen: Neske, 1954.

———. *Identität und Differenz.* Pfüllingen: Neske, 1957. *Identity and Difference.* Trans. Joan Stambaugh. New York: Harper and Row, 1969.

———. *Unterwegs zur Sprache.* Pfüllingen: Neske, 1959. *On the Way to Language.* Trans. Peter D. Hertz and Joan Stambaugh. New York: Harper and Row, 1971.

———. *Der Ursprung des Kunstwerks.* Stuttgart: Reclam, 1960.

———. *Nietzsche.* Pfüllingen: Neske, 1961. *Nietzsche.* Vol. 1: *The Will to Power as Art.* Trans. David Krell. San Francisco: Harper and Row, 1979.

———. *Holzwege.* 4th ed. Frankfurt: Klostermann, 1963.

———. *Einführung in die Metaphysik.* Tübingen: Max Niemeyer: 1966. *An Introduction to Metaphysics.* New Haven: Yale University Press, 1959.

———. *Vom Wesen der Wahrheit.* 5th ed. Frankfurt: Klostermann, 1967.

———. *Poetry, Language, Thought.* Trans. Albert Hofstadter. New York: Harper and Row, 1971.

———. *Basic Writings.* Ed. David Farrell Krell. New York: Harper and Row, 1977.

———. *The Basic Problems of Phenomenology.* Trans. Albert Hofstadter. Bloomington: Indiana University Press, 1982.

———. *Die Selbstbehauptung der deutschen Universität.* Frankfurt: Klostermann, 1983. "The Self-Assertion of the German University." Trans. Karsten Harries. *Review of Metaphysics* 38 (1985), 467–502.

Hekman, Susan. "Action as a List: Gadamer's Hermeneutics and the Social Scientific Analyses of Action." *Journal for the Theory of Social Behavior* 14 (1984), 333–54.

———. *Hermeneutics and the Sociology of Knowledge.* Notre Dame: University of Notre Dame Press, 1986.

Hendrik, D., and W. Iser, eds. *Theorien der Kunst.* Frankfurt, 1982.

Henrichs, Norbert. *Bibliographie der Hermeneutik und ihrer Anwendungsbereiche zeit Schleiermacher: Kleine Bibliographien aus dem Philosophischen Institut der Universität Düsseldorf.* Düsseldorf: Philosophia Verlag, 1968.

Hinman, Lawrence M. "Gadamer's Understanding of Hermeneutics." *Philosophy and Phenomenological Research* 40 (1980), 512–35.

———. "Quid facti or quid juris?: The Fundamental Ambiguity of Gadamer's Understanding of Hermeneutics." *Philosophy and Phenomenological Research* 40 (1980), 512–35.

Hirsch, E. D., Jr. "Truth and Method in Interpretation." *Review of Metaphysics,* (1965), 489–507.

———. *Validity in Interpretation.* New Haven: Yale University Press, 1967.

———. *The Aims of Interpretation.* Chicago: University of Chicago Press, 1976.

Hogan, John. "Gadamer and the Hermeneutical Experience." *Philosophy Today* 20 (1976), 3–12.

Hollinger, Robert. "Practical Reason and Hermeneutics." *Philosophy and Rhetoric* 18 (1985), 113–22.

———, ed. *Hermeneutics and Praxis.* Notre Dame: University of Notre Dame Press, 1985.

Hörisch, J. *Die Wut des Verstehens: Zur Kritik der Hermeneutik.* Frankfurt, 1988.

How, Alan R. "Dialogue as Productive Limitation in Social Theory: The Habermas-Gadamer Debate." *Journal of the British Society for Phenomenology* 11 (1980), 131–43.

———. "A Case of Misreading: Habermas's Evolution of Gadamer's Hermeneutics." *Journal of the British Society for Phenomenology* 16 (1985), 131–43.

Howard, Ray T. *Three Faces of Hermeneutics: An Introduction to Current Theories of Understanding.* Berkeley: University of California Press, 1982.

Hoy, David Couzens. *The Critical Circle: Literature and History in Contemporary Hermeneutics.* Berkeley: University of California Press, 1978.

———. "Hermeneutic Circularity, Indeterminacy and Incommensurability." In *New Literary History* (1978).

———. "Taking History Seriously: Foucault, Gadamer, Habermas." *Union Seminary Quarterly Review* 34 (1979), 85–95.

———. "Must We Say What We Mean?" *Review of the University of Ottowa* 50 (1980), 411–26.

———, ed. *Foucault: A Critical Reader.* New York: Blackwell, 1986.

Humboldt, Wilhelm. *Schriften zur Sprachphilosophie* (also found in *Werke in fünf Bänden.* Vol. 3). Ed. A. Flitner and K. Giel. Darmstadt, 1963.

Husserl, Edmund. *Logische Untersuchungen.* In *Husserliana,* vols. 18–19. The Hague: Martinus Nijhoff, 1975. *Logical Investigations,* 2 vols. Trans. J. N. Findlay. New York: Humanitites Press, 1970.

Hyde, Michael J. "Philosophical Hermeneutics and the Communicative Experience." *Man and World* 13 (1980), 81–98.

Ibbett, J. "Application and the History of Ideas." *History of Political Thought* 8 (1987), 545–55.

Ihde, Don. *Hermeneutic Phenomenology*. Evanston: Northwestern University Press, 1971.

———. "Interpreting Hermeneutics." *Man and World* 13 (1980), 325–44.

Ingram, David. "The Possibility of a Communication Ethic Reconsidered: Habermas, Gadamer and Bourdieu on Discourse." *Man and World* 15 (1982), 149–161.

———. "The Historical Genesis of the Gadamer-Habermas Controversy." *Auslegung* 10 (1983), 8–151.

———. "Hermeneutics and Truth." *Journal of the British Society for Phenomenology* 15 (1984), 62–76.

Innis, Robert E. "Hans-Georg Gadamer's Truth and Method. A Review Article." *The Thomist* 40 (1976), 311–21.

Jalbert, John E. "Hermeneutics or Phenomenology: Reflections on Husserl's Historical Mediations as a 'Way' into Transcendental Phenomenology." *Graduate Faculty Philosophy Journal* 8 (1982), 98–132.

Jauss, Hans Robert. "The Limits and Tasks of Literary Hermeneutics." *Diogenes* 17 (1980), 92–119.

———, and Godzich, Wlad. *Aesthetic Experience and Literary Hermeneutics*. Minneapolis: University of Minnesota Press, 1982.

Johnson, Patricia. "The Task of the Philosopher: Kierkegaard/Heidegger/Gadamer." *Philosophy Today* 28 (1984), 3–19.

Kamper, Dietmar. "Hermeneutik—Theorie einer Praxis?" *Zeitschrift für allgemeine Wissenschaftstheorie* 5 (1974), 39–53.

Kelly, Michael. "On Hermeneutics and Science: Why Hermeneutics is Not Anti-Science." *Southern Journal of Philosophy* 25 (1987), 481–500.

———. "Gadamer and Philosophical Ethics." *Man and World* 21 (1988), 327–46.

———. "The Gadamer-Habermas Debate Revisited: The Question of Ethics." *Philosophy and Social Criticism* 14 (1988), 368–89.

———, ed. *Hermeneutics in Ethics and Social Theory*. Special issue of *Philosophical Forum* 21 (1989-90).

———, ed. *Critique and Power: Recasting the Foucault/Habermas Debate.* Cambridge: MIT Press, 1994.

Kerby, Anthony P. "Gadamer's Concrete Universal." *Man and World* 24 (1991), 49–61.

Kestenbaum, Victor. "Meaning on the Model of Truth: Dewey and Gadamer on Habit and *Vorurteil.*" *Journal of Speculative Philosophy* 6 (1992), 25–66.

Kierkegaard, Soren. *The Concept of Anxiety*. Ed., trans. R. Thomte, in collaboration with A. Anderson. Princeton: Princeton University Press, 1980.

Kimmerle, Heinz. "Hermeneutische Theorie oder ontologische Hermeneutik." *Zeitschrift für Theologie und Kirche* 61 (1962), 114–30.

———. "Metahermeneutik, Applikation, hermeneutische Sprachbildung." *Zeitschrift für Theologie und Kirche* 61 (1964), 221–35.

———. "Die Funktion der Hermeneutik in den positiven Wissenschaften." *Zeitschrift für allgemeine Wissenschaftstheorie* 5 (1974), 54–73.

Kirkland, Frank M. "Gadamer and Ricoeur: The Paradigm of the Text." *Graduate Faculty Philosophy Journal* 6 (1977), 131–44.

Kisiel, Theodore. "The Happening of Tradition: The Hermeneutics of Gadamer and Heidegger." *Man and World* 2 (1969), 358–85.

———. "Repetition in Gadamer's Hermeneutics." *Analecta Husserliana* 2 (1972), 196–203.

———. "Hegel and Hermeneutics." In *Beyond Epistemology*. Ed. E. D. Weiss.

———. *The Genesis of Heidegger's "Being and Time"*. Berkeley: University of California Press, 1993.

Knapke, Margaret Lee. "The Hermeneutical Focus of Heidegger and Gadamer: The Nullity of Understanding." *Kinesis* 12 (1982), 3–18.

Kockelmans, Joseph J. *On Heidegger and Language*. Evanston: Northwestern University Press, 1972.

———. "On Myth and Its Relationship to Hermeneutics." *Cultural Hermeneutics* 1 (1973), 47–86.

———. "Toward an Interpretive or Hermeneutic Social Science." *Graduate Faculty Philosophy Journal* 5 (1975), 73–96.

———. "Destructive Retrieve and Hermeneutic Phenomenology in *Being and Time*." *Research in Phenomenology* 7 (1977), 10–37.

Kogler, Hans-Herbert. *Die Macht des Dialogs: kritische Hermeneutik nach Gadamer, Foucault und Rorty*. Stuttgart: Metzler, 1992.

Krajewski, Bruce. *Traveling with Hermes: Hermeneutics and Rhetoric*. Amherst: University of Massachusetts Press, 1992.

Kristeva, Julia. *Étrangers à nous-mêms*. Paris, 1988.

Kroker, Arthur, and David Cook. *The Postmodern Scene: Excremental Culture and Hyper-Aesthetics*. New York: St. Martin's Press, 1986.

———, and Marilouise Kroker, eds. *Body Invaders: Panic Sex in America*. New York: St. Martin's Press, 1987.

Kuhn, Thomas S. *The Structure of Scientific Revolutions*. 2d ed. Chicago: University of Chicago Press, 1970.

———. *The Essential Tension: Selected Studies in Scientific Tradition and Change*. Chicago: University of Chicago Press, 1977.

Lang, P. C. *Hermeneutik, Ideologiekritik, Ästhetik: Über Gadamer und Adorno sowie Fragen einer aktuellen Ästhetik*. Königstein, 1981.

Lawrence, Fred. "Self-Knowledge in History in Gadamer and Lonergan." In *Language, Truth, and Meaning*. Ed. Philip McShane. Notre Dame: University of Notre Dame Press, 1972.

———. "Truth and Method by Hans-Georg Gadamer." *Religious Studies Review* 3 (1977), 35–44.

———. "Gadamer and Lonergan: A Dialectical Comparison." *International Philosophical Quarterly* 20 (1980), 25–47.

Linge, David E. "Dilthey and Gadamer. Two Theories of Historical Understanding." *Journal of the American Academy of Religion* 41, 536–53.

Lipps, Hans. *Untersuchungen zu einer hermeneutischen Logik*. Frankfurt: Klostermann, 1959.

Llewelyn, John. *Beyond Metaphysics?: The Hermeneutic Circle in Contemporary Continental Philosophy*. Atlantic Highlands: Humanities Press, 1985.

Lohmann, Johannes. "Gadamer's *Wahrheit und Methode.*" *Gnomon* 38 (1965), 709–18.

———. *Philosophie und Sprachwissenschaft*. Berlin: Duncker and Humblot, 1965.

Lyotard, Jean-François. *The Postmodern Condition: A Report on Knowledge*. Trans. Geoff Bennington and Brian Mussumi. Minneapolis: University of Minnesota Press, 1984.

———. *The Postmodern Explained: Correspondence 1982–85*. Ed. Julian Pefanis and M. Thomas. Trans. Don Barry et al. Minneapolis: University of Minnesota Press, 1992.

MacIntyre, Alasdair. "Contexts of Interpretation." *Boston University Journal* 24 (1976), 431–46.

———. *After Virtue*. Notre Dame: University of Notre Dame Press, 1981.

———. *Whose Justice? Which Rationality?* Notre Dame: University of Notre Dame Press, 1988.

MacKenzie, Ian. "Gadamer's Hermeneutics and the Uses of Forgery." *Journal for Aesthetics and Art Criticism* 45 (1986), 41–48.

Maddox, Randy L. "Hermeneutic Circle-Viscious or Victorious?" *Philosophy Today* 27 (1983), 66–76.

Madison, Gary. B. *Understanding: A Phenomenological Pragmatic Analysis*. London: Greenwood Press, 1982.

———. *The Hermeneutics of Postmodernity: Figures and Themes*. Bloomington: Indiana University Press, 1988.

———. "Coping with Nietzsche's Legacy: Rorty, Derrida, Gadamer." *Philosophy Today* 36 (1992), 3–19.

Makkreel, Rudolph A. *Dilthey: Philosopher of the Human Studies*. Princeton: Princeton University Press, 1975.

———. "Tradition and Orientation in Hermeneutics." *Research in Phenomenology* 16 (1986), 73–85.

Malpas, J. E. *Donald Davidson and the Mirror of Meaning: Holism, Truth, Interpretation*. Cambridge: Cambridge University Press, 1992.

Mandelbaum, Maurice. *The Problem of Historical Knowledge: An Answer to Relativism*. New York: Harper and Row, 1967.

Maraldo, John C. *Der Hermeneutische Zirkel: Untersuchungen zu Schleiermacher, Dilthey and Heidegger*. Freiburg und München: Verlag Karl Alber, 1974.

Maranhao, Tullio, ed. *The Interpretation of Dialogue*. Chicago: University of Chicago Press, 1990.

Marcus, G. "Diogenes Laertius contra Gadamer: Universal or Historical Hermeneutics?" In *Life after Postmodernism: Essays on Value and Culture*. Ed. John Fekete.

Margolis, Joseph. *Pragmatism without Foundations: Reconciling Realism and Relativism*. Oxford: Basil Blackwell, 1986.

———. *Texts without Referents: Reconciling Science and Narrative*. Oxford: Basil Blackwell, 1989.

———. "Interpretation at Risk." *Monist* 73 (1990), 312–30.

———. *The Flux of History and the Flux of Science.* Berkeley: University of California Press, 1993.

Marquard, Odo. *Abschied vom Prinzipiellen.* Stuttgart: Reclam, 1981.

Martin, Luther H., et al., eds. *Technologies of the Self.* Amherst: University of Massachusetts Press, 1988.

Martland, T. R. "Quine's Half-Entities and Gadamer's Too." *Man and World* 19 (1986), 361–73.

Marx, Werner. *Heidegger and the Tradition.* Evanston: Northwestern University Press, 1971.

———. *Towards a Phenomenological Ethics: Ethos and the Life-World.* Albany: State University of New York Press, 1992.

McCarthy, Thomas. "The Operation Called *Verstehen:* Towards a Redefinition of the Problem." In *PSA* 1972.

———. "On Misunderstanding 'Understanding.'" *Theory and Decision* 3 (1973), 351–69.

———. *The Critical Theory of Jürgen Habermas.* Cambridge: MIT Press, 1978.

Meinecke, Freidrich. *Historism: The Rise of a New Historical Outlook.* Trans. J. E. Anderson. London: Routledge and Kegan Paul, 1972.

Mendelson, Jack. "The Habermas-Gadamer Debate." *New German Critique* 18 (1979), 44–73.

Michelfelder, D., and R. E. Palmer, eds. *Dialogue and Deconstruction: The Gadamer-Derrida Encounter.* Albany: State University of New York Press, 1989.

Misgeld, Dieter. "Critical Theory and Hermeneutics: The Debate between Habermas and Gadamer." In *On Critical Theory.* Ed. John O'Neill. New York: Seabury Press, 1976.

———. "Discourse and Conversation: The Theory of Communicative Competence and Hermeneutics in Light of the Debate between Habermas and Gadamer." *Cultural Hermeneutics* 4 (1977), 321–44.

———. "On Gadamer's Hermeneutics." *Philosophy of the Social Sciences* 9 (1979), 221–39.

Mitscherling, Jeff. "Philosophical Hermeneutics and 'The Tradition.'" *Man and World* 22 (1989), 247–50.

———. "Hegelian Elements in Gadamer's Notions of Application and Play." *Man and World* 25 (1992), 61–67.

Mueller-Vollmer, Kurt, ed. *The Hermeneutics Reader: Texts of the German Tradition from the Enlightenment to the Present.* New York: Continuum, 1985.

Mul, Jos de. "Dilthey's Narrative Model of Human-development: Necessary Reconsideration after the Philosophical Hermeneutics of Heidegger and Gadamer." *Man and World* 24 (1991), 409–26.

Müller, J. "Hans-Georg Gadamer, *Wahrheit und Methode.*" *Tübinger Theologische Quanalschrift* 141 (1961), 467–71.

Murchadha, Felix. "Truth as a Problem for Hermeneutics: Towards a Hermeneutic Theory of Truth." *Philosophy Today* 36 (1992), 122–30.

Murray, Michael. "The New Hermeneutic and the Interpretation of Poetry." *Review of the University of Ottawa* 50 (1980), 374–94.

Nassen, Ulrich, ed. *Studien zur Entwicklung einer materialen Hermeneutik.* München: Fink, 1979.

Nenon, Thomas. "Dilthey's Inductive Method and the Role of Philosophy." *Southwest Philosophy Review* 5 (1989), 121–34.

Nicholson, Graeme. "The Role of Interpretation in Phenomenological Reflection." *Research in Phenomenology* 14 (1984).

———. *Seeing and Reading.* Atlantic Highlands: Humanities Press, 1984.

Okrent, Mark. "Hermeneutics, Transcendental Philosophy and Social Science." *Inquiry* 27 (1984).

Olson, Alan, ed. *Myth, Symbol, and Reality.* Notre Dame: University of Notre Dame Press, 1980.

Ormiston, Gayle, and Alan Schrift, eds. *The Hermeneutic Tradition: From Ast to Ricoeur.* Albany: State University of New York Press, 1990.

———, eds. *Transforming the Hermeneutic Context: From Nietzsche to Nancy.* Albany: State University of New York Press, 1990.

Orr, Leonard. *De-Structuring the Novel: Essays in Postmodern Hermeneutics.* Troy: Whitston Publishing Co., 1982.

Otto, Eckart. "Die Applikation als Problem der politischen Hermeneutik." *Zeitschrift für Theologie und Kirche* 71 (1974), 145–80.

Palmer, Richard. *Hermeneutics: Interpretation Theory in Schleiermacher, Dilthey, Heidegger, and Gadamer.* Evanston: Northwestern University Press, 1969.

———. "Phenomenology as Foundation for a Post-Modern Philosophy of Literary Interpretation." *Cultural Hermeneutics* 1 (1973), 207–22.

———. "Postmodernity and Hermeneutics." *Boundary* 2 (1977), 363–93.

———. "Allegorical, Philological and Philosophical Hermeneutics." *Review of the University of Ottawa* 50 (1980), 338–60.

———. "The Scope of Hermeneutics and the Problem of Critique and the Crisis of Modernity." *Texte* 3 (1984), 223–39.

Pannenberg, Wolfhart. "Hermeneutic and Universal History." In *Basic Questions in Theology.* Vol. 1. Trans. George H. Kehm. Philadelphia: Fortress Press, 1970.

Paslick, Robert H. "The Ontological Context of Gadamer's Fusion: Boehme, Heidegger, and Non-Duality." *Man and World* 18 (1985), 405–22.

Peters, Ted. "The Nature and Role of Presuppositions: An Inquiry into Contemporary Hermeneutics." *International Philosophical Quarterly* 14 (1974), 209–22.

Pfafferott, G. *Ethik und Hermeneutik: Mensch und Moral im Gefüge der Lebensform.* Königstein, 1981.

Pöggeler, Otto. "H.-G. Gadamer, *Wahrheit und Methode.*" *Philosophischer Literaturanzeiger* 16 (1963), 6–16.

———. *Hermeneutische Philosophie: Zehn Aufsätze.* München: Nymphenburger, 1972.

———. "Die ethisch-politische Dimension der hermeneutischen Philosophie." In *Probleme der Ethik*. Ed. G.-G. Grau. München, 1972. 45–81.

———. "Hermeneutiche Philosophie und Theologie." *Man and World* 7 (1974), 158–76.

———. *Heidegger und die hermeneutische Philosophie*. Freiburg: Alber, 1983.

Poster, Mark. *The Mode of Information: Poststructuralism and Context*. Chicago: University of Chicago Press, 1990.

Rabinow, Paul, and W. M. Sullivan, eds. *Interpretive Social Science: A Second Look*. Berkeley: University of California Press, 1987.

Radnitzky, Gerard. *Contemporary Schools of Metascience*. New York: Humanities Press, 1968.

Reagan, Charles E. *Studies in the Philosophy of Paul Ricoeur*. Athens: Ohio University Press, 1979.

Ricoeur, Paul. *The Conflict of Interpretations: Essays in Hermeneutics*. Evanston: Northwestern University Press, 1974.

———. *Interpretation Theory: Discourse and the Surplus of Meaning*. Fort Worth: Texas Christian University Press, 1976.

———. *Paul Ricoeur: Hermeneutics and the Social Sciences*. Ed., trans. John B. Thompson. Cambridge, England: Cambridge University Press, 1981.

———, and Hans-Georg Gadamer. "The Conflict of Interpretations." In Bruzina, R., and B. Wilshire, eds., *Phenomenology: Dialogues and Bridges*.

Riedel, Manfred. "Zwischen Platon und Aristoteles. Heideggers doppelte Exposition der Seinsfrage und der Ansatz von Gadamers hermeneutischer Gesprächsdialektik." *Allgemeine Zeitschrift für Philosophie* 11 (1986), 1–28.

———. *Für eine zweite Philosophie*. Frankfurt: Suhrkamp, 1988.

———. *Hören auf die Sprache: Die akroamatische Dimension der Hermeneutik*. Frankfurt: Suhrkamp, 1990.

Ripanti, G. *Gadamer*. Assisi, 1978.

Risser, James. "The Imaging of Truth in Philosophical Hermeneutics." In *Selected Studies in Phenomenology and Existential Philosophy*. Vol. 19. Albany: State University of New York Press, 1994.

Rockmore, Tom. "Ideality, Hermeneutics and the Hermeneutics of Idealism." *Idealistic Studies* 12 (1982), 92–102.

———. *Hegel's Circular Theory of Knowledge*. Bloomington: Indiana University Press, 1986.

———. "Epistemology as Hermeneutics: Antifoundationalist Relativism." *Monist* 73 (1990), 115–33.

———. "Knowledge, Hermeneutics, and History." *Man and World* 25 (1992), 79–101.

Rodi, Frithjof. "Dilthey, Gadamer and 'Traditional' Hermeneutics." *Reports on Philosophy* 7 (1983), 3–12.

Ronell, Avital. *The Telephone Book: Technology—Schizophrenia—Electric Speech*. Lincoln: University of Nebraska Press, 1989.

Rorty, Richard. *Philosophy and the Mirror of Nature*. Princeton: Princeton University Press, 1979.

————. *Consequences of Pragmatism.* Minneapolis: University of Minnesota Press, 1982.

————. *Contingency, Irony, and Solidarity.* Cambridge: Cambridge University Press, 1989.

————. *Objectivity, Relativism, and Truth.* Cambridge: Cambridge University Press, 1991.

————. *Essays on Heidegger and Others.* Cambridge: Cambridge University Press, 1991.

————, et al., eds. *Philosophy in History.* Cambridge: Cambridge University Press, 1984.

Rosen, Stanley. *Hermeneutics as Politics.* New York: Oxford University Press, 1987.

Rothberg, Donald J. "Gadamer, Rorty, Hermeneutics, and Truth: A Response to G. Warnke's Hermeneutics and the Social Sciences: A Gadamerian Critique of Rorty." *Inquiry* 29 (1986), 355–61.

Russen, Jorn. "Wahrheit und Methode in der Geschichtswissenschaft-philosophische Probleme der Historik." *Philosophische Rundschau* 18 (1972), 267–89.

Sallis, John. *Delimitations.* Bloomington: Indiana University Press, 1987.

————. *Echoes.* Bloomington: Indiana University Press, 1990.

————. *Crossings.* Chicago: Chicago University Press, 1991.

————, ed. *Deconstruction and Philosophy.* Chicago: University of Chicago Press, 1987.

————, ed. *Reading Heidegger: Commemorations.* Bloomington: Indiana University Press, 1993.

Sandkühler, Hans Jorg. *Praxis und Geschichtsbewußtsein: Fragen einer dialektischen und historisch-materialistischen Hermeneutik.* Frankfurt: Suhrkamp, 1973.

Schleiermacher, F. D. E. *Hermeneutik.* Ed. Heinz Kimmerle. Heidelberg: Carl Winter, Universitätsverlag, 1959.

————. *Hermeneutics: The Handwritten Manuscripts.* Ed. Heinz Kimmerle. Trans. James Duke and Jack Forstman. Missoula: Scholars Press, 1977.

Schmidt, Dennis. *The Ubiquity of the Finite.* Cambridge: MIT Press. 1988.

————, ed. *Hermeneutics and the Poetic Motion.* Binghamton: State University of New York Press, 1990.

Schmidt, Lawrence. K. *The Epistemology of Hans-Georg Gadamer: An Analysis of the Legitimization of "Vorurteile."* Frankfurt: Peter Lang, 1987.

————. "When the Text Speaks the Truth: The Preconception of Completion." *Southern Journal of Philosophy* 35 (1987), 395–405.

————. "The Exemplary Status of Translating." In *Hermeneutics and the Poetic Motion.* Ed. Dennis Schmidt. Binghamton: State University of New York Press, 1990.

Schnädelbach, Hans, ed. *Rationalität: Philosophische Beiträge.* Frankfurt: Suhrkamp, 1984.

Schneider, Wolfgang. *Objektives Verstehen: Rekonstruction eines Paradigmas: Gadamer, Popper, Toulmin, Luhmann.* Opladen: Westdeutscher Verlag, 1991.

Schrift, Alan. "Nietzsche's Hermeneutic Significance." *Auslegung* 10 (1983), 39–47.

Schuckman, Paul. "Aristotle's Phronesis and Gadamer's Hermeneutics." *Philosophy Today* 23 (1979), 41–50.

Schultz, Walter. "Anmerkungen zur Hermeneutik Gadamers." In *Hermeneutik und Dialektik*. Ed. Bubner et al. 1970.

Schweiker, William. "Beyond Imitation: Mimetic Praxis in Gadamer, Ricoeur, and Derrida." *Journal of Religion* 68 (1988), 21–38.

Scott, Charles E. "Gadamer's *Truth and Method*." *Anglican Theological Review* 59 (1977), 63–78.

———. *The Language of Difference*. Atlantic Highlands: Humanities Press, 1987.

———. *The Question of Ethics*. Bloomington: Indiana University Press, 1990.

Seebohm, Thomas M. *Zur Kritik der hermeneutischen Vernunft*. Bonn: Bouvier, 1972.

———. "The Problem of Hermeneutics in Recent Anglo-American Literature: Part 1." *Philosophy and Rhetoric* 10 (1977), 180–98.

———. "Falsehood as the Prime Mover of Hermeneutics." *Journal of Speculative Philosophy* 6 (1992), 1–24.

Seigfried, Hans. "Phenomenology, Hermeneutics and Poetry." *Journal of the British Society for Phenomenology* 10 (1979), 94–100.

Serequeberhan, Tsenay. "Heidegger and Gadamer: Thinking as Meditative and as Effective-Historical Consciousness." *Man and World* 20 (1987), 41–64.

Shapiro, Gary. "Gadamer, Habermas, and the Death of Art." *British Journal of Aesthetics* 26 (1986), 39–47.

———, and Alan Sica, eds. *Hermeneutics: Questions and Prospects*. Amherst: University of Massachusetts Press, 1984.

Shapiro, Michael J. *Language and Political Understanding: The Politics of Discursive Practices*. New Haven: Yale University Press, 1981.

Sheehan, Thomas. "Getting to the Topic: The New Edition of *Wegmarken*." *Research in Phenomenology* 7 (1977), 299–316.

Siemek, M. "Marxism and the Hermeneutic Tradition." *Dialectics and Humanism* 2 (1975), 87–103.

Silverman, Hugh J. "Phenomenology: From Hermeneutics to Deconstruction." *Research in Phenomenology* 14 (1984), 19–34.

———. "Hermeneutics and Interrogation." *Research in Phenomenology* 16 (1986), 87–94.

———, and D. Ihde, eds. *Hermeneutics and Deconstruction*. Albany: State University of New York Press, 1985.

———, ed. *Gadamer and Hermeneutics*. New York: Routledge, 1991.

Smith, P. Christopher. "Gadamer on Language and Method in Hegel's Dialectic." *Graduate Faculty Philosophy Journal* 5 (1975), 53–72.

———. "Gadamer's Hermeneutics and Ordinary Language Philosophy." *The Thomist* (1979), 296–321.

———. "H.-G. Gadamer's Heideggarian Interpretation of Plato." *Journal of the British Society for Phenomenology* 12 (1981), 211–30.

———. "The Ethical Dimension of Gadamer's Hermeneutical Theory." *Research in Phenomenology* 18 (1988), 75–92.

————. "Sichberatenlassen, Nachgiebigkeit, Verständnis (*Bouleuesthai, Epiekeia, Synesis*)." *Heidelberger Jahrbücher* 34 (1990), 197–205.

————. *Hermeneutics and Human Finitude: Towards a Theory of Ethical Understanding.* New York: Fordham, 1991.

Smith, Gary. "Gadamer's Hermeneutics and Ordinary Language Philosophy." *The Thomist* 43 (1979), 296–321.

Soffer, Gail. "Gadamer, Hermeneutics, and Objectivity in Interpretation." *Praxis International* 12 (1992), 321–68.

Sprung, Marvin, ed. *The Question of Being: East-West Perspectives.* University Park: Pennsylvania State University Press, 1978.

Stack, George. *Kierkegaard's Existential Ethics.* Tuscaloosa: The University of Alabama Press, 1977.

Stegmüller, Walter. "Der sogenannte Zirkel des Verstehens." In *Natur und Geschichte: Zehnter deutscher Kongreß für Philosophie.* Ed. K. Hüber and A. Menne. Hamburg, 1974.

Strauss, Leo, and H.-G. Gadamer. "Correspondence Concerning *Wahrheit und Methode.*" *Unabhängige Zeitschrift für Philosophie* 2 (1978), 5–12.

Sullivan, Robert. *Political Hermeneutics: The Early Thinking of Hans-Georg Gadamer.* University Park: Pennsylvania State University Press, 1989.

Takeda, Sumio. *Reflexion, Erfahrung und Praxis bei Gadamer.* Diss. Tübingen, 1981.

Taylor, Charles. "Interpretation and the Sciences of Man." *Review of Metaphysics* 25 (1971), 3–51.

————. *Human Agency and Language: Philosophical Papers I.* Cambridge, 1985.

Taylor, Mark. *Journey to Selfhood: Hegel and Kierkegaard.* Berkeley: University of California Press, 1980.

Templeton, A. "The Dream and the Dialog: Rich's Feminist Poetics and Gadamer's Hermeneutics." *Tulsa Studies in Women's Literature* 7 (1988), 283–96.

Thiselton, Anthony C. *New Horizons in Hermeneutics.* Grand Rapids: Zondervan Publishing House, 1992.

Thompson, John B. *Critical Hermeneutics: A Study in the Thought of Paul Ricoeur and Jürgen Habermas.* Cambridge: Cambridge University Press, 1981.

————, and Held, David, eds. *Habermas: Critical Debates.* Cambridge: MIT Press, 1982.

Torrance, I. R. "Gadamer, Polanyi, and Ways of Being Closed." *Scottish Journal of Theology* 46 (1993), 497–505.

Toulmin, Stephen. *The Uses of Argument.* Cambridge, 1958.

————. *An Introduction to Reasoning.* 2d ed. New York, 1984.

Tugendhat, Ernst. *Der Wahrheitsbegriff bei Husserl und Heidegger.* Berlin: de Gruyter, 1970.

————. "The Fusion of Horizons." *Times Literary Supplement* 19 (May 1978).

————. *Traditional and Analytic Philosophy: Lectures on the Philosophy of Language.* Trans. P. Gortner. Cambridge: Cambridge University Press, 1982.

Turk, Horst. "Wahrheit oder Methode? H.-G. Gadamers 'Grundzüge einer philosophischen Hermeneutik.'" *Hermeneutische Positionen: Schleiermacher, Dilthey, Heidegger, Gadamer.* Ed. H. Birus. Vandenhoeck and Ruprecht, 1982. 120–50.

Vattimo, Gianni. *The End of Modernity: Nihilism and Hermeneutics in Postmodern Cul-

ture. Trans. Jon R. Snyder. Baltimore: Johns Hopkins University Press, 1988.

——. *The Transparent Society.* Trans. David Webb. Baltimore: Johns Hopkins University Press, 1992.

——, ed. *Jenseits vom Subjekt: Nietzsche, Heidegger und die Hermeneutik.* Graz/Wien, 1986.

Velkley, Richard. "Gadamer and Kant: The Critique of Modern Aesthetic Consciousness in *Truth and Method.*" *Interpretation* 9 (1981), 353–64.

Verra, V. "Gadamer's Hermeneutics in Italy." *Aut Aut* 242 (1991), 49–60.

Virilio, Paul. *Vitesse et politique.* Paris: Galilee, 1977.

Wachterhauser, Brice. "Must We Be What We Say? Gadamer on Truth in the Human Sciences." In *Hermeneutics and Modern Philosophy.* Ed. Brice Wachterhauser. Albany: State University of New York Press, 1986.

——, ed. *Hermeneutics and Modern Philosophy.* Albany: State University of New York Press, 1986.

——, ed. *Hermeneutics and Truth.* Evanston: Northwestern University Press, 1994.

Waldenfels, Bernhard. *Der Spielraum des Verhaltens.* Frankfurt, 1980.

Walhout, Donald. "Hermeneutics and the Teaching of Philosophy." *Teaching Philosophy* 7 (1984), 303–12.

Wallulis, Jerald. "Philosophical Hermeneutics and the Conflict of Ontologies." *International Philosophical Quarterly* 24 (1984), 283–302.

——. *The Hermeneutics of Life History: Personal Achievement and History in Gadamer, Habermas, and Erikson.* Evanston: Northwestern University Press, 1990.

Walsh, Robert D. "When Love of Knowing Becomes Actual Knowing: Heidegger and Gadamer on Hegel's *Die Sache Selbst.*" *Owl of Minerva* 17 (1986).

Warburg, Max. "Zwei Fragen zum Krytylos." *Neue Philologische Untersuchungen.* Vol. 5. Berlin, 1929.

Warnke, George. *Gadamer: Hermeneutics, Tradition and Reason.* Stanford: Stanford University Press, 1987.

——. *Justice and Interpretation.* Cambridge: MIT Press, 1993.

Watson, Stephen. *Extensions: Essays on Interpretation, Rationality, and the Closure of Modernism.* Albany: State University of New York Press, 1992.

Weberman, David. *Historische Objektivität.* New York: Lang, 1991.

Weinsheimer, Joel C. *Imitation.* London: Routledge and Keagan Paul, 1984.

——. *Gadamer's Hermeneutics.* New Haven: Yale University Press, 1985.

——. *Philosophical Hermeneutics and Literary Theory.* New Haven: Yale University Press, 1991.

Weiss, F. G., ed. *Beyond Epistemology.* The Hague: Martinus Nijhoff, 1974.

Westphal, Merold. "Hegel and Gadamer." In *Hermeneutics and Modern Philosophy.* Ed. B. Wachterhauser. 65–86.

Widdershoven, Guy. *Handelen en rationaliteit.* Meppel: Boom, 1987.

Wiehl, Reiner, ed. *Die antike Philosophie in ihrer Bedeutung für die Gegenwart: Kollo-*

quium zu Ehren des 80. Geburtstag von Hans-Georg Gadamer. Heidelberg: Carl Winter Universitätsverlag, 1981.

Wolff, Janet. *Hermeneutic Philosophy and the Sociology of Art.* London: Routledge and Kegan Paul, 1975.

Wright, Georg von. *Explanation and Understanding.* Ithaca: Cornell University Press, 1971.

———. *Philosophical Papers. Vol. 1: Practical Reason.* Oxford, 1983.

Wright, Kathleen. "Gadamer: The Speculative Structure of Language." In *Hermeneutics and Modern Philosophy.* Ed. B. Wachterhauser. 193–218.

———, ed. *Festivals of Interpretation.* Albany: State University of New York Press, 1990.

Contributors

FRANCIS J. AMBROSIO, Associate Professor of Philosophy at Georgetown University, received his Ph.D. from Fordham University with a dissertation on Gadamer's hermeneutics. He has published essays on hermeneutics in such journals as *Man and World, International Philosophical Quarterly, Owl of Minerva*, and *Journal of the British Society for Phenomenology*. His current work is the development of hermeneutics and deconstruction toward a metaphorics of the human person.

ROBERT BERNASCONI is Moss Professor of Philosophy at the University of Memphis. He is the author of *The Question of Language in Heidegger's History of Being* and of *Heidegger in Question*, as well as a number of essays on various aspects of continental philosophy and the history of social thought. He is currently completing a book called *Between Levinas and Derrida*. He has edited a collection of Gadamer's essays entitled *The Relevance of the Beautiful and Other Essays*. With David Wood he edited *Derrida and Difference* and *The Provocation of Levinas*, and with Simon Critchley he edited *Re-Reading Levinas*. Before coming to Memphis, he taught at the University of Essex for 13 years. He has also held visiting positions at Loyola University of Chicago, Vanderbilt University, and Braunschweig University in West Germany.

GÜNTER FIGAL is Professor of Philosophy at the University of Tübingen. He received his Ph.D. in 1976 and Habilitation in 1987 from the University of Heidelberg. He is the author of *Theodor W. Adorno: Das Naturschöne als spekulative Gedankenfigur* (1977); *Martin Heidegger: Phänomenologie der Freiheit* (1988, 2nd ed. 1991); *Das Untier und die Liebe: Sieben platonische Essays* (1991); *Martin Heidegger zur Einführung* (1992); and *Für eine Philosophie von Freiheit und Streit: Politik—Ästhetik—Metaphysik* (1994). He is author of numerous articles on contemporary European philosophy.

HANS-GEORG GADAMER is Professor of Philosophy Emeritus at Ruprecht-Karls-Universität, Heidelberg. His magnum opus, *Wahrheit und Methode*, introduced philosophical hermeneutics and has been widely translated. His collected works, *Gesammelte Werke*, are being published by J. C. B. Mohr (Paul Siebeck). He has written numerous books and essays concerning hermeneutics, contemporary philosophy, Greek philosophy, and aesthetics and poetry, that have applied and continued his thinking on philosophical hermeneutics.

JEAN GRONDIN studied at the Universities of Montréal, Heidelberg, and Tübingen. He was a Fellow of the Conseil de recherches en sciences humaines du Canada and of the Alexander-von-Humboldt Stiftung. He presently teaches philosophy at the Université de Montréal and has taught at the Université Laval and the University of Ottawa. His books include *Hermeneutische Wahrheit? Zum Wahrheitsbegriff Hans-Georg Gadamers; Le tournant dans la pensée de Martin Heidegger; Kant et le problème de la philosophie: l'a priori; Emmanuel Kant. Avant/Après; Einführung in die philosophische Hermeneutik; L'universalité de l'herméneutique; L'hoizon herméneutique de le pensée contemporaine;* and *Der Sinn für Hermeneutik.*

MICHAEL KELLY is Adjunct Assistant Professor of Philosophy and Managing Editor of *The Journal of Philosophy*, both at Columbia University. He is editor of *Hermeneutics and Critical Theory in Ethics and Politics* (1990); *Power and Critique: Recasting the Foucault/Habermas Debate* (1994); and *The Encyclopedia of Aesthetics* (forthcoming). He has published articles on Gadamer, Habermas, Foucault, ethics, and art.

MARC LAFOUNTAIN is Professor of Sociology at West Georgia College where he teaches critical and postmodern theory and phenomenological sociology. He received his Ph.D. from the University of Tennessee. His current interests focus on the body, the erotic, art, ethics, and the environment. He is presently completing a book offering a postmodernist interpretation of Salvador Dali.

JOSEPH MARGOLIS is Laura H. Carnell Professor of Philosophy at Temple University. He has recently published a trilogy entitled *The Persistence of Reality* (1986, 1987, 1989). His many publications include *The Truth about Relativism* (1991), *The Flux of History and the Flux of Science* (1993), and *Interpretation: Radical but Not Unruly* (forthcoming).

TOM NENON is Associate Professor of Philosophy and Director of the Center for the Humanities at the University of Memphis. He received his Ph.D. from Freiburg Universität where he taught and worked for several years at the Husserl Archives. He is the author of *Objectivität und endliche Erkenntnis* and numerous articles concerning contemporary German philosophy.

JAMES RISSER is Associate Professor of Philosophy and held the Pigott-McCone Chair of Humanities at Seattle University. He has published extensively in the area of hermeneutics, principally on the work of Gadamer and Nietzsche.

TOM ROCKMORE is Professor of Philosophy at Duquesne University. His extensive publications on modern and contemporary German philosophy include *Heidegger and French Philosophy* (1994); *Irrationalism: Lukacs and the Marxist View of Reason* (1992); *Habermas on Historical Materialism* (1989); and *Hegel's Circular Epistemology* (1986). He received a Morse Fellowship to study in Heidelberg in 1975–76 and a Humboldt grant for Tübingen in 1981–82.

LAWRENCE K. SCHMIDT is Associate Professor of Philosophy at Hendrix College. He studied at the Universität Freiburg and later received his Ph.D. from the Universität Duisburg. He is author of *The Epistemology of Hans-Georg Gadamer* (1985) and has written several articles on hermeneutics. With Monika Reuss he translated several essays for *Hans-Georg Gadamer on Education, Poetry, and History* (1992). He has organized international conferences and workshops in Heidelberg to discuss Gadamer's philosophy.

P. CHRISTOPHER SMITH is Professor of Philosophy at the University of Massachusetts at Lowell. A doctoral student of Gadamer's in Heidelberg from 1961 to 1966, he is the translator of three of Gadamer's books into English and the author of *Hermeneutics and Human Finitude: Toward a Theory of Ethical Understanding* (1991) as well as a number of articles in German and English on Gadamer's theory of interpretation.

KEES VUYK teaches at the Christelijke Hogeschool voor de Kunsten Constantijn Huygens and received his Ph.D. from the University of Amsterdam. His most recent project was to translate Richard Rorty's *Contingency, Irony and Solidarity* into Dutch.